The Gulag Survivor

Beyond the Soviet System

The Gulag Survivor

Nanci Adler

Transaction Publishers
New Brunswick (U.S.A.) and London (U.K.)

Library of Congress Catalog Number: 2001041595
ISBN: 0-7658-0071-3 (alk. paper)
Printed in the United States of America

Library of Congress Cataloging-in-Publication Data

Adler, Nanci.
    The Gulag survivor : beyond the Soviet system / Nanci Adler.
        p. cm.
    Includes bibliographical references and index.
    ISBN: 0-7658-0071-3 (alk. paper)
    1. Political prisoners—Rehabilitation—Soviet Union.   2. Political prisoners—Rehabilitation—Former Soviet republics.   3. Political persecution—Soviet Union—Psychological aspects.   4. Concentration camps—Soviet Union.   I. Title.

HV9375 .A35 2001
365'.45'0947—dc21   2001041595

For Zoë and Noah

The distant sound of a bell
comes into my cell with dawn
I hear the sad bell calling me:
"Where are you? Where are you?"
"Here I am!..."And tears of greeting,
sparse tears of non-freedom...
Not for God,
But for you, Russia.

—Semyon Vilensky
1948, Sukhanov Prison

Contents

Preface

He was last seen in a Manhattan shelter for the homeless, on January 7, 2000. That was about a week after his last contact with the authorities—in the form of a New York City police officer, who issued him a "violation ticket" for "obstructing a park bench." He had placed his briefcase on the bench in a park frequented by the homeless. The briefcase contained a Russian-English dictionary, a book on philosophy, and a few personal items, including a hairbrush.

Who is, or was, he? Nikolai Tolstykh, who had spent six years in Soviet labor camps, having been convicted under Article 70 (anti-Soviet propaganda). A former dissident! Released by decree of Gorbachev in 1987, he won his freedom—only to find that he had become estranged from his wife and family. His ultimate escape was the liberty which, seemingly, America could grant. He did not make it there either. He vanished.[1]

Nikolai Tolstykh's fate is a current and tragic example of the lot that his predecessors of the Stalinist camps had experienced for decades. And Tolstykh returned to a nascent civil society. I have written this book so that the lives of those who survived the terror of the Soviet camps will not be regarded as vain sacrifices. Their stories deserve to be recorded and remembered.

Note

1. See Nina Bernstein, "On Park Bench, Another Jolt in a Bumpy Life," *New York Times*, 26 March 2000, pp. 37, 41.

Acknowledgments

In the course of this research I had the privilege of meeting a number of extraordinary people. These individuals helped me to gain access to information, to archives, and to life stories. Though they are named in the text, I would like to take this opportunity to acknowledge their help and cooperation, without which this book would not have been possible: Isaak Filshtinsky, Sergey Kovalyov, Aleksandr Krushelnitsky, Zoya Marchenko, Izrail Mazus, Paulina Myasnikova, Pavel Naumov, Dina Nokhotovich, Nikita Petrov, Lev Razgon, Tamara Ruzhnetsova, Andrey N. Sakharov, Zorya Serebryakova, Roza Smushkevich, Leonard Ternovsky, and Zayara Vesyolaya. I owe a special debt of gratitude to Vladlen Loginov and Arseny Roginsky for their guidance, and to Semyon Vilensky, who took on my task as if it were his own. The critical appraisal of Bruno Naarden and careful eye of Marc Jansen forced me to sharpen my observations. Stephen Cohen provided advice, friendship, and unlimited access to his rich archive on returnees. I am indebted to Irving Horowitz for his enthusiasm and for his input. My husband, Rob, had the forbearance to put up with a long project that took place, for the most part, far away from home. My family provided tremendous support by being there for me when I needed to share my thoughts and ideas. My beautiful twins, Zoë and Noah, were born just after this project was completed. I am grateful to them for being here. Finally, I was fortunate to be able to study the Memorial archive in the serene and professional setting of the International Institute of Social History in Amsterdam. The Faculty of the Humanities of the University of Amsterdam and the Netherlands Organization for Scientific Research (NWO) provided indispensable and generous support and travel grants for this research.

Introduction

In December of 1998 the Russian State Duma voted in an overwhelming majority to restore the statue of Feliks Dzerzhinsky to the platform in front of the Lubyanka from which the founder of Lenin's Cheka (secret police) had been so ceremoniously toppled seven years earlier. The Duma resolved that returning Dzerzhinsky to his place would prove an important step in the preservation of the "historical-cultural heritage of Russia," and would serve as a symbol in the struggle against crime.[1] In 1991, this symbol had been hoisted by popular demand, and four cranes, from its perch, and dumped in a Moscow park alongside other fallen idols. The other monument—to the victims of totalitarianism—that had co-existed on the same square for one year, could finally stand alone in quiet vigil. This unsculpted boulder from Lenin's first concentration camp challenged Russia to confront its history, and it seemed that the removal of "Iron Feliks" was a significant step in this process. But, as attested by sentiments reflected in the Duma's motion, Dzerzhinsky was not really dead and gone, he apparently only lay dormant. This confrontation of symbols is yet another powerful example of Anna Akhmatova's "two Russias": those who were imprisoned and those who put them there.[2]

Russia's ambivalent struggle to come to terms with its repressive and onerous past has been going on for nearly half a century. On a political and societal level, starting in the fifties, entrenched officials attempted to address these issues in their efforts to distance themselves from the Stalinist past. At the same time, Gulag victims returning to society confronted every individual with whom they came into contact with a reality about the nature of the system and the mentality it nurtured that many did not want to see or think about.

1

Indeed the way in which the victims of Soviet terror returned and were returned to society touches upon some of the most complicated questions in Soviet history and in Russia's continuing search for accountability and direction. What, for example, does it say about the credibility of a system in which many believed when an individual (or millions of individuals) endures seventeen years in prisons and labor camps, and then is declared an "innocent victim," yet the perpetrator is left unnamed? In one sense, the perpetrator was, to borrow Vaclav Havel's argument, everyone—neighbors, colleagues, friends, and family members who were induced to go along with the system for personal gain or out of fear. In another sense, the perpetrator was no one in particular. It was the system as a whole, with pervasive terror as its adaptive tool. The Soviet dictatorship lasted for over seven decades, so the pathology that extended from the top down, and from the bottom up, had a long time to take root and develop. These fundamental issues will be considered throughout the present work because they are at the very core of the Gulag returnee question.

This book will present accounts of how individual victims and the Soviet system survived *after the Gulag*. Through memory, memoir, extensive interviews, and official record and directive, we shall explore what the ex-prisoners experienced when they returned to society, how officials and others helped or hindered them, and how the questions surrounding the existence of these returnees evolved from the fifties to the nineties. We will begin by placing the Soviet returnee question in context (chapter 1). We shall then analyze society's reaction to early returnees by presenting the experiences of those who were "liberated" into exile in Stalin's time, since future attitudes toward ex-prisoners were partially shaped in these years (chapter 2). The reforms, policies, and practices of the Office of the General Procuracy in the mid-fifties serve to indicate the Soviet system's adaptation to repression, and form the basis for the following discussion (chapter 3). Diverse aspects of the return, such as camp culture, family reunion, and the psychological consequences of the Gulag, will then be looked at in depth (chapter 4). There follows an examination of the effects of the XX Party Congress on the lives of prisoners and ex-prisoners as well as issues involving the housing, employment, status, and rights of returnees, and the return of their confiscated property (chapter 5). We shall next focus on belief in the Communist Party and the association between returnees and dissidents (chapter 6). In the conclusion, we will examine the return of the returnee question in the eighties and nineties and reflect on the impact that these reemerging people and issues had on the failing Soviet system (chapter 7).

At the outset of this journey into the lives and fates of those who survived the condemnation of the Gulag, we should bear the following reality in mind: despite the fact that the "blank spots" in Soviet history have now largely been filled with knowledge of the atrocities committed under the Soviet regime, the Communist Party of the Soviet Union was neither legally condemned nor morally indicted. In consequence, its symbols are not tabooed. While Dzerzhinsky may not come back, he is apparently not altogether unwanted. And Lenin was still resting on Red Square, as the Russian Communist Party enjoyed some degree of popularity at the close of the twentieth century. Indeed, this Russian century did make Kafka fact.

Notes

1. "Pust' vernetsia 'zheleznyi Feliks'!," *Sovetskaia Rossiia*, 5 December 1998. See also "Vozvrashchenie Feliksa," *Moskovskie Novosti*, no. 48, 6-13 December 1998; "Demokraty protiv vozvrashcheniia pamiatnika Dzerzhinskomu," *Segodnia*, 7 December 1998; Michael R. Gordon, Celestine Bohlen, "...But Twilight Cloaks Russia," *New York Times*, 3 January 1999; Bart Rijs, "In Magadan zijn beulen en slachtoffers buren," *de Volkskrant*, 3 December 1998.
2. Stephen Cohen, *Rethinking the Soviet Experience: Politics and History since 1917* (New York: Oxford University Press, 1985), pp. 99-100.

1

Defining the Parameters

The last leader of the Soviet Union, Mikhail Gorbachev, signified the second period of official de-Stalinization at the seventieth anniversary of the October revolution in 1987. On this occasion he re-opened a discussion that had long been officially closed when he publicly declared that "thousands" of Party members and other Soviet citizens had been repressed under Stalin. This understatement reflected political, rather than historical reality. After all, there had been Khrushchev thirty years earlier, whose Secret Speech referred to "massive" crimes, presumably well over "thousands." But when Khrushchev's term of office ended, so, too, did the selected efforts at truth-telling. The Khrushchev era was followed by nearly twenty-five years of official amnesia.

A year after Gorbachev's public admission on crimes under Stalin, the General Secretary seemed to recognize its implications, that is, the implications of coming to terms with his nation's past. The realization was revealed at a 1988 Politburo session, where the agenda item "Memorial" was up for discussion. "Memorial" had commenced functioning in 1987 as a tiny organization—an eleven-person initiative group—which was conducting a campaign aimed at gathering signatures to support the creation of a monument to victims of Stalin's repressions. But by the time of the 1988 Politburo session, its scope had expanded to encompass the establishment of a scientific and public research center in Moscow with an archive, a museum, a reception room, and a library containing information and data on victims of Soviet repression. Among others, Memorial's efforts immediately cast doubt on the suggestion that a mere "thousands" had been victimized under Stalin. Once the discussion became public, there existed a grave threat to the Soviet system itself.

Apprehensive about the political potential of Memorial, Gorbachev suggested the path of caution: he opted for retaining the investigation of the Soviet past in the hands of the Party, by limiting Memorial to the regional level under Party supervision.[1] What did Gorbachev have to fear from Memorial's mandate? After all, other states (but not regimes) had dealt with, and are still dealing with, the contentious issue of officially acknowledging national responsibility and guilt. The appropriate commemoration of the fiftieth anniversaries of the liberation of Auschwitz and the bombing of Hiroshima and Nagasaki, with all the history they evoked, are two current examples.

However, the problems associated with confronting their history were different for Gorbachev's Soviet Union than for either Germany or Japan. Neither Nazi Germany nor Imperial Japan had in fact ever confronted their history nor attempted to make an evolutionary change toward a more open society. These political systems perished, defeated by force of arms, and it was only the subsequent democratic political system that took up the struggle to confront the onerous past. Soviet state terrorism, on the other hand, experienced a much slower death, long outlasting the demise of the dictator. The Communist Party of the Soviet Union (CPSU) remained ruthless, had a rigid hierarchy with only top-down accountability, and had no feedback mechanism for responding to the needs of the populace. In contrast to postwar Germany and Japan, in the Soviet system, many of the same people who committed the political crimes were still in political office and were not about to cede power to those who would challenge them.

The death of Josef Stalin in 1953 and the subsequent trickle of prisoners that began to be released from the Gulag system constituted the beginning of the Soviet process of coming to terms with the Stalinist past. These ordinary, for the most part non-political, innocent citizens had been arrested for "counter-revolutionary" activities and dispatched to the barely habitable regions of the north and far east to mine nickel, chop wood, excavate gold, or build railroads leading nowhere,[2] but mostly just to waste away through hard labor and hunger under horrendous conditions. Those who, against all odds, had survived the Gulag were, by virtue of their status alone, a political statement, awakening a social conscience that had to be reckoned with. They and the ghosts of the millions of victims who had died in the camps were evidence and damning testimony to a deranged system. The reappearance of innocent victims of a criminal system now compelled society and the state to confront its past.

But the process was neither smooth nor uninterrupted, and virtually came to a halt by the time of Brezhnev. When it resumed, under Gorbachev, the "unbearable shock" generated by the agonizing examination of Soviet history produced political tremors. In *Lenin's Tomb*, David Remnick observes, "[u]nder this avalanche of remembering, people protested weariness, even boredom, after a while. But, really, it was the pain of remembering, the shock of recognition, that persecuted them."[3] The philosopher Grigory Pomerants describes it thus: "imagine being an adult and nearly all the truth you know about the world around you...has to be absorbed in a matter of a year or two or three."[4] He considered the predicament of the country as a condition of "mass disorientation." But it was more than the condition of being politically lost. It was the shock of finding out and being found out. Moreover, revelations on the past further wounded the pride of an already economically failing nation.[5] Society and the state suddenly had to deal with feelings of guilt, shame, and disgrace as well as the dismaying culture shock of learning a dreadful political truth.

Historiography, Literature

Considering the paucity of knowledge regarding the readaptation of the victims of Soviet terror, little scholarly literature has been devoted to this problem. However, a number of works that deal with similar problems can help constitute a framework for a better understanding of this issue. Of particular interest are the works *The Survivor* and *Die Schuldfrage*, which will be discussed below in the context of this study. In *The Wages of Guilt: Memories of War in Germany and Japan*,[6] Ian Buruma describes how these two states have come to terms with their totalitarian pasts. He specifically refers to Japanese shame and German guilt.[7] This work is useful in providing perspective for the Russian process of coming to terms with an ignominious past. While there is a proliferation of scientific literature written in post-totalitarian states dealing specifically with victims of political repression under the previous regime, particularly those of Nazi Germany (Holocaust), Cambodia (Khmer Rouge), and Latin America,[8] most of what we know about the experience of victims of the Soviet era thus far is unsystematized. Our knowledge comes from camp memoirs, unofficial and unsystematic reports, testimonials, defector and emigré anecdotes, dissident literature (including *samizdat*), and a limited number of substantiated studies.[9]

This short survey of the literature relevant to our theme will not address the multitude of works that deal primarily with the terror and the camps, since our present focus is on the aftermath of Soviet repression.[10] Given that the Soviet authoritarian structure has crumbled only relatively recently, there has been little opportunity to systematically study the effects and political implications of its victimizations. Access to official archives was prohibited or limited, and only since 1988 have victims begun to openly discuss their history of repression on a broad scale. There are, however, a few Western, Soviet, and post-Soviet works or parts of works that do specifically address the issue of the victims' return to society. Among them are Stephen Cohen's 1985 *Rethinking the Soviet Experience*, in particular his chapter on "The Stalin Question Since Stalin." In his discussion of victims' requirements regarding housing, jobs, medical care, and so on, Cohen evaluates the political impact of this group of survivors. His assessment that "these demands of the surviving victims had enormous political implications, if only because exoneration and restitution were official admissions of colossal official crimes"[11] proved to be prescient, as the experience under Gorbachev's de-Stalinization was to illustrate.[12]

In *Remembering Stalin's Victims: Popular Memory and the End of the USSR*, Kathleen E. Smith compares transitions from totalitarianism or authoritarianism to democracy, specifically with reference to Khrushchev's and Gorbachev's respective reigns of power. She traces the history of each of their de-Stalinization campaigns, their efforts at truth-telling, and their search for accountability. The author notes that the complicated and unpublicized rehabilitation procedures "reinforced social atomization" and hindered the mourning process.[13] Implicitly, the very process of rehabilitation laid bare the state's ambivalence about exoneration of those who were labelled "enemies of the people." With regard to the victim, she asserts that in 1956, "rapid release ... did not generally translate into rapid reintegration of returnees into society."[14] Smith does not pursue this key issue in any depth.[15]

In his 1994 *The Unquiet Ghost: Russians Remember Stalin,*[16] Adam Hochschild provides some insight into survivors' memories of their time in the Gulag. He even includes former henchmen in his selection of interviewees. But with the exception of a few isolated references to their post-camp fate, he focuses on the ex-prisoners' vision of the Stalinist epoch and of the present. Hochschild's work does not devote particular attention to the status of the returnee in society.

Jane Shapiro's unpublished 1967 dissertation, *Rehabilitation Policy and Political Conflict in the Soviet Union 1953-1964,*[17] is one of the earliest studies on this issue. It emphasizes the rehabilitation process of Party and military leaders who were victims of the '36-'38 Purge. Shapiro also discusses changes in the MVD's jurisdiction of the camps after Stalin's death. However, with its focus on the rehabilitation of prominent Party members and understandably limited information on former victims, this study provides little about the fate of ordinary citizens.

Albert van Goudoever published a unique study on the rehabilitation of former Communist Party members, entitled *The Limits of Destalinization in the Soviet Union: Political Rehabilitations since Stalin.* Though it is a detailed examination of the process and meaning of rehabilitation, the period during which it was written did not permit access to certain types of materials on social rehabilitation. Moreover, the victims themselves were not yet able to openly discuss their experiences, so oral history was not a readily available means of supplementing the written, official history. Van Goudoever himself asserts, "[f]rom a social point of view, the rehabilitation of the victims of Stalin presents one of the most pressing and, at the same time, least accessible issues in the history of Soviet society."[18] In his criticism of the Medvedev brothers' contention that victims were fully accommodated, he pointed out (in 1986), "[t]he material is too deficient to justify any conclusion on the way in which reintegration into social life was realised."[19] Fortunately, the material is no longer too deficient for such inquiries.

Much of the historiographical literature on Khrushchev's de-Stalinization focuses on changes in the political and cultural arena, the rehabilitation of prominent Party members, and the elimination of the "cult of personality." With regard to returnees, it generally limits itself to the description of administrative measures. The actual effect that these measures had on the victim was not a subject of extensive inquiry. Answers had to be sought in the memoirs and fiction of the period. Examples of how fiction was employed to cloak reality will be presented throughout this book.

Russian scholars, of course, have also addressed some of the returnee issues of the post-camp years. Assertions in Roy and Zhores Medvedev's works on Khrushchev presumably are based on oral history, though it is not clear exactly what the sources are. Though these were very important early works, new information has revealed a number of inaccuracies, rendering some of their figures obsolete. In *Memory and Totalitarianism*, oral historians Darya Khubova and Irina Sherbakova have touched upon the returnee theme. Sherbakova specifically discusses the issue of gender and memory with regard to the Gulag.[20] The symptoms of post-traumatic stress and readaptation into society in victims of one particular (post-Stalin) manifestation of Stalinism—dissidents who were incarcerated in psychiatric institutions—have also been studied.[21] Memorial's own work with victims has been described and analyzed by the organization itself in, among others, their almanac *Zvenya* (Links).[22] Though a few of the essays contain some material on the victim's return to society, the return is not handled as a separate theme.

In her study on the Gulag, *GULAG v sisteme totalitarnogo gosudarstva* (The Gulag in the System of Totalitarian Government), Russian historian G.M. Ivanova describes, with the help of archival references, the structure and function of the Gulag. She also briefly discusses the nature of rehabilitation—the so-called "triumph of justice." Witness her observations on this practice: "the insulted feelings of the citizen could not be [altered] by this false restoration of honor."[23] Ivanova's inclusion of the victim's experience of administrative measures makes this a particularly enlightening Russian reference work.

Memoirs necessarily constitute a key source for learning about the Soviet world from the perspective of the former victim. Aleksandr Solzhenitsyn and Varlam Shalamov have allowed us to enter the prisoner's mind, and be in the camps with him. Throughout this book we will refer to numerous published and unpublished memoirs. However, a few accounts that provide insight into the prisoner's post-camp journey deserve some extra attention here. Evgeniya Ginzburg dedicates a great deal of *Within the Whirlwind*, the second volume of her memoirs, to experiences she had after her release from camp. This work succinctly captures the psychological and physical aspects of the prisoner's journey out of the camps and into society. After years of hard labor, Ginzburg's last place of incarceration was the Elgen camp in Kolyma, where she worked as a nurse in the children's home. Having served ten years for "participation in a Trotskyite terrorist counter-revolutionary group,"[24] Ginzburg was liberated from camp (exiled) in 1947. Her description of the first official procedures after release epitomized what life was to be like for many ex-prisoners. Witness the officially imposed physical alienation of the former prisoner when she went to exchange her temporary certificate of release for a so-called Form A, that would eventually lead to the receipt of a one-year internal passport: "the window through which documents were handed out was so deeply recessed that looking at the man sitting there was like looking through binoculars from the wrong end."[25] When the official mentioned something about Ginzburg's hand, she thought to herself, "[c]ould they have introduced anything so human as a ritual handshake to congratulate people on their release?"[26] To her attempt to extend a hand in his direction, he responded, "Ten years you've done inside and you still don't know the ropes! ... Where are you putting your hand? Haven't you got eyes? On your right!"[27] He motioned to an apparatus for taking fingerprints. Ginzburg's response reflects the anguish of injustice felt among many former prisoners:

> I'd been imagining that I was free. All my release meant was that I could come and go without escort for the time being. I was stuck with my jailers for life, forever. Even now, after ten years as a prisoner, they wanted my fingerprints all over again, wanted to harass and persecute me to my dying day. You could spin around in this accursed wheel till every bone in your body was ground to bits.[28]

This sentiment was shared by many returnees in the years before 1953 and, in many cases, it persisted throughout the Soviet period. Ginzburg also takes readers through the process of amnesty, rehabilitation, and the search for housing and appropriate work.

In *Vse Dorogi Vedut Na Vorkutu* (All Roads Lead to Vorkuta), Pavel Negretov, who was arrested for belonging to the NTS (National Labor Union of the New Generation) and spent from 1945-1955 in the mines of Vorkuta, presents a collection of anecdote-memoirs about the people he met in Vorkuta during and after incarceration, for many stayed in this city even after being freed. In one episode, Negretov describes how Ursula Valterovna Elberfeld (later to become his wife), daughter of repressed parents, went to Leningrad to study in 1949.

"Ursula always felt the stamp of being an outcast,"[29] writes the author, as he goes on to tell how a soldier who wanted to court her never came back after hearing that her parents had been incarcerated. With its emphasis on the post-camp period, this work provides valuable examples and insight into the disparity between policy and practice with regard to former prisoners.

Though they do not fit neatly into a section on historiography, two additional sources of memoirs should be mentioned here. Vozvrashchenie, a support organization for former victims, has published a number of their stories. One of their volumes, *Dodnes Tyagoteet*[30] (Till My Tale is Told), a collection of memoirs by women survivors, contains some information on the returnee theme. Lastly, the organization Memorial has played a significant role in exposing the nature and extent of victimization under Stalin and Stalinism. It provides victims with a forum for telling their stories and voicing their demands. Memorial's data base of information has been systematically collected since the beginning of the second period of de-Stalinization in 1987. The organization has a wealth of unpublished, unedited, sometimes handwritten memoirs, collected in the late eighties and early nineties, that provide insight into how ordinary people experienced the terror and its aftermath. These documents range from two to two-thousand pages and are the writings of mostly non-professional writers. To the extent that they are the testimony of witnesses, the historical value of these materials is undeniable. There is considerable rambling in these stories, but specific information on the victims' return can be found. The sources noted in this literature survey help form but a framework for understanding the Soviet victim's predicament. It is the object of this study to fill the canvas between these frames.

The Study

The return of these alienated, institutionalized, survivors, each representing many who had perished, was unsettling for them as individuals and traumatic for the body politic. The society to which they returned had no comfortable physical or emotional place to put them. Enormous adjustments would be required by the returnees, by their families, by their communities, and by the political system. All of these adjustments would have personal, social, and political consequences. The focus of the present study is the description of the attempt by victims of Stalinist terror to readapt and resocialize into Soviet society, and the reciprocal struggle of Soviet society and the Soviet system to adapt to returnees. The discussions that follow in this chapter should serve to offer a perspective on this problem. They will raise many questions, but they provide few answers as yet. These will be offered at a later stage.

It will be from the perspective of adaptive and maladaptive behaviors that we will examine the Gulag returnees, their families, and repression as a state instrument of governance. All living systems—individuals, families, and governments—either perish, or survive by adapting. The process of adaptation between two opposing parties requires an accommodation by at least one of the parties, but often by both. The Soviet system of state-run terror forced its citizens to accommodate to it through the unconstrained use of coercion. The surviving, returning prisoner was in some important ways a changed person from the one who first went into the camp. The families of the returnees were also changed by the experience. They were under pressure to change their feelings toward the prisoner in order to protect themselves from frustration and even, perhaps, imprisonment.

Soviet leaders adapted to repression and the use of terror as an instrument to maintain power, inmates (who survived) adapted to the Gulag; families and the social network of prisoners who were left behind had to adjust to their absence. As part of their effort to survive by adapting, prisoners were under considerable pressure to reshape themselves to fit into a pathologic system. As noted in Terence Des Pres' *The Survivor*, the first stage in camp is similar for all prisoners of totalitarian regimes, Nazi, Soviet, or other:

> every newcomer immediately had to traverse a course of profound personal degradation and humiliation.... There were two possibilities and within three months it became apparent which one would apply. By that time a man would have gone into an almost irresistible mental decline—if, indeed, he had not already perished in a physical sense; or he would have begun to adapt himself to the concentration camp.[31]

Prisoners had to learn what to do and how to act in their new situation, however abnormal it may have been.

For its part, the strength of the Soviet political system was its unwavering control over its citizens. This was also its weakness. Because it did not accommodate, it could not institute the kind of changes necessary to meet the changing conditions. It turned out to be a brittle monolith that finally crumbled.

We can view the cautiousness with which even a committed reformer like Gorbachev had to move as appropriate, though, given that the whole Soviet system was maladapted to repression. Indeed, terror and the use of forced labor (no stranger to tsarist times) had been an integral means of preserving the Soviet state's power since mid-1918 when Lenin legalized a decree sanctioning the existence of work camps.[32] By 1922, sixty-five concentration camps existed.[33] A year later the first Correctional Labor Camps were opened in the Solovetsky island monasteries in the far north.[34] (It was for this very reason that Memorial chose an unsculpted stone brought from Solovki, as the islands are also called, for its monument to victims of totalitarianism. It appropriately symbolized the continuity of Soviet terror.) Moreover terror, along with bureaucratization, a ruthless leader, and loyal executants and believers, were characteristic of Stalin's rule and Stalinism in general.[35]

Before proceeding with our discussion on de-Stalinization, we should note that the term "Stalinism" has a number of definitions. Some define it as the personal evil of Stalin (the person), while others view it as a larger phenomenon (the system). The beginning of the Stalinist repression has been variously attributed to the 1934 murder of Sergei Kirov or to the collectivization in 1930. There are even those who regard Lenin's "Red Terror" in the early days of the Soviet state as its starting point. Memorial adheres to the definition of A.D. Sakharov—"illegal and terroristic methods of governing," and considers that it can be applied to the entire period of Soviet rule, as its effects persisted.[36] Without getting into the discussion of the "hero in history," Stalinism seems well defined as "the meeting point of a man and a system, which has not only survived him in part but which also antedated him."[37] However, for our purposes we are primarily focusing on its manifestation in the years from 1934-1953 and the ensuing consequences.[38] These manifestations and these consequences of Soviet repression can be best understood as a system of interdependent parts that are to varying degrees adapted to each other in such a way that it is difficult to change only one part of the system.

The Stalinist system had no mechanism for accommodating to a constituency. It used repression as an adaptive tool, forcing accommodation to the totalitarian system. When we consider the central role played by terror in the maintenance of the Soviet state, then viewing it as a maladaptive system can help us to explain the resistance of the leadership to (liberalization-oriented) reform, which would require some accountability to a constituency. Because the Soviet system was adapted to repression, reform was a slow and dangerous undertaking. Revelations on the Stalinist past, and rehabilitation—the official admission of official crimes—ran the risk of destabilizing the system and unseating the leaders themselves.

By contrast, postwar Germany and Japan could move quickly because their "adapted" political systems were defeated by the Allies. They did not have to go through the slow process of evolving from within (noteworthy is the distinction between reproach "von aussen aus der Welt oder von innen aus der eigenen Seele" [from without—the world, or from within—the soul]).[39] Real change requires acknowledging past mistakes, attempting to correct them, and attempting to prevent their recurrence. This process is generally operationalized by revealing the extent of the crime, providing financial compensation, returning confiscated property, creating new laws, and prosecuting those responsible. Though these measures deal with juridical and political aspects, they do not cover the moral and metaphysical issues. While it is true that political systems can create climates of terror, the terror is carried out by individual people against other individuals. This brings into focus the question of personal responsibility for one's actions or inactions.

In 1947, Karl Jaspers discussed the German process of *Vergangenheitsbewältigung* in his work *Die Schuldfrage* (*The Question of Guilt*). He distinguishes between four types of guilt: criminal—clear violation of law; political—"es ist jedes Menschen Mitverantwortung, wie er regiert wird" (everyone is responsible for how he is governed); moral—the individual is responsible for all his actions, political and military, "Befehl ist Befehl" ("an order is an order") being unacceptable because a crime remains a crime even if it has been ordered by someone else; and finally metaphysical—the solidarity of man with man, making everyone co-responsible for wrongs and injustices, for not doing whatever is possible to prevent the crime.[40] He considers it morally absurd to accuse a whole people of a crime, because "es gibt keinen Charakter eines Volkes derart, dass jeder einzelne der Volkszugehörigen diesen Charakter hätte" (there is no such national character that everyone who belongs to the population group in question shares).[41] Thus, Jaspers argues, there cannot be collective guilt of a people or a group, though they may be politically liable.[42] In addition, when a whole people is labeled as guilty, this has the morally undesirable effect of mitigating the responsibility of any particular individual. The moral, metaphysical, and criminal guilt bring other issues to the fore, such as recognition of one's blindness to the evil of others. Jaspers raises the question of membership in the Nazi Party, a question that finds some analogy in the Russian membership in the CPSU. He maintains that we need to look at the context and motivation of those who joined the Nazi Party, since in 1936-37 belonging to the Nazi Party was part of keeping one's profession, and not necessarily a political act.[43] Jaspers asserts, "ohne Reinigung der Seele keine politische Freiheit" (without purification of the soul, there is no political freedom), which requires consciousness of guilt, of solidarity and of co-responsibility.[44]

The Gulag returnee's plight was compounded by the fact that this consciousness was only partially attained in the Soviet Union of the fifties, and had progressed only a little further in the late eighties and early nineties. One can argue that Gorbachev was clearly a proponent of raising consciousness about the Stalinist past, but the Soviet system was still in place (and he wanted to keep it that way). Revelations on the crimes of Stalinism even further discredited the already failing state structure.

Scope

A discussion of the aftermath of the terror would be incomplete without some assessment of the number of victims it claimed. The exact number of victims of Stalinist terror has long been a fiercely debated issue, even further intensified by the opening of official archives. We shall briefly review some of the available statistics demonstrative of the victimizations. Estimates range from the J. Arch Getty/Gabor T. Rittersporn "revisionist"[45] claims in the hundreds of thousands, to millions. The researchers presenting the lower-range figures assert that 786,098 victims were executed between 1930 and 1952-53, the majority of the death sentences having been carried out between 1937-1938. They conclude that a little over 2.3 million victims (excluding deaths among deportees and exiles) perished in the entire Stalin period.[46]

In his pioneering work prior to the opening of archives, Robert Conquest's original calculations were approximately twenty million victims. But the issue rages on, as evidenced by his attack on the revisionists' attempt to minimize the numbers of Stalin's victims:

> Those of us who accepted, in some areas, estimates that now seem too high, have amended or reconsidered. But some theory resembling psychosomatic blindness seems to prevent any act of self-criticism from Getty—without which he can scarcely expect absolution.[47]

Steven Rosefielde, considering the economic significance of the Gulag, calculated the forced labor population between 1929-1956. With regard to numbers at the height of the terror, he basically concurred with Conquest, Swianiewicz, Dallin, and Solzhenitsyn that 8 to 12 million prisoners were victimized.[48] Stephen Wheatcroft, citing other scholars (Timasheff, Jasny, and Bergson) who support his (lower-range) position, suggests that the labor camp population at the end of the thirties was approximately three and a half million.[49] Edwin Bacon, also basing his estimates of victimizations on a number of official archival materials, asserts that millions were incarcerated in the Gulag in its decades of existence. He contends that Gorbachev's glasnost was selective regarding which information from the archives to reveal and which to curtail. These selections were made at the discretion of the Party. Based on inflow and outflow statistics, Bacon calculates that there were approximately 12 million repressed in camps and labor colonies between 1934-1947.[50] Alec Nove goes even further in his estimate to assert that there were approximately 10 to 11 million "surplus deaths" in the thirties.[51]

Russian figures have tended to be in the higher range. In 1987 the economist, Nikolai Shmelyov, cited an estimate given by Khrushchev of those who were or had been in labor camps as 17 million for the years 1937-1953.[52] Dmitry Volkogonov, a historian who had ample access to official archives, asserted that 21.5 million were repressed from 1929-1953,[53] while Shatunovskaya, a former prisoner who worked on Khrushchev's rehabilitation commission gives 19.8 million as the number of persons repressed from 1935-41.[54] Colonel Grashoven of the Russian Security Ministry offers similar figures.[55] Aleksandr Yakovlev, one of the architects of perestroika, and head of Gorbachev's (and later Yeltsin's) Rehabilitation Commission, also subscribes to the high range assessments. He suggests that around 15 million Soviet citizens fell victim to man-made famine, dekulakization, deportation, and terror.[56] V.P. Zemskov cautions that the high numbers may include such innaccuracies as counting rear-rested victims twice.[57] And these are just the main actors in a debate that is as yet unresolved.

Witness this example of the ongoing discussion. In his recent work, *Life and Terror in Stalin's Russia, 1934-1941*, Robert Thurston argues that the 681,692 executions that he records for 1937-38 did not constitute mass terror and that the terror had no profound, long-term effects on everyday life.[58] In rebuttal, Robert Conquest disputes Thurston's numbers as well as Thurston's comparison of the hysteria surrounding the Stalin Terror to that of McCarthyism, during which the two Rosenbergs were executed. Conquest wryly suggests that the analogy would be more fitting if, in a two-year period, the Americans "shot that half a million suggested above, including most of the US Government and three-quarters of Congress, hundreds of writers, thousands of military officers—which might even have intimidated the citizenry a little."[59]

After the opening of the archives, the revisionist estimates of victims came out higher, and some of the traditionally accepted estimates were reduced. But the archives cannot present the true dimensions of the problem. Stephen Cohen calls our attention to the "great multitude" of descendants of Stalin's victims, who, as family members, were also afflicted by the terror. They can certainly be counted in the millions.[60] Thus we are still dealing with pervasive repression and terror on a massive scale. Though crucial in its conviction of the system, the exact calculation of repressed is a subject for a different kind of study. A significant issue is the distribution of repression within the time period—especially with regard to the fifties. (More attention will be devoted to this question at a later point.) Our concern here is those who survived[61] and the meaning of their experience for them, for Soviet society, and for the Soviet political system.

Periodization, Demography of Arrests, Releases

Now that we have dealt with the scope of the terror, let us turn to the development of repression in the course of time. The purpose of this section is not to discuss the political aspects of the period of terror, or Stalin's personal role, or the development of the camp system, but rather to present a chronology of the repression. Like the Gulag itself, the instrument of repression was an integral part of the

Soviet system from its early days, although, according to archival sources, 1926 seems to have marked the true birth of large-scale forced labor as a "method of reeducation."[62] In the words of one Russian historian,

> The Bolshevik authorities set out to destroy their real and potential opponents, casting aside all generally accepted [legal] norms.... The camps in all their forms—concentration, forced labor, special designation, corrective labor, etc. ... were ideally suited for this goal. The creation of the camps did not demand much time or special materials.[63]

The camps of the twenties, especially Solovki, were populated with, among others, priests, White Guards, socialists, anarchists, and other political opponents.[64] While the Stalinist terror was a constant threat, it varied in its intensity. There were waves of arrests, waves of releases, and different kinds of releases in different periods. Thus different cohorts of prisoners and returnees had different experiences.

In 1929, in the midst of the collectivization and de-kulakization campaigns, the idea of colonizing the northern regions with prisoners who had terms of longer than three years was proposed and accepted. This was as much practical as ideological because the prisons could no longer accommodate so many prisoners. In early 1930, a normative act that regulated the activity of the GULag (Main Administration of Labor Camps) was passed—the camp system had thus become a legally sanctioned instrument for exerting political influence on society[65] (i.e., deterring even potential opposition). The prisoners were used to exploit resources and build such infrastructures as railways, roads, and canals. By mid-1930, the corrective labor camps had already expanded to encompass 41,000 prisoners in the northern camps and 15,000 in the far eastern camps. The Vyshersky, Siberian, and Solovetsky camps confined another 84,000 prisoners.[66]

Those arrested in the countryside in the years 1930-1932 were primarily peasants while those arrested in the cities were mostly engineers, scientists, and the "bourgeois" intelligentsia. The terror gained new momentum after Kirov's murder in 1934, and 1935-36 saw arrests of oppositionists, mostly professional revolutionaries, and Party and Soviet workers. The Great Trials began in 1936 and were followed by the great purges of *Yezhovshchina* by 1937-38. This campaign of terror named after state security chief Yezhov "renewed" the whole state and Party apparatus, the military cadres, the diplomatic corps, and managers on all levels.[67] A great many of the victims were Party members, but also among the arrested were count-

less (non-Party) ordinary citizens, workers, and peasants. Blame for
the excesses of the purges was deflected to Yezhov, and he was
replaced by Lavrentii Beria at the end of 1938. The releases of the
late thirties "liberated" approximately 327,400 victims of the collectivization as well as "Trotskyites" and other oppositionists.[68] Their
freedom was largely restricted and often short-lived (see chapter 2).

The system of repression remained, however, and the Gulag and
prisons were constantly replenished. As the state's circle of suspicion widened, "Article 58," which defined "counter-revolutionary
crimes," was liberally applied. According to the Russian (and Soviet) Criminal Code, these offenses included: "any action directed
toward the overthrow, undermining or weakening of the authority
of the worker-peasant soviets ... espionage ... terrorist acts... [anti-
Soviet] propaganda or agitation, etc."[69] In essence, almost any type
of action—or inaction—could make one vulnerable to arrest under
these charges. Likely suspects came to include: active members of
the church, members of religious sects, rebels (i.e., anyone who in
the past had, however remotely, been involved in an anti-Soviet uprising), those who had contacts abroad, active members of student
organizations, the National Guard, anyone who had fought against
the Reds in the Civil War, representatives of foreign companies, anyone who had contact with foreign countries (i.e., businessmen, ho-
tel/restaurant owners, shopkeepers, bankers, clergy, the former Red
Cross), and so on. Even a veterinarian who had treated consular
dogs or a woman who supplied the German consul's milk, or her
brother(!), were subject to arrest.[70]

By 1940, such offenses as arriving at work twenty-one minutes
late were criminally punishable.[71] In this period political repression
was also carried out along national lines.[72] In 1939, for example,
Poles and Balts were targeted. In 1942-1945 other repressed national groups included Finns, Germans, Kalmyks, Chechens, Tatars,
Armenians, Latvians, Koreans, and others.

There were also releases of prisoners on the eve of the war. Approximately 420,000 prisoners were initially transferred to the Red
Army.[73] In the course of the war, the total of releasees sent to the
front comprised about one million prisoners.[74] Article 58'ers, even
if they requested the chance to fight for the motherland, and many
did, were generally not released in this period due to their discredited status.[75] The unfortunate few who were, however, were mobi-

lized into labor battalions and sent right to the front. Witness one such prisoner's description of his train journey: "I was sitting in the coupe, still dressed in my camp rags. The man across from me asked where I was headed. [I replied]: 'I escaped from the grave and I am searching for a new cemetery.'"[76]

After the war came the arrests of returning POWs—Soviet citizens coming back from incarceration in German camps only to enter the "NKVD verification-filtration points," that is to say, the Gulag. They were considered "not completely clean"[77] and often received ten-to-twenty-five-year sentences on charges of spying or treason.[78] To the postwar ranks of the repressed we can also add Ukrainians and, in Medvedev's words, "militant officers like Solzhenitsyn, who manifested too much audacity or curiosity."[79] Some of the ex-officers proceeded to lead the Vorkuta revolt of the late forties.[80] The years 1947-1948 brought a number of releases of those who had survived the arrest and incarceration of the Great Terror, since a served term could (but did not necessarily) allow for release. The next arrest wave, 1949-1952, struck "cosmopolitans," that is, the Jewish intelligentsia in, among others, the notorious "Doctors Plot" and "Leningrad Affair."

Stalin's death on March 5, 1953, "a biological event" that constituted "the first act of de-Stalinization"[81] led to an amnesty of March 27 that released 1.2 million ordinary criminals (53.8 percent) out of an official Gulag population estimated at 2.5 million.[82] Prisoners referred to this as the Voroshilov amnesty, though it was possibly a brief act of de-Stalinization on the part of Beria before his unanticipated arrest and death sentence. The amnesty did not apply to political prisoners. However, a few who were convicted or requalified on "criminal" charges may have fallen under this category. Moreover, approximately 600,000 new arrivals were added to the camp population of that year.[83] Writing in 1975, Roy Medvedev asserted that 4,000 prisoners were released in 1953.[84] It is not entirely clear to which contingent he is referring, or on what his information was based, but the archives have shown this to be a gross underestimate.

The years 1953-55 were a period of "silent de-Stalinization," during which some non-publicized rehabilitations took place.[85] The release (not to be confused with rehabilitation) of those convicted of "counter-revolutionary crimes" (Article 58'ers) was sanctioned by a decree of the General Procuracy of the USSR of May 19, 1954.[86]

Between 1954 and 1955 almost 90,000 political prisoners were released either under this decree, or on the basis of early reevaluation of their cases. Tens of thousands of others were also set free on the basis of a September 1955 amnesty for "wartime collaborators."[87] Additionally, certain groups of exiled kulaks—the victims of collectivization—were also released from special settlement by an MVD decree in the fall of 1954.[88] According to the Medvedevs, Khrushchev personally arranged for the release of a "very special 12,000" prisoners in 1954-1955, most of whom were influential Party members.[89] They also point out that only about 5 percent of those arrested in the thirties were still alive in 1956.[90] If true, then the group of returnees released in the fifties would have been largely composed of arrestees of the forties (former soldiers, etc.). Indeed, the strong presence of this contingent of ex-soldiers and officers in the Gulag population is, among others, evidenced by their heading of strike commissions in the camp rebellions of Norilsk and Vorkuta in 1953, and Kengir in 1954.[91]

Khrushchev's Secret Speech at the XX Party Congress on February 25, 1956 led to the liberation of a great majority of surviving prisoners and exiles, perhaps seven million, in 1956-1957.[92] In addition, some were granted posthumous rehabilitations.[93] Some figures on post-XX Party Congress releases have run in the millions, while others point to only "hundreds of thousands" of liberated citizens.[94] The Dutch historian Van Goudoever calculated that on the basis of registered voters approximately two million people had their rights restored.[95] Chapter 5 will devote more attention to these figures, but it may be that the discrepancies and inexactitude can best be explained by the fact that some of the historians who first started working with these numbers confused release with rehabilitation. In addition, there is a vast difference between the number of prisoners actually returning from the camps and the great number of their (implicated) family members returning from exile. They, too, faced the ordeal of reassimilation. For the purposes of this study, the exact number of returnees is less relevant than the experience of the returnee. What will be examined is the struggle of ordinary citizens, formerly labeled "enemies of the people," to reenter society, and the Soviet system's efforts to adapt to this prima facie evidence of its criminal nature, which began on a broad scale in these years.

Khrushchev

In what Stephen Cohen has called "the intensely historicized politics" of 1953-64,[96] Khrushchev partially decried Stalin's abuse of power, but blame was deflected from the socialist system that supported it and redirected to Stalin's "personal defects." Efforts were made in the legislative arena to modify and stabilize the system, but not to correct its fundamental flaws. Much was still left to the discretion of the authorities. In fact, elements of re-Stalinization were also introduced under Khrushchev, for example, the "parasite" campaign of 1957 which targeted mostly writers and poets. The Pasternak affair, in which the writer declined the Nobel Prize for literature for fear of exile from his country, was another example of Khrushchev's balancing act.[97]

Khrushchev was very much a man of his time and his ambivalent role—that of liberator and victimizer—reflected the zeitgeist, a recoiling from the past and a dread of the unknown future. This is the social and historical context that shaped the fate of the returnee, so we will proceed by examining it. His Secret Speech, which portrayed a governmental system whose modus operandi included criminal acts, lawlessness, mass murder, incompetent leadership and systematic falsification of history[98] resulted in a "mass exodus."[99] These revelations at the XX Party Congress were indeed a bold effort at de-Stalinization. However, materials from the Presidential Archive show that Khrushchev was late in arriving at this liberal position. He himself had played a direct role in the terror in Moscow and Ukraine in 1936 and 1937 as first secretary of the Moscow Committee and the Moscow City Committee of the Communist Party, and in 1938, as first secretary of the Communist Party of Ukraine.[100]

The KGB archives have yielded documentary materials that prove Khrushchev's participation in the conducting of mass repressions in Moscow, the Moscow province, and Ukraine in the prewar years. He had personally forwarded proposals for the arrests of leading figures of the Moscow City Council and the Moscow provincial Committee. In the years 1936-37 the Moscow and Moscow province NKVD was responsible for the repression of 55,741 people. Under Khrushchev's Party leadership in Ukraine in 1938 106,119 were arrested, in 1939—12,000, and in 1940—approximately 50,000. The Ukrainian Party Secretary personally sanctioned the repression of hundreds of people suspected of plotting terrorist acts against him.[101] Khrushchev did indeed have blood on his hands.

Other newly available evidence even further tarnishes both Khrushchev's reputation and his efforts toward de-Stalinization. While we know that in the fifties there were large numbers of releases of those arrested on political articles (58 and 59), statistics of the Procuracy of the RSFSR demonstrate that in these same years there were also a significant number of arrests for "especially dangerous crimes against the order of governing" (Article 59). In consequence, while some politicals were released, others were incarcerated. Article 59 defines as criminal, among a host of other activities, the maintenance of contact with foreign governments or their representatives with the goal of instigating armed intervention in the Soviet republic, helping with the declaration of war or organization of military expeditions after the declaration of war, banditism, and so on. Maximal penalty for such crimes was capital punishment.[102] Witness these examples of the pattern of convictions on Article 59-3, 59-3b, and 59-7, and so on, for the period of 1936 - 1957: 1936: 3,667, 1937: 4,372, 1938: 5,373, 1941: 14,415, 1942: 26,136, 1945: 5,981, 1949: 11,188, 1953: 13,257, 1954: 12,490, 1955: 12,765, 1956: 12,869, 1957: 14,930.[103] These figures suggest that some degree of tempo was maintained in the punitive repressive apparatus (see also chapter 5). They further attest to the Soviet system's dependence on repression as well as to the cosmetic character of the first period of de-Stalinization. While officials from Khrushchev on down denounced the Stalinist repression, it is clear from their actions that the system of governance did not renounce repression. This dualism, if not hypocrisy, expressed itself at all levels of the system and of society and hampered the rehabilitation of the returnees. The ambivalent attitude toward ex-zeks can be seen as having extended both from the top down and from the bottom up.

Pavel Negretov allegorized Soviet society's search for identity during this period in the tale of a former camp-mate: "The XX Party Congress gave Sasha freedom, and he became, like Dusya [his wife], a Stalinist, he did not trust the new course of the Party and did not believe that it would last."[104] (We can assume that Stalinism in this case refers to opposition to Stalin's successors, or to their methods of governance.) Negretov decided not to argue with them about their type of Stalinism: "they were simply looking to it for support in our unstable existence."[105] Like Hamlet, some people were more prone to bear the ills they had than to fly to others that they knew not of. And so the system in those years oscillated in a narrow range between de-Stalinization, stagnation, and re-Stalinization.

In his biography of Khrushchev, Roy Medvedev cites some concrete cases of returnees for whom Khrushchev intervened with preferential treatment, but he goes on to describe how fifteen years later (in the early 1970s) returnees making similar requests were rebuffed with the statement: "The fashion for rehabilitated people is now dead."[106] Newly available documentation provides additional examples of the shifting political forces. In a 1974 confidential meeting of the Politburo much discussion was devoted to the Solzhenitsyn case. Brezhnev commented cynically, "Solzhenitsyn was incarcerated, served his term for *gross violation of Soviet law* [my italics] and was rehabilitated. But how was he rehabilitated? He was rehabilitated by two people—Shatunovskaya and Snegov."[107] These two returnees to whom Brezhnev referred with such disdain played important roles in the de-Stalinization process. The former was a member of an official commission that examined the crimes of the thirties and the Moscow purge trials, the latter was a key organizer of the troika commissions that were empowered to release prisoners in 1956-57.[108] At the meeting there was apparent consensus regarding Brezhnev's views. It is therefore significant in measuring political (official) sentiment toward rehabilitation that among those present at this Politburo session were: Andropov, Grishin, Gromyko, Kirilenko, Kosygin, and Podgorny. (In a Politburo meeting ten years later, where "no-one found a good word to say about Khrushchev,"[109] the issue of Solzhenitsyn's rehabilitation was raised again. Chebrikov, then head of the KGB, asserted that a number of illegal rehabilitations of people who were "rightly punished" had taken place. He cited Solzhenitsyn as one such example. It is interesting to note that Gorbachev, who was later appointed General Secretary, was present at this session.) Stephen Cohen has described returnees as an "important historical and social dimension of political de-Stalinization."[110] Indeed, their fate was a key indicator of the state's persistent entrenchment in Stalinism.

To what extent could the Communist structure adapt to de-Stalinization without destabilization? What were in fact the tolerable limits of such political changes for the Soviet system? Brezhnev apparently felt that they had been exceeded under Khrushchev, and a process of re-Stalinization (absent unbridled mass terror) was carried out in the sixties and seventies. Prisoners and potential prisoners were generally more fortunate than their Stalinist-era counterparts, perhaps partially because detente rendered the opinion of the West of some significance. By and large, however, the Soviet political system of those years did not tolerate its dissidents (a group that sometimes overlapped, but was not synonomous with the Article 58'ers of the Stalin era). It incarcerated them, put them in psychiatric hospitals, or expelled them (i.e., Solzhenitsyn, Bukovsky).

If we conceptualize history as a dialectic process, then it is not surprising that the eighties brought a new corrective force to the repressions of the Stalinist system in organizations such as Memorial. The widely circulated stories of the survivors or their family members and the sympathetic public reaction to them provided Gorbachev's de-Stalinization efforts with a broader base of support than that enjoyed by Khrushchev. When Gorbachev mentioned "thousands" of victims of Stalin, many were disappointed by the grossly understated estimate. But it was a politically calculated underestimate.[111] This statement was at some level as monumental as Khrushchev's XX and XXII Party Congress revelations, because Gorbachev dared to reopen the subject. People were permitted to do investigation into the real numbers, and perhaps Gorbachev hoped that those "numbers would speak for themselves so that the leadership at the time would not have to take responsibility for some of the jarring disclosures."[112]

We might recall that Gorbachev did not want to let this rediscovery of history get too far out of (Party) control, because the Soviet system was still in place. Even so, there was a political tide, uncertain of its fate, but drifting unsteadily away from repression. Gorbachev's wide-ranging de-Stalinization and rehabilitation campaign coincided with and, perhaps even significantly contributed to the dissolution of the Soviet Union. But let us not get ahead of ourselves. Coming to terms with the Stalinist past began at the moment of release from incarceration.

Types of Release and/or Rehabilitation

Release did not by any means automatically imply rehabilitation, a term defined under Khrushchev as the "revision of all legal consequences of a judgment pertaining to a person who was unlawfully prosecuted, in consequence of the acknowledgement of innocence."[113] Some zeks received partial rehabilitations, that is, they were cleared of certain charges, while other charges remained in their record. Some prisoners who spent ten years in the camps were liberated (at some point) after their terms had been served. Many of them received "restoration of rights"—a term meaning that the prisoner was entitled to his former political and civil rights.[114]

In *The Limits of Destalinization in the Soviet Union*, Albert van Goudoever characterizes different types of rehabilitation: individual formal rehabilitation—reassessment of one's case and implication of innocence; social rehabilitation—compensation for lost wages and suffering, return of confiscated property, restoration of former position, pension and financial settlement, etc.; reinstatement in the Party; posthumous rehabilitation; and public rehabilitation.[115] This last category, which was utilized mostly for prominent Party members, is described by Jane Shapiro as, "restoration of [the victim's] name and deeds to Soviet historiography. A victim is considered to have been rehabilitated fully when his biography has been published in the Soviet press or his own work republished."[116]

As regards legal rehabilitation, Leopold Labedz accurately describes this as the invalidation of juridical sentences which does not necessarily imply political rehabilitation.[117] Alternatively, writing in the sixties, Shapiro asserts that repudiation of the victim's conviction (judicial rehabilitation) was also accompanied by restoration of Party or military rank where relevant. She goes on to claim that physical rehabilitation, that is, release from prison or labor camp, followed judicial rehabilitation.[118] This was not the case. Prisoners were sometimes released on the basis of amnesties, or when their terms expired, but apart from being liberated from the camps, their status was uncertain. The process of rehabilitation and reinstatement in the Party appears to be and to have been systematically long and drawn out. As we shall see, a great number of victims did not receive rehabilitation until forty years after their release. Rehabilitation was a politically explosive issue because, as Labedz asserts, "what is at stake in the battle of rehabilitations is not so much the resurrection of the dead as the survival of the living—at least the political survival."[119] Many Party members had built their careers under Stalin and were personally involved in the repression. They were certainly aware that exoneration of its victims could implicate them.

Some zeks were released with "loss of rights": while the charges were dropped, they were sent to particular places for "permanent settlement" or "eternal exile." Those without rehabilitation had a so-called "minus" in their passports which restricted the ex-prisoners' freedom of movement, and forbade them to be closer than 101 kilometers from Moscow, Leningrad, Kiev, and a number of major cities. This was enforced by, among other means, requiring the ex-prisoner to report at least twice monthly to the local authorities. One former prisoner observed that, "of course, that [practice] did not exclude constant secret surveillance, the system of stool-pigeons that entangled the whole country.... I think the system of surveillance in some variant still exists even today [1995]." In addition to that, she explained, "the work book (*trudovaya knizhka*), without which it was impossible to get work, also had a notation on the potential employee's stay in the camps, which barred access for me even to such work as that of a stenographer..."[120] Another prisoner defined exile thus:

> What is exile? Exile means you are assigned to a region and transported there. You have no passport, you are registered for that region. You have no right to exceed the borders of that region. Then there is a commandant that you have to check in with twice a month. And these are all of your rights and obligations. No one is interested in where you work, what you eat ... it is not camp, where you are fed...[121]

Some prisoners were released with restored rights, constituting, in a certain sense, rehabilitation, but they were not given a *spravka* (certificate of proof of rehabilitation, see Roginsky's comm͟ ͐ ͐ chapter 5). Such documents carried a great deal of meaning in the Soviet social system. There was considerable variation in how they were dispensed. Some prisoners were released and rehabilitated in the fifties and sixties, others were released in the fifties and rehabilitated only in the nineties, and some were never rehabilitated. As will be noted, rehabilitations are still being carried out, the status of the children of the repressed and/or rehabilitated is being reconsidered, and the scope of the rehabilitations is still being calculated.

The year in which the prisoner was released had political implications which affected their resocialization. Even in the years prior to Khrushchev's XX Party Congress "Secret Speech," there must have been apprehension about how political accounts would be balanced.

Witness the remarks of Anna Akhmatova in 1956, "[n]ow they [officials] are trembling for their names, positions, apartments, dachas. The whole calculation was that no one would return."[122] But many, some millions, somehow managed to survive and did return. The Gulag survivors who returned to society after 1953 were confronted with many of the same problems as their predecessors. Previously published memoirs in addition to many stories which were collected in the late eighties attest to this. Even later in the fifties the rehabilitation of victims was impeded by the fear of those in power for their own safety and for the stability of the system. The rehabilitation of its victims was almost antithetical to the authoritarian (Soviet style) system, because it threatened the legitimacy of that system—a legitimacy maintained by terror.

Some prisoners not only returned, but wanted reinstatement in the Communist Party. The motivation behind this desire is a perplexing issue. Sometimes it was utilitarian. When Evgeniya Ginzburg received her rehabilitation certificate, she was given the telephone number of the Party Control Commission. She could not understand why the Soviet official thought the she would want reinstatement in the Party. He replied, "Otherwise what will you put in your curriculum vitae when you are offered a job?" and when they ask, "Were you ever a member of the Party and, if so, when and how did you leave it ... you'll have to use the formula recorded in your case file: 'Expelled from the Party for counter-revolutionary Trotskyite terrorist activity.' So I suggest you phone this number!"[123]

Sometimes the motivation was ideological. One prisoner was sent to Kolyma, worked at hard labor twelve and a half hours daily, was "freed" in 1942 in order to join a labor army, and went to the front in 1943. After that he was sent into exile. While working in Moscow in 1950, he was rearrested, interrogated for three and a half months, and released for "lack of crime." Despite these victimizations, he worked for many years toward getting reinstated in the Party, and finally achieved this goal in 1956.[124] This story is not uncommon. Many victims considered themselves to be the "builders of socialism" and thus had abiding faith in the Party. Another survivor claimed that he always "found solace in his belief in the truth of the Party"[125] during his years of repression. This long-time prisoner who spent from 1937-1956 in arctic camps and then in exile in Norilsk literally dreamed of reinstatement in the Party. He even wrote a poem to the effect that he would walk onto Staraya Ploshchad (i.e., the building of the Central Committee of the CPSU) into a familiar office, someone would shake his hand and give him his Party card. "It may take a long time, but this day will come," ends the verse.[126]

Comparative Context

Though the scale of repression (number of victims) may vary from one state to the next, the experience of all former victims of political repression raises similar issues on a personal and on a societal level. German and Soviet survivors have been most often compared to one another. Isaak Moiseevich Filshtinsky, ex-prisoner, philologist, and philosopher makes the following distinction: "German survivors came into a world that was screaming, here it was silent."[127] Though his description of the world to which Nazi survivors returned is not completely accurate, by comparison the world was up in arms. Moreover, what the scream shares with the silence is that they are both traumatic victim-society interactions. It is beyond the scope of the present work to compare Soviet totalitarianism with Nazi totalitarianism or any other state repression.[128] It is also inappropriate to measure one level of evil against the other. Suffice it to say that the large-scale repression of any system often leads to similar psychological symptoms and personal readaptation issues among survivors. However, rather than examine the human tragedy on a massive scale, we will trace its path through the personal lives of some of its victim-survivors.

Rehabilitations and De-Stalinization

The nature and scope of the problems faced by Soviet victims are particularly difficult to determine, because during the lengthy period of the dictatorship (1917-1991) relatively little information was *officially* provided. In the course of the forties, fifties, and sixties, as noted earlier, some millions did return to Soviet society. According to one official source, during the first wave of rehabilitation, from 1954 to 1962, approximately 30,000 victims were rehabilitated per year for a total of 258,322.[129] Khrushchev stated at the secret session of the 1956 XX Party Congress that 7,679 people had been rehabilitated since 1954,[130] while Dmitry Yurasov of Memorial maintains that 612,000 people achieved this status in the period between

1953 and 1957.[131] Yet another source notes that between 1954 and 1961 737,182 individuals received rehabilitation (or were posthumously rehabilitated).[132] Notwithstanding these discrepancies, given the large prison camp population, this is still a small percentage of victims. Major General Vladimir Kupets, head of the section on rehabilitation for Russian and foreign citizens of the Military Procuracy in 1996, offered an answer to the not very puzzling question of why there were not more rehabilitations at that time: "The CPSU couldn't very well admit that it was the henchman of its own people."[133] It is worth noting that the cumbersome rehabilitation process was made even more so because it was carried out by "professional" procurators, many of whom had not even received higher education.[134]

By 1962 rehabilitations started dropping off sharply, as only 117 cases (some involving more than one person) were examined. In 1963 only fifty-five cases were reviewed, and in 1964 the numbers dwindled even further still — twenty-seven cases were examined in all.[135] The rehabilitation process had nearly come to a halt. It is not clear exactly how many rehabilitations were granted between 1964 and 1987, but the numbers can be counted in no more than some hundreds[136] because of the political questions surrounding the issue of culpability. Under Gorbachev, the process resumed and in the two years between 1987 and 1989 almost 840,000 individuals were rehabilitated.[137] Between the time the law "On rehabilitation of victims of political repression" was passed on October 18, 1991 and 1994, approximately 207,400 repressed persons were rehabilitated in the Russian Federation,[138] while half a million were officially granted this status in the USSR.[139]

These low figures on rehabilitation demonstrate the limited character of official de-Stalinization. They do not, however, reflect the number of ex-prisoners who were unofficially exonerating themselves. Former victims of Stalinist terror had been coming to terms with their social status and personal history since their release, starting in most cases in the fifties. Their unofficial efforts at de-Stalinization were expressed in *samizdat*, private conversations, and so on by those who were not too afraid to talk.

Official silence from the late fifties to the eighties made it difficult to follow the fate of the returnees. While it is hard to determine the exact nature of the resocialization experience, what we regularly find is a marked discrepancy between the official perspective (and traditional vision of Khrushchev's de-Stalinization) and the victim's own experience—enough to make us skeptical of the official version. Vladlen Loginov (Gorbachev Foundation), a historian and member of a work group of Khrushchev's 1956 rehabilitation commission, asserts that returnees of those years were more or less received (or perceived) by society as heroes.[140] This was probably the case for a few prominent Party members and some members of the intelligentsia. Likewise, Vladimir Pavlovich Naumov, a historian, an official in President Boris Yeltsin's administration, and member of the rehabilitation commission set up under Aleksandr Yakovlev during Gorbachev's de-Stalinization campaign, maintained that the victims on the whole did not remain on the fringes of society. In most cases they were released, they applied for rehabilitation, and they looked for and found work. Roy Medvedev concurs on this last point that those who returned (emphasizing that 80 percent did not live to return) had no trouble finding work quickly and in their specialty.[141] Naumov went on to discuss that while there were some problems—for example, those liberated around 1949 often feared rearrest (and with good reason, as many were in fact rearrested), in some instances, their children had died or had been given different names (like Nikolai Bukharin and Anna Larina's son)—at the same time, they considered themselves to be the "builders of socialism" and sought reinstatement in the Party.[142] This, of course, would be more likely to be the case with repressed members of the Communist Party like Lev Kopelev. But many non-Party members (i.e., kulaks or members of other parties) were among the ranks of the repressed.

Naumov calls attention to the diverse composition of the victim group. For example, many henchmen like Yagoda, head of the NKVD from 1934-1936, or Sudoplatov, high state security official, came to be included in this category. (Yagoda was executed as a traitor in March of 1938—see chapter 7 for a discussion of his case when it came up for rehabilitation review in 1998. Sudoplatov was incarcerated from 1953 to 1968. After release, KGB chief Andropov personally helped him find housing. Sudoplatov later lectured to young KGB officers, wrote memoirs, and petitioned for rehabilitation, which he finally achieved in 1992. He was granted the pension of a lieutenant general of state security, and his medals were posthumously returned in 1998.[143]) Furthermore, Naumov asserted that in gen-

eral, returnees were not dogged throughout their lives by their status as former victims. The statistics on rehabilitation for 1992-1994,
sometimes nearly fifty years after their release, however, would
suggest a somewhat different reality—that there had been at least
an ambivalent attitude toward this group both during Khrushchev's
de-Stalinization and in the ensuing years. We can infer this from
the backlog, even fifty years later, of people still attempting to be
rehabilitated.

Specifically, in the two-year period following the dissolution of
the Soviet Union, over two million applications were filed for judicial rehabilitation, of which one million were examined. Half a million applicants were granted a *spravka* (rehabilitation certificate),
while another half million of these were still being reviewed in
1995.[144] In this "peak year" for rehabilitation, a total of 1.8 million
applications were examined.[145] Naumov expected another several
million, because of a 1994 law regarding restoration of property and
compensation which are contingent upon the status of "rehabilitated."[146] With regard to the motivation to change their status from
"repressed" (those who directly suffered—were incarcerated in prisons or camps) or *postradavshy* (this term applied to children of
victims, who were not themselves incarcerated, but "suffering" by
virtue of their family status)[147] to "rehabilitated," we cannot look
into the individual reasons of these post-Soviet period applicants. In
the years between 1992 and 1997, four million applications for rehabilitation were filed. Approximately 1.5 million of these applicants received rehabilitation certificates, while 296,000 were declared
to have suffered political repression.[148] We can infer that if these
few million, and likely many more, did not, or could not obtain rehabilitation in the years immediately following their return, and now
are trying to, there were a host of official barriers during the post-
release period.

It is interesting to note that the victims' children are also heirs to
the problems of rehabilitation, as witnessed by the debate on their
status that raged on in 1996.[149] In May of the previous year, the
Constitutional Court of the Russian Federation changed the official
status of children of "enemies of the people" from "*postradavshy*"
to "repressed."[150] In November of that same year, Yeltsin signed a
law declaring that "children who were together with their parents in
places of detention, in exile, or special settlement are considered to

have undergone political repression and are subject to rehabilitation."[151] Under this law, the process is almost automatic—if the parents have been rehabilitated, their children need only apply with proof. This, in turn, has caused consternation among many elderly survivors who appear to feel that their status as repressed has to some degree been devalued by extending it to people who have never had the common experience of being a zek.[152] To confer this status upon those who have suffered only indirectly downgrades the martyrdom of those who suffered directly and those who died in the process.

While Naumov and others promote the official position that the victim was welcomed back into society, the story that many of the victims themselves tell is quite different. They persisted in their fear that repression was an event waiting to happen again. For example, when asked if they felt a continuing sense of injustice after release, one former victim answered "always,"[153] another said, "yes, in my contact with people I was a white raven."[154] And yet another, Zoya Dmitrievna Marchenko, at age eighty-eight, after having been arrested three times, spending twelve years in labor camps (nine of them in Kolyma and Dalstroy), and eight years in bessrochnaya ssylka (eternal exile) recounted the following:

> I always lived with the sense of being a "second-class citizen." I was always prepared for any trouble. I understood that my life and fate did not depend on my personal qualities, but on the forces that governed the country and I simply had to somehow try to survive...[155]

The clear discrepancy between the "top-down" official description of the readaptation process and the "bottom-up" victim's recollection of that same process suggests either distortion of facts by one side or the other or wide variations in the experience of returnees. These variations range between full social and political reintegration and non-assimilation, that is, the rejection of the individual by society and the system. The latter can be described as a "mis-fit" between the system and the returnee.

The Return: Status as Ex-Prisoner

The general status of being an ex-prisoner has both personal and social consequences in all societies. In addition, the status of having been a Gulag prisoner has its own special problems. Let us approach the special problems of the Gulag returnee by first examining the larger issue of being an ex-prisoner. Even in open and relatively permissive democratic societies, the reentry of ex-convicts is problematic, because it often requires a process of resocialization. It has been argued that prison can serve as an advanced course in how to be a more proficient criminal.[156] The incarceration separates the prisoner from day to day contact with the outside world, forces him/her into close physical contact with criminals, and provides the conditions for their bonding by stigmatizing them. To adjust and adapt to this is to become more socialized into the criminal subculture. The American system of criminal justice as well as many others use rehabilitation programs and parole officers in an attempt to counteract the criminalizing tendencies of prison and to facilitate the ex-convict's resocialization process. Even so, reentry into society is difficult.[157]

The problem of resocialization becomes even greater when the detention was not the result of a criminal act committed by the (ex-) prisoner, but rather a consequence of political circumstances. The prisoner is thus innocent—the victim of a criminal system. When that innocence is recognized by the society to which they are returning (as was mostly the case with victims of Nazi terror), then the problems are on a different scale than those of ex-prisoners returning to a society that does not recognize or not satisfactorily recognize their innocence.[158] Victims of state terror in the Soviet Union were officially regarded as members of a conspiracy who had betrayed society at large, and so were to be viewed thenceforth as traitors with a pariah status. For those returnees released before the XX Party Congress, and especially for those released before Stalin's death, the state, not its victim, was considered to be the offended party, and seemed to regard itself thereafter as perpetually entitled to harass the former "enemies of the people." One consequence of this was that the prisoner and, by association, their family were made to feel like outcasts.

The pariah status of ex-prisoners was not unknown in the West. In *Stigma: Notes on the Management of a Spoiled Identity*, Erving Goffman describes the spread of what we can appropriately call a "social disease" throughout the stigmatized network. He refers to a letter from a girl to an advice columnist asking how to deal with being the daughter of an ex-con. She signed the letter: "AN OUTCAST." Goffman notes that, "in general, the tendency for a stigma to spread from the stigmatized individual to his close connexions provides a reason why such relations tend to either be avoided or to be terminated, where existing."[159] This is even more likely to occur when fear of official retribution and/or belief in the guilt of the relative are added to the predicament. To compound the assault on the returnee's social status, it was not uncommon to find upon return from the Soviet labor camp that one's spouse had married someone else.

To recapitulate, and emphasize the Soviet problem, there are at least three types of return situations: prisoners returning to a changed system (i.e., Holocaust survivors), prisoners returning to a social system that is essentially unchanged from the one that they left (Stalin-era returnees), and rehabilitated prisoners (those who served their terms in a "correctional labor camp" and subsequently received exoneration, mostly post-1956 returnees) returning to an unreformed system. Once on the outside, Gulag returnees were confronted with many barriers: physical (restriction of movement), psychological, professional, etc. Thus, they often referred to society as the "big zone" (*bolshaya zona*), the "little zone" (*malaya zona*) being the camps. The fact that even after release, many continued to think of themselves as inhabitants of a zone illustrates how deeply ingrained their prisoner status was.

The ensuing discussion focuses not so much on the nature of the terror, but on its aftermath, the place that the camp experience occupied in the victim's post-camp life—the effect that the *status* of having been in the camps had on the victims, and on others. It will include examining the psychological impact of the camp experience and its sociopolitical consequences. This status is reflected by the way victims viewed their future, and in the behavior and feelings between the victim and family members, the social network, and the regime.

The issue has been raised regarding whether the incarceration politicized the victims and led them to question or challenge the legitimacy of the system. In *The Survivor*, Des Pres quotes from Bernard Malamud's *The Fixer*, a novel based on the Beilis trial in Kiev in 1913. He uses this well-known case of anti-Semitism in a discussion on victims as scapegoats of power. The protagonist, a Jew, is accused of killing a Christian child and is held in prison for two years under barely survivable conditions. Anti-Semitism is the government's only basis for its case, thus it must try to break his spirit, obtain a confession, and create conditions that will ensure illness or death. If the prisoner has perished, the problem is resolved. But the prisoner is determined to stay alive, and force the government to bring him to trial, so that he can prove his innocence: "at first he insists that he is not a 'political person.' But gradually his suffering brings home to him the pain of all men in extremity, and he comes finally to realize that when the exercise of power includes the death of innocent people, 'there's no such thing as an unpolitical man.'"[160]

Aside from such spontaneous, implicit politicization that can arise from the condition of being in the death grip of the state, some ex-prisoners' attitudes demonstrate a very conscious, deliberate development of a reorientation toward the Soviet political system. In addition, there were also involuntary, psychopathological changes that were caused by the physical and mental suffering imposed on the victims of repression. These were the psychological and emotional derangements associated with a post-traumatic stress disorder which persisted even after incarceration. A further determinant of the ex-prisoner's course would be whether the injustice that they had experienced continued to plague them. It is thus essential to explore to what extent, if any, after release from internment (in labor camps or prisons) victims of Stalinist terror experienced an ongoing process of injustice. Such unjust treatment would be exemplified by job rejections and/or assignment to work far below levels of qualification, harassment, loss of rights to housing, or social ostracism. The practical and personal problems associated with the victim's resocialization were manifested in the victim's professional prospects and family relationships, including the creation of new families. Alternatively, we must look at the attitude of society, the regime, and family members toward the victim, specifically considering what the existence of such a group of returnees with demands for housing, pensions, justice, and so on meant to society and the system.

Briefly coming back to the issue of the Soviet state's maladaptation, let us consider a few additional points with regard to the returnee. Gulag prisoners had to have been distorted, at least temporarily, by the very process of adaptation that permitted them to survive. This was manifested by the jargon and other symbols and carryovers—the subculture—of camp life with which they returned. To this extent they would be reshaped as "misfits" in the context of a "normal" system to which they would be returning. Hence they could be expected to have had major adjustment problems even if people had been awaiting them with open arms. For their part, the social networks that the repressed had left had been forced by their needs for political and psychological adaptation to find ways to get along without them. The mechanism included self-protective "distancing" attitudes which, in effect, blamed the victim for their predicament.

Oral History, Social Memory

There are a number of problems that complicate the task of accurately depicting the course of the victims' return and subsequent resocialization into society. To begin with, the information on this subject can only be culled from a number of scattered sources. In addition, even when found it is meager. In the many published and unpublished camp memoirs, typically as many as a few hundred pages are devoted to the camp experience, but only two pages describe the release, exile, rehabilitation, and possibly reinstatement in the CPSU. It is not surprising that the writers of camp memoirs dwell on their most traumatic years. Their preoccupation bears similarities to a Post-Traumatic Stress Disorder which is relived in flashbacks, hoping to resolve itself. Not only is their mind drawn back to the camp experience by its intensity, but the status of being a martyred victim has its own sacred satisfactions. They are witnesses for themselves and for those whom they saw perish. By contrast, post-camp frustrations with family, jobs, and housing would seem to be trivial. But they are not. They are the reverberating evidence of a dysfunctional social and political system. All of the survivors encountered during this present research felt that the camp experience had a tangible effect on their subsequent lives, yet when asked about post-camp events, they invariably bring the discussion back into the camp setting. Thus, oral history is an essential tool for exploring the aftermath of incarceration, because it gives us the opportunity to probe, and to discover how ex-prisoners often remained victims of the Soviet system. This examination is not just an exploration of individual memories, although the information that we will use will be gathered from individuals. Rather, we will be employing an oral history methodology not to look *at* individuals, but to look *through* them to the political system.

The oral memoir, however, has its own set of limitations, especially in places where freedom of speech has been curtailed for decades. Galina Skopyuk, a Gulag survivor who remained in Norilsk, Siberia after release in 1954, did not begin to discuss her camp experience until 1985. But even a decade later, in 1995, this former "enemy of the people" was still hesitant to disclose details of the Stalinist terror, so deeply ingrained was her fear that the Soviet *system* may somehow have survived the dissolution of the Soviet state. Reflecting on the post-camp decades, she told an interviewer:

> the whole time we were silent, careful not to say anything anywhere, so that we were not sent back to where we had been. And now I'm talking to you, and maybe I'll say something wrong and be punished again and I'll sit [in prison camp] again. So you're afraid your whole life...[161]

Isak Dinesen (the author of *Out of Africa*) writes, "All sorrows can be borne if you put them into a story or tell a story about them."[162] Clearly she was not spied on by secret police. There is a persistent conflict between the former victim's therapeutic necessity to release memory, and "through expression ... put it to rest,"[163] and the victim's fear of speaking lest they become vulnerable to their enemies or to their own traumatic memories. It is said that there are two kinds of survivors—those who cannot speak and those who cannot stop speaking.[164] In the early days of Memorial, during the late eighties, streams of clients lined up at the Moscow reception room to describe their experiences. Their task was a therapeutic one: "the pressure in these victims to tell their story was so great that they poured out their hearts to one foreign observer even though they had been informed that he did not understand Russian."[165] We can term this the psychological function of oral history.

There are also altruistic motives for giving testimony. Many Gulag returnees, like Holocaust survivors, feel that it is their moral imperative to bear witness. Des Pres calls this "response-ability," conscience being the guide to one's responses.[166] He also quotes a prisoner's markings on the walls of a latrine in a Soviet camp, "May he be damned who, after regaining freedom, remains silent."[167] For this group of returnees there are at least two reasons to tell and retell their stories: one is the issue of guilt among survivors toward the many who did not return (addressed in the citation above), and the other is to serve as a warning so that such catastrophic evil can never manifest itself again. When the threat of a Communist president in

Russia seemed very real in 1996, many of the Gulag survivors who had given oral histories or written memoirs, said that they did whatever they could to prevent Communism's upsurge by telling their personal stories of Soviet repression. Hence oral history can serve a political function.[168]

Another problem associated with gathering an oral history is accuracy. What it is about the past that is relevant to remember is always to some degree determined by the needs of the present. Thus post-camp experiences can influence what is recalled. Also, the need to be a member of a group can influence what is remembered. Social memory "as an expression of collective experience ... identifies a group, giving it a sense of its past and defining its aspirations for the future."[169] But how and what memory was to be preserved among survivors of the Gulag whose traumatic experiences were for years at variance with both accepted morality and official description? It was risky to attempt to get social validation for the camp experience after leaving the camp. Openly recalling events of the Stalinist repression did not serve to legitimize the (then) present from the late-fifties to the mid-eighties. Official social memory was systematically imposed from above through schooling, newspapers, books, radio and television, and so on,[170] so the reference points of the victims of Soviet terror were often blurred by the total absence of collective remembering of the repression during those (post-Khrushchev, pre-Gorbachev) years. It is little wonder, then, that the flood of memories of individual experiences that surfaced in the Soviet Union in the late eighties was deeply influenced (and supplemented) by the experiences of others.

For the victims of Stalinism, memory of repression became so collective after 1988, that one has to diligently and critically explore the individual's own experience. An interview with Paulina Stepanovna Myasnikova, a woman who had been a camp-mate of Evgeniya Ginzburg's, revealed such a similarity between her story and that of Ginzburg's personal description from *Into the Whirlwind*, that it appeared that she had merged her memory with Ginzburg's story. Like Goethe, who accounts how he threw the family china onto the street after the birth of his sibling, and was later unsure as to whether his memory of the incident was real or a reconstruction in his childish imagination of a story repeated by his parents,[171] Paulina seemed, albeit unwittingly, to be conveying someone else's story as her own.[172]

Besides the problems of meager sources, official censors, self-censure, poor memory, inaccurate memory, and collective memory, there is also the problem of helping the person to focus on the issue at hand. Leopold Haimson, who headed an interviewing program between 1960 and 1965 on the Menshevik movement, remarks that a major task was "to eliminate major digressions from the narrative flow (usually biographical details concerning secondary figures...).''[173] He also discusses the problems that subjects have in reconstructing memories of events that took place a number of decades earlier. Myasnikova's case illustrates how the cognitive difficulties associated with advanced age can distort the accuracy of recollections. Furthermore, events are not always recalled as they really happened, but rather as individuals and the group wished them to be. Memory is sometimes not far from mythology[174]—assigning a heroic role to one's self in order to make the unbearable a little more bearable.

In Haimson's Menshevik project, a variety of sources was utilized to converge on the memory. The subjects were provided with primary sources, speeches they had written, and records of events in which they had participated, in an effort to refresh their memories. He was also trying to fill in the gaps and to illuminate the "sometimes deliberate obscurities in the written record."[175] The life journeys of those who contributed to the political history of the Menshevik Party were, clearly, different from those who were victims of Stalinist terror, so Haimson's observations may be of only limited value here. He reports that the

interview experience ... appeared at least partially to confirm the common sense rule that, especially many years after the event, the mind recalls most easily and vividly moments of victory rather than moments of defeat, times of hope rather than times of despair.[176]

These findings are not confirmed by my own interviews with former victims which reveal that survivors of Stalinist terror tend to focus on the victimization rather than their survival. Nor do the recorded oral histories of Memorial (done around 1990) generally concur with this rule. Haimson's generalization is understandable when applied to a political party—the Mensheviks were striving toward a particular goal, they would most likely remember well the steps that were made in achieving it. Moreover, Gulag victims had few victories to recall. Despite its limitations and its selective nature, oral history is one of the best methods we have for reclaiming and reconstructing part of the social history of the group that shared the common experience of Soviet repression.

Limitations of the Study

This study does not represent a complete picture of the experience of resocialization of the Gulag survivor or the significance of the returnee to the Soviet social and political system. The sample is obviously limited to the information available, and is thus biased. Those who survived and emigrated are largely not relevant to this research, because it is assumed that they did not readapt to Soviet society. There remains a relatively small number of returnees still alive and able to give interviews, so the selection of subjects is based more on availability than on any other factor. A great majority of the oral histories are taken from the urban intelligentsia; the experiences in the provinces and of workers and the peasantry will surely have parallels, but will not be identical.

Furthermore, we are only dealing with the group that wrote memoirs, that came to social organizations such as Memorial and Vozvrashchenie, that either needed assistance or wanted to unite with others who had shared their fate. Those returnees who never registered with organizations for the repressed or took part in public life as former victims were perhaps completely reassimilated. Maybe they were so successful in re-adapting to Soviet society that their status was not remarkable, and they were not in need of any support. On the other hand, perhaps they never adapted at all, not even enough to publicly and privately join the ranks of their fellow ex-zeks. Aside from others' descriptions and official archives, we have no way of learning about the experience of those who never came forward about their past. We can, however, learn a great deal about a part of the group that shared the common experience of being incarcerated in labor camps and prisons during the Stalinist terror. That part should be a very good indication of the whole.

Notes

* In transcribing Russian names and words I have used the popular English spelling system in the text, except in cases where other spellings are more familiar to Western readers, that is, "Yeltsin" instead of "Eltsin." The endnotes and selected bibliography are, with a few exceptions, transcribed in accordance with the Library of Congress system.

1. Zasedanie Politbiuro TsK KPSS, 24 November 1988, TsKhSD, f. 89, op. 42, d. 23, ll. 1-5.
2. The railroad from Igarka to Salekhard, for example, was one of the last main forced labor projects under Stalin. It was never completed and the camps were abandoned after Stalin's death.
3. David Remnick, *Lenin's Tomb: The Last Days of the Soviet Empire* (New York: Random House, 1993), p. 7.
4. Ibid.
5. See "Stalin's Shadow Will Pursue Russians for Many Years More," *International Herald Tribune*, 12 March 1996.
6. Ian Buruma, *The Wages of Guilt: Memories of War in Germany and Japan* (New York: Farrar, Straus & Giroux, 1994), pp. 21, 63, 104, 116 and 128, among others.
7. See also the introduction to John Löwenhardt, *The Reincarnation of Russia: Struggling with the Legacy of Communism, 1990-1994* (Essex: Longman, 1995).
8. See, for example, Bruno Bettelheim, "Individual and Mass Behavior in Extreme Situations," *Journal of Abnormal and Social Psychology* 38, no. 4 (October 1943): 417-452; Leo Eitinger and Axel Strom, *Mortality and Morbidity after Excessive Stress* (Oslo: Universitet Fologet, 1975); Dierk Juelich, Hrsg., *Geschichte als Trauma* (Frankfurt am Main: Nexus Verlag GmBH, 1991); Eve Berstein Carlson and Rhonda Rosser-Hogan, "Trauma Experiences, Post-traumatic Stress, Dissociation, and Depression in Cambodian Refugees," *American Journal of Psychiatry* 148, no. 11 (1991); J. David Kinzie, William H. Sack, et al., "The Psychiatric Effects of Massive Trauma on Cambodians: I. The Children," *American Journal of the American Academy of Child Psychiatry* 25, no. 3 (1986): 370-76; Nancy Speed, Brian Engdahl, et al., "Post-traumatic Stress Disorder as a Consequence of the POW Experience," *Journal of Nervous and Mental Disease* 177, no. 3 (1989): 147-53; Paloma Aguilar, Alexandra Barahona de Brito, Carmen Gonzalez Enriquez, eds., *The Politics of Memory: Transitional Justice in Democratizing Societies*, (Oxford: Oxford University Press, 2001).
9. Articles on the subject include: Nanci Adler and Semën Gluzman, "Soviet Special Psychiatric Hospitals: Where the System Was Criminal and the Inmates Were Sane," *The British Journal of Psychiatry* 163 (1993): 713-720; Id., "Pytka Psykhiatriei. Mekhanizm i Posledstviia," *Obozrenie Psikhiatrii i Meditsinskoi Psikhologii imeni V.M. Bekhtereva* 3 (1992): 138-152; Stephen Kotkin, "Terror, Rehabilitation, and Historical Memory: An Interview with Dmitry Yurasov," *Russian Review* 51 (1992): 238-62; "Punished Peoples of the Soviet Union: The Continuing Legacy of Stalin's Deportations," a Helsinki Watch Report, September, 1991. See also *Totalitarizm i totalitarnoe soznanie* (Tomsk: Tomskii oblastnoi antifashistskii komitet, 1996).
10. For accounts of the terror see, for example, Robert Conquest, *The Great Terror: A Reassessment* (London: Pimlico, 1990); David J. Dallin and Boris I. Nicolaevsky, *Forced Labour in Soviet Russia* (London: Hollis & Carter, 1948); Roy Medvedev, *Let History Judge: The Origins and Consequences of Stalinism*, revised edition (New York: Columbia University Press, 1989); Ralf Stettner, *'Archipel GULag': Stalins Zwangslager—Terrorinstrument und Wirtschaftsgigant. Entstehung, Organisation, und Funktion des sowjetischen Lagersystems 1928-1956* (Paderborn: Ferdinand Schöningh, 1996).
11. Stephen F. Cohen, *Rethinking the Soviet Experience: Politics and History since 1917* (New York: Oxford University Press, 1985), p. 97, and "The Victims Return: Gulag Survivors and the Soviet Union after Stalin." I am particularly grateful to Professor Cohen for providing me with this unpublished 1983 paper. As far as I know, it is the first analysis on the social dimensions of the return.

12.   My own *Victims of Soviet Terror: The Story of the Memorial Movement* (Westport, CT: Praeger Publishers, 1993) examines the history of the organization Memorial, the history of Stalin's crimes, and the personal stories of a number of those who were repressed. The oral histories (interviews with former victims and Memorial leaders) were gathered after 1988, during the second period of de-Stalinization. The book addresses some of the issues of the post-camp period, particularly the revelations about the Stalinist past and their impact under *glasnost*, as well as the psychological effects of decades of silence. However, *Victims of Soviet Terror* does not specifically deal with the re-assimilation process.

13.   Kathleen E. Smith, *Remembering Stalin's Victims: Popular Memory and the End of the USSR* (Ithaca, NY: Cornell University Press, 1996), p. 171.

14.   Ibid., p. 32.

15.   For a more detailed examination of this work, see my review in the *Russian Review* 57, no. 1 (January 1998): 157-58.

16.   Adam Hochschild, *The Unquiet Ghost: Russians Remember Stalin* (New York: Penguin Books, 1994).

17.   Jane P. Shapiro, "Rehabilitation Policy and Political Conflict in the Soviet Union 1953-1964," (Ph.D. dissertation, Columbia University, 1967).

18.   Albert P. Van Goudoever, *The Limits of Destalinization in the Soviet Union: Political Rehabilitations in the Soviet Union since Stalin* (New York: St. Martin's Press, 1986), p. 47.

19.   Ibid., p. 48.

20.   Irina Sherbakova, "The Gulag in Memory," in Luisa Passerini, ed., *Memory and Totalitarianism* (Oxford: Oxford University Press, 1992), pp. 103-115.

21.   Adler and Gluzman, "Soviet Special Psychiatric Hospitals: Where the System was Criminal and the Inmates were Sane."

22.   *Zven'ia: Istoricheskii Almanakh*, volumes 1 and 2, (Moscow: Progress, Fenix, Atheneum, 1991, 1993).

23.   G.M. Ivanova, *GULAG v sisteme totalitarnogo gosudarstva* (Moscow: MONF, 1997), p. 81.

24.   Eugenia Ginzburg, *Within the Whirlwind* (New York: Harcourt Brace Jovanovich, Publishers, 1981), p. xvi.

25.   Ibid., p. 198.

26.   Ibid.

27.   Ibid., p. 199.

28.   Ibid.

29.   Pavel Ivanovich Negretov, *Vse Dorogi Vedut Na Vorkutu* (Vermont: Chalidze Publication, 1985), p. 128.

30.   *Dodnes' Tiagoteet*, Vypusk 1 (Moscow: Sovetskii Pisatel', 1989). In 1999, Indiana University Press published the English translation of this work, entitled *Till My Tale Is Told: Women's Memoirs of the Gulag*.

31.   Terence Des Pres, *The Survivor. An Anatomy of Life in the Death Camps* (New York: Oxford University Press, 1976), p. 79.

32.   Conquest, p. 310.

33.   Ibid.

34.   Edwin Bacon, *The Gulag at War: Stalin's Forced Labour System in the Light of the Archives* (London: Macmillan Press Ltd., 1994), p. 44. For information on the history, structure and function of the Soviet forced labor camps see also the valuable Memorial reference work, N.G. Okhotin, A.B. Roginskii, eds., *Sistema ispravitel'no-trudovykh lagerei v SSSR* (Moscow: Zven'ia, 1998); and Stettner.

35.   Adler, *Victims*, p. 39.

36. Ibid., p. 3.

37. François-X. Coquin, "Comments on the Current 'Ferment' and Revision of History in the Soviet Union: Stakes, Limits, Outlook," in Takayuki Ito, ed., *Facing Up to the Past: Soviet Historiography under Perestroika* (Sapporo, Japan: Hokkaido University Slavic Research Center, 1989), p. 23.

38. The year 1934, rather than 1930, has been chosen because most of the information in this study relates to victims of the Great Terror.

39. Karl Jaspers, *Die Schuldfrage* (Zürich: Artemis-Verlag, 1947), p. 17.

40. Ibid., pp. 10-11.

41. Ibid., p. 18.

42. Ibid., pp. 20, 39.

43. Ibid., p. 48.

44. Ibid., pp. 94-95.

45. Even the very term "revisionist" has been subject to debate. Stephen Cohen notes, in the past the term referred to historians who accepted and reinterpreted data. It is now applied to a "particular school of thought that has accepted falsification, dismissed established evidence and misinterpreted newer materials," cited in Robert Conquest, "Small Terror, Few Dead," *Times Literary Supplement*, 31 May 1996, p. 3.

46. J. Arch Getty, Gabor T. Rittersporn, Viktor N. Zemskov, "Victims of the Soviet Penal System in the Pre-war Years: A First Approach on the Basis of Archival Evidence," *American Historical Review* 98, no. 4 (October 1993): 1023-24.

According to Memorial researchers who have culled data from the KGB archives, no less than one million prisoners were executed between the years 1921-53 (Ofitsial'naia Spravka "Memoriala" k dniu politzakliuchënnogo v 1997gg., 30 October 1997).

47. Robert Conquest, "Playing Down the Gulag," a review of Edwin Bacon's *Gulag at War*, *Times Literary Supplement*, 24 February 1995, pp. 8-9.

48. Edwin Bacon points out that Rosefielde's numbers are higher than the official tallies he derived from the archives for those years (Bacon, pp. 16-17). For other overviews see R.W. Davies, *Soviet History in the Yeltsin Era* (London: Macmillan Press Ltd., 1997); Ibid., "Forced Labor Under Stalin: The Archive Revelations," *New Left Review* no. 214 (November-December 1995): 62-80. See also Steven Rosefielde, "Stalinism in Post-Communist Perspective: New Evidence on Killings, Forced Labour and Economic Growth in the 1930s," *Europe-Asia Studies* 48, no. 6 (1996): 959-987; Stephen Wheatcroft, "The Scale and Nature of German and Soviet Repression and Mass Killings, 1930-1945," *Europe-Asia Studies* 48, no. 8 (1996): 1319-1353; J. Arch Getty, R.T. Manning, eds., *Stalinist Terror: New Perspectives* (Cambridge: Cambridge University Press, 1993).

49. Bacon, p. 18.

50. Ibid., p. 27.

51. Alec Nove, ed., *The Stalin Phenomenon* (London: Weidenfeld and Nicolson, 1993), pp. 29-33.

52. Bacon., p. 35. Shmelëv, Khrushchev's son-in-law, cited an even higher figure of arrests between 1935 and 1941—close to 20 million—in a conversation with Stephen Cohen. See chapter 4 in Stephen Cohen, *Rethinking Russia* (New York: Oxford University Press, forthcoming).

53. *Nezavisimaia Gazeta*, 4 March 1993.

54. *Argumenty i fakty*, No. 20, 1990.

55. Cited in Vera Tolz, "Ministry of Security Official Gives New Figures for Stalin's Victims," *RFL/RL Research Report* 1, no. 18, 1 May 1992, p. 9.

56. "Staraia Komnata," Russian television broadcast, May 1996.

57.   *Times Literary Supplement*, 24 February 1995, p. 8.
58.   Robert W. Thurston, *Life and Terror in Stalin's Russia, 1934-1941* (New Haven, CT: Yale University Press, 1996), pp. 63, 90.
59.   *Times Literary Supplement*, 31 May 1996, p. 3. See also Robert Conquest, "Victims of Stalinism: A Comment," *Europe-Asia Studies* 49, no. 7 (1997): 1317-19.
60.   Cohen, *Rethinking Russia*, chapter 4.
61.   It is not possible to calculate exactly how many victims survived the terror to return to society, but former exiles and deportees, effectively living in prisons without walls, should be counted in the category of "returnees," since they generally shared the problems attendant to that status. It is likely that well over five million victims (including population groups) returned in the fifties. See also endnote 92.
62.   Bacon, p. 45. The author's cautious assertion is based on new archival material.
63.   Ivanova, pp. 19-20. See also p. 29.
64.   Marc Jansen, *A Show Trial Under Lenin: The Trial of the Socialist Revolutionaries, Moscow 1922* (The Hague: Martinus Nijhoff Publishers, 1982), p. 175.
65.   Ivanova, pp. 31, 47.
66.   Bacon, pp. 46-47.
67.   Roy Aleksandrovich Medvedev, response to questionnaire developed by Stephen F. Cohen in a letter written on September 10, 1980.
68.   V. Rogovin, *Partiia Rasstreliannykh* (Moscow, 1997), p. 457. See also *Argumenty i Fakty*, no. 5, 1989.
69.   *Ugolovnyi Kodeks RSFSR* (Moscow, 1950), pp. 35-43.
70.   Conquest, *The Great Terror*, pp. 257, 271.
71.   See Peter H. Solomon, Jr. *Soviet Criminal Justice under Stalin* (Cambridge: Cambridge University Press, 1996), pp. 301-305.
72.   "National operations" in 1937-38 were directed against various ethnic groups for alleged collaboration or suspicion of being agents of foreign intelligence services. Approximately 250,000 of these victims (half of them Poles) received the death penalty. See N.V. Petrov, A.B. Roginskii, "'Pol'skaia operatsia' NKVD 1937-1938gg.," in *Repressii protiv poliakov i pol'skikh grazhdan* (Moscow: Zven'ia, 1997), p. 33.
73.   "GULAG v gody voiny: Doklad nachalnika GULAGa NKVD SSSR V.G. Nasedkina, Avgust 1944g.," *Istoricheskii Arkhiv* 3 (1994): 64.
74   Ivanova, p. 110.
75.   Ibid., p. 111. See also V.N. Zemskov, "GULAG (istoriko-sotsiologicheskii aspekt)," *Sotsiologicheskie Issledovaniia* 6 (1991): 23-24.
76.   Gleb Iosifovich Anfilov, "Materialy k biografii: Vyderzhki iz pisem, dnevnikov i drugie dokumenty," Memorial, f. 2, op. 1, d. 4, l. 0001 2909 0267.
77.   V.P. Naumov, "Sud'ba voennoplënnykh i deportirovannykh grazhdan SSSR, materialy komissii po reabilitatsii zhertv politicheskikh repressii," *Novaia i Noveishaia Istoriia* 2 (1996): 101; Id., "O Massovykh repressiiakh v otnoshenii voennoplënnykh i deportirovannykh grazhdan," unpublished paper, December 1996.
78.   Marta Craveri, "The strikes of Norilsk and Vorkuta camps and their role in the breakdown of the Stalinist forced labor system," unpublished paper, p. 16; see also Ulrike Goeken, "Von Kooperation zu Konfrontation: zur Repatriierung sowjetischer Kriegsgefangener und Zwangsarbeiter nach dem Zweiten Weltkrieg," *Arbeitskreis Militärgeschichte e.V. newsletter* 7 (September 1998): 16-20.
79.   Medvedev, questionnaire.
80.   Andrea Graziosi, "The Great Strikes of 1953 in Soviet Labor Camps in the Accounts of their Participants: A Review," *Cahiers du Monde russe et sovietique* XXXIII, 4 (octobre-decembre 1992): 421-22.

81. Cohen, *Rethinking*, p. 103, and "The Victims Return," p. 7.
82. GARF (State Archive of the Russian Federation), f. 9401, op. 2, d. 450, l. 471.
    See also Marta Craveri, Oleg Khlevniuk, "Krizis Ekonomiki MVD (konets 1940 - 1950 gody)" *Cahiers du Monde russe* XXXVI, 1-2 (janvier-juin 1995): 182.
83. Graziosi, p. 430.
84. Roy A. Medvedev and Zhores A. Medvedev, *Khrushchev: The Years in Power*, (New York: Columbia University Press, 1977), p. 19.
85. Van Goudoever, p. 11.
86. Prikaz General'nogo Prokurora Soiuza SSR, Ministra Iustitsii Soiuza SSR, Ministra Vnutrennikh Del Soiuza SSR i Predsedatelia Komiteta Gosudarstvennoi Bezopasnosti pri Sovete Ministrov Soiuza SSR za 1954, No. 96ss/oo16/00397/00252, May 19, 1954. GARF, f. 8131, op. 32, d. 3284, ll. 40-41.
87. V.N. Zemskov, "GULAG: istoriko-sotsiologicheskii aspekt," *Sotsiologicheskie Issledovaniia* 7 (1991): 14.
88. Ibid., "Sud'ba 'Kulatskoi ssylki' (1930-1954)," *Otechestvennaia Istoriia* 1 (1994): 118-147.
89. Medvedev and Medvedev, p. 19.
90. Ibid., p. 20.
91. Alla Makarova, "Noril'skoe Vosstanie, Mai - avgust 1953," *Volia, Zhurnal uznikov totalitarnykh sistem* 1 (1993): 70, 82; see also Marta Craveri, "Krizis Gulaga: Kengirskoe Vosstanie 1954 goda v dokumentakh MVD," *Cahiers du Monde russe* XXXVI, 3 (juillet-septembre 1995): 319-344.
92. According to V.N. Zemskov, 113,735 individuals charged with "counter-revolutionary" crimes remained in the camps and colonies on January 1, 1956 ("GULAG," *Sots. Is.* 7: 14). However, to this estimate should be added a great number of others who were also victimized by the terror. Many incarcerated prisoners and exiles had exiled spouses, children, siblings, aunts, etc. In this study, these individuals are also considered returnees.
93. Medvedev and Medvedev, p. 20.
94. Van Goudoever citing Medvedev and Sakharov respectively, p. 46.
95. Ibid.
96. Cohen, "The Victims Return," p. 2.
97. Adler, pp. 42-44.
98. Michel Heller and Aleksandr Nekrich, *Utopia in Power* (London: Hutchinson, 1986), p. 531.
    Khrushchev's son, Leonid, fell into the hands of the Germans during the war and was recaptured by the Soviets. On the basis of collected documents, he received a sentence of capital punishment. Apparently Khrushchev pleaded to, among others, Stalin for the sentence to be revoked, but his efforts were to no avail. For thoughts on Khrushchev's motivation for the Secret Speech, see Vadim Udilov, "Za chto Khrushchev otomstil Stalinu," *Nezavisimaia Gazeta*, 17 February 1998.
99. Cohen, *Rethinking the Soviet Experience*, p. 97.
100. "Massovye Repressii Opravdany Byt ne Mogut," *Istochnik* (Vestnik Arkhiva Presidenta RF) 1 (1995): 126-127.
101. Ibid. See also the introduction by L. Golovkova in *Butovskii Poligon: 1937-1938* (Moscow: Moskovskii antifashistskii tsentr, 1992), pp. 26-28.
102. *Sbornik zakonodatelnykh i normativnykh aktov o repressiiakh i reabilitatsii zhertv politicheskikh repressii* (Moscow: Izdatel'stvo Respublika, 1993), p. 14; *Ugolovnii Kodeks* (Moscow: OGIZ, 1936). pp. 31-37.
103. GARF, f. 461, op. 8s, d. 395, l. 2.
104. Negretov, p. 114.

105. Ibid., p. 115.
106. Roy Medvedev, *Khrushchev* (Oxford: Basil Blackwell, 1982), p. 98. Many return-ees have confirmed this assertion.
107. A.V. Korotkov, S.A. Melchin, A.S. Stepanov, compilers, *Kremlëvskii Samosud: Sekretnie Dokumenty Politbiuro o pisatele A. Solzhenitsyne* (Moscow: Rodina, 1994), p. 361.
108. Cohen, "The Victims Return," p. 24.
109. Davies, *Soviet History in the Yeltsin Era*, p. 213. At this meeting, Gorbachev spoke in favor of the restoration of Party membership to Malenkov and Kaganovich.
110. Ibid., pp. 1-2.
111. Only after he fell from power did Gorbachev (feel safe enough to?) reveal full information about how his own family was repressed. He told two American report-ers, Jonathan Sanders and David Remnick, that members of his and Raisa Maksimovna's family had been arrested as kulaks and exiled to Siberia. Clearly he knew that this fate was shared by many more than "thousands."
112. Adler, p. 45.
113. Van Goudoever, p. 8.
114. Ibid.
115. Ibid.
116. Jane P. Shapiro, "Soviet Historiography and the Moscow Trials: After Thirty Years," *Russian Review* 27, no. 1 (January 1968): 69.
117. Leopold Labedz, "Resurrection - and Perdition," *Problems of Communism,* vol. XII, no. 2 (March-April 1963), p. 52.
118. Shapiro, "Rehabilitation Policy," p. 310.
119. Labedz, p. 51.
120. Zoia Dmitrievna Marchenko, answer to questionnaire, April 6, 1995.
121. Evgenii Aleksandrovich Gramp, interview with Memorial members (transcribed oral history), 16 July 1990.
122. Cohen, *Rethinking the Soviet Experience*, p. 99.
123. Ginzburg, pp. 412-413.
124. Boris L'vovich Brainin, "Vospominaniia vridola," Memorial, f. 2, op. 1, d. 27, ll. 2909 306-323.
125. Lev Gavrilovich Gavrilov, "Zolotoi Most," Memorial, f. 2, op. 1, d. 5, l. 2909 1511.
126. Ibid., l. 2909 1691.
127. Isaak Moiseevich Fil'shtinskii, interview held at his Moscow home, April 20, 1995.
128. For further examination of this question see Ian Kershaw, Moshe Lewin, eds., *Stalinism and Nazism: Dictatorships in Comparison* (Cambridge: Cambridge University Press, 1997).
     Among the newest of memorials to victims of state repression, Cambodia's museums of sun-bleached skulls are a particularly graphic reminder of that regime's loss of humanity and humankind, *International Herald Tribune*, 8-9 June 1996.
129. *Moskovskie Novosti*, no. 12, 31 March 1996, p. 14.
130. Stephen G. Wheatcroft, "Glasnost and Rehabilitations," in Takayuki Ito, ed., *Facing Up to the Past*, p. 201.
131. Kotkin, "Terror, Rehabilitation...," p. 252.
132. Rogovin, p. 487.
133. *Moskovskie Novosti*, no. 12, 31 March 1996, p. 14.
134. GARF, f. 461, op. 8s, d. 3223, l. 18.
135. Vladimir Naumov, "Znamia ili mishen?," *Moskovskie Novosti*, no. 42, 20-27 Octo-ber 1996.
136. See Wheatcroft, "Glasnost," p. 208; Rogovin, p. 487.

137. Rogovin, p. 487.
138. Galina Vesnovskaia, "Rabota po reabilitatsii," *Volia* 2-3 (1994): 208.
139. Vladimir Pavlovich Naumov, interview held at his office on Staraia Ploshchad', Moscow, April 21, 1995. See also "Massovye Repressii Opravdany Byt ne Mogut," *Istochnik* 1 (1995): 117-32.
140. Vladlen Terent'evich Loginov, interview held at his Moscow home, March 3, 1994.
141. Roy Medvedev, response to Cohen questionnaire.
142. Naumov, April 21, 1995.
143. Marc Jansen and Ben de Jong, "Stalin's Hand in Rotterdam: The Murder of the Ukrainian Nationalist Yevhen Konovalets in May 1938," *Intelligence and National Security* 9, no. 4 (October 1994): 689-90. See also "Uznik XX S"ezda," *Obshchaia Gazeta*, 29 August - 4 September 1996.
144. Naumov, interview. See also "Ob ispolnenii organami vnutrennikh del zakonodatelstva o reabilitatsii i ob arkhivnom fonde RF," in *Otechestvennye Arkhivy* 6 (1995): 27; *Memorial Aspekt* 15, August 1995.
145. For more statistics on rehabilitations in the nineties, see T.I. Anikanova, "O reabilitatsii zhertv politicheskikh repressii," *Otechestvennye Arkhivy* 1 (1999): 110-114.
146. See "Pokaianie i iskuplenie: Postanovlenie Pravitel'stva Rossiiskoi Federatsii," *Rossiiskaia Gazeta*, 20 May 1994.
147. For a discussion on the meaning and legal consequences of the status of "postradavshii" see *Rossiiskaia Gazeta*, 31 May 1995, p. 5.
148. Anikanova, p. 113.
149. See among others: "Reabilitirovannie i postradavshie: prava i l'goty," *Rossiiskaia Gazeta* 76, 20 June 1996, p. 3; "Kto reabilitirovan," *Tikhookeanskaia zvezda* (Khabarovsk), 6 March 1996, p. 2; "Postradavshim ot repressii," *Vladivostok*, 12 April 1996, p. 12.
150. *Rossiiskaia Gazeta*, 31 May 1995. An interesting discussion on this theme was presented in *Sudebnie vedomosti* (Krasnodar) 12, December 1995, p. 5; see also "Zhertvy repressii nuzhdaiutsia v zashchite," *58er* nos. 9-10 (October 1995), p. 3; Anatolii Karpychev, "Deti GULAGa: ran'she ikh nazyvali 'stalinskimi sirotami' seichas nazyvaiut 'postradavshimi'," *Trud*, 19 August 1997.
151. "Federal'nii Zakon o vnesenii izmenenii i dopolnenii v Zakon Rossiiskoi Federatsii 'O reabilitatsii zhertv politicheskikh repressii'," *Rossiiskaia Gazeta*, 11 November 1995; *Izvestiia*, 25 April 1996.
152. Semën Samuilovich Vilenskii, interview held at "Vozvrashchenie" headquarters (his Moscow home), May 2, 1996.
    "Zek" is often applied as a term for prisoner (*zakliuchënnyi*).
153. Lev Razgon, interview held at his Moscow home, April 16, 1995.
154. E. Repa, spring 1995 response to a questionnaire developed for this project.
155. Zoia Dmitrievna Marchenko, interviews held at her Moscow home on April 6 and April 13, 1995.
156. Karl Menninger, *The Crime of Punishment* (New York: Viking Press), 1968.
157. Case overloads and greater emphasis on victimology have altered or diminished these practices in recent years. See Freda Adler, Gerhard O.W. Mueller, William S. Laufer, *Criminology*, second edition (New York: McGraw-Hill, Inc., 1995), pp. 386, 402, 494.
158. Recognition of a survivor's innocence by society is not necessarily the prescription for a hearty welcome. For insight into the problems of re-assimilation encountered by Dutch Holocaust survivors see, among others, Connie Kristel, "'De Moeizame Terugkeer': De repatriëring van de Nederlandse overlevenden uit de Duitse concentratiekampen," ('The Difficult Return') in *Jaarboek van het Rijksinstituut*

voor Oorlogsdocumentatie (Amsterdam: Oorlogsdocumentatie '40-'45, 1989), pp. 77-100; Dienke Hondius, "A Cold Reception. Holocaust Survivors in The Netherlands and their Return," *Patterns of Prejudice* 28 (1994): 47-65.

159. Erving Goffman, *Stigma: Notes on the Management of a Spoiled Identity* (Engelwood Cliffs, NJ: Prentice-Hall, 1963), p. 43.
160. Des Pres, pp. 11, 13.
161. RTL5 (Dutch television documentary), "Gijzelaren van de Goelag," 3 July 1995.
162. Isak Dinesen, *2,715 One-Line Quotations for Speakers, Writers and Raconteurs* (New York: Crown Publishers, Inc., 1981).
163. Des Pres, p. 36; and Paul Thompson, *The Voice of the Past, Oral History* (Oxford: Oxford University Press, 1988), p. 151.
164. Mark Kurlansky, *A Chosen Few: The Resurrection of European Jewry* (Reading, MA: Addison-Wesley Publishing Company, 1995), p. 123.
165. Adler, p. 109.
166. Des Pres, p. 46.
167. Ibid., p. 38.
168. In his "Intellectuals on Auschwitz: Memory, History and Truth," Omer Bartov argues that it is a false distinction to separate the emotional need to bear witness from the moral imperative, to distinguish between "those who write so as to rid themselves of a burden which otherwise would make their existence impossible and those who feel charged with a moral mission and direct their writing at the public ... thereby [fulfilling] a social and moral function without becoming necessarily politicized." He does not take into account here that politicization depends on the political climate in which that story is told. *History & Memory* 5, no. 1 (Spring/Summer 1993): 102.
169. James Fentress and Chris Wickham, *Social Memory: New Perspectives on the Past* (Oxford: Blackwell, 1992), p. 25.
170. Ibid., p. 134.
171. Ibid., p. 22.
172. At age eighty-eight, Miasnikova, who plays a small role in the "Sovremennik" production of Ginzburg's story, was already in her ninth season. See "Krutoi Marshrut Sud'by," *Trud*, 15 January 1998.
173. Leopold H. Haimson, ed., *The Making of Three Russian Revolutionaries* (Cambridge: Cambridge University Press, 1987), p. viii.
174. Valerie Raleigh Yow, *Recording Oral History* (Thousand Oaks, CA.: Sage Publications, 1994), p. 181.
175. Haimson, p. 14.
176. Ibid., p. 17.

2

The First Return: Between Liberation and Liberalization, 1947-1953

The Return of the Repressed

The title of this section refers to one of Freud's basic hypotheses regarding the cause and treatment of mental disorders in individuals. In the context of this discussion, however, the term will be used to describe how a dysfunctional social system deals with disowned parts of itself.

Briefly, Freud's hypothesis is that people regularly experience forbidden thoughts, feelings, or impulses and instead of finding socially acceptable ways to express or satisfy them, they repress them. They become "forgotten" by being relegated to an amnestic section of the mind. There, these forbidden impulses persist, exerting constant pressure to have their demands satisfied. In consequence, it requires considerable mental energy to continually keep them from intruding into consciousness. The individual's peace of mind depended on preventing "the return of the repressed," and when the repressed impulses break through the ego's mechanisms of defense, the person experiences psychiatric symptoms and is at risk for decompensating.[1]

Freud's hypothesis is being appropriated here for use in the social and political arena. The "return of the repressed" refers to the victims of the Soviet system who were repressed by the state, incarcerated in the Gulag, and then returned to Soviet society. Freud's concept is useful in understanding both the cause and the result of this political process because Gulag returnees were not just people, they were also living memories that could no longer be denied. Writing on the Holocaust in 1971 Ernest Rappaport asserts, "survivors of

51

the camp were treated as unwelcome disturbers of a lulled world conscience and their persistent mental anguish after liberation was shrugged off as their resistance against adjustment." He further describes the "preferred attitude of forgetting" that the victims resisted.[2] The "return of the repressed" is not just an exploration of individual memories. It is an examination of the tension created by the constant struggle between the Soviet system's efforts to repress its citizens and the citizens' efforts to express themselves. Organizations like Memorial were able to force a recognition of both the repressed people and their repressed history. This eventually led to a crescendo of revelations during Gorbachev's de-Stalinization.

Though repression was the Soviet way of functioning, we will investigate the deeper meaning of the Soviet returnee question within the theoretical framework of a dysfunctional social system with its recurring conflict between the repressed and the repressive forces. Our examination will begin with the period of exile of the late forties, since this commenced the first significant wave of returnees to society. These returnees were mostly the prisoners who had gotten ten-year sentences in 1937. Their experiences are an important indicator of society's sentiment toward their "politically criminal" fellow countrymen. Prisoners were freed from the confines of their prison, but as their stories will attest, their new status could hardly be called liberated. Commenting on release in the pre-Khrushchev years, Solzhenitsyn aptly observed,

> There is a curse on those 'released' under the joyless sky of the Archipelago, and as they move into freedom the clouds will grow darker.... Release is arrest all over again, the same sort of punishing transition from state to state, shattering your breast, the structure of your life and your ideas, and promising nothing in return.[3]

(Solzhenitsyn's comment could also be applied to the Khrushchev years, as later returnee tales will evidence.) In terms of the ex-prisoners' personal freedom, exile effectively constituted a prison without walls. With his characteristic grim irony, Solzhenitsyn reminded his countrymen that exile was supposed to be among "the inventory of instruments of oppression which the glorious revolution was to sweep away forever."[4] In *The Gulag Archipelago*, he points out that exiles did not intimately discuss things past, as was common practice in prisons, nor did they make photographs, lest they be suspected of organizing anti-Soviet activities. For these reasons, Solzhenitsyn found it difficult to collect stories about the lives of those in exile.[5] However, these stories were eventually incorporated into memoirs that were published in *samizdat* or later collected in the eighties. They comprise a rich store for our reconstruction of Soviet attitudes toward Gulag returnees.

In this section we will explore a number of stories about the returnee experience in exile. These stories include their living conditions, family relationships, working conditions, contact with and mutual attitude toward Soviet authorities, their (realistic) fear of rearrest, and their sense of self. Enduring problems associated with all of these issues were to be recurrent themes in the life of returnees even as late as the seventies. This will be amplified later.

Return to Soviet society began at the moment of release, but the reception that awaited the returnees varied with the historical period. While the releases at the end of the thirties and the beginning of World War II will not be dealt with extensively here, some of the patterns established at that time were to become standard practice for the release and rehabilitation experience of later years. For example, Medvedev has chronicled the fact that important military men such as Rokossovsky and Meretskov, and well-known civilians such as Tupolev and Korolyov belonged to this category of returnees, and received complete rehabilitation. They returned to work and were given high positions. But, according to Roy Medvedev, their comfortable status was accompanied by a warning:

> Give your signature that you will never tell anyone what you saw and what you know. Otherwise, you will end up in camp. You saw terrible things. You don't want them to happen to you again. You don't want that?—Then be silent! Don't even tell your wives in bed anything about the camp. Don't say anything about the torture! Don't say anything about the interrogation! Then you will do whatever you want: work, the army, the front, battle, work as People's commissars, ministers. You will be trusted.[6]

Silence in exchange for rehabilitation—"a bargain with the devil" as it were, was initiated here and later employed under Khrushchev. While release with rehabilitation was possible, the practice was not widespread. In those unusual circumstances when it did occur, the sentence was revoked, the case was closed, and the rights were restored. As release and return became a more common practice, the procedure became more complicated. Most prisoners were released because their term had expired unless their sentence was arbitrarily extended; others were pardoned under an amnesty, but this did not mean that they were exonerated. The increasingly institutionalized and bureaucratized rehabilitation process can be used as an important gauge for measuring the Soviet system's adaptation to repression. It reflected the ability of the system to tolerate its mistakes.

Medvedev's description of the conspiracy of silence is confirmed by a number of stories from early returnees. Their stories are sometimes reminiscent of Josef K.'s visit to The Lawyer's residence in Kafka's *The Trial*. There he makes the acquaintance of another "accused" man, a long-time client, who is desperately employing every possible measure to extricate himself. He tells K. that he has hired five additional lawyers to work on his case.[7] Innocence cannot be assumed and must be proven against an overwhelming assumption of guilt. (One ex-prisoner employed the old folk saying "prove that you are not a camel" to describe this principle of "Stalinist justice."[8]) Furthermore, innocence is of little consequence. Soviet reality frequently echoed Kafka's eloquent descriptions. The modus operandi of the Soviet system was often characterized by two contradictory messages: the first is that you probably cannot reach your goal (justice, employment, acquisition of proper housing, etc.); the second is that you are expected to continue to behave as if you think you can. These contradictions can coexist because they employ different levels of communication—action and words. Their coexistence is also maintained by implicitly discouraging the participants from acknowledging the contradiction.

In the post-Khrushchev era, one of the only ways available for dealing publicly with the camp experience and the plight of the returnee was through the use of fiction. By employing the literary mode, real-life stories could be presented as if they were fiction and if they were sufficiently artful they could contain messages critical of the Soviet system. In *Pushkinsky Dom* (*Pushkin House*) written in the 1970s, Andrei Bitov presents such a work of fiction. The novel tells the life story of Lyova, whose father and grandfather were returnees. One of the characters is "Uncle" Mitya, a relative who has returned from prison in the post-war period, and is in reality Lyova's father. We do not learn much else about Uncle Mitya. One of the main points in the plot is that Lyova did not know for a long time that his father was a prisoner. After his return, the father remained separated from his family, only visiting under the disguised name of "Uncle Mitya." This family was not reunited out of fear of the effect that having a returnee father would have on the boy.

Lyova's grandfather, Ded, is a more dramatic character with a more poignant story of personal tragedy following his return, and because of his return. Ded's tale focuses on some very significant questions with regard to returnees. He tells Lyova that he became a broken man only *after* his return, and that the return was the greatest humiliation in his life: "I don't belong to those good-for-nothings, those without pride, who were first undeservedly incarcerated and now deservedly liberated.... The authorities are what they are. If I were in their position, I would have jailed me. [He was apparently arrested on real charges of active political opposition.] But what I do not deserve is this insult of rehabilitation." Ded was given an apartment and a pension as if it were some kind of gift, not something that he had earned. He cannot be bought by these things, he explains, because he is a changed man. He becomes ill after his return, cannot find any peace, starts to fall apart, and begins drinking. "It is cruel to do that to a person twice!"[9] he exclaims to his grandson, referring to the punishment of incarceration and the subsequent punishment of rehabilitation. Ded makes the analogy of operating on a virgin after she has been raped to make it appear as if she were still a virgin. Ded tells how in camp he had a purpose in life—to get out. Now his life is empty. Ded could not readjust to living with the family and eventually returned to the exile settlement where he had been. There he remarried, and refused his family's request to return to them with his new wife. He subsequently dies of a heart attack.

Though a number of issues are illustrated by this story, Bitov's dramatization of the impact of return and the difficulty of readapting to society as an ex-prisoner is particularly insightful. He is especially articulate in criticizing the state for granting forgiveness *to* the returnee rather than asking forgiveness *from* the returnee. This perspective challenges the self-serving, self-righteous official view of rehabilitation.

Witness the following Kafkaesque circumstance of one early returnee. Moisey Aronovich Panich, a Jewish military engineer, was arrested in 1938 at age thirty-six on Article 58-10 (anti-Soviet agitation) and sentenced by the OSO (Special Conference), that is, without trial, to three years in Ivdellag in the Northern Urals. Upon release in February 1941, with the "terrible disgraceful label 'enemy of the people'" he was forbidden to live in provincial and city capitals, as well as in a number of administrative centers. He had no family of his own, no home, and could not see his brothers and sisters because it would endanger them. Panich decided to go to Moscow and fight to rid himself of the stigma of being a political criminal.

After finally gaining entrance to the Military Procuracy, Moisey Panich was told that his case would be looked into at some point, but whatever the outcome, the official advised him to forget everything, "No one is pushing you to say where you have been ... you have a diploma, a passport, your last military service certificate says that you were demobilized without any details on the reason. So go, live and work."[10] Though his friends in Moscow received him well, and were even willing to write letters to the Military Procuracy on his behalf, Panich was unsuccessful in accelerating the process, and was forced to leave the Soviet capital under threat of arrest for transgression of his passport regime.

His efforts to find work as an electrical engineer met with failure as soon as his potential employer became acquainted with his history. The ex-prisoner finally went to the head of the local branch of the NKVD and demanded either to be given work or to be rearrested. Employment was arranged in a local factory, but a few months later, the Germans invaded, and he had to quickly abandon both his work and the city of Mariupol where he had settled. As a suspicious element, he was not taken into the army, and he was consistently reproached for talking about his background: "Why remember your whole past now? Who is pushing you to tell about it?"[11] In order to survive, Panich found it necessary to change his biography. Thereafter he got a job in a Kuznetsk metallurgical plant where he worked until 1962. Despite the stability he had found, he lamented in his memoirs, "I simply could not reconcile myself with this situation and could not prevail upon myself to forget everything. I only adapted to life. I could not reconcile myself with the fact that I should be ashamed of my past, and even more so, ashamed of heroic pages of my history."[12] As long as he was willing to repress his memory, the system was willing to accept him, because this repressed person was apparently too much of a reminder of the system's repressed history and its repressive nature. Fortunately, for this particular ex-zek, as a former military engineer, he had a higher status than many others, so he was officially aided in his amnesia about his past.

Interestingly, Panich was among many of the incarcerated who paradoxically maintained a strong belief in the Party. Hence, the earnest effort to appeal to the Party to expose the truth and correct injustices was understandable. Panich's individual struggle to supress his personal history in order to adapt to the demands of the present, mirrored similar efforts and similar failures by the larger society. The past could not be wished away because its consequences were always present. The distortions required for this futile attempt were dysfunctional at both the individual and the societal level.

Exile

One of the dysfunctional consequences of the Soviet system's repressive nature was that it was riddled with contradictions and in-consistencies. For example, the system itself was not always willing to put aside the past, even for those who were able to repress their memories or at least their disclosures. There were numerous instances in which individuals were urged not to talk about their pasts while at the same time officials doggedly pushed to expose them. In the fol-lowing section we present unvarnished stories of exile that speak eloquently about the impact of the "ex-prisoner" status on the lives of these early returnees. Though there is a certain amount of unifor-mity in their experiences, each of these stories has been selected to illustrate a particular aspect of the returnee experience: the exile's (former) profession, patriotism, devotion to the Party, and so on. They fill in some of the blank spots of this part of Soviet history.

It is also useful at this juncture to reflect on the phenomenon of prisoners who remained at work in the Gulag or voluntarily main-tained contact with their former supervisors (i.e., jailers), even after liberation. One woman who was released in 1940 from the women's labor camp in Akmolinsk returned with a letter of recommendation from her former camp surpervisor, to head an MVD technological project at a local factory.[13] This illustrates the way in which "the camp" and "the outside (Soviet world)" overlapped and merged with each other. This is not surprising when we recognize that the culture of the camp reflected that of the Soviet system. As such, some pris-oners enjoyed special privileges. For example, those who were at-tached to the regime had better jobs. For its part, the repressive So-viet system was in many ways a prison camp with wider boundaries. Consequently, the camp experience largely determined adaptation to society after release.[14] Stephen Kotkin asks, "How much longer will the massive gulag, with all its horrors and paradoxes, continue to be treated as entirely apart from the rest of Soviet society and at the same time as *the* defining institution and experience of the USSR?"[15] For heuristic purposes our present discussion will treat the zone (the camp) and the outside world as separate entities, but it is important to recognize that in practice (i.e., in the Soviet scenario of socialism) this distinction was blurred. We must, in either case, view the Gulag as the integral mechanism of the Soviet system's adaptation to repression.

Maria Maksimovna Galner was stripped of her Party membership in 1936 and incarcerated in the Karlag and Dolinka from 1937-1946 for being a family member of a traitor to the motherland. Her husband had been shot in 1936 for participation in the "Trotskyite-Zinovievite terrorist center." Galner's imprisonment started in the Butyrka, where a cell originally built for forty housed one hundred women. Among her cell-mates were the wife of the editor-in-chief of *Vechernyaya Moskva* and the second wife of Marshal Mikhail Tukhachevsky who had been executed in 1937. Once in camp, Galner met and befriended various women prisoners—artists, ballerinas, singers, teachers, wives of high military officers, and government officials—who shared the common lot of manual labor under miserable conditions. Despite their separation from loved ones, heavy work, and poor food, they still maintained their belief in the country, as expressed in a patriotic song they liked to sing, "My country, my Moscow—you are most precious." In short, its message was "despite our grief ... we have to believe in our marvelous country."[16] Galner eventually got a good job in the camp working as a lathe operator. She even remained at this job as a free worker for a year after her sentence had expired.

When Galner left the camp, she went to Ryazan, but was unable to find work. She joined some former camp-mates in a town 100 kilometers from Moscow. Though a professional translator, the ex-zek did not even attempt to find work in her field, since former prisoners were not given "ideological" work. Instead, she went to factories looking for employment as a lathe operator. Galner despaired, "Lathe operators were needed everywhere, but as soon as they saw my camp certificate, they rejected me."[17] She eventually did get a job at a factory whose director sympathized with former prisoners.

Every subsequent move created the same problems with work. Only in 1966, thirty years after her arrest, was Galner able to find work without any restrictions. Despite limitations, she was relatively fortunate in that she did manage to get hired.

The intention of the policy governing the release into exile of political prisoners seems to have been "that no prisoner should ever taste freedom again."[18] Accordingly, a February 1948 *ukaz* (decree) of the Presidium of the USSR Supreme Soviet ordered "political offenders and individuals presenting a danger on account of their anti-Soviet ties [to be] exiled indefinitely" when their prison terms were up.[19] A March 1948 order of the Ministry of State Security further specified the remote regions (eastern Siberia, Kazakhstan, etc.) to which these exiles were to be sent for settlement.[20] A typical example of release into exile can be found in the following story. Grigory Grigoryevich Budagov, a railroad engineer (a suspect profession that by Stalinist definition often implied "Trotskyite-Japanese sabotage"), was arrested in 1930 and taken to Moscow's Butyrka prison. His journey through the prisons and camps ended when his term was completed in 1948. He waited three days, then walked sixteen kilometers to the train station and headed for Novosibirsk. At this destination, he was picked up by authorities and taken to prison. He waited four days and then went on a hunger strike to protest being held illegally. It was finally explained to the prisoner that they had "lost" him and were thus obligated to send him for consignment. Then he learned that all Article 58ers were being sent to remote places in Siberia for "permanent settlement." Dozens of others were in the same situation, all waiting to be dispatched:

> Under convoy two officers took us to the village of Chumakovo in Novosibirsk province ... where I was reminded of *Uncle Tom's Cabin*. It was something like a slave auction. All the big bosses of the region came: the director of a production plant, ... the chairmen of kolkhozes, etc. I was chosen by the head of the regional community services [*raikomkhoz*], who took me right away, telling me along the way that he did not have a technical engineer, and if the chairman of the regional executive committee (RIK) gives permission, then he would engage me in this function. After his visit to the chairman of the RIK, the head of the *raikomkhoz* reported the former's answer: "Give him the heaviest physical work."... I dragged logs for a week.[21]

That particular chairman was later charged with corruption and removed from office. His successor allowed the ex-zek to work as a technical engineer. Problems remained, however, in his living circumstances. The locals, as a rule, did not allow exiles in their homes, because they considered them "enemies of the people."[22]

Every ten days, Budagov was obliged to report to the MVD where he was told that any attempt to transgress his prescribed borders would be considered an escape and would be punished with ten years of incarceration. His experience and his conclusions were not uncommon among the population of exiled former prisoners:

> Soon I began to sense that in the Tomsk camp I felt better than in exile. Here, with every step the local inhabitants made me understand that I was an "enemy of the people." Whereas in camp I enjoyed some authority by virtue of my engineering work, here my title and skills are not applicable.... In this circle of bureaucrats and uncultured population, I remained an outcast.[23]

Yet another disheartened exile, Aleksandr Dmitrievich Yegorov, writes in anguish in his memoirs, "Exile was incomprehensible and clearly unfounded and monstrously illegal."[24] This former prisoner, a physician, worked as a doctor on the front in World War I. He was arrested in Ufa in 1940 on Article 58-10&11 and sentenced to six years of deprivation of liberty with three years loss of rights. He was freed in 1946 and rearrested in 1950 (at age sixty-two) whereupon he was sent for "eternal settlement" to Krasnoyarsky Krai. Transport to the region was in the notorious Stolypin cars with no space, no sanitation, little food and no water. A thief who was placed in the same wagon stole what little bread Yegorov had. His money had already been confiscated during the search prior to the journey, and so he arrived at his destination with no food and no means. He ended up having to spend the first two months of his exile in the hospital as a patient, after which he could remain temporarily as a physician, working for a salary. The ex-zek describes his search for work in his profession:

> There was an announcement that applications were being taken for employment [at a local hospital or clinic], but I was rejected because [they said] there were no vacancies. They were afraid to hire us; discrimination was tolerated with regard to us exiles, even though the procurator and the examining magistrate in Ufa assured me that a decree was issued on the unhindered acceptance [of exiles] for employment, but it was deception, indeed it was the very same procurator who did not allow me to receive my doctor's diploma from home, and without a diploma, he well knew, one is not hired as a doctor.[25]

The procurator's office elevated obfuscation, deception and passive resistance to a fine art. Witness Yegorov's attempt to find work in his specialty: ear, nose, and throat. It is testimony to the prevalent

attitude toward exiles—they were feared, but they were also undes-
ired, outcast. After somehow managing to obtain a copy of his diploma, the physician applied to the Krai Health Department. They
replied that they had no positions available. "If I were to show this
answer in Moscow," the doctor mused, "they would be horrified,
amazed and surprised that the whole of Krasnoyarsky Krai is satu-
rated with ear, nose and throat specialists, though it is well known
that there aren't even enough in Krasnoyarsk alone."[26] (This reference to a "reasonable Moscow" seems ironically out of place from
someone who was already a long-time victim of a system that was
engineered from the capital.) The doctor's plight only confirmed
that as bad as things are, the procurators can make them worse.

The next year (1951) Yegorov asked for a transfer to be closer to
European Russia, and was granted a move to Kazakhstan. Change
in location did not change the local attitudes. When there was not
enough bread at bakeries, he would overhear the order, "Don't give
exiles or Russians any bread!"[27] Yegorov eventually found some
work in his specialty there. When he was freed from exile in 1954,
the doctor experienced new problems as an ex-exile. Officials wanted
to keep him in Kazakhstan for work, and so they systematically set
up obstacles to hinder his release. Reflecting on his life as an exile,
Yegorov recalled that he did not experience humiliation, but rather
melancholy, loneliness, and a sense of feeling abandoned.

Indeed, as long as there was no blanket condemnation of Stalin
and Stalinism (an idea approached at the XX and XXII Party Congresses, but not fully realized or lasting), the presumption of guilt
generally characterized society's approach to ex-prisoners. Consequently, the reassimilation of "political offenders" into what was
claimed to be a legitimate system was a complex and exceedingly
difficult task. If exiles transgressed their prescribed boundaries in
their search for better work, living conditions, and families, they
were automatically subject to rearrest and sentences of up to twenty-
five years of hard labor. Most of these individuals had already served
years of prison terms. To ensure limited movement of these "dangerous elements," they were required to check in at local MVD headquarters every ten days.

After her release Nina Georgievna Bardina struggled with both
the experience of having been incarcerated and with her status as a
returnee. In 1975 she writes that forty years had passed since the

moment of her arrest, which was followed by seven years in camp and seven years in exile, and "[n]ot once, not in any circumstances, did I allow a single episode from that life to enter my mind"[28] (a statement contradicted by the length and richness of her memoirs). Bardina explains that the period after release was the most painful time of her life: "it seems that the transition from imprisonment to liberty, to free life, is much more difficult than that from freedom to jail."[29] In a long discourse, she contends that though it is extremely traumatic for an innocent person to end up in prison, it is not alienating because everyone else (among the politicals) is experiencing the same bitter fate. The prisoner does not see his family, but neither do his fellow inmates; the prisoner is deprived of his rights, but so, too are the others, and so on. There are no hopes that can be dashed—life is expected to be rough. The transition, however, from incarceration to liberty, with its limited rights for ex-zeks and the burden of charges from which most were not cleared was in its own way more difficult. The liberated prisoner, in Bardina's words, "is constantly confronted with his inadequacy. Instead of a passport he has a simple piece of paper ... everyone has a passport and you have a paper! When people see this paper, the expressions on their faces change, fear appears in their eyes."[30] During this period, it was rarely possible to conceal one's history from, for example, a potential employer.

Bardina describes the frustration of ex-zeks who have to live in restricted places, who lose connections with friends, acquaintances, and former colleagues, and who feel compelled to invent something to tell others about where they have been. Though no one high or low was immune to the same fate, their sense of estrangement was compounded by the circumstance that if they disclosed their past they were branded as "enemies of the people" and shunned by society; if they tried to hide it they were alienated from themselves.

In 1942, Bardina was a chemistry student at Moscow State University when she was arrested by the NKVD in the dean's office.[31] Seven years later, after her release, that same dean told her that she was not allowed to study, not even as a non-matriculated student, because she did not have the right to stay in Moscow where she had come to be with her mother. They went to Kaluga, where the returnee and her mother had to move from one house to another, as local police informed their landlords of their status. The work situation was no better. Bardina lost every job she was given because of her passport. Ultimately, like Panich, she went to the supervisor of the local Ministry of Internal Affairs (MVD) and explained that she could not find a place in this new life. She requested that she be sent back to camp.[32] By severely limiting the vocational and geographical options of returnees the prison camp life often came to appear to be the least bad among worse alternatives.

As we have also seen, there was some compassion for these victims (officially perpetrators), even among the ranks of the MVD. In this particular case, Bardina was offered work in her field in a secret military factory (the year was 1950), and told not to show her passport. The MVD "benefactor" could at least be assured that she would work hard, since prisoners were accustomed to little else.

Family Ties

In all societies, the incarceration of a family member exposes the family to varying degrees of stress. In the Soviet Union, politics raised the degree of stress to the level of physical danger. All relatives were stigmatized by their association with "enemies of the people" and were themselves at risk for arrest. Let us briefly explore the impact of arrest on the family, since family reunion was to be one of the most crucial questions for returnees.

In the early fifties, Harvard University conducted an extensive and unique project on the Soviet social system, utilizing interviews and questionnaires of 3,000 refugees and displaced persons who had left the Soviet Union during and after World War II. This was a group of people who had not reassimilated and were not necessarily direct victims of the terror. Their attitudes, at least those expressed during the interviews, were decidedly anti-Soviet—a feature not common to the group examined in the present study. This sample provides a useful contrast to the ex-prisoner returnees.

Oral interviews revealed a variety of reactions of the family to the arrest of a member. While they ranged from clinging together to dissolution to denouncement of the arrestee, one of the researchers, H.K. Geiger, reported that the average family reaction was to become more close-knit, which he interpreted as a "survival response" at some level. He suggests that this bonding may have been a "psychological adaptation to being rejected by the system. The family becomes a place of psychological refuge for a person rejected by the system."[33] According to this early study, family cohesion, rather than disintegration, was the most common reaction to the arrest of one of its members. Family members were unable to lead a normal life because they were rejected by the system (economic restrictions, feeling outcast by the community), and so they responded by developing anger toward the regime.[34] These interviewees also appeared willing to forgive and forget the regime's actions if only they could resume normal lives.[35] However, the possibility of resuming a normal life for the stigmatized family members of Soviet returnees was very remote.

Numerous memoirs that have become available in subsequent decades, particularly in the late eighties, contest Geiger's conclusions on family cohesion. Rather, these memoirs suggest that family ties with prisoners were systematically, and often successfully, discouraged. (It should be noted that some wives and children of "enemies of the people" were summarily shot in the 1930s. Still others were kept alive to become co-conspirators and adult defendants.[36]) If a potential arrestee were to denounce her husband, she might be able to avoid incarceration, though denunciation of others was by no means a guarantee against one's own imprisonment. One memoir writer quotes the following letter received by a campmate:

> Dear husband, I heard that you miss me. Don't miss me and don't write to me anymore, because I have been living with another man for a year and a daughter was born to us one month ago. I only learned about life after you were put in prison.... I learned about what rights women are given in the USSR, and you concealed these rights from me, and never read me *Vechernyaya Moskva*, [you acted like] a class enemy.[37]

Another memoir author describes the financial incentives provided to the spouses of victims to dissolve the relationship. Normally divorce cost five-hundred rubles, but divorce from a prisoner cost only three rubles—the equivalent of two portions of ice cream.[38]

It was the common experience of the returnees that even initially solid personal relationships would erode under the stress of stigmatization, threats, and long separation, especially when there is no reassurance of reunion. Perhaps the separation is also driven by a sentiment the narrator expresses in Shalamov's *Graphite*: "I wouldn't want to go back to my family. They wouldn't understand me, they couldn't.... No man should see or know the things I have seen and known."[39]

1948 and Its Aftermath

Soviet repressive policies have been characterized by freezes and relative thaws, by periods of repression followed by periods of retrenchment from these policies. And so it was that at the end of the forties a new cycle of repression began. Evgeniya Ginzburg refers to the "house of cards" in which ex-zeks then lived, and she writes about sensing the dread approach of 1949, "twin brother of 1937."[40] Ginzburg, at the time was working in a kindergarten as an exile when she was picked up by the authorities on suspicion of continuing her terrorist activities. Outraged at the absurdity of the new trumped-up charge, she exclaimed, "Am I supposed to have continued with my terrorist activity in the kindergarten?"[41] This period was not ultimately to become the twin in terror of 1937, but prisoners did not know that and feared the worst. In many cases the purpose of their detention was only to change their status to that of "permanent, lifelong" exiles by decision of the Special Conference of the MGB.[42]

Some ex-prisoners—exiles—were picked up and sent to new places of settlement. The previously mentioned *ukaz* of February 21, 1948 stipulated that those "especially dangerous state criminals," who had already served prison or camp terms, and were released, now would be sent into *bessrochnaya ssylka* (unlimited or eternal exile). In the words of the Council of Ministers, this category was comprised of: "spies, diversants, terrorists, Trotskyites, rightists, Mensheviks, SR's, anarchists, nationalists, White emigrés, participants of other anti-Soviet organizations, and groups or individuals presenting a danger because of their anti-Soviet hostile activities." This category also included those "state criminals" who were released from incarceration at the end of the war.[43] Those who were arrested under this directive were prosecuted under the same article for which they had already served and completed sentences, thus being punished twice for the same alleged offence. An October 1948 instruction recommended that MGB supervisors arrest and interrogate particularly suspicious individuals in the above-mentioned category of "criminals."[44]

Newly accessible archival materials provide some insight into the scope of this wave of repression. By order of "Division A" of the MGB, without the decision of the OSO (Special Conference), 37,951 individuals were sent into unlimited exile in the years between 1948 and 1953. Additionally, another 20,267 ex-prisoners were dispatched to far places by decision of the Special Conference in the period between 1949 and 1953.[45]

Zoya Dmitrievna Marchenko[46]

Zoya Dmitrievna Marchenko was arrested three times, the first time in 1931, the second time in 1937, and the third time in 1949. Her brother had been a Trotskyite who was arrested in 1929 and sentenced to ten years in the Solovetsky camps for his alleged attempt on Stalin's life. On the only visit she had with her brother after his arrest, Marchenko asked what he was in for. He responded that he was "for purity of the Leninist line." He was shot on Solovki in 1937. Zoya Marchenko's first arrest was for possession of "anti-Soviet literature"—notes from the parting conversation with her brother in which he told of the torture during his interrogation.[47] She was initially held in the Butyrka where she eventually worked as a stenographer. Then she was sent to Svitlag (acronym for the Northeastern Correctional Labor camps), where she also continued stenographic work for the remainder of her three-year sentence. Marchenko contends that she knew she would be arrested again, since (superstitious as Russians are) she turned around and looked at the prison when she left it.[48] In view of the contrived charges that the Soviet authorities routinely used to justify their arrests, this reasoning was not so unusual.

In the interim between arrests, Marchenko met and married the chief engineer of a construction enterprise, German Iosifovich Staubenberger. He was subsequently arrested in 1936 and died during incarceration. Marchenko's second arrest, in 1937, was for refusal to sign a false deposition against her husband, and also for counter-revolutionary Trotskyite activity. She spent the first year in prison, was sentenced to eight years in Kolyma, and was held there for an additional year after her term expired. Regarding her ability to survive the notorious journey by boat from Vladivostok to the North and the subsequent years of incarceration in the harshest of labor camps, she reflected, "Our organism has more strength than we think."[49] At age eighty-nine she claimed that her goal for living was a certain responsibility, "for the sake of remembering, preserving, and passing on ... that which [she] had to endure."[50]

Zoya Dmitrievna was released in 1946 with a "minus" in her passport. She was not allowed to live in big cities, but she could return to her native Ukraine. She stayed at the same job where she had worked her last year as a prisoner, and lived in a dormitory in Magadan, outside the camp zone. In 1948 Marchenko went to live with her parents in the province in Ukraine, but not for long. She was arrested again in 1949, "they let you out of camp too early," she was told.[51] The Special Conference first sent her to Sumy, where she had to endure an internal prison coupled with interrogations. Under such circumstances, being sentenced to unlimited exile to Krasnoyarsky Krai near the Arctic Circle came as a relief. Otherwise, Marchenko contends, she would have committed suicide.

The liberty of Krasnoyarsky Krai was relative, since travelling outside the boundaries of this region was punishable by twenty-five years of hard labor. There Marchenko worked as an economist on the "dead roads," an expensive wasteful forced labor project that was abandoned after Stalin's death. In 1954 Marchenko moved to Krasnoyarsk where she married an ethnic German, who was also a returnee with a minus in his passport. As exiles, wherever they went, they had to check in every ten days with the local authorities. One day they were told that their documents had been received, and that their exile was over. They still were not allowed to live in major cities.

Returnees were constantly plagued by the threat of renewed repression. To the authorities, the fact that someone had once been incarcerated made them almost automatic suspects. This suspicion spread to the social network. Marchenko explained that after her arrest, a number of her friends believed that she was indeed a criminal, and avoided her after release. Others who understood the inequity of her predicament tried to help her after release, even at their own risk. Some old friends got together with the ex-prisoner, but carefully avoided any mention of the past. Marchenko had a deep sense of feeling like an outcast and was ashamed to tell others about her past, lest she scare people away.[52] Considering the pervasive attitude of fear and blame toward returnees, Marchenko was so grateful toward the Siberian geologists who "dared give [her] work" after release that she still maintained contact with them in the nineties. Marchenko was rehabilitated in 1956, and many of her (non-ex-prisoner) acquaintances whose "eyes were suddenly opened" by the XX Party Congress sought her friendship. However, her circle of friends remained comprised exclusively of returnees. A group of ex-Kolyma prisoners was created, they corresponded with each other, and held regular meetings in Moscow. In short, they formed their own support network. The feeling of being second-class citizens was lessened by the XX Party Congress, but it never fully went away. Moreover, the fear of renewed repression was to pervade the lives of many ex-prisoners. Even in 1978, when passports were being changed, Marchenko recalls how she and her friends stayed up all night, afraid, asking themselves: "What letter or number [of the Criminal Code] will we get now?"[53]

Incarceration was a defining experience in Zoya Dmitrievna Marchenko's life. Her identification was with ex-prisoners who shared the common experience of first being labelled political criminals, and after years of imprisonment, having the charges cleared. This was a central theme of her existence. Marchenko, like many others, felt a sense of loss for her own broken life, as well as a certain responsibility (and perhaps guilt) for those who did not survive. Hence, she was motivated to undertake such tasks (in the Gorbachev era) as typing Anna Akhmatova's "Requiem," an ode to prisoners of the Gulag, as well as writing her own memoirs.[54] In the late eighties and nineties, Marchenko became an active participant in the organizations Vozvrashchenie (The Return) and Memorial. When Memorial unveiled its monument to victims of totalitarianism in 1990, Marchenko, together with former long-time Solovki prisoner Oleg Volkov, cut the ribbon. She was there to represent the relatives of those who perished on Solovki.

As has already been described, exile was for some a phase of liberation, while for others it was another period of incarceration. But there were still others for whom exile was the first experience of deprivation of liberty. This category came to include family members of convicted (and generally executed) "enemies of the people" who were sentenced under Article 7-35 as "socially dangerous elements." To the extent that this group of exiles are not returnees, their experience in exile is outside the scope of this study. However, in order to look at the exile experience from another perspective, we will briefly examine one such example.

Zayara Artyomevna Vesyolaya

One of the reasons for the contradictions and inconsistencies in the Soviet system of repression was that while it used laws to repress people, the system was less a rule of law than of men. These men often exercised their power when and how they saw fit. One of many examples is the policy toward children of the repressed. Stalin's popular words, "children are not responsible for their parents" were only applied when they were convenient, which was not much of the time. In 1949, Zayara and Gayara Artyomovna Vesyolaya, teenage daughters of the executed writer Artyom Vesyoly,[55] were arrested under Article 7-35 (similar to 58-10). They were convinced that their father was not an "enemy of the people," and they read and loved his books. Despite their knowledge of his arrest and imprisonment (but not his fate at the time), Zayara contends that even though the interrogator assumed that they harbored an anti-Soviet attitude, neither in the immediate aftermath of their father's arrest, nor later did she feel any hostility toward the Soviet system, or even toward the organs (of the NKVD). "I loved the Soviet regime even when I was in exile, I cried bitterly in March 1953. My attitude changed only after the XX Party Congress," she later recalled.[56] At that time, Zayara assumed that her father was mistakenly imprisoned during the big sweep of spies and "diversants."[57]

The other prisoners in the Lubyanka guessed that Zayara and her sister would be let through the gates, and given a choice of Siberian cities in which to settle for a short time. This was not to be the case. After being transferred to the Butyrka, Zayara received a sentence of five years of exile in Novosibirsk—a seeming eternity to the teenager. Her mother had been sentenced to eight years in a labor camp. She said that the hardest blow was that her sister, Gayara, was unexpectedly sent for her term of exile to Karaganda. As we have already discussed, one of the goals of arrest was to weaken or break family ties. Individuals would then presumably look to the state for support, become beholden to the system, and become more compliant subjects.

Zayara returned to Moscow in 1953, released under an amnesty, only to find that her status as a former exile prevented her from getting a job.[58] After repeated rejections, she decided to try the literary channel. She applied for work to the editor-in-chief of a publisher of technical literature. Fortunately, this man had met her father, and his conscience did not permit him to reject her. Zayara was hired with the warning that her co-workers were not to find out that she had been in exile, otherwise her boss could get into trouble. At first it was easy to maintain this secret, since her co-workers did not ask anything about Vesyolaya's past. It was not until she was invited to apply for membership in a trade union that she was once more confronted with the illegitimacy of her past. At a meeting, at which her benefactor editor-in-chief was present, Zayara was asked to reveal her biography. She refused without explanation, causing a scandal at the meeting. The purpose of the refusal was not only to protect her boss, but to protect herself from ostracism.

Vesyolaya recalls that event as being the second occasion on which she wanted to disappear into the floor. The first was in 1949 when she was marched under armed escort through Novosibirsk together with German prisoners of war. People stood on the sidewalks, recalls Zayara, "I don't know with what expressions they were looking at us—I didn't see anyone, I clenched my teeth, not moving my eyes from the yellow and gray back [in front of her]."[59] In later years, Zayara wrote memoirs and directed her energy toward helping the organization Vozvrashchenie.

Returnees were not viewed by everyone with fear or suspicion. They were sometimes even aided in escaping impending rearrest. One ex-zek, employed as a 'free worker' in a factory in 1949, was warned by its director: "The organs [MGB] called, they were interested in you, whether you were at the factory, whether you had left. I'm very afraid for you, because there are rumors that they have started picking up people again."[60] He left immediately for another city—Karaganda—where a friend had remained after liberation from camp. Upon arrival he called his former employer, who confirmed that the authorities did indeed come to arrest him. This ex-zek was able to work as an engineer in a Karaganda factory for a year. Then the rumors came again. The MGB had its own agenda, with which local political organizations did not always agree. In this case, the secretary of the Party Committee warned the hassled returnee that the organs had started inquiring about him. And so he was constantly on the move to escape arrest until 1953. Many of his friends were in the same position. The "organs" even caught up with one in 1956, rearresting him and sending him to Akmolinsk.[61]

Fortunately for some of the ex-prisoners, bureaucrats sometimes put their own personal interest as well as humanitarian feelings above the party policy. There are tales of ex-prisoners whose movement and means were restricted but who were able to trade services for tickets to take them away from the camp zone. One ex-zek, Arkady Grigoryevich Grosman, worked as a head mechanic in the same factory where he had labored as a prisoner. His supervisor offered him a flight to Khabarovsk, since he knew the crew of this route, in exchange for the repair of a friend's car. The ex-prisoner agreed and carried out the work. Though his papers were in order, he did not have permission to leave Magadan, so when the plane made an unexpected stop there to pick up passengers, he faced the threat of "violation of [his] passport regime"—three years of incarceration.[62] While other passengers' documents were checked, Grosman smoked with the crew, nervously anticipating exposure of his status and a new sentence. But he was assumed to be a crew member and left alone by the authorities. Later, en route to Khabarovsk, one of the pilots approached the ex-prisoner with the request for money so that the crew could eat and drink in Khabarovsk. Though his services had already been rendered, Grosman could not refuse the request, remembering the fear he had experienced in Magadan and knowing on what a delicate balance his state of liberty rested.[63] Their vulnerable status made ex-zeks easy to exploit.

During this period, there was apparently a directive prohibiting supervisors from giving former prisoners decent work.[64] For example, in 1950 engineers who had served terms of incarceration under Article 58 were fired from their positions by orders from above.[65] The work-related problems occured both early and late and were always a potential threat to the ex-zeks. Much of the behavior toward ex-zeks was governed by unwritten laws. One memoirist claims that many supervisors utilized both written and *unwritten* instructions to exploit former prisoners. Another returnee calls attention to the duplicity of the system, "By law exiles were not deprived of voting rights; moreover, an exile could even be elected to a Council of Workers' Deputies. The reader understands, of course, that no single exile was ever a deputy."[66] The achievement of high positions, even for those who were rehabilitated in the Khrushchev years and beyond, remained problematic. The truth about how the Soviet system dealt with the absorption, and rehabilitation of "political offenders" was not contained in official rhetoric or in official decrees, so it may have been hidden from the general populace. It was, however, an open secret to the ex-zeks whose efforts were frustrated by the Office of the Procuracy (see chapter 3) at every turn. These problems persisted under Khrushchev and will be reexamined in relationship to his policies.

It was relatively easy in the late forties and early fifties to find work if the ex-zek was a manual laborer, chauffeur, mechanic, electrician, accountant, or even a doctor. The article under which one was sentenced also could play a role in obtaining employment.[67] But keeping one's job, or advancing in one's position, was another issue. As one ex-zek accountant explains, "In these years [the early fifties] the question constantly arose as to why a former 'enemy of the people' could work as a chief accountant."[68] He was fired and hired elsewhere, with the same responsibilities, but without the title or salary of chief accountant. On the other hand, teachers and journalists, as conveyers of knowledge and information, found it almost impossible to get work in their fields of specialization.[69] Friends in high places sometimes tried to help. One former prisoner writes about how he and his mother were supported by their old friend, Dmitry Shostakovich, who attempted to help them with acquiring work and university admittance.[70] The authorities tried to subvert this relationship. The mother (wife of an "enemy of the people") was offered work—as an informant. She was to divulge information about Shostakovich, his loved ones, his friends, and his acquaintances. She categorically refused the job.[71] She was eventually rearrested for "anti-Soviet agitation"—as evidenced by her belief in her husband's innocence.[72] The former prisoner described the cumulative impact of the repressive measures on his life in September of 1953: "the stigma that has been placed upon me can neither be washed off nor masked and everything that I succeed in doing will cost tremendous effort."

There were few cases in which the "return of the repressed" did not evoke some degree of fear, anger, shame, loathing, or anxiety from officials and society. However, it would be inaccurate to claim that these accounts present a complete picture of the experience of returnees in their first post-camp years, prior to Stalin's death. Some additional information should be added here. Not all prisoners felt victimized by the system *while in camp* because while they did not like what was happening to them, they subscribed to the ideology that it was for a greater good. They considered themselves participants in the construction of socialism. Their attitude was expressed in the Russian saying, "when you cut wood, chips fly"—oft-quoted in the memoirs of those who maintained their belief in the system. Some prisoners were released from labor camp with award certificates for their industry and initiative.[73] We can assume that their process of readaptation to society went smoother than that of the majority of returnees who were broken when they left the camps.

It is also the case that not all prisoners felt victimized by the system *after the Gulag*. There were even instances in which honors for achievement were granted to returnees whose criminal charges were yet to be revoked. One woman, the family member of a "traitor to the motherland," was sentenced in 1938 to eight years of corrective labor camp by the Special Conference. She was conditionally released in 1942, worked in a Karaganda *sovkhoz* (collective farm), and received a Stalin prize in 1951 for her work on the creation of a new breed of livestock. Her sentence, however, was not revoked until 1952, and official rehabilitation did not follow until 1956.[74] We can also assume in her case that she was not persecuted as a result of her returnee status.

Yet another category of prisoner-survivors is comprised of those who felt that they were both innocent victims of the regime, and involuntary participants in the terror. This group consisted of those who covertly cooperated with the "organs" while in camp, primarily in the role of informants. This enabled them to get lighter work. Some files on these prisoners were preserved, but according to Roy Medvedev, millions of the dossiers on which was written "to be preserved forever" were burned under Khrushchev.[75]

In this chapter we have discussed how the political atmosphere in the country prior to Stalin's death was reflected in attitudes toward returnees. During the same period, other forces were stirring. New pressure was being applied from above as the "Doctors Plot"—aimed primarily at Jews—was launched. The journal *Kommunist* published an article promoting "vigilance against internal enemies" (meaning Jews), and in January 1953 it was announced that a group of "terrorist doctors" had been arrested.[76] A massive purge was being prepared. In this wave of anti-Semitism, Beria was suspected of partiality to Jewish interests, and a case was already being made against his associates by MGB chief, Abakumov. At the same time, prisoner unrest and insubordination were erupting in Kazakhstan and at Vorkuta (already in 1952). The atmosphere of rebellion had not yet reached the proportions that it would in Norilsk and Vorkuta in the summer of 1953, or in Kengir in the summer of 1954, but something was brewing.

An additiional source of instability was the death of Stalin on March 5, 1953. Even though Malenkov, Beria, and Khrushchev had already arrived on the scene, Stalin apparently laid for a number of hours without medical help after a blood vessel burst in his brain. The circumstances surrounding this delay are still somewhat mysterious, though it is likely that there was fear if Stalin recovered, they would be blamed for his inadequate medical treatment. To be sure, the leaders had their own personal motivations as well.[77] The event of Stalin's death marked the beginning of de-Stalinization. His legacy was to linger for decades. John Keep asserts that "the whole issue of Stalin and Stalinism served as a talisman by which one could judge the attitude towards reform of particular individuals."[78] But that was not the only indicator of which way the political winds were blowing. The reassimilation and rehabilitation of political prisoners was also a talisman. It served as a measure of how much of its past errors the Soviet system could acknowledge, and in acknowledging, make restitution and learn from its mistakes.

Notes

1.   Sigmund Freud, *Collected Papers Volume IV, Repression* (London: Institute of Psycholanalysis and Hogarth Press, 1924).
2.   Ernest A. Rappaport, "Survivor Guilt," *Midstream* vol. XVII, 7 (August, September, 1971): 41.
3.   Alexander I. Solzhenitsyn, *The Gulag Archipelago 1918-1956*, vol. three (New York: HarperCollins Publishers, 1992), p. 445.
4.   Ibid., p. 340.
5.   Ibid., p. 383.
6.   Roy Medvedev, transcript of interview with Stephen Cohen, early 1980s, p. 3.
7.   Franz Kafka, *Der Prozess* (Frankfurt am Main: Fischer Taschenbuch Verlag, 1980), p. 153.
8.   Isaak Solomonovich Shur, "Pod kolesom istorii (Khronika nezabyvaemykh dnei)," chast' 1, Memorial, f. 2, op. 1, d. 138, l. 0008 3111 0424.
9.   Andrei Bitov, *Pushkinskii Dom* (Moscow: Sovremennik, 1989), p. 73.
10.   Memorial, f. 1, op. 1, d. 3500, l. 0026 1901 0129. This memoir was also contributed to the Russian Center for Preservation and Study of Documents of Recent History (RTsKhIDNI, former Central Party Archive in the Institute of Marxism-Leninism), f. 560, op. 1, d. 30.
11.   Memorial, f. 1, op. 1, d. 3500, l. 0132.
12.   Ibid., l. 0133.
13.   Marianna Lazarevna Antsis, "Vospominaniia," Memorial, f. 2, op. 1, d. 5 ll. 0001 2909 511-531.

14. Professor Isaak Moiseevich Fil'shtinskii, interview held at his Moscow home, April 20, 1995.
15. *Slavic Review* 55, no. 1 (Spring 1996): 170.
16. Memorial, f. 1, op. 1, d. 989, ll. 0013 0612 1110-1111.
17. Ibid., l. 1144.
18. John Keep, *Last of the Empires: A History of the Soviet Union 1945-1992* (Oxford: Oxford University Press, 1996), p. 12.
19. *Istochnik* 2 (1994): 92-92; TsKhSD, f. 89, op. 18, d. 26, l. 1
20. Prikaz Ministerstva Gosudarstvennoi Bezopasnosti Soiuza SSR za 1948 god, "Ob organizatsii raboty po ssylke, vysylke i ssylke na poselenie," Moscow, 23 March 1948.
21. Grigorii Grigorievich Budagov, "Zapiski...," Memorial, f. 2, op. 1, d. 30, l. 0001 2909 516.
22. Ibid.
23. Ibid., l. 517.
24. Aleksandr Dmitrievich Egorov, "Iz nedavnego proshlogo," Memorial, f. 2, op. 1, g. 61, l. 1993 0710 0444.
25. Ibid., l. 0451.
26. Ibid.
27. Ibid., l. 0457.
28. Nina Georgievna Bardina, "O vremeni i o sebe," Memorial, f. 2, op. 1, d. 20, l. 0001 2909 2142.
29. Ibid., l. 2160.
30. Ibid., l. 2161.
31. She mistakenly called the NKVD the KGB in her memoirs.
32. Ibid., l. 2177.
33. Raymond A. Bauer, "Arrest in the Soviet Union," Research Memorandum Number 30, Human Resources Research Institute Project "An Analysis of the Soviet Social System," Maxwell Air Force Base, Alabama, January 1954, p. 9.
34. Ibid., pp. 8, 10.
35. Ibid., p. 8.
36. Stephen F. Cohen, "Introduction: Bukharin's Fate," in Nikolai Bukharin, *How It All Began: The Prison Novel* (New York: Columbia University Press, 1998), p. xvii.
37. Gleb Iosifovich Anfilov, "Materialy k biografii: vyderzhki iz pisem, dnevnikov i drugie dokumenti," Memorial, f. 2, op. 1, d. 4, l. 0001 2909 0327.
38. Mikhail Davidovich Baital'skii, "Tetradi dlya vnukov," Memorial, f. 2, op. 1, d. 8, l. 0001 2909 950.
39. Varlam Shalamov, *Graphite* (New York and London: W.W. Norton, 1981), p. 281.
40. Ginzburg, p. 279.
41. Ibid., p. 293.
42. Ibid., p. 294.
43. TsKhSD, f. 89, op. 18, d. 26, l. 1.
44. Tsentral'nyi Arkhiv Ministerstva bezopasnosti Rossiiskoi Federatsii, kollektsiia rassekrechennykh prikazov, prikaz ot 26 oktabrya 1948.
45. TsKhSD, f. 89, op. 18, d. 26, l. 2.
46. Throughout this book, sub-chapters are generally designated in cases where personal interviews or extensive questionnaire responses are involved.
47. Zoia Dmitrievna Marchenko, response to questionnaire designed for this project, p. 1.
48. Id., interview held at her Moscow home, April 6, 1995.
49. Ibid.

50.   Ibid.
51.   Id., questionnaire, p. 1.
52.   Id., interview held at her Moscow home, April 12, 1995.
53.   Letters like SOE (socially dangerous element), KRTD (counter-revolutionary Trotskyite activity), ChSIR (family member of a traitor to the motherland), also called 'liter', were often used before numbers (like 58-10) started to be employed for criminal articles.
54.   See *Dodnes' Tiagoteet*, Vypusk 1, (Moscow: Sovetskii Pisatel', 1989), pp. 309-325.
55.   The posthumous rehabilitation certificate of 1956 indicated December 2, 1939 as Vesëlyi's date of death. In 1988, the Military Collegium of the Supreme Court of the USSR revealed that he had been shot on April 8, 1938.
         Zaiara Vesëlaia, *7-35*, (Moscow: Moskovskii Rabochii, 1990), p. 13.
56.   Vesëlaia, response to a questionnaire specially designed for this project, December 1995.
57.   Id., *7-35*, p. 26.
58.   Ibid., pp. 56-57.
59.   Ibid., p. 58.
60.   Zaven Efremovich Gabrelian, transcript of interview done by Memorial members, 1990, p. 8.
61.   Ibid., p. 8.
62.   Arkadii Grigor'evich Grosman, "Pust' ne povtoritsia nikogda (povest' o perezhitom)," Memorial, f. 2, op. 1, d. 50, l. 1993 0511 0215.
63.   Ibid., l. 0218.
64.   Viacheslav Viacheslavovich Dombrovskii, "Sovsem obychnaia zhizn'," avtobiograficheskaia povest', Memorial, f. 2, op. 1, d. 56, l. 1993 0511 0985.
65.   V.V. Lapshin, "Vsë techet, vsë izmeniaetsa...," Memorial, f. 2, op. 1, d. 80, l. 1993 0810 0691.
66.   V.V. Polonskii, "Doroga v Piat' let v Kazakhstan i obratno, zapiski ssylnogo," *Istochnik* 1 (1996): 75.
67.   Vitkovskii, "Polzhizni," *Dvatsatii Vek* 1 (London, 1976): 197.
68.   Memorial, f. 1, op. 1, d. 3481, l. 0025 1701 1871.
69.   V.V. Dombrovskii, Memorial, f. 2, op. 1, d. 56, l. 1993 0511 0985.
70.   Ibid., l. 0987
71.   Ibid., l. 0989.
72.   Ibid., l. 0991.
73.   Memorial f. 1, op. 1, d. 948, l. 0013 0612 0720.
74.   Ibid., d. 2620, ll. 0021 0401 1393, 1415, 1417, 1418, 1419, 1420.
75·   R. Medvedev, letter to S.F. Cohen, 25 September 1983.
76.   Keep, p. 36.
77.   Ibid., pp. 37-38.
78.   Ibid., p. 60.

3

The System's Adaptation to Repression, 1953-55

Many political systems maintain their stability through a dynamic tension between opposing forces. But that was not the state of the Soviet Union in the aftermath of Stalin's death. The beginning of the post-Stalin period was characterized by an oscillation between a surge toward reform and the renewed pursuit of repressive policies. This was not a stable equilibrium. Rather the political system wobbled unsteadily in the weakened grip of Stalin's squabbling heirs. In this chapter we will examine the vicissitudes of the post-Stalin policies. We will examine how the system—a system that had thus far maintained its legitimacy by force—struggled to maintain itself in the absence of mass terror. In the mid-fifties, there was significant movement toward reforms in the camp system and the Office of the Procuracy but the new policies were in the hands of old, ambivalent bureaucrats, so progress was slow, spotty, and inconsistent. Though there were notable differences in the experience of returnees after the XX Party Congress, many of the official obstacles and unofficial attitudes toward rehabilitation and the rehabilitated were retained.

Unlikely as it would have seemed, Beria, the Minister of Internal Affairs, was the first de-Stalinizer. Perhaps because of the company he kept, he was in need of a new image if he hoped to preserve, and perhaps consolidate his power in the changing political climate. Though it was difficult to conceal his own culpability in the terror, Beria wanted to present himself as a reformer who had carried out repressions on the instructions of Stalin. As one Russian researcher noted, "Beria recognized that de-Stalinization was a strong weapon in the struggle for power."[1] In fact, bending with the political winds every subsequent de-Stalinizer saw the need to signal a break from the immediate past, and to distance himself from the ideology and/ or actions of his predecessors. On Beria's initiative the resolution of March 18, 1953 of the Council of Ministers was adopted.[2] It decreed the transfer of the majority of correctional labor camps and colonies, including their sub-divisions and local organs, from the Ministry of Internal Affairs (MVD) to the Ministry of Justice. Apparently this move was not designed to bring a pretence of justice into the Gulag system. Rather, it was an attempt to lighten the MVD's administrative load. Greater efficiency rather than greater legality was its aim. At any rate, the "politicals" remained in the camps, which were still under the jurisdiction of the Ministry of Internal Affairs.[3]

On March 27, less than a month after the dictator's death, on Beria's suggestion, a broad-ranging amnesty was issued.[4] Like many similar political signals, it offered less than met the eye. The amnesty explicitly did not apply to those who were sentenced for "counter-revolutionary crimes." In the first instance, it applied only to those who were sentenced for up to five years (mostly ordinary criminals, although their infractions may not have qualified them as offenders in a different political system). This provision virtually excluded politicals, since most of them got eight to twenty-five years. Additionally, it reduced by half the sentences of those individuals who were incarcerated for terms of longer than five years. In the year 1953, 1,201,738 prisoners were released under the March amnesty.[5] According to correspondence of the Central Committee, they comprised 53.8 percent of the camp population,[6] though Zemskov places this number at closer to 40 percent,[7] and correspondence by Beria to the Presidium of the Central Committee estimates the total number of prisoners on March 26 to have been 2,526,402.[8] Upon release, these prisoners were given money for food for the journey, clothes and shoes if they were needed, and a ticket to the chosen place of residence.[9] A set of rules and regulations obliging labor unions to help in the job placement of these individuals was put into effect in July of 1953.[10] Meanwhile, almost all of the politicals languished for at least another year and many for a number of years.

In April of 1953 the physicians implicated in the "Doctors Plot" were exonerated[11] as were a few military officers (posthumously). Changes in the legal system were also considered at this time. The question of the legality of exile was raised in a letter from Minister of Internal Affairs Kruglov and MVD political officer A.I. Ivanov to the Presidium of the USSR Supreme Soviet, since the "basic principle of Soviet criminal policies [was that of] in the first place individual guilt"[12] (as opposed to guilt by association, i.e., family members). Moreover, since Soviet criminal legislation had been modified to provide sentences of fixed terms, indefinite sentences such as unlimited exile could no longer be given. Exile was still an acceptable punishment, but only for up to five years. It was also proposed that the February and October 1948 *ukazy* (sending those who were released into exile) be abolished, because they punished people twice for the same crime. Furthermore, release was recommended under the amnesty of exiles who had been sentenced for up to five years.

In June of 1953, Beria proposed limiting the rights of the extrajudicial Special Conference. It appeared that he was trying to present himself as the initiator of the reformist transformations in the country, and his rivals came to look upon him as a viable contendor and dangerous rival for the position of Stalin's successor. Consequently, at a meeting of the Presidium of the Council of Ministers of June 26, Beria was arrested in what has been termed a palace coup.[13] The Plenum of the Central Committee stripped him of his posts, excluded him from the Party, and passed the case onto the Supreme Court for investigation.[14] It is one of history's ironies that Beria's arrest was not in accordance with existing legislation but rather with his own Stalinist practices. On July 10, 1953 *Pravda* reported that Beria was excluded from the Party as an enemy of the people. On December 23 Beria, along with his closest associates, was sentenced to death on the basis of the anti-constitutional law of December 1, 1934 that had provided the juridical basis for the Stalinist repressions. It is possible that Beria's execution had already been carried out before the verdict was announced.[15]

Though Beria disappeared from the political scene, a number of his proposals lived on. In September of 1953 the Special Conference that had been in existence since November 5, 1934 was abolished. It had sentenced 442,531 persons (including 10,101 to capital punishment) in its time.[16] Most of those sentenced by this organ had been accused of "counter-revolutionary" crimes.[17] Additionally the October 1948 *ukaz* was declared to be a "gross violation" of Soviet law. It was recommended that all cases that were examined by the Special Conference be reassessed by the Supreme Court within six months of the Conference's abolition for the purpose of reversing the decision or ending exile.[18]

Beria's character is beyond the scope of this work, nor is it particularly relevant to the fate of returnees. It is also not the intention here to make the former henchman seem a humanist. However, a few interesting facts on Beria as repressor and reformer have come to light with the opening of the archives. They reveal a more ambivalent Beria, reflecting, perhaps, the inconsistencies and contradictions of the larger Soviet system. It seems that as early as 1945 he had suggested the elimination of the Special Conference, a proposal which Stalin rejected. Beria apparently also argued against the Stalinist decisions of the Central Committee of 1937 and 1939 that allowed the application of physical force (torture) during interrogation.[19] In a Ministry of Internal Affairs document dated April 1, 1953, Beria orders the elimination of the accommodations and instruments for torture in the Lefortovo and internal prisons of the MGB.[20] Beria also took part in a plan to release 1.7 million special settlers in the course of 1953. The plan was abandoned at that time in connection with Beria's arrest.[21] This is in no way a defense of Beria, whose behavior was indefensible because whatever his compunctions may have been, he executed his duties with great efficiency. However, this glimpse into some reformist sentiments in even such a hardliner suggests that there may have been a nascent pressure for de-Stalinization at the highest levels even before Stalin's death. This would explain the rapidity with which many of the old leaders were eager to distance themselves from the dead Stalin.

It is hard to think of Beria as a scapegoat because he was so deserving of punishment, but his execution did have a quality of ritual political sacrifice and exorcism about it because it could be used to represent a break of the new leaders with some of the worst excesses of the Stalinist era. And prisoners did view it as such. As one ex-zek recalls: "After the destruction of that dog Beria, life in the camps got much better. They stopped locking barracks ... bars were taken off the windows ... a commercial dining room was opened and they started to pay us *kontriki* [counter-revolutionaries] a salary."[22] The work day was also reduced to eight hours, and the numbers were removed from prisoners' uniforms. Of course these reform measures were also driven from below. By the end of July, 1953 thirteen of the large camps at Vorkuta, containing three to four thousand prisoners each, were on strike. The strikers were even attracting local workers to their ranks.[23]

How was this wave of "liberalization"—the freeing of prisoners—received and perceived by the general public? Or rather, how was the general public instructed to think about this? Let us look at excerpts from readers' letters to *Pravda* (preserved in the archive of the Supreme Soviet) in response to the directive of the Presidium of the Supreme Soviet on amnesty. A teacher in Kishinev writes,

> I was never a criminal, and there were no criminals in my family. But I received the news on the radio about this new law [the March 1953 amnesty] with deep concern and joy.... The directive is a historical document that mobilizes and inspires our whole people to new achievements in our work for the glory of the complete victory of Communism, in whose name the unforgettable Comrade Stalin lived and worked his whole life, until the last heart beat.... Glory to comrade Malenkov ... Voroshilov ... Khrushchev![24]

A group of Siberian exiles also express their overwhelming support of the "great state's gesture":

> We are children of our Soviet motherland-mother. Maybe we committed an offense, disobeyed, and mother punished us. But can we really hate her for that? She punished, but she also forgave, and she once again embraces her children! ... Let the American leaders think about whether it is possible in their country for such a thing to happen that former prisoners leave prisons with even more love for their country, and devotion to their own government.[25]

Other letters in this collection from former prisoners were also generously laced with Soviet slogans declaiming gratitude to the great motherland, to the Presidium, and so on. Do these sentiments represent the true feelings of a representative cross-section of the population? On the one hand, these writings are unabashed uncritical propaganda devices that contain no acknowledgement of the reality of the camps, the reason they were so crowded, or the fact that so many prisoners still remained incarcerated. On the other hand, there is little reason to doubt that many average people subscribed to the official party line. Many of those released under the 1953 amnesty were ordinary criminals, who were likely convicted of real crimes (however minor they may have been), and may have had little reason to consider politics as relevant to their lives. However, allegiance to the Party was even observed among politicals (both ex-zeks and those still incarcerated). Without the countervailing influence provided by a free press, religion, independent universities, and other competing voices in a free society, there were only weak and unsupported alternative points of view. The Soviet system, like the total institution of an asylum, was able to promulgate the most preposterous lies because of its control through censorship. Could we imagine that *Pravda* at that time would publish a letter containing a closely reasoned rebuttal of the official Party line? This may well be the reason why the published letters are full of glorification of the government's point of view, rather than compassion for those returning from the Gulag system; they expediently focus on the present and future rather than the past. Praise is heaped on the government for finally beginning to end something that it never should have started. The reality is that by the time the liberalization movement in the Soviet government started to make concessions, millions of its citizens had already been irretrievably lost. Moreover, even as the government was trumpeting reform, political prisoners in the Gulag still awaited their fate. One former political prisoner recalls how the inmates were gathered for the announcement of the amnesty. To her question, "What about us 58'ers?" a camp supervisor replied, "There cannot be any mercy for enemies of the people."[26]

Throughout this work we will be exploring society's attitude toward returning political prisoners which was at best ambivalent and at all times influenced by the historical period. In the Soviet Union, the spirit of the times was generally superimposed on reconstruction and recollection of the blank spots of Soviet history. During Gorbachev's de-Stalinization campaign, efforts were made to recover the amnestic periods in Soviet history in every arena. His leadership allowed various informal and independent organizations to become more active. One of these was the Cinematographer's Union which was one of the initial supporters of Memorial and a forerunner in the liberalization campaign. It provided a much needed office prior to the organization's official registration. In artistic terms the cinematographers found that they could utilize a whole new range of subjects. *The Cold Summer of 1953*, a film directed by Aleksandr Proshkin, provides the 1987 perspective on society's prevailing attitude toward political prisoners in the aftermath of Stalin's death. It is the melodramatic story of how two political prisoners, who happened to be among the very few to get released under the amnesty, save a village from the threat of murderous marauding criminals who had been the main beneficiaries of the decree. This is a romantic notion, but it is unlikely that returning political prisoners had a hero's reception that summer, or for that matter, at all.

During Stalin's reign there was a fairly smooth coordination between his directives and the state apparatus which carried them out. In the aftermath of his death, the newly liberalized old leaders—Beria, Khrushchev, Voroshilov, and others, did attempt modest reforms. But the system's entrenched bureaucracy, comfortably adapted to repression, thwarted many of their efforts. This was particularly problematic for the camp system and the administration of justice which needed to be reviewed and reformed. In September of 1953 the Office of the Procuracy issued a report "On the deficiencies of educational and corrective work of corrective labor camps." It documents the failure of efforts to reassimilate into society and the workplace those who were liberated under the amnesty. These were mostly common criminals, not political prisoners. It reported that scarcely a day passed without one or several murders.[27] This group was the state's choice for the first wave of releasees, and as such, they provided society's first mass contact with those returning from the camps. It was traumatic for both sides. One village "had to use all of its arms to prevent a 'St. Bartholomew's Eve' massacre and chase away the bandits."[28] (We can assume that these events inspired some degree of fear of any group returning from "the zone.") The report goes on to complain that the "correctional labor camps" did nothing correctional. It points out that the criminals had created their own organizations within the camps. These organizations provided them with mutual support, ties to other criminals inside and outside, and they became proficient in their own type of "correctional education." Once freed, they remained in their own groups with their own rules

The concern about protecting the general populace from the dangers of the organized criminal element never extended to concern for protecting the political prisoners in "the zone." Political prisoners were constantly subject to exploitation by incarcerated criminals. Moreover, criminals enjoyed a higher status, so politicals generally got heavier workloads. We should note that there were cases in which politicals were also aided by their fellow prisoners. As a token of their friendship, thieves gave Semyon Vilensky (see chapter 4) a knife as a going away present when he was released.[29]

The report's conclusions are significant because they reflect an awareness of the need to allow former prisoners to return to "normal lives." (We should remember that for the most part, politicals did not enjoy the status of being *former* prisoners at that time.) It recommends that after serving one's sentence in any type of camp, "citizens of the USSR should not be subject to any kind of supplemental passport, work, or other restrictions and should have the possibility (especially those freed from concentration camps) of immediately leaving the area of the camp and going to their place of residence."[30] It also adds that a vigilant—they probably meant wary—eye should still be kept upon this group.

The Ministry of Justice followed through on some of the recommendations. In October of 1953 the Council of Ministers issued a decree "On curtailing the amount of regimented cities and localities and lists of passport limitations." It is clear that politicals did not benefit from this decree, since their restrictions remained in force. Major cities and a long list of other places still remained off limits to *all* Article 58'ers whose sentences had not been revoked, but it was a gesture toward more freedom of movement for some ex-prisoners.[31] The leash was gradually being loosened but it was a choke collar that could be tightened at any moment.

The recently declassified *osobaya papka* (Special Files) of Khrushchev provide new information on the scope of the terror, and also on the issues that arose in the initial period of de-Stalinization. By February of 1954, the sixty-five correctional labor camps and 798 correctional labor colonies and sub-divisions of the Gulag system were in the process of being transferred back from the Ministry of Justice to the (presumably reorganized) Ministry of Internal Affairs.[32] The first steps toward reform had been taken. It was now time to deal with the daunting and haunting political issues personified by the *dokhodyagi* (goners) who were still languishing in the camps, and by the abandoned, exiled widows and orphans of executed "enemies of the people."

In February of 1954, at Khrushchev's request, an assessment was made of the contingent of political prisoners that remained in the camps. According to data of the Ministry of Internal Affairs (in a report to Khrushchev), in the period between 1921 and 1954, 3,777,380 people were convicted of counter-revolutionary crimes by the Collegium of the OGPU, troikas of the NKVD, the Special

Conference, the Military Collegium, courts and military tribunals. According to this source, the death penalty was administered to 642,980 prisoners, while another 2,369,220 were sentenced for up to 25 years in camps and prisons, and 765,180 persons filled the ranks of exile.[33] These numbers may not accurately reflect the actual number of victims but they were the figures that the officials were working with as they approached reform.

In the beginning of 1954, according to the document addressed to Comrade N.S. Khrushchev, the General Secretary of the Central Committee of the CPSU, there remained in the camps and prisons 467,946 prisoners who had been convicted of counter-revolutionary crimes. Moreover, an additional 62,462 individuals, who had already served their sentences for counter-revolutionary crimes, were still in exile by directive of the MGB and Office of the Procuracy.[34] The legality of the Special Conference was once again called into question —and condemned—because this organ had examined cases in the absence of both the accused and witnesses. It was an understatement to conclude that this created a great opportunity for "grave distortion of Soviet law."[35]

The report proposed the creation of a Central Commission comprised of a republic Procurator (as chairman), the republic Minister of Internal Affairs, and the republic Minister of Justice. These officials should be assisted in their work by camp supervisors and procurators. Their chief mission was to be the "careful verification of the grounds for incrimination ... of every individual" sentenced by the above-mentioned organs (Collegium of the OGPU, etc.).[36] The conclusions were then to be presented to the Supreme Court of the USSR for the revocation of sentences or exile. The document was signed by Rudenko, General Procurator, Kruglov, Minister of Internal Affairs, and Gorshenin, Minister of Justice.

In this same period, the examination of Stalinist repression was also extended to "special settlers"—whole nationalities that had been exiled to the Kazakh, Uzbek, Kirgiz, and Tadzhik SSR, the Komi, Bashkir, and Yakut ASSR, Altai, Krasnoyarsk and Khaborovsky Krai, just to name several of the areas of settlement. These nationalities included ethnic Germans, Chechens, Ingush, Balkars, Crimean Tatars, and Kalmyks, among others. It was recommended that they be given freedom of movement within the boundaries of provinces, krais, and republics (without changing their place of residence), and that they be allowed to make work-related trips to any place in the country. Their registration with local authorities would be limited to once every three months.[37]

On April 24, 1954, a long-awaited accommodation was made toward correcting the repressive mechanism. The Minister of Internal Affairs and the General Procurator issued an order releasing from exile those who had been sentenced for up to five years for counter-revolutionary crimes. This included those prisoners who were sentenced under the February *ukaz* of 1948. There had already been a slight reduction in the number of prisoners in camps and in prisons for counter-revolutionary crimes. On April 1 this number was reported to be 448,344[38] as opposed to the figure of 467,946 quoted above. As time went on, the 1953 amnesty decree was extended to include new groups or categories of indviduals. In consequence, this group of exiles was liberated and their charges were cleared.[39]

A month later, on May 19, a decree of the General Procurator, the Minister of Justice, the Minister of Internal Affairs and the Chairman of the Committee for State Security (KGB), issued regulations for examining criminal cases of individuals who were incarcerated in camps, colonies, and prisons, or who were exiled for counter-revolutionary crimes. The decree adopted the recommendations on procedure that were set forth in the February report to Khrushchev. The commissions were empowered to carry out resolutions regarding a wide scope of crimes and punishments. Their mandate included the reversing of decisions and the complete rehabilitation of the accused, the reclassification of the type of crime, the shortening of sentences, the application of the March 27 amnesty, the abolishment of exile, and the confirmation of prior refusals to reexamine decisions of cases. The commissions' decisions were to be considered final for cases of those convicted by the Collegium of the OGPU, troikas of the NKVD and the Special Conference. Recommendations could be made with regard to prisoners sentenced by judicial organs, but the final decision was to be rendered by the courts. In a major reorientation toward prisoners' status, the commissions were instructed not to depend on lists that might be provided by the Ministry of Internal Affairs, but rather to proceed on the basis of prisoners' complaints registered with the Procuracy and the organs of State Security. As an additional safeguard, camp administrators were also instructed to send prisoner's complaints and requests to the Central, republican, krai, or provincial commissions.[40]

In a May 1954 report to the Central Committee, the Ministry of Internal Affairs assessed the state of affairs in the camps and colonies. By this time the provisions and procedures with regard to the release of prisoners had already been established and were operational. The May report is significant because it laid down more humanitarian rules with regard to the transition to liberty. It stipulated that the administration of the place of incarceration should assist prisoners if they wanted to continue to work in the camps or colonies or in one of their enterprises. Liberated prisoners were also to be given free transport to a chosen destination or to their place of residence, either food or the money to buy it for the journey, clothing if necessary, documents on specialization (if one was acquired), and term (*stazh*) of work. Personal documents and valuables were to be returned. Finally, prisoners were to be given a certificate of release and a *kharakteristika* (judgment) regarding their behavior in the camp.

The efforts at reform were gradually gaining momentum, but the hundred or more teams delegated to tour the camps could scarcely manage the burden of cases.[41] While the slow process of liberalization may have been tedious for the authorities, it was painstaking for the prisoners. Impending liberation was not a mitigating circumstance. The use of arms against Article 58'ers attempting to escape was generally considered justified.[42] In June of 1954, zeks took over the camp complex in Kengir, Kazakhstan for forty days. The mutiny was violently supressed by authorities. According to Solzhenitsyn, approximately 700 persons were killed or wounded.[43] The archives, however, have disclosed that a significantly lower number of prisoners – thirty-five in all—were killed in this uprising.[44] The true number of victims may lie somewhere in between, but it is likely in this case that the archival estimate is more accurate.

Solzhenitsyn describes the exasperation of waiting for justice in his writing about the rebellion's leader, Kapiton Kuznetsov, "How did he feel about his imprisonment? What stage did he imagine his appeal to have reached? How long was it since he had asked for a review, if the order of release (with rehabilitation, I believe) arrived from Moscow during the rebellion?"[45] (Kuznetsov was sentenced to death in August of 1955, but his sentence was commuted to twenty-five years. In 1960 he was released and rehabilitated. This special treatment may be explained by the fact that just after the suppression of the rebellion, it seems that Kuznetsov wrote a forty-three-page confession in which he denounced a number of other prisoners who had been part of the "conspiratorial center."[46])

In an attempt to alleviate the tensions building in the zone, and to raise morale the political organs of the camps circulated dozens of different newspapers, with propagandistic articles on "socialist competition," hard-working zeks, etc.[47] The newspaper coverage included production, education, and cultural work in the camps.[48] In addition, the "news" was also sprinkled with such light topics as what had been prisoner-reader's fare in the thirties and forties, for example, the visit of friendly bears to the camps.[49]

Consistent with the inconsistencies in the Soviet system, while release in some camps moved at a sluggish pace, in others the process of liberation was accelerated to the point that some individual prisoners were just let go before any form of justice could be meted out.[50] In June of 1954 another decree regarding the release of exiles sentenced by the Special Conference stated that the work on their release should be completed within two months.[51] In August, a resolution of the Central Committee provided for the withdrawal of the limitation of special settlement for a number of groups. These included former kulaks deported during the collectivization campaign of 1929-1933, ethnic Germans, and Germans mobilized during the "Great Patriotic War" for work in industry.[52] Unfortunately, the native lands of the special settlers had been occupied by others—mostly Russians—after they had been displaced. The consequences of returning the deported nationalities back to a place that was now occupied by others had not been fully anticipated or effectively addressed. The tension created by the confrontation between two groups with claims to the same place is reflected in a story by Semyon Lipkin entitled "Dekada" (Decade). In one part, a Russian is killed by a Chechen during a fight at a disco. A woman who worked at the factory with the slain Russian wonders aloud:

> Why did they return the Chechens? They want the houses back in which Russians are now living. They say they built these houses. But we, the Russians, are not to blame that we were given these houses. Chechens are seizing houses by force, throwing out the belongings of those who live there now.[53]

Her co-workers assert that these bandits should be handled "in the Stalinist way." This was apparently what was really happening in the early sixties in Grozny. (It is in this context interesting to note that most of the later Chechen rebel leaders, for example, Dudaev and Maskhadov, were returnees.) Though elements of ethnic discrimination compounded the plight of these returnees, some of the general returnee problems are illustrated by this tale. Lipkin's story does not only invoke the issues of prejudice or even politics. It is a commonplace theme about a scarce resource claimed by two groups. People had, after all, moved into the vacated apartments, jobs, and families of returnees. So, there was an understandable resistance to giving up things that they had acquired in their absence. When the "ghosts returned from a world that was not supposed to exist,"[54] they were returning to a world that no longer existed.

According to the Khrushchev files, the Ministry of Internal Affairs reported that on July 1, 1954 425,809 political prisoners still remained in the camps. Zemskov estimates the number of political releasees in 1954-55 to be 88,278.[55] It is difficult to arrive at accurate figures because some political prisoners were reclassified under other articles, and thus could qualify for the amnesty of 1953.[56] For example, Pavel Vasilyevich Aksyonov (Evgeniya Ginzburg's husband) was arrested in 1937 on Articles 58-7 & 11 and sentenced to fifteen years at a correctional labor camp with the confiscation of property. In September of 1954, the Presidium of the Supreme Court of the RSFSR stipulated that activities that previously fell under Article 58-7 & 11 were reclassified to Article 109 (abuse of office or position) of the Criminal Code, which is punishable by a sentence of five years, without confiscation of property. Since the sentence was up to five years, the amnesty could be applied, and Aksyonov's sentence was thus revoked.[57] This stipulation of September 24, 1954 implied political rehabilitation.[58]

The Clash between Rehabilitative and Repressive Processes at Work in 1954-1955

In his memoirs Khrushchev said that he was afraid of the thaw lest it become a flood that would wash away the regime.[59] By 1954, a number of reforms regarding prisoners had been initiated. These affected the Gulag, the Procuracy, the Ministry of Internal Affairs, and the Ministry of Justice. Individual freedom and democratic rights were never the goals of the official reformers. Rather they were trying to achieve what they termed "socialist legality," an oxymoron that operationally could be described as "dictatorship without mass terror."[60] As it was practiced, "socialist legality" was neither socialist nor legal by Western standards of governance. It came to mean that whatever the government did was to be considered both legal and socialistic by fiat. There was, indeed, a movement toward reform but it proceeded with so many fits and starts that it always seemed on the verge of retrenchment.

A lot of change was taking place, but it was accomplishing little in the direction of real reform. A report on the work of the Procuracy of the RSFSR for 1954, for example, indicates that despite an increased workload, its total staff was reduced in size three times (as was that of the whole USSR Procuracy).[61] This was connected to general reorganization, the formation in the RSFSR of six new provinces (territorial administrative divisions), and the consolidation of positions. At the same time, additional measures of an unclear and perhaps even contradictory character were being taken. In February of 1954, the corrective labor camp procurators (365 posts) were placed under direct supervision of the RSFSR Procuracy instead of the MVD).[62] This was done in an effort to monitor the activities of the organs of state security and the Ministry of Internal Affairs. It was thought necessary to monitor the Ministry of Internal Affairs because it was found that they had not properly reeducated prisoners and that they had utilized them only as a work force. Moreover, the Party organizations and political departments of correctional labor camps did not conduct political work and there was "significant violation of socialist legality in the regime and conditions of detainment."[63] Consequently, in March, the Party Central Committee instructed the Office of the Procuracy to "strengthen legality ... and the methods of procurator supervision at places of detention." This order was clearly one of the state's efforts at rehabilitating itself. Special commissions with representatives of the camp administration had already been set up to work on the targeted deficiencies. The organs of the Procuracy were ordered to strengthen their surveillance of the camps in order to reinforce legality and terminate the prevalent "liberal attitude" toward arbitrariness.[64] The central apparatus of the Procuracy as well as a number of provincial procuracies made very modest increases to their staffs in an attempt to accommodate the admittedly "heavier volume of work."[65]

The Central Committee charged the Procuracy with verifying the grounds for incarceration. The special commissions would no longer conduct reviews of cases based solely on "formal" qualifications, that is, the proper stamps and signatures. Instead, the review would be based on the facts of the crime and the justification of the punishment.[66]

Although the process had begun before the Central Committee formally wrote the directive, the initial results were very meager. In one camp, for example, only twelve cases of illegal detention were discovered. Accordingly, the procurator did contest these cases, and the prisoners were released.[67] Perhaps the Office of the Procuracy was willing to concede only some token cases. It is also likely that the reorganization and overall reductions in staff during that period reduced the quality and productivity of the Procuracy. In this climate of downsizing, the bureaucrats had reason to be concerned about both their jobs and their political fate—major distractions to the "intensive work" of reexamining cases. However, the meager number of cases processed was not just the result of overload or distraction. There was a pervasive attitudinal problem on the part of the camp officials toward the prisoners. The transfer of former camp procurators to the RSFSR Procuracy only changed their chain of command, not their outlook or political orientation. There is no information on serious rearrangements or purges in these local subdivisions of the Procuracy. Hence, they were the same staff who only yesterday had despised, vilified, and exploited the prisoners for what they believed to be good reasons.[68] Now these officials were responsible for the timely release of prisoners whose terms had expired, and for enforcing the general or partial amnesty. With the stroke of a pen—and not much more—these former MVD Procurators now had to behave toward prisoners in ways completely at variance with their previous training. In so doing, they had to try to put aside a good bit of their own history. As of January 1, 1955 approximately 70 percent of the staff had been working in the Soviet Procuracy for ten or more years, and had been there through the whole period of postwar political repressions.[69] They now had to reexamine cases with a view toward liberating the prisoners rather than extending their term of incarceration—a most difficult task, under the circumstances.

During the de-Stalinization period of the mid-fifties the state's attitude toward political prisoners (subsequently returnees) was at best ambivalent, at worst destructive. We can see how this was expressed in the administration of justice. In addition to being over-worked, over-worried, and over-repressive, there was the question of the Procuracy employees being under-qualified to make judicial decisions. (Writing about the education of legal officials in the late Stalin era, Peter Solomon questions what kind of jurists were produced, since many obtained their degrees through correspondence. He argues that they had some knowledge of the law but were not imbued with "a commitment to the legal process or legality that might enable them to resist bureaucratic and political pressures at work."[70]) Only in May of 1955, two years into the de-Stalinization process, did a decree of the Presidium of the Supreme Soviet stipulate that new procurators were required to have a higher legal education.[71] The decree was less than timely for a number of prisoners. Witness the qualitative composition of the Procuracy staff in 1954 and 1955: only 45.2 percent of the RSFSR Procuracy employees had a higher legal education, 42.5 percent had only a rudimentary knowledge of law, and the rest had no legal education whatsoever.[72] Not only did they not comprehend much of what was now expected of them, but what they did understand they did not like because it contradicted their previous experience. And these were the people entrusted to decide the fate of the prisoners and the viability of the rehabilitation program. However, from the perspective of the Soviet system as a whole, maybe the inefficiencies and the incompetence of the staff in overseeing the rehabilitation program were irrelevant, because some tempo in the punitive repressive mechanism was still maintained. During the mid-fifties "thaw," the population of incarcerated political prisoners was also replenished as some of those who were released were replaced by others (see the statistics on incarceration for political offenses in the fifties presented in chapter 1).

For those prisoners whose incarceration was validated, the procuracy's task was to oversee the utilization of prison labor. It was to be used for purposes of reeducation and learning a skill. Regular medical check-ups were also supposed to be given to certain categories of prisoner-laborers. Things often did not happen the way they were supposed to. In a Chita camp it was discovered that prisoners in the indicated labor category received 50 percent less medical attention than was legally prescribed.[73]

The Procuracy was also mandated to review prisoners' living conditions. Since prisoners could generally be expected to spend a number of years in the camp, they were to "have the right to demand a separate sleeping place in a room with a normal temperature, to have the necessary things for sleep [presumably sheets, etc.], to have normal food and conditions for rest after work."[74] Because of a number of incidents in which prisoners were hurt by criminals, those who were identified as especially dangerous criminals were to be separated from the others.

In spite of the Central Committee's instructions, the camp administrators enjoyed a considerable degree of autonomy and many continued to take care of problems in their old repressive ways. There was little oversight, so each camp was relatively free to bend the rules. In one region only 974, or 15 percent, of the complaints were directed to other departments where they might have gotten a fairer hearing.[75] The complaints included lack of medical treatment, withholding of prisoner wages, and so on. As a rule these complaints were sent to the Gulag MVD of the USSR (the main camp administration) which did nothing to verify their authenticity. The same problems with lack of oversight regarding prisoners' complaints were found in such widely separated places and significant centers of the camp network as the Arkhangelsk province and the Mordovian ASSR. As one official report stated, "in Arkhangelsk province the same practices are being carried out as in the central apparatus, that is, most of its complaints are sent to the supervisors of the correctional labor camp at whom they are directed, and are not checked. Last year, in the Mordovian ASSR 24 percent of the complaints fell into this category."[76] The prisoners' complaints were thus going right to the accused!

While reform was the official policy at the top, it was unofficially hampered at lower levels.[77] Mid-level bureaucrats who had been indoctrinated into the old system of repression were unwilling to change and were in a good position to impede any real reform in the system. They could and often did create a procedural maze that counfounded the efforts of prisoners to get their just due. But the impediments to reform resulted from more than bureaucratic defensiveness and passive resistance. It was the system itself that was an obstacle. Kafka would not have been surprised. In *The Trial*, he employed the metaphor of the legal system to describe a mindless, rote social organization that was dedicated to doing things right rather than doing the right thing. It was process as product. He presciently described the Soviet automaton that has its own momentum, obeys its own laws, has little, if any, capacity for self-correction and is impervious to corrections from without. As a consequence, the status of prisoners shifted from absolute injustice during the repressive era to relative injustice during the ineffective reformist era. Justice delayed was justice denied.

For all of these reasons, camp conditions were not significantly improving under Khrushchev. In the second quarter of 1954, "serious violations of law" could still be found in the Gulag. The most common examples included placing murderers, bandits, and other dangerous criminals together with those convicted of less dangerous crimes.[78] Through such manipulations the camp staff found ways of further punishing prisoners. In addition, the living quarters were filthy, prisoners were sleeping in their clothes, there was insufficient medication, and too few medical evaluations of patient-prisoners to determine their eligibility for release on medical grounds.[79] Medical care in the correctional labor camps was officially recognized as being insufficient. Labor conditions had also shown little improvement. For example, women were still assigned heavy work though it was officially forbidden.[80]

A document of the Procuracy of the RSFSR from December 1954 acknowledges that despite all the efforts to change, much had remained the same. "Gross violations of law" regarding the conditions of detainment could still be found. Prisoners who had already been legally freed continued to be held, some barracks were considered to be uninhabitable, and prisoners often lacked basic necessities. While they languished, their complaints slowly wound their way through the formal review process. The plight of the prisoners was hardly improving because the government was turning a blind eye to the ongoing abuses. The document blandly concludes that the republican Offices of the Procuracy were not carrying out their functions of guiding and checking the work of the camp procuracies.[81] (Camp procuracies were subordinate to republican procuracies who were subordinate to the General Procuracy of the USSR.) Thus implementation of reform was a failed effort from the onset because of opposition at lower organizational levels, lack of will to enforce the reform at higher levels, and the inertia of the bureaucratic behemoth.

The fitful progress toward reform can be further explained by the fact that the Procuracy was explicitly charged with a twofold mission. On the one hand, they were instructed to review cases with regard to their legality. On the other, as one instruction warns, officials were to bear in mind that "together with rehabilitation of those who were illegally accused of counter-revolutionary crimes, the struggle with real enemies of the Soviet state should not be weakened."[82] There was still a siege mentality in which the threat to the integrity of the state was seen to come from the prisoners rather than from those who had unjustly imprisoned them. A sign of the repressive atmosphere of the times was that Stalin's opponents, like Bukharin, were not eligible for reconsideration in these years. Procurators were to be vigilant in their reexamination of cases, lest they release "real" counter-revolutionaries. In the climate of the times, camp officials were permitted to interpret such directives as support for further repression. After all, Soviet legal officials were accountable to "their bureaucratic and political masters" and not to the "public or the values of objectivity."[83]

Let us examine, by turning to particular provinces and cities, how in 1954 and 1955 the Procuracy partially corrected its repressive mechanism, while at the same time remaining a servant of the state (system). A late 1955 report of the Tomsk provincial procuracy cites a number of cases in which the prisoners' review had not taken place within the legally prescribed time. The reexamination process was initiated by letters of complaint sent by the prisoner or their relatives to the Tomsk KGB division. The explanation that was offered for the delay is informative because it reflects the inherent and perhaps purposeful inefficiency of the system. The excuse for justice delayed was that they were understaffed. Only six people were allotted the task of handling thirty-five "archival-investigative" cases, involving a few hundred individuals. Moreover, their task was further complicated by the fact that for every case it was necessary to find additional cases in order to verify testimony. Apparently the files only contained copies from the other cases in question, the originals— which were necessary in order to proceed with work—were preserved in Moscow and other provinces.[84]

In the province of Chita, between June of 1954 and November of 1955, 980 cases involving 1,646 individuals convicted of counter-revolutionary crimes were examined. About one-third (365 cases or 37 percent) were found to have been justifiably convicted. The other two-thirds (615 cases or 63 percent) were declared illegal. This led to complete rehabilitation in 150 cases for 296 individuals, while another 362 prisoners received reduction in their sentences. Approximately 137 persons were recategorized to come under the amnesty law, and they were released with rescinded sentences. Seven individuals were freed from exile. This "great number of suspended cases" led the Chita provincial Procuracy to assert that there were "gross violations of Soviet legality permitted during the investigation by the organs of state security and during the judicial review of these cases."[85]

The conclusions publicized by this report demonstrate efforts on the part of some officials to distance themselves from past abuses. In the course of this investigation, they "discovered" that: illegal methods of interrogation had been employed, while arrests and accusations were based on falsified documents; confessions were extracted at all costs; and maximal sentences were rendered regardless of the article under which the prisoner was convicted.[86] Despite the admission that these practices were common, the Chita provincial procuracy nevertheless approved of 37 percent of the sentences.

They were not alone in their "vigilant" behavior. In 1955 in Stalingrad province, of 2,181 political offenders' complaints examined, 360 received reduction in their sentences, 121 were given amnesty, and sixteen were released from exile. However, 1,602 sentences were upheld upon review.[87] The fact that approximately three-quarters of the convictions in this particular province were still considered by the post-Stalin Procuracy to be justified in spite of widespread knowledge of political repression, suggests that little had changed. In Astrakhan province, as of January 1955, of 407 prisoners incarcerated for counter-revolutionary crimes, the sentences of 198 of them were upheld upon reexamination.[88] In that same month in the province of Balashov, out of seventy-nine prisoners' appeals, fifty-one were rejected in the review.[89] In the Leningrad province in early 1955, out of 2,869 political cases, 1,622 sentences were upheld on reexamination.[90] In the province of Rostov, the commission of the Procuracy met eighteen times between June of 1954 and January of 1955 to review cases involving 1,709 persons convicted of counter-revolutionary crimes. Only fifty-six, or 3.2 percent, of them received rescinded decisions with complete rehabilitation.[91] And so it went, place after place. Stalin was dead, but Stalinism lived on in the officials charged with reform.

The accusatory bias of the late forties and early fifties noted in chapter 2 continued to dominate the justice system. Acquittals were seen as a stigmatization for the system, because a groundless prosecution discredited the agency (i.e., the Procuracy) responsible for dispensing justice.[92] While it may not be surprising that an active campaign against acquittals was pursued from 1949 on, it is apparent from the abovementioned cases that post-Stalin officials as well were under pressure to avoid acquittals.[93] An overturned sentence for groundless prosecution raised the issue of responsibility, and ultimately culpability. The issue of culpability was to plague Soviet and post-Soviet efforts to come to terms with the Stalinist past for decades to come (see below and chapters 5 and 7).

There were also more mundane and very Soviet reasons for the delay of many appeals. Many cases could not be reviewed because prerequisite lists from the places of detainment had not been turned over to the reviewers, or they were late in arriving. The Ivanovo provincial procuracy complained that their work had to be carried out solely on the basis of prisoners' complaints, since the required lists of prisoners had not yet arrived.[94] In Kostroma province 250-300 criminal cases awaited review, but could not be considered without these lists.[95] In a January 1955 letter to the Procuracy of the RSFSR, the Kuibyshev provincial procurator contends, "It is hard to say something definite about whether the camp administration is [responsible for holding up the process by] holding back the presentation of these lists of prisoners that must be examined by the commission."[96] The Yakut republican procurator was reluctant to point an accusatory finger. In the Yakut ASSR, out of 223 applications for review, thirty prisoners had their sentences revoked with complete rehabilitation. "The demands of the May 1954 decree [on the reexamination of criminal cases of counter-revolutionaries] with regard to lists of prisoners from places of detention," laments the Yakut Procurator, "are being carried out unsatisfactorily by the places of detention."[97] There was clearly a discrepancy between official policy and practice with regard to prisoners of the Stalinist camps.

Officials, who loudly proclaimed the need for reform, were exhibiting a very different attitude when they rejected the overturning of so many sentences. Furthermore, camp administrators hobbled liberation and rehabilitation efforts by failing to provide essential documents. It appears that this ambivalence was systemic. We can assume that this dualism was reflected at all levels of society. Reform had been set in motion but it faltered at every step because many of the people charged with carrying it out did not believe in it.

All this notwithstanding, there was ample evidence that the system was attempting to correct itself. During this period there were cases in which individuals were arrested, sentenced, incarcerated and then released for lack of valid grounds. One late arrestee, for example, was incarcerated on October 30, 1954 with the approval of the Deputy Procurator of Leningrad for allegedly having written three anonymous anti-Soviet letters in 1952-53 and sending them to the Central Committee and the Commmittee of Radio Information. Neither during interrogation, nor in Court did the accused admit guilt. The court based its sentence exclusively on the conclusions of handwriting experts. The Procuracy of the RSFSR and the Supreme Court of the RSFSR admitted, however, that expert opinion may not be considered as hard proof, so the case was suspended. The Procuracy of the RSFSR sent a letter to the Procurator of Leningrad on March 16, 1955 stating that in this case there had been no grounds for arrest and there was no call for Article 58-10 to be applied to the accused.[98]

In another case, a man was sentenced to ten years imprisonment in May of 1953 on Article 58-10 for spreading anti-Soviet agitation in his circle of contacts from 1949-1953. It was ascertained that the KGB had abused its authority. The sentence was reversed in June of 1955, and the prisoner was released.[99] In a number of cases reviewed in this period it was recognized and admitted that illegal methods were used for obtaining a confession during interrogation.[100]

While the system was attempting to correct itself, it was also struggling against an entrenched repressive tendency. At this same time, there were some cases in which release was indicated but not desired by the authorities. There were other ways of taking a prisoner out of the camp system, and not returning him to society—commitment to psychiatric hospitals. Forensic psychiatry was to become one of the refined (and frequently employed) instruments of repression against "political offenders" in subsequent years (from the fifties to the eighties). G.I. Butov was arrested in September of 1952 by the MGB of the Adygey autonomous province. He was sentenced on Article 58-10 to ten years of correctional labor camp for allegedly systematically carrying out agitation of an anti-Soviet character in the presence of acquaintances. The charge read that Butov was contending that war between the USSR and capitalist countries was inevitable, and the Soviet Union would lose. In October of 1955, the Presidium of the Supreme Soviet of the RSFSR rescinded the sentence, and sent the case for a new examination in the stage of preliminary investigation. The Presidium of the Supreme Court ruled that Butov be required to undergo a forensic psychiatric examination. Butov was sent to the Serbsky Institute.[101]

A better-known case, described by Peter Reddaway and Sidney Bloch, reveals the fact that these practices were apparently sanctioned from above. A Party member, Sergei Pisarev, openly criticized the secret police in 1953 for fabricating the "Doctors Plot." He was arrested, first sent to the Serbsky Institute, and then for eighteen months to the Leningrad Prison Psychiatric Hospital. In these places, he was able to observe a number of cases of intentional misdiagnoses. Upon returning he campaigned for the abolition of this abuse of science, requesting that the Party Central Committee help in the cause. A commission of inquiry was set up to inspect the Serbsky, Leningrad, and Kazan Hospitals. It seems that the commission's findings must have confirmed Pisarev's observations, because they were disregarded by the Party. Reddaway and Bloch, pioneers in researching this phenomenon, provide insight into its motivation: "[t]he advantages inherent in psychiatrically-based repression, especially the discreet silencing of dissenters without recourse to a major trial or blatantly trumped-up charges probably appealed to Khrushchev as he tried to project a new image of the Soviet regime."[102]

The practice of misusing psychiatry to detain political dissenters in mental hospitals seems to have been initiated under Lenin,[103] and was continued under Stalin.[104] Some of the prisoners of the late thirties, however, were actually aided by this practice. Hospitals generally had a lighter regime than the camps, and for those who were only sent for an "expert opinion," there were even cases in which psychiatrists attested to the prisoner's inability to withstand night interrogations, isolation, and so on.[105] Through the years, official Soviet psychiatry became increasingly transmogrified to accommodate to political influences, but that process is beyond the scope of this work. The system had many ways of achieving repression. While the state proclaimed and lauded its efforts to free itself from the legacy of the Stalinist Gulag, it was simultaneously further developing the (ab)use of psychiatry for punitive purposes.

It is difficult to know how much of the delay in reform was due to official weakness at the top, unofficial resistance at the bottom, or complicity at the top with collusion at the bottom. What we do know is that officials of higher departments criticized the work of their regional subordinates at least on paper. If they were sincere, they would have to be described, at best, as under-achievers. In 1955, surveys of the investigative work of regional, provincial and krai organs of the Procuracy determined that efforts at reexamining cases of counter-revolutionary crimes were still unsatisfactory.[106] Inefficiency, lack of initiative, and inaction were cited as reasons for the failures. Although deputy procurators were expected to participate in the review of cases of counter-revolutionary offenders, the report claimed that the Deputy Procurator of Chelyabinsk province did not take part in the review of even one of three cases under consideration. In Chkalov province the Deputy Procurator not only failed to participate in the investigation of a case that was brought, but did not even know that the case was under review.[107] The infrequent participation by other deputy procurators was duly noted by the investigators: "the proof that some procurators [merely] formally relate to their responsibilities can be found in the fact that in a number of protocols of cases, the inscription reads that they were 'read' by the procurator."[108]

An October 1955 RSFSR Procuracy report demands that regional, krai, and autonomous republican procuracies, as well as those of Moscow and Leningrad, seriously improve their work of reexamining cases of counter-revolutionary crimes. Addressing the Kafkaesque maze of procedures, it asserted that there were too many cases in which investigators focused on small details rather than on real substance, and that the legally established time frames for reinvestigation continued to be exceeded.[109] These and similar improper practices are also registered in documents of early 1956.[110]

Some prisoners, frustrated by the inadequacy of local liberation and rehabilitation efforts, sent their appeals directly to officials in

Moscow and even to the chairman of the Presidium of the Supreme Soviet, K.E. Voroshilov. Some were even encouraged to do so. There was the case of a man who worked for a number of years as a free employee in a correctional labor camp after his term had ended in 1941. His tale confirms one author's definition of a returnee: "a semi-free person with a suspicious looking passport."[111] This man was apparently mistakenly issued a passport without limitations. In 1954, more than twelve years after his liberation, he was called into the provincial police and questioned about how it was possible that he had a passport with no "minuses." It was ascertained that a mistake had been allowed twelve years earlier, and that this returnee's clean passport had to be replaced by one with limitations. Moreover, the bureaucrats noted "if you had been sentenced to five years, you could have come under the amnesty, but you got six years, so we can't do anything about this. Go to the Presidium of the Supreme Soviet, only they can decide this question."[112] His sentence was eventually revoked, but the bureaucratic apparatus that created and maintained such folly was preserved.

For many, the camp experience came to be endured either as an acceptable way of life or an acceptable policy of government. One long-time prisoner, Vasily Petrovich Barkhanov, spent seventeen years incarcerated in the correctional labor camp of Norilsk before he was sent into exile. He underwent a long process of release from this phase. In a November 1954 letter from exile in Norilsk, the ex-zek writes that his sentence was reduced for good work, and that he was released prior to the end of his term (after seventeen years!) at age fifty-six. "It was like being born again," he writes to an influential friend, "everything was new for me, even buses. I am still walking around in camp clothing, I have to acquire some things again.... But I am happy that the people in the Party leadership and government are leading the country along the Leninist path, and my life was not in vain."[113] It is interesting to note that despite seventeen years of incarceration—perhaps because of seventeen years of incarceration—this prisoner still expressed belief in the system.

Barkhanov requested that his friend forward this letter to the Minister of Internal Affairs. In it he asked for rehabilitation, and for permission to be released from Norilsk so that he could be reunited with his family whom he had not seen since the day of his arrest in 1938. He requested permission to join his wife in a village 150 kilometers from Leningrad, adding that no major enterprise was located within a fifty kilometer radius of his home. He explained that his wife and parents could not join him in the North because of the harsh climatic conditions. His friend sent the letter on to Moscow. In addition, the ex-prisoner's wife wrote an appeal directly to Voroshilov. It took nine months from the start of his petitioning before Barkhanov was eventually released from exile in August of 1955. Since the documents of his case were culled from the archive of the USSR Procuracy[114] it took this long even with the intervention of officials in Moscow. It took much longer for those without friends in high places.

Between January and July of 1955, approximately 165 prisoners' requests for the rescinding of sentences were sent to the Presidium of the Supreme Soviet of the RSFSR and they were honored. Many of these appeals were based on the desire to return home, or on the need for employment which was very difficult to obtain if the charges were not cleared. For a number of Article 58'ers the stock document read as follows: "he [or she] was justifiably sentenced," or "the criminal activities were correctly categorized. However, considering that [this person] comes from the peasant [or worker] middle [or lower]-class, has no previous criminal record, and has a good work 'kharakteristika' at this time, the Procuracy of the RSFSR does not object to rescinding the sentence."[115] It is noteworthy that the document does not challenge the applicability of Article 58 nor the culpability of the victim. It simply avoids these issues and presents the Procuracy as a forgiving benefactor. Even so, a number of these individuals did not receive rehabilitation until the late eighties.[116]

At this time, returnees were not in a position to be too demanding. They had to be satisfied with whatever concessions they could get, regardless of whether or not real justice prevailed. One ex-zek, who had been arrested as a student for anti-Soviet agitation and was freed in 1951, explains his needs for petitioning for his charges to be cleared and his civil rights restored: "the shadow of my disgraceful past haunts me everywhere I go. I cannot be a trade-union member, I cannot vote, I cannot get a higher education, or enjoy the privileges of other workers..."[117] The procurator concluded that there were no grounds for protesting the sentence, since it was justified. That being said, he did not object to restoring civil rights and rescinding the sentence. In some exceptional cases, in the process of petitioning for withdrawal of a sentence, it was ascertained that the prisoner had been incorrectly sentenced, because there had been no crime.[118] There were even cases in which high officials personally got involved. Rudenko, the USSR General Procurator, wrote to Voroshilov on behalf of a returnee requesting release from exile. He stated that the man's 1939 and 1949 sentences had been groundless. Consequently, the ex-prisoner was freed from exile.[119] However, these cases were rare. More common was what might be termed the ambivalent pardon. The Soviet legal system was engaged in a delicate balancing act between trying to correct some of the abuses of the past, and denying that the system was wrong. While the official actions that were taken—restoring civil rights, etc.—were indeed proper, they took the form of pardoning a criminal. The reason for this approach may have been an attempt on the part of the authorities to finesse the central juridical question: If all of these petitioners who languished for years in labor camps for their political offenses were not criminals, then who or what was?

In addition to all of the other impediments of the returnees, there was one further bureaucratic obstacle. Contrary to other obstacles that occured lower down in the system, this hindrance came from the higher echelons. Toward the end of 1955, those ex-zeks who had succeeded in having their sentences withdrawn and their civil rights restored, and who were among the lucky few to get rehabilitated, encountered an additional problem. This was the disjunction resulting from the two halves of the reform system not communicating with each other. It seems that neither the Supreme Court of the USSR nor that of the RSFSR was issuing certificates attesting to a victim's rehabilitation. Such "sacred documents"[120] were very important, if not the most important material object necessary for reassimilation into "normal" Soviet life. When the courts sent notice that a case was suspended, that implied that the former prisoner was rehabilitated. However, the courts were not sending along a corresponding *spravka* (certificate). Ex-prisoners were complaining to the local MVD that they needed to have documented proof of their innocence in their hands. The MVD in their turn passed the complaints onto provincial procuracies, who then appealed to the General Procuracy of the USSR.[121] There was apparent agreement among lower officials on the necessity of such a document, but it was a very long time in coming.

How many prisoners were indeed released in this decisive year preceeding the XX Party Congress? According to the Special Files of Khrushchev, 24,036 prisoners, who had been convicted of counter-revolutionary crimes, were released after the review ordered by the May 19, 1954 decree.[122] Added to this number of returnees were those liberated under a September 1955 amnesty for Soviet citizens who had been accused of collaboration with the occupiers during the Great Patriotic War[123] as well as special settlers. Zemskov arrives at a figure of 195,353 politicals released in 1955,[124] though it is difficult to be accurate because of all the different kinds of categorization. Moreover, as we have noted, there was movement in both directions, to as well as from the prison system. In 1955, for example, 12,765 individuals who were arrested on parts of the political Article 59 (especially dangerous crimes against the order of governing) were added to the prison and Gulag population.[125]

Despite the "Khruschevian thaw" the system remained repressive and this was, among others, reflected in attitudes about laws past. There existed, in the words of Zemskov, an active principle of continuity whereby certain former repressive practices were not criticized, and were even looked upon as having been politically expedient (he cites the previous practice of mass deportation which was ordained by then existing laws).[126]

The liberal forces impelling the country toward de-Stalinization in 1956 and subsequent years were in place, but so too were the counterforces. Officials maintained an ambivalent attitude at best toward the liberalization process. While the top Party officials proclaimed reform, the Office of the Procuracy practiced the fine art of passive resistance with regard to returnees and rehabilitation. As we have seen, their mandate still left room at all levels for repressive interpretation. Moreover, rehabilitation was presented as an act of magnanimous forgiveness by the authorities, rather than a plea to the victims to forgive the system. Regardless of the official view of rehabilitation, the "bottom-up" perspective provided by the victims' stories describes conditions of rejection, feelings of being outcast, feelings of being second-class citizens, persecution in and out of prison, restricted movement and job opportunities, and inability to reunite with families or to reintegrate into the work and social community. They attest to continued implicit or explicit repressive policies from the top down. Reforms were undeniably underway, but they were still a long way from arriving. The reason for the sluggishness of reform was that the Soviet system was still dependent on repression. It repressed not only people, but also ideas. That was its maintenance tool. To acknowledge this open secret by admitting to the victimizations was to undermine the legitimacy of the regime.

Rehabilitated persons and returnees were a constant reminder of the criminal nature of the system. The struggle over how to handle them and how to come to terms with what they represented was to continue through Gorbachev and the end of the Soviet Union. Khrushchev crafted a number of ways of dealing with the problem, including silence when possible and partial accommodation when necessary. Even though no one was immune to the label, attitudes toward former "enemies of the people" were deep seated. It was hard to find an appropriate psychological and social place for these reminders and remainders of the Stalinist legacy. At the time of his Secret Speech, Khrushchev could do little more than make a diagnosis. But the times were not yet right for a cure.

Notes

1.   O. Khlevniuk, "Beriia: predely istoricheskoi 'reabilitatsii'," *Svobodnaia Mysl'* 2 (1995): 110.
2.   A.I. Kokurin, A.I. Pozharov, "'Novyi Kurs' L.P. Berii," *Istoricheskii Arkhiv* 4 (1996): 132-33; see also *Osteuropa* nos. 11-12 (1998): 367-68.
3.   Nikita Vasil'evich Petrov, interview held at his Moscow home, November 30, 1996.
4.   "Ob amnistii: Ukaz Prezidiuma Verkhovnogo Soveta SSSR ot 27 Marta 1953," *Pravda*, 28 March 1953, p. 1.
5.   GARF, f. 8131, op. 32, d. 4581, l. 122. This figure is also recorded in the "Osobaia Papka Khrushcheva," GARF, f. 9401, op. 2, d. 450, l. 464.
6.   GARF, f. 9401, op. 2, d. 450, l. 471.
7.   Keep, *Last of the Empires*, p. 78.
8.   GARF, f. 9401, op. 2, d. 416, l. 31.
9.   Ibid., d. 1329, ll. 17-26, in Kokurin and Pozharov, p. 147.
10.   GARF, f. 7523, op. 85, d. 41, ll. 1-5, 20.
        There was also a plan drafted in April of 1954 to sanction the early release from correctional labor camps and colonies of 8,000 prisoners who were specialists in agriculture in order to work at machine-tractor stations of the Ministry of Agriculture (GARF, f. 9401, op. 2, d. 450, ll. 233-39).
11.   *Pravda*, 3 April 1953, p. 4.
12.   TsKhSD, f. 89, op. 18, d. 26, l. 3.
13.   Kokurin and Pozharov, p. 134-35.
14.   See R.J. Service, "The Road to the Twentieth Party Congress: An Analysis of the Events Surrounding the Central Committee Plenum of July 1953," *Soviet Studies* XXXIII, no. 2 (April 1981): 232-245; *Izvestiia TsK KPSS* no. 2 (1991): 171-77.
15.   Keep, p. 44. See also A. Korotkov, A. Stepanov, R. Pikhoia, "Agent inostrannoi razvedki," *Moskovskie Novosti*, no. 22, 1-8 June 1997.

16.   TsKhSD, f. 89, op. 8, d. 23, l. 1.
17.   Ibid., l. 2.
18.   Ibid., l. 3.
19.   Kokurin and Pozharov, p. 135.
20.   GARF, f. 9401, op. 1, d. 1299, l. 246.
21.   V.N. Zemskov, "GULAG: istoriko-sotsiologicheskii aspekt," *Sotsiologicheskie Issledovaniia* 7 (1991): 14.
22.   Ivan Mikhailovich Evseev, "Vid na zhitel'stvo, vospominaniia," Memorial, f. 2, op. 1, d. 60, l. 1993 0710 0397.
23.   Andrea Graziosi, "The Strikes of 1953 in Soviet Labor Camps," *Cahiers du Monde russe et sovietique* XXXIII, 4 (octobre-decembre, 1992): 435-436.
24.   GARF, f. 7523, op. 107, d. 235, l. 6.
25.   Ibid., ll. 7-8.
26.   M.A. Goldman, transcibed oral history, Memorial oral history group, October 20, 1989.
27.   GARF, f. 8131, op. 32, d. 4581, ll. 120-121.
28.   Ibid., l. 121.
29.   Semën Samuilovich Vilenskii, interview held at his Moscow home, December 2, 1995.
30.   GARF, f. 8131, op. 32, d. 4581, l. 128.
31.   Ibid., f. 9492, op. 5, d. 166, ll. 28-31.
32.   Ibid., f. 9401, op. 2, d. 450, l. 463.
33.   Ibid., l. 30.
34.   Ibid., l. 31.
35.   Ibid.
36.   Ibid., l. 33.
37.   Ibid., ll. 410-411.
38.   Ibid., l. 463.
39.   Ibid., f. 8131, op. 32, d. 3284, ll. 23-24.
40.   Ibid., ll. 40, ob., 41, ob.
41.   Keep, p. 78.
42.   GARF, f. 9401, op. 2, d. 463, l. 30.
43.   Solzhenitsyn, *The Gulag Archipelago*, volume three, p. 329.
44.   Davies, *Soviet History in the Yeltsin Era*, p. 181.
45.   Solzhenitsyn, p. 312.
46.   Recorded in Davies, p. 181.
47.   GARF f. 9401, op. 2, d. 463, l. 125.
48.   Ibid., d. 451, l. 337.
49.   Newspapers of the Gulag, microfilm collection of the International Institute of Social History (Amsterdam); the originals are housed at the Central Archival Library of the State Archive of the Russian Federation (GARF).
50.   Keep, p. 78.
51.   GARF, f. 8131, op. 32, d. 3284, ll. 55, ob.
52.   Ibid., f. 9401, op. 2, d. 451, l. 127.
53.   Semën Lipkin, *Dekada* (New York: Chalidze Publications, 1983), p. 164.
54.   Keep, p. 79.
55.   Zemskov, p. 14.
56.   Reclassification was not always necessary in the post-May 1954 climate. One rehabilitation certificate of July 1954 issued by the Chief Military Procuracy read: "In response to your complaint addressed to K.E. Voroshilov on May 20, 1954, which was sent to the Chief Military Procuracy, we inform you that as a [prisoner]

convicted in 1940 to 5 years in a correctional labor camp you fall under the decree of the Presidium of the Supreme Soviet of the USSR of March 27, 1953 "On Amnesty." This decree revokes your sentence and you are liberated from exile." (Memorial, f. 1, op. 1, d. 2181, l. 0019 2412 0805.)

57.   "Delo no. Politicheskie zhertvy totalitarizma v Rossii. Dva Sledstvennykh dela Evgenii Ginzburg," (Kazan: Taves, 1994), p. 207.
58.   Ibid., p. 216.
59.   Nikita Khrushchev, *Vospominaniia* (New York: Chalidze Publications, 1979), pp. 274-6. My thanks to Peter Reddaway for locating this citation.
60.   Keep, p. 76.
61.   GARF, f. 461, op. 8s, d. 3223, ll. 12-20.
62.   Ibid., l. 12.
63.   Ibid., d. 3250a, l. 292.
64.   Ibid., l. 293.
65.   Ibid., d. 3223, l. 12.
66.   Ibid., d. 3250a, l. 296.
67.   Ibid.
68.   Already in 1935, secret police chief Yagoda made clear that his attitude toward prisoners and soon to be ex-prisoners was that once a person was tainted with a crime, they remained tainted (see David R. Shearer, "Crime and Social Disorder in Stalin's Russia," *Cahiers du Monde russe* 39, 1-2 (janvier-juin, 1998): 12). This sentiment persisted from the top down, and from the bottom up, even through—and beyond—the Khrushchev years.
69.   GARF, f. 461, op. 8s, d. 3223, l. 17.
70.   Peter H. Solomon, Jr., *Soviet Criminal Justice Under Stalin* (Cambridge: Cambridge University Press, 1996), pp. 337-38.
71.   *Sovetskaia Prokuratura: sbornik dokumentov* (Moscow: Iuridicheskaia Literatura, 1981) p. 147.
72.   GARF, f. 461, op. 8s, d. 3223, l. 18.
73.   Ibid., d. 3250a, l. 299.
74.   Ibid., l. 304.
75.   Ibid., l. 340.
76.   Ibid.
77.   For more on what was going on at the top, see Yoram Gorlizki's discussion on the changes in criminal legislation, 'After Stalin: The Criminal Law Reforms,' in "De-Stalinization and the Politics of Russian Criminal Justice 1953-1964" (Ph.D. dissertation, University of Oxford, 1992), chapter 2.
78.   GARF, f. 461, op. 8s, d. 3250a, l. 353.
79.   Ibid.
80.   Ibid., l. 354.
81.   Ibid., d. 3217, ll. 93-94.
82.   Ibid., d. 3669, l. 61.
83.   Solomon, p. 469.
84.   GARF, f. 461, op. 8s, d. 3631, ll. 65-66.
85.   Ibid., l. 82.
86.   Ibid. Such "discoveries" were also made at strategic moments during the Terror, for example, after Ezhov was dismissed.
87.   Ibid., l. 89.
88.   Ibid., d. 3251, l. 10.
89.   Ibid., l. 13.
90.   Ibid., ll. 67-68.

91.   Ibid., ll. 95-101.
92.   Solomon, pp. 371, 400-401, 453.
93.   Solomon also makes this point, p. 453.
94.   GARF, f. 461, op. 8s, d. 3251, l. 33.
95.   Ibid., l. 56.
96.   Ibid., l. 61.
97.   Ibid., ll. 147-49.
98.   Ibid., d. 3669, ll. 3-4.
99.   Ibid., ll. 146-47.
100.   Ibid., ll. 156, 167, 171-72.
101.   Ibid., l. 149.
102.   Sidney Bloch and Peter Reddaway, *Soviet Psychiatric Abuse: The Shadow over World Psychiatry* (London: Victor Gollancz Ltd., 1984), pp. 18-19. See also Id., *Russia's Political Hospitals: The Abuse of Psychiatry in the Soviet Union* (London: Victor Gollancz Ltd., 1977), pp. 51-65.
103.   Richard Pipes, ed., *The Unknown Lenin*, (New Haven, CT and London: Yale University Press, 1996), pp. 155-56.
104.   Bloch and Reddaway, p. 17.
105.   Semën Samuilovich Vilenskii speaking from personal experience, interview held at his Moscow home, December 5, 1995.
106.   GARF, f. 461, op. 8s, d. 3669, l. 60.
107.   Ibid., l. 61.
108.   Ibid., l. 68.
109.   Ibid., l. 95.
110.   Ibid., ll. 108-9.
111.   Lebedenko, "Budni bez vykhodnykh," *20 Vek* 2 (London, 1976): 254-56.
112.   GARF, f. 385, op. 23, d. 1474, ll. 52-53.
113.   Ibid., f. 7523, op. 107, d. 123, ll. 14-15.
114.   Ibid., ll. 14-19.
115.   Ibid., f. 385, op. 23, d. 1468, ll. 12-14, 39, 47, 96, 118, 121, 142, 175.
116.   "Dolg platezhom krasen, a ne krov'iu," *Zaural'e*, 1 January 1996, p. 3.
117.   GARF, f. 385, op. 23, d. 1469, l. 36.
118.   Ibid., l. 122.
119.   Ibid., f. 7523, op. 107, d. 123, l. 3.
120.   Arsenii Borisovich Roginskii, interview held at the Memorial office in Moscow, April 5, 1996.
121.   GARF, f. 8131, op. 32, d. 4290, ll. 8-9.
122.   Ibid., f. 9401, op. 2, d. 500, l. 319.
123.   *Izvestiia*, 18 September 1955, p. 3.
         This group had their own special problems with reassimilation and stigmatization. Historian and rehabilitation committee member V.P. Naumov reports, "The political distrust of former prisoners of war and their families continued for many years. Suffice it to say that the widely distributed questionnaire with the question, 'Were you or were any of your relatives captured, interned, or located on occupied territory?' was only abolished in 1992." V.P. Naumov, L.E. Reshin, "Nezakonchennoe srazhenie Marshala Zhukova: O reabilitatsii sovetskikh voennoplennykh, 1954-1956gg.," *Istoricheskii Arkhiv* 2 (1995): 110.
124.   Keep, p. 78.
125.   GARF, f. 461, op. 8s, d. 395, l. 2.
126.   V.N. Zemskov, "Massovoe osvobozhdenie spetsposelentsev i ssylnykh (1954-1960gg.)," *Sotsiologicheskie Issledovaniia* 1 (1991): 12.

4

The Impact of Repression on Readaptation

Overview

The scope of the repression did not begin with the arrest of the victims and it did not end with their release. Nor was it limited to the individuals who were arrested. Even those who were never arrested were still intimidated by the constant fear that they or their loved ones could suddenly be taken away. This pervasive threat stifled individual social expression in almost all spheres of life. After release, the deforming effects of the camps continued to wreak their havoc on the ex-prisoners, along with their social networks. That is why the deleterious effects of the repression could never be examined merely from the perspective of the individuals who were incarcerated. They extended to their families, their social circles, their jobs, and to the body politic.

Introduction

Although the repressed were taken out of the camps, for many, the camps could never be taken out of the repressed. The consequences of their experience as prisoners and the further consequences of their status as ex-prisoners hindered all efforts toward readjustment and reassimilation. Not only did prisoners experience major assaults to their psychological stability from the trauma of the camps, but in their damaged condition they had to manage the stress of reentering society. After their release they had to try to gain acceptance into a world that had changed while they were gone. The returnees had also changed. In discussing the moral impact of the camp experience on the individual, Shalamov says "it only makes a person worse ... there is a lot that happens in camps that a person should not see ... the main question becoming whether one remains a human being."[1]

As the repression abated and the political climate thawed in the mid-fifties, it might have been expected that society at large as well as their own social networks would have embraced the returnees and welcomed them back into the fold. However, the years of separation from their families as well as the emotionally disturbing culture of the camps had alienated many of them. Not only did many of them come back as strangers, they came back as problems. They all needed, and some demanded, jobs, housing, rehabilitation, and often the restoration of Party membership. The general failure to achieve these goals served as constant reminders to ex-zeks of the system's repressive nature and its indifference to their plight. Compounding the problem of reentry was the fact that both sides—the government and the returnees—lacked the material and social preparedness for the task. Housing and jobs were scarce. Political expression was dangerous. In addition, there was no socially established institutional process for reentry. The social system exhibited what one journalist, in a different context, described as "the national failure to devise appropriate rituals of return that might have helped [these people] come to terms with [their] experience."[2] While this journalist was referring to American soldiers returning from Vietnam, he could with more cogency have been talking about discharged camp inmates in the post-Stalin Soviet Union.

This chapter will diverge from the chronological format used thus far in order to present a collection of returnee experiences. From these narratives the predicament of the returnees in the Soviet state will emerge with a more human face.

Psychological and Moral Issues Associated with the Return

The Need to Speak About the Unspeakable

Much of what we know about the experience of incarceration and the struggle to survive comes from the oral history and the memoirs of the victims of repression. They tell of the killing ground in which many people lost their families, their convictions, their spirits, their humanity, and their lives. But some victims endured and some fewer prevailed. Their stories provide a kaleidoscopic view of both man's inhumanity to man and the triumph of the human spirit.

These accounts are necessarily a selective sample. We do not know what the illiterate might have written. We do not know what many of the perished would have written or said. We do, however, have the accounts of some of the survivors. We also have the accounts that survived (even if their writers did not), as well as the information that we can infer from reading between the lines. What, we may ask, is the motivation for writing memoirs? Some people write memoirs out of a sense of responsibility, and in order to remember and commemorate. Mikhail Baitalsky, long-time prisoner, rails against the blind eye that society turns to their victimized fellow countrymen in his *Notebooks for the Grandchildren*:

> Some say: The fate of those innocently condemned affects you because you yourself were imprisoned. No, the fate of those tormented and shot troubles me the more strongly the less others seem to know about it. It is not the dead who haunt me in my sleep, but the living who cause my anxiety.[3]

Isaak Moiseevich Filshtinsky has similar sentiments. In *My shagaem pod konvoem* (We Are Walking Under Armed Escort), he also warns of the dangers of relying too heavily on the accounts of a more fortunate few:

> I don't like it when former zeks who were not forced to do hard labor say that it wasn't so bad in the camps, that people read there, learned languages ... it only attests to emotional dryness and moral detriment. I was lucky. I returned from the camp alive and relatively healthy, but I do not have the right to forget those whose lives were destroyed there.[4]

Other memoirists write to redeem a vow, appease a ghost, or retaliate against tormentors. One former prisoner wants Soviet society and the state to suffer guilt, shame, and disgrace about what happened in the camps:

> sometime long ago, when I was standing next to the corpse of a girl with a number tattooed on her back who had been murdered by the guards, I swore that I would someday tell people about it. As I finish writing my story, I turn to the distant shadow of this girl and say: "to the best of my ability I fulfilled this promise."[5]

It was the incremental crescendo of stories like these that contributed to the destabilization of the Soviet system that cracked under Khrushchev and crumbled under Gorbachev. While the political system had already recognized the need to change, the cumulative impact of the (now permissible) public airing of individual accounts of repression further discredited the struggling system. But the writers had a more personal motivation—the need to tell their story. One of the habitual ways that people deal with distress is to transform it into a story and try to recruit a receptive audience. The mitigation of a trauma by co-processing it with a compassionate listener is both an ordinary social remedy and an established psychotherapeutic practice.[6] "Testimony psychotherapy"—telling the story of trauma—has proven to reduce symptoms and improve survivors' psychosocial functioning.[7] However, for many of the early returnees the political atmosphere bred fear of discussion and disclosure of their experiences. So some wrote it down for a future audience. Others waited in silence for times to change. In the late eighties many of these suppressed stories found an audience, and their writers and tellers found some surcease.

More recently, as many of the tales of repression have already been recounted and recorded, the urge to tell and retell these stories of repression has decreased, as have the long lines waiting to get into Memorial's reception room. But many of those who registered with Memorial still requested that oral histories be taken. "Silence," as one author writes, was a "prime alternative when the exit option is foreclosed and one is subjected to a repressive power."[8] Silence may help to maintain physical safety, but it increases emotional suffering. Now, it was no longer necessary to suffer in silence, and the repressed were eager for an audience.[9]

Nightmares

One of the characteristics of the "concentration camp syndrome" is the persistence of symptoms of anxiety and depression long after the physical cessation of the threatening events. Leo Eitinger, an Auschwitz survivor and researcher on this phenomenon, reports that over half of the survivors that he examined still experienced posttraumatic stress symptoms for many years after the war.[10] How does this finding compare with the experience of Gulag survivors? One author aptly observes that a friend who spent eighteen years in an Arctic labor camp chopping wood "developed iron muscles and broken nerves."[11] Evidence of the lasting psychological effects of incarceration is widespread and appears in many forms. Roy Medvedev records that upon their return many prisoners had the doorbells taken out of their homes: "they were afraid of doorbells, because that's what their arrest and misfortune began with.... You had to knock on the door when you visited. Some even feared telegrams."[12]

One former prisoner tells that though he was not threatened by "anything more than threatens every other human being" (it is presumably after 1956), fear persists in his dreams. There, he writes,

> I am back in Lubyanka, Lefortovo, and Butyrki prisons and in camps.... In prison I had flown free as a bird when I snatched brief hours of sleep in damp, foul-smelling barracks. Here [in the outside world] I have nightmares in which I wallow in snow up to my neck, I shiver under the blasts of icy winds, I slip and fall on my face in the mud...[13]

Many others like him experienced this manifestation of trauma. Another ex-prisoner described recurrent dreams of being in a prison or camp and feeling degraded and despondent in the grip of fears that her incarceration might never end. These dreams persisted for twenty years after her release.[14] Yet another was haunted by nightmares in agonizing detail as she slept, and plagued by unremitting traumatic memories in her waking hours. She lamented, "rarely a day goes by when I don't remember those malignant years. This will go on until the day I die."[15]

In the case of one Gulag survivor, that was, indeed, what happened. In 1983, almost three decades after release from her seventeen-year incarceration in Kolyma, Berta Aleksandrovna Babina, age ninety-seven, sat up in her hospital bed. In response to efforts to get her to lie down, she uttered the words: "the convoy [armed escort] is waiting."[16] The bedside nurse, who was unfamiliar with her history, was understandably perplexed. The convoy was Berta Aleksandrovna's last image before dying. We may not know how often this victim of Stalinist terror was transported from one camp to the next, on foot, in temperatures of less than 40 degrees below zero, for sometimes a hundred kilometers across untrodden virgin taiga.[17] But we do know that her journey never ended. At the moment of her death, the traumatic experience was still lodged in her psyche. The nurse's ignorance of what Babina meant and what the epoch she had lived through meant reflected something else—official amnesia, because in 1983 it was once again forbidden to recall the history of Soviet repression.

Psychiatric Treatment

Survivors of the Soviet Gulag have regularly described the persistence of symptoms of anxiety, depression, and nightmares, long after the physical cessation of the threatening events. Despite this, doctors who worked with returnees in the fifties and sixties at Moscow Hospital No. 60, the clinic for Old Bolsheviks, dealt only with the somatic complaints presented by their patients. Although the doctors later admitted to having recognized the psychological aspects of the "camp syndrome" at the time, they were not at liberty to treat the ex-prisoners' ailments psychotherapeutically, because of the proscribed political issues that they represented.[18]

In the post-Soviet era, the doctors felt free to disclose their experiences of those years. On an afternoon visit to Hospital No. 60 in the course of this research, doctors informed of the theme anxiously gathered around a table. They seemed as eager to tell their repressed stories as many returnees had been to tell their stories of repression, often interupting one another with yet another account of post-traumatic sequelae in the camp survivors of the fifties and sixties. "These people were not like the others, they had the stamp of having been in the camps," asserted one of the doctors. Her colleague elaborated, "They were hardened, insulted, pushy, aggressive, and in need of extra attention."[19] All agreed that the men were more difficult than the women patients, who seemed to adapt better. (The gender issue is beyond the scope of this study, but part of the explanation for this phenomenon may lie in the fact that the women victimized as wives of "enemies of the people" were sometimes sentenced to exile rather than camp internment, so they were exposed to fewer stressors. Moreover, those who were incarcerated seemed to process the experience better even while in camp, focusing on friendships and human relationships to help them adapt to their surroundings.[20]) Another physician recalled that in 1960, quite a dramatic scene ensued in the cafeteria when a patient recognized his camp supervisor, who had later become a victim, and subsequently a patient in the clinic.

At that time, these patients were treated only for their physical ailments. There were also an unfortunate few who did not receive treatment of any kind. Shalamov, for example, reportedly suffering from "camp syndrome" later in life, was refused treatment by psychiatrists (and other doctors) out of fear for their professional safety.[21] Not surprisingly, despite the presence of such a large group of cases, no scientific articles were published on this theme. Nor was there a field of specialization for dealing with post-traumatic stress syndrome in camp survivors, as had been developed in countries like West Germany or Holland.

The beginnings in Russia, however, are evident. Since 1992 Hospital No. 60 has been cooperating with the organization Compassion (*Sostradanie*), a (former) branch of Memorial[22] that tends to the psychological rehabilitation of its elderly clientele of camp survivors. According to Dr. Eduard Karyukhin, director of the "in-home help program," Compassion seeks to remedy the "postponed psychosomatic consequences of torture, enforced by age, pathology, and unfavorable living conditions."[23] When home care cannot provide sufficiently effective treatment for these patients, they are admitted to Hospital No. 60 for psychotherapy, medication, and physical therapy.[24] The Compassion doctors have observed that almost all of their clients, long after release from incarceration, manifest such symptoms as sleeping disorders accompanied by nightmares, muscular pains, and digestive disorders. Among some of the clients with "normal psychosocial adaptation," alcoholism and sexual disturbances have been noted.[25]

Compassion has a twofold mission: research and treatment. This particular group of survivors constitutes a unique sample due to three main features: age (sixty to eighty years and older), the postponed consequences of torture, and the extended length of the stressful period in their lives. The team of psychiatrists that surveyed the victim-clients came to some interesting conclusions. We shall review some of them here.

Among 200 subjects, one-quarter had managed to overcome the social, psychological, and somatic consequences of repression, and were in need of no special assistance. A larger group, 38.4 percent, had not completely overcome the consequences of repression, and this was manifested on a somatic level. Outpatient and inpatient treatment as well as psychotherapy was recommended for this group. In a third group, representing almost 15 percent of the sample, partial psychosocial dysadaptation was found. These former victims had not overcome the consequences of repression in the post-repression period, either on a social or psycho-emotional level, and continued to focus on the experience of repression. Dynamic observation and treatment, including outpatient and inpatient psychotherapy, was indicated for this group. Slightly more subjects (16.4 percent) experienced social dysadaptation in one or more major domains of their

life, accompanied by pathological fixation on the experience of repression and frequent outbursts. Active monitoring and consultation
as well as outpatient and inpatient psychiatric treatment was prescribed for this contingent of camp survivors. Finally, about 7 percent of those surveyed were found to suffer from complete social
dysadaptation in all major domains of life, for which constant inpatient and outpatient observation and treatment were recommended.[26]

To what did the victims themselves attribute their (sometimes damaged) mental state? Almost half of the clients connected their psychic trauma solely to the events of the repressive period, one-quarter traced their mental and emotional state to both the repressive
period and the post-repressive period, and 20 percent connected their
psychic trauma only with events of the post-repressive period. The
researchers concluded that for the majority of these survivors, the
experience of repression was their strongest stress factor, influenc-
ing their lives and remaining significant to this day. Social adaptation was frequently achieved by compensation on a somatic level.[27]

The fact that these former labor camp prisoners of the thirties,
forties, and fifties were still alive in the nineties speaks volumes about
their ability to adapt. Marina Berkovskaya, director of Compassion,
which began in 1989 as the medical group of Memorial, points out
that the people who come to the organization have by definition
great survival mechanisms, since many former prisoners died in the
first five years after release.[28] One of the physicians who treats sur-
vivor-patients at Hospital No. 60, Lia Grinshpun, concurs with this
observation, further asserting that returnees are generally strong
people. She adds that their psychological condition in the pre-camp
period also had a great bearing on their post-camp experience.[29]

It is not surprising that the physicians providing treatment to this
group of patients are often wounded healers. Grinshpun was the
child of repressed parents. And Karyukhin's grandfather was part of
the forced labor brigade exploited to constuct the White Sea Canal.
He recalls how his grandfather "cried all his life but never said anything."[30] He died relatively young. Eduard's mother only revealed
the cause of her father's traumatized state after the onset of
perestroika. Times were starting to change quickly. Sakharov was
released from exile, and the organization Memorial began to flour-
ish. In October of 1989, Eduard joined its ranks. He filled out the
Memorial questionnaire with details on himself, and with what little

information he had on his grandfather, hoping that Memorial could help him find more. When the Memorial staff member noticed Karyukhin's profession and sensed his involvement, she asked if he could help take care of the ailing Gulag survivors in Memorial's constitutency. Karyukhin felt a professional, spiritual, and civil obligation to take on the task.

Almost ten years later, he is still dedicating his professional life to working with ex-prisoners—talking to them, treating their pains, and trying to alleviate their fears. In 1998, for example, many of his patient-clients in their seventies, eighties, and even nineties, were afraid that under a new government they might be locked up again. They lament their broken families whose bonds were not repaired by the act of reunion. They regret their nearly life-long sense of stigmatization as second-class citizens. They complain of not having been able to get desirable work, or into universities. They suffer ill health. All this notwithstanding, Karyukhin reports some contradictory feelings toward the system among this group. Despite the relatively ruined lives which they describe, about one-third believed in the Soviet system (and to some extent still do) and thought that their personal suffering was a mistake, the result of certain problems in the system that were merely in need of correction; one-third felt just the opposite, and attributed their suffering solely to the "barbaric system"; and one-third changed their (earlier positive) views on the system as a result of what happened to them.

Karyukhin concludes that the heart problems, asthma, hypertension, and other symptoms which his patients present constitute a "somatic mask that conceals neuroses" that are attendant to their experience of repression. He keeps constant and close contact with his patients, which in itself has a psychotherapeutic effect. He takes time to see them and listen to them, checks up on their living conditions, monitors whether they are being visited by social workers, and organizes hospitalization when necessary and admission to nursing homes when indicated. When he is not treating patients, Karyukhin is developing his specialization, occasionally attending training seminars abroad in order to learn more about psychotherapeutic approaches to former victims.[31]

A 1995 article in the Russian daily newspaper *Trud*, entitled "The Gulag is Not Only the Past," points out that in the Russian Federation alone more than four million people were registered with organizations for the repressed. Its author, a physician, argued that there is no way to compensate for the damage of the Stalinist terror, but specialized medical care could help alleviate some of its consequences. He proposed a medical center for this group of survivors to treat both the physical ailments sustained in the Gulag and their "traumatized psyches."[32] Such a medical center would be out of financial reach and likely would not gain official approval in the present political climate of Russia. Nevertheless, it seems that the concept is slowly but surely being realized, in the efforts of organizations like "Compassion," doctors like Karyukhin, and treatment facilities like Hospital No. 60.

Channeling the Traumatic Experience—Art and Religion

The writer Yuri Dombrovsky, who was in the camps from age twenty-five to fifty, would awaken from his sleep crying, "they are going to cut me with an ax."[33] Though he had spent much of his life in the camps, he could not write about them directly, but he did channel these unspeakable things into his art. This is not unusual. A number of visual artists who slaved at hard labor as well managed to secretly draw or paint, on notebook paper or plywood, while imprisoned in the camps. The portraits, self-portraits, landscapes, animal pictures, and icons attest to the muted struggle for expression by the prisoners.[34]

Memorial has undertaken the task of gathering and displaying the works of repressed artists, both those who perished and those who survived. Its collection is extensive. In his appraisal of the portraits, Lev Razgon stated that, "If an album of these drawings were published without captions or any references to where they were made it would still be clear who these people are and why their faces carry the stigma of upcoming death."[35] This is an apt, albeit finely tuned assessment because very few inner-Gulag themes are directly expressed. Instead, many of the landscapes portray a world *beyond* the barbed wire—perhaps the artist's creative escape into his recollection of or hope for freedom.[36]

One particular ex-prisoner artist, Yefvrosiniya Antonovna Kersnovskaya, recorded in extensive memoirs and meticulously etched in hundreds of drawings much of what she endured. These are impressionistic scenes of exile, interrogation, transport, the camp hospital, prisoners at work in the mines, and so on. Semyon Vilensky referred to Kersnovskaya's life and work as representing "the triumph of the spirit over the system ... proof that a person can be independent of the state even under totalitarian conditions."[37] Isaak Filshtinsky referred to her as an "unfettered soul."[38] Kersnovskaya's illustrated memoirs, written in 1963-64 to describe to her mother what happened in the fifteen years that they did not see each other, span 1,500 pages, and have yet to be published in their entirety. They are about the author herself and the people she met during the various phases of her journey: exile (1941), transport, wood-cutting, escape during which she wandered 1,500 kilometers in the Siberian forests until someone informed the authorities, rearrest, interrogation, receiving a death sentence that was later reduced to ten years of camp, hard labor work in a mine, release (1952), exile. She returned to her life with her mother only in 1957.

Kersnovskaya managed to assert her own will in the Soviet penitentiary system. She frequently performed such altruistic acts as donating blood to get extra rations of food for the "goners" in the camp hospitals. Considering the weakened physical state of prisoners, this gesture was a significant sacrifice. She also taught other prisoners to maintain their dignity even in extreme conditions. It was often the practice of "convoy" guards to command the women being transported under armed escort to lay down in the mud. Prisoners could be shot for disobedience. When Kersnovskaya did not perform this senseless, demeaning act in the power game of victims and henchmen, one by one, the other prisoners literally took a stand, too, by rising from the ground. Kersnovskaya's courageous example helped the prisoners to win this round.

Kersnovskya also refused in other ways to quietly comply with the criminal system. Since she could not "demand justice" when she was sentenced to execution, she would also not ask for mercy. Moreover, she told her judges exactly what she thought of them and of the system they served. Instead of taking the opportunity to defend herself, she enumerated all the "horrible things" she encountered in exile, on the run, and in the prisons. And when she was released, she refused to sign a pledge of silence about what she saw in the prisons and camps. Moreover, while performing relatively "light" work in the camp morgue, she discovered that certain prisoners had been beaten to death by rifle butts. She refused to give false testimony on their cause of death in order to help conceal this official transgression.

She later was able to capture the scene in the morgue in vivid detail. It is one of 700 other illustrations included in a volume published by former dissident Igor Moiseevich Chapkovsky and his family members, who inherited her twelve notebooks.[39] In 1988, Chapkovsky's then fifteen-year-old daughter, Dasha, left Moscow to care for the ailing Kersnovskaya in Yessentuki, in the Northern Caucasus, for the remaining six years of her life. Kersnovskaya's art work and writings were clearly the way in which she channeled her experience of repression. That was their individual function. But her legacy is richer than what was recorded on paper. By the influence she had and still has on former Stalinist era prisoners and dissidents, her life and work also had a political and social function. When in 1990 the popular magazine *Ogonyok* published an extensive illustrated spread on Yefvrosiniya Antonovna,[40] hundreds of readers' letters confirmed the veracity of her accounts. Kersnovskaya instilled in them and in countless former prisoners a greater sense of the dignity of the human spirit.[41]

"Self-expression helped to stave off, however minimally, degradation and despair [allowing some escape] from [one's] unbearable surroundings into a private world,"[42] writes Memorial member and art historian Valentina Tikhanova. Art is an attempt to express deeply felt needs and to make sense of the world. So is religion, as Viktor Frankl so persuasively argued in *Man's Search for Meaning*.[43] Those who endured the inhumanity of the camps confronted the associated issue of God's relationship to man. Mass terror and repression inevitably raise the question of victims' unanswered prayers. Believers were faced with the question how God could be both good and omnipotent and yet permit such cruelty. The experience of repression and surviving the experience of repression generally compel people to evaluate or reevaluate their religious convictions. Solzhenitsyn's post-camp discovery of religion is one of the better known examples of a spiritual transformation as a consequence of repression. Another former Gulag inmate who shared this experience wrote that "imprisonment played a decisive role in my inner-development. Only there did I truly learn about life without distortions."[44] Upon his return in 1955 he became a devout Christian, entered a seminary and studied Orthodoxy. He went on to explain that he turned to Christianity to cure his tormented soul after the experience of the Stalinist camps. It appears that there are some hurts that are perceived to be beyond the power of humans to heal, and under these circumstances, only divine help may be sought.

A number of Gulag survivors claimed that they felt the presence of God during their incarceration. They sensed that he protected them, and helped them through the many trials and tribulations that they had to endure. This belief was not manifested in prayer or any other overt religious exercise, but rather was internalized.[45]

For those people who were socialized, or politicized, to a completely secular society, turning to a deity was not an alternative even to be considered in any of their deliberations. God played no role at all in either their joy or their suffering. Without attempting to reach any conclusions because of sampling limitations, it is interesting to note some returnee responses to the following questions on religion: "Were you religious before repression? Did your attitude toward religion change after repression?" These questions were part of a 1995 questionnaire constructed for this research project and conducted among returnees primarily in Moscow, but also in St. Petersburg and Magadan. Among thirty-one respondents: two were atheist and became religious in the camps, eight started out as religious and remained so, four became religious after the camp or later in life, twelve were not religious either prior to or after the Gulag, two experienced little change in their attitude toward religion (unclear what that attitude was), two were religious before camp and lost their faith afterwards, while one returned to religion later in life. Apparently for some, suffering confirmed the existence of God. Zoya Marchenko (one of this sample's non-believers) describes female camp-mates who considered the suffering that was inflicted upon them in the camps to be punishment for their lack of faith.[46]

This survey equated "belief" perhaps too narrowly with belief in God. For many Party members, "religious" zeal was invested in Stalin or the Party. One of the twelve irreligious respondents explained, "I was and remained a non-believer because I was raised in a family of Communists and professional revolutionairies."[47] Another had his own brand of belief (as did many): "I was neither an atheist nor was I religious, neither perspective affected me. That didn't change. I simply believed in Stalin and he turned out to be a scoundrel and a villain."[48] Belief in the Party or socialism, sometimes even belief in Stalin, was a common sentiment among returnees. This influenced their later efforts to gain reinstatement in the CPSU.

Victims and Informants

The pathology of the Soviet system extended to all of its components—victims, victimizers, and informants alike.[49] One of the systemic techniques used to fragment the opposition was to turn members of a social group against each other. There were strong inducements for people to become *donoschiki* (informers) and turn in their neighbors, friends, and even family members. This had lingering consequences, since some victims or their families had subsequent dealings with the informants.

In 1932, thirteen-year-old Pavlik Morozov denounced his father to the local authorities of his Ural village for harboring fugitive kulaks. As a result, he was hacked to death by vengeful relatives. Subsequently he became a Communist folk hero because he put allegiance to the state above family loyalty. Pavlik Morozov's disturbing legacy was that this practice became an implicitly accepted way of protecting oneself or avenging one's neighbor during the subsequent years of Stalinist terror. One woman is said to have suffered a paralyzing stroke when prisoners started to return after Stalin's death, because she had denounced so many of her neighbors.[50]

Polina Furman, a Jewish doctor, was arrested along with her husband and son in August of 1952. Another son, a medical student, had already been arrested in 1951. In the course of her interrogation in the Lubyanka, Polina was told that a certain Khukhrina had reported the "anti-Soviet activities" of the Furmans to the authorities. Furman was shocked that her friend of thirty years, a friend with whom she had gone through medical school, could be capable of such an act. Furman was released under the 1953 amnesty but her husband continued to serve his ten-year sentence of hard labor. Immediately upon returning to Moscow, Polina telephoned her "old friend" who frightfully gasped, "You returned?!" They agreed to meet in the metro station. When confronted with how she could do such a base thing, the informer turned pale and lamely replied that "the interrogator said that you would never come back."[51] Furman never saw Khukhrina again and tried to forget her. In 1954, after repeated inquiries, Polina was finally informed by the Supreme Court that her son Vladilen (from Vladimir Lenin) had been executed in March of 1952. In 1955 Furman's husband returned from the camps and the whole family was rehabilitated a year later. They emigrated in 1980.

Medvedev described the special psychological problems faced by camp informers. These were people who, in return for cooperating with the authorities, were rewarded by being placed in favorable assignments such as those of camp cooks. Medvedev records that "This was the fate and the heavy moral suffering of many [he cites Pyotr Yakir] ... it tormented them in their subsequent lives, because those lives had been bought at a very terrible price indeed."[52] They lived in chronic fear of exposure because they were unaware of the "complete destruction of camp documentation" that revealed their roles. (Medvedev's assertion about the destruction of these materials is only partially true. In 1954 Khrushchev ordered that certain "*operativnye dela*" [operative files] be destroyed. These included files that contained incriminating information on "honest Soviet citizens." In Stalin's time such materials were preserved for potential future exploitation.[53])

The trauma and tragedy of these complicated issues plagued both victims and informers upon return. The former experienced anger, sorrow, and suspicion; the latter guilt and often self-reproach. These politically circumscribed questions could be addressed if they were cloaked in fiction. This literary mode was an acceptable way of portraying the plight of victims and informers, as witnessed by Solomon Shulman's heart-wrenching "Tupikovaya Situatsiya" (Dead End Situation). While this tale did not actually happen, it easily might have, and will therefore be outlined here for illustrative purposes.[54] The protagonist, Oleg, works in a research institute and is engaged to be married. When his fiancée admits to him that her parents were repressed, he decides to remain engaged but to keep it a secret for the time being. One day he is summoned by a supervisor and asked to fill out a questionnaire. Oleg becomes frightened because he assumes that the NKVD is watching him and is aware of his marriage plans. He is especially afraid of the NKVD because his father had fought on the side of the Whites during the Civil War. The fact that he had misrepresented himself as an orphan might have been discovered by the NKVD. Oleg cancels his wedding plans because he is afraid that if he were to marry the daughter of an "enemy of the people" the NKVD would expose his past. As it turned out, his worst fears were realized. Oleg's fiancée was arrested and never returned from the camps.

Oleg suspected that someone had informed the NKVD of his marriage plans. He wondered if it might have been his friend and colleague Sergey. Oleg's suspicions intensified when, quite by chance, he happened to see Sergey coming out of NKVD headquarters at Dzerzhinsky Square. Convinced that his colleague had informed on him, Oleg decided to avenge himself by killing Sergey. He staged a mishap with high voltage currency at the institute in such a way that Sergey's death appeared to be accidental.

Some years later, Oleg received a letter from Sergey's mother who had just returned from the camps. She wanted to meet with Oleg because he had been Sergey's best friend. When Oleg went to see her, he found an old broken woman who had spent nearly twenty years in the camps. She had not been allowed to correspond with her son and knew little about him. Sergey's mother clutched a book in her hand—a work written by Oleg and Sergey. Afterwards, Oleg became so overwhelmed with guilt that he went to the Party secretary, revealed the truth, and asked to be arrested for murder. The Party secretary called the NKVD to search their archives concerning the matter. A paper was promptly brought in, revealing that the reason for Sergey's visit to the NKVD was to request permission to see his mother in the camps. He was innocent of the offense for which Oleg murdered him. He was not an informer after all!

The Party secretary suggested that Oleg forget the whole thing, because it would be easier for everyone involved. The secretary, thus, conveyed the message that coming to grips with the legacy of terror of individual trauma, guilt, and responsibility should be a private, rather than a public process.

The issue of victims and henchmen (NKVD'ers, camp guards, etc.) raises separate questions. In the post-Stalin era, a number of guards were perpetually afraid of running into the prisoners that they had guarded and often taunted.[55] The victims generally remembered them well, and were also aware of the fact that many enjoyed personal pensions that were higher than the amount that their victims were compensated for their suffering. Whatever desire victims may have had for revenge, and many did, went unsatisfied, since henchmen were never brought to trial. To make matters even more complicated, the victim-henchman line was sometimes blurred, as no small amount of NKVD'ers later became victims. Pavel Sudoplatov, former NKVD'er, who unlike many other incarcerated former henchmen, lived to fight for his rehabilitation, called himself the system's "scapegoat."[56] These core issues will be dealt with at greater length in the concluding chapter.

Semyon Samuilovich Vilensky: Participant-Observer[57]

An inspiring example of a returnee who dedicated his life to exposing the historical truth and helping others to do the same can be found in Semyon Samuilovich Vilensky. For this reason, we will explore, in depth, the story of this man whose own fate is so inextricably intertwined with that of other returnees.

The historical literary society which Vilensky founded in 1989 is appropriately called Vozvrashchenie (The Return). He, and it, have two goals: to publish memoirs that salvage repressed history so as to preserve it in the public domain, and to assist survivors of the terror. To these ends, Vilensky has given the survivors a forum in which to tell their tales, and he has, among a host of other things, successfully lobbied the commission on rehabilitation of victims of political repression. He has pushed them to assist in the transfer of a rent-free estate—Chukavino—to Vozvrashchenie. Though Vilensky's own two-room Moscow apartment is cramped because it functions as a combination publishing house, archive, storage space, reception room, and living quarters, his efforts are aimed at finding space for others. For this purpose Vozvrashchenie has created from Chukavino a cultural, charitable center to which former prisoners can retreat.[58] It is located on the Upper Volga in the province of Tver.

Semyon Samuilovich Vilensky is an ex-prisoner who has developed the extraordinary ability to observe his personal experiences from an outside perspective, and has dedicated his life to humanitarian pursuits. His camp experience shaped his life and perspective. His returnee experience is intimately connected with shaping the lives and perspectives of other returnees. As a prisoner, ex-prisoner, and a returnee Vilensky's story exemplifies the issues associated with the return of political prisoners to society.

Vilensky describes two aspects of the return: the external and the internal. The external aspect includes such problems as acquiring the *propiska* (internal passport system, i.e., residence permit), finding work, securing rehabilitation, and petitioning for compensation. The internal aspect addresses the problems associated with how the individual comes to terms with his/her inner psychological life. Here, fearful recollections of the past persecution merge with fearful suspicions of present surveillance. Vilensky reports that many ex-zeks were (and still are) perpetually afraid of committing even such minor infractions as jaywalking, for fear of being caught and punished. The mindset of the terrorized prisoner is an enduring expectation of punishment. Vilensky recalls that he continued to walk with his hands clasped behind his back after release, and that it took him years to break the habit. It was a struggle to get used to walking on the sidewalk, because prisoners were always marched under armed escort in the middle of the road.[59]

Early on, there were indications that Vilensky had the kind of inquisitive mind, benevolent spirit, and steadfast courage that would put him on a collision course with a terrorist dictatorship. In 1945 he entered Moscow State University as a philology student and began his development as a free-thinking intellectual in these years. Vilensky did not mind studying Lenin, but was skeptical about the theories of Stalin. He did not like the attitude toward the intelligentsia who, he believed, could play a special role in society that was being neglected. Furthermore, he was against nationalistic politics and opposed the deportation of peoples. All told, these stances were later to amount to "anti-Soviet activities." At age seventeen he was already questioning the system and defending the rights of others when he voiced that a friend was unjustly arrested. This was considered a form of "anti-Soviet agitation."

As a student he liked walking in the forest with his friends and reading poems aloud. One afternoon in 1948, in the presence of some fellow students, he recited a poem about Stalin and the intelligentsia. Its final line read, "agents are all around, and Stalin is the first."[60] Someone informed the authorities of this, and it was interpreted as Vilensky's expression of a desire to destroy Stalin ("terrorist intentions"). He was arrested, and Semyon's nine-month interrogation began. The following year he was sentenced to ten years under the *liter* ASA (abbreviated letters for "anti-Soviet agitation"[61]) and the Article 58-8 (point 8 referred to "terrorist intentions").

Vilensky spent one month in the Lubyanka, from July 17 until August 18, 1948. He was then taken to the Sukhanovka, notorious for fifty-two types of torture.[62] Those who survived the Sukhanovka were the most physically destroyed.[63] There Vilensky languished for 100 days with no walks, no interrogations, little light, and the awful sound of moans and screams. He contended that one could easily go crazy there. In spite of intense pressure to sign a false confession, Vilensky refused to do so. When he went on a hunger strike to protest the false charges he was taken to a *kartser* (a cold, dark special punishment cell). When he insisted on seeing a Procurator, the authorities, in a Kafkaesque gesture, provided him instead with an interrogator. This is quite the opposite of what Vilensky needed since he had been put in the *kartser* in the first place for not signing a confession. The interrogator did not like his original story, but Vilensky had nothing to add to it.

Vilensky recalls that in the *kartser* he began hallucinating. The next thing he remembers is waking up in the cell to find a local doctor standing over him. She diagnosed Vilensky as having mental problems and recommended that he be taken to the Serbsky Institute for expert examination. The role of this institution at that time was almost diametrically opposed to its later task of punishing dissidents. In the Stalinist period, the Serbsky Institute assessed the authenticity of the psychiatric diagnosis to make sure that the patient was not faking illness. There were ample incentives to fake mental illness because such a diagnosis could save the patient-prisoner's life. Later, as we have already noted, the Institute practiced the fine art of faking diagnoses and providing inappropriate, physically painful treatment in order to punish patient-prisoners. Vilensky was in fact rescued by the institute's validation of his psychological condition of nervous exhaustion. The doctors said that he could not be interrogated at night, and Vilensky was sent back to the Lubyanka.

According to the ex-prisoner, there was a short interval at the Lubyanka during which the beating of prisoners was suspended in favor of other forms of coercion. One such form was the use of psychological torture by the arrest of family members. Another was the so-called "conveyer" method in which prisoners are deprived of sleep[64] in order to extract false confessions. Vilensky was subjected to a prolonged interrogation, but because of the medical recommendations he was allowed to sleep at night. Subsequently, he was transferred to the Butyrka, where he was charged under the *liter* ASA (see above), and also accused of the preparation of a terrorist act. He was sentenced by the Special Conference to ten years in a special camp in Kolyma.

In May of 1949 Vilensky set out on his nearly two-month train journey. Then came the ship, where they were "transported like slaves, but that's another story," Vilensky chuckled, as he realized how many issues he was bypassing, and how during our interview we were able to reduce such a tremendous amount of personal tragedy into this narrative of events.

At the special camp at Kolyma, zeks wore numbers on their backs, caps, and knees. Vilensky's number was I-1620. He recalled one camp-mate who drew his numbers larger than the standard size. When the supervisors asked why he had done this, the prisoner replied, "I want the Americans to see me from their planes."[65] No one saw him for the next ten days. He was confined to the *kartser*. While prisoners were allowed to write home twice a year, the "supervisors" (*nadzirateli*) were not required to send the letters. Prisoners soon learned that if they wanted the heavily censored letters they had written to be mailed, they would have to confine their writing to the subjects of working, being healthy, and living well. Prisoners could ask for packages with things they needed, so that people could guess how they were really living.

(One story culled from the Memorial archive of memoirs provides a poignant example of how family members learned to read between the lines for the real content of the message. A prisoner's wife correctly inferred from a simple statement about clothing, scribbled on a receipt [for items delivered] that she got back from the prison administration, that her husband had been sentenced to death. She had been told that he was being sent to Kolyma. From a list of items that he would still be needing he crossed out the words "blanket" and "coat." The climate in Kolyma has been described by prisoners as twelve months of winter and the rest summer. His wife realized that he knew he would not be getting there.[66]

Sometimes prisoners pushed letters through the cracks in the floor of transport trains while en route. Remarkably, these letters often reached their destinations.[67] Although people who found them along the tracks must have known the status of the letter writers, they nevertheless stamped them and mailed them. Even in the depths of the terror there were still "free" individuals who maintained their humanity.)

Vilensky remained in the special camp in Kolyma for over six years, until the fall of 1955. In the winter of 1953-54 after Beria's execution, he helped to organize the expulsion of a rebel from the camp. This "prisoner" had started to agitate young people toward insurrection. From his experience, Vilensky knew that such open provocations would never be possible unless the camp leadership wanted it to happen, so he rallied opposition against the provocateur. Because he had foiled their plot, Vilensky was persecuted by the supervisors. He was sent to a camp in Kolyma where only common criminals, not political convicts, were held. Then he was sent to a camp that incarcerated privileged criminals, the so-called "*suki*" (thieves who agreed to be in the service of the camp supervisors). Vilensky was perceived by his new campmates to be an agent of their arch-enemies, because he had not been killed in the camp from which he came. One of the *suki* clans set out to burn Vilensky and the young Ukrainian nationalist prisoners with whom he had arrived in their barracks, but ultimately failed.

Vilensky was freed from camp in the fall of 1955. He explained that at that time Kolyma had a liberation system that was linked to work output. For example, if a prisoner exceeded the normal work quota by 110 percent, then one working day equalled two days of the sentence; 151 percent made one work day count for three days. Thus, extra productivity could reduce the days spent in prison and result in early release. If the prisoner had less than a year to go, he was allowed to grow hair, a mark of privileged status among the shaven inmates. Zeks could also earn some money to which they were entitled upon release. However, from this sum the camp administration subtracted the costs of feeding the prisoner, clothing him, and guarding him! The clothing in which the prisoner was arrested ten, twelve, or fifteen years earlier was taken out of storage (if it had survived the various transports) and returned to him. On discharge, Vilensky received a certificate of release, and some money that his brigade-mates had saved up for him.

Vilensky was initially instructed to go to Yagodnoe, the center of the Northern Mining Industrial Complex where he was to obtain necessary additional documents. Those who were in the special camps did not receive a passport, but instead received a paper. Those who had certain "points" (sub-divisions of criminal articles, like Vilensky's 58-10) were not subjected to colonization (compulsory settlement) in Kolyma, and thus had the right to obtain passports, albeit restricted ones. One former prisoner described these passports as an open advertisement of official disapproval. With their distinctive numbers and letters, "as soon as the passport is opened, people know with whom they are dealing. It is like a stigma."[68] Nevertheless, it was better than a simple piece of paper, because it gave the bearer permission to live in a certain place. In 1955 when the first soviets and *raikoms* (district committees) came to Kolyma, Vilensky turned to the new administrators for help, since the camp administration had refused to issue him a passport. He was one of the first zeks that had come to the secretary of the *raikom*. Fortunately, Vilensky's father was successful in enlisting the help of the writer Ilya Ehrenburg, whose intervention had a powerful effect on the authorities. Vilensky received his passport, albeit with all the standard restrictions. Ehrenburg proceeded to work on the young writer's rehabilitation.

Vilensky's return could now begin. He describes the scene at the Ugolnaya railroad station on the Moscow-Vladivostok line: "there were a thousand former zeks at the station, almost all criminals that the trains wouldn't take. I left Kolyma alive and almost got killed at the station!"[69] It was impossible to get tickets going West, so Vilensky headed for his cousin in Blagoveshchensk, near the Chinese border in the southeast. He had no legal right to go there because of his passport restrictions, but he got help from an unexpected source. Seated next to him on the train was a lieutenant colonel to whom he told his story. Near the border, when documents were being checked, the officer said that Vilensky was with him.

Vilensky was picked up at the Blagoveshchensk train station by his physicist cousin, Iosif, who took Semyon back to his house. That evening, when they were out taking a walk in town, Iosif pointed to a little side street and said, "Our relative lives here with his family. He works for the KGB and also wants to see you." There was a meeting of sorts. Vilensky looked across the street and saw a man, a woman, and two children staring at him. There they stayed, at a safe distance—close enough to see that Vilensky was alive and well, and far enough not to have to inform on him.

Shortly after his arrival in the east, Vilensky called Moscow to inquire about his prospects for a legal return. He was informed that his case was being examined, and that his father and Ilya Ehrenburg were working on it. That was incentive enough for Semyon to go back to Moscow. He returned to the communal apartment where he had been living. As a former prisoner he was received cautiously. One friendly neighbor promised Vilensky that she would not tell the authorities about his presence in Moscow. Other neighbors judiciously refrained from asking questions.

In the meantime, Ehrenburg called Vilensky's procurator. This young man supported the rehabilitation, but his superiors were against it, preferring amnesty, because they suspected that there was a subversive quality in Vilensky's poetry, confiscated upon arrest in 1948. In consequence, his poems were sent for review to determine if any anti-Soviet themes could be found. They were not, and the Military Collegium of the Supreme Court, which was responsible for issues of terrorism, instituted a reexamination of his case. The sentence was revoked and rehabilitation eventually followed in July of 1956. While he was awaiting the determination of his legal status, Vilensky officially lived with his uncle in the province of Kostroma, beyond the 101-kilometer range.

During this time, Semyon could not get work in his field of literature, so he took a job as a dispatcher at a truck company. Through this job he was able to (illegally) travel from Kostroma to Moscow frequently, while his rehabilitation process dragged on. Vilensky found his co-workers in the truck company to be much more receptive to his ex-prisoner status than were his peers in the intelligentsia. As it happened, so many of these workers had been imprisoned that they had developed an attitude that someone who had not been incarcerated was somehow inferior. In assessing this stance, we must bear in mind that many of the workers were likely to have been sentenced under criminal articles for intentional acts. As a rule, this sentiment was not held by ex-Article 58'ers, since they generally were not incarcerated as a result of any act they had committed.

In 1957, the year following rehabilitation, Vilensky obtained contract work at a publisher, Sovetsky pisatel, translating poems by Balkars, an ethnic group that had been deported en masse during the war, and had now returned from exile. He was not allowed to express his own sentiments through publishing his own poetry, but the themes of war and deportation depicted in the Balkars' writings served to convey Vilensky's message. In the meantime, the KGB kept a close watch on Vilensky. His apartment was once searched for the poems of an ex-zek from Kolyma, but nothing was found there. The rehabilitated Vilensky wrote an indignant letter to the authorities about the invasion. Meanwhile, Vilensky kept one step ahead of them by concealing in other locations manuscripts that he had gathered. During this time, he reregistered at the University in order to finish his studies in Russian philology. As compensation for over seven years of imprisonment, Semyon was given a two-month stipend.

In 1962 Vilensky returned to Kolyma in the capacity of both a special correspondent for *Literaturnaya gazeta* and as a representative of the Writers' Union. He was not troubled by his return to the place of his imprisonment, but apparently the local authorities were because he was not well received by them. Kolyma lagged behind Moscow in accommodating to the political changes that were taking place. In Moscow at that time many publicists valued and sought out friends who had been former prisoners because they expected that the "thaw" would last. In Kolyma, change was much slower in coming, and hard to sustain. A branch of the Writers' Union was created there in the early sixties. In this setting Vilensky made the acquaintance of Nikolai Vladimirovich Kozlov, director of a publishing company and secretary of the Magadan branch of the Writers' Union. The vicissitudes of Kozlov's struggle to publish a book on Kolyma compiled by Vilensky, and the fate of Kozlov can serve as indicators of the persistent repression in the post-Stalin era Soviet Union.

The book that Kozlov tried to publish was an attempt to fill a void in official Soviet history. It was an effort to present the memoirs and stories of Kolyma prisoners. Up to that time, nothing had been published in Kolyma on the camps, so the book's compilers were venturing into politically uncharted and, as it turned out, forbidden territory. Opposition did not develop immediately because the First Secretary of the Magadan Regional Communist Party was in favor of the idea. However, when the work was compiled and his assistant, the ideological secretary, informed Moscow of its content, things changed quickly. An order was issued from the censor requesting that the manuscript be sent to the Soviet capital, because by then it had been labeled an "ideologically unsound volume." In consequence Moscow decreed that the book could be published only if it was limited to the stories of those who had a *propiska* (registration) in Magadan. In other words, only the writings of those who had survived the camps (and did not mention their existence), or those who were employed in the camp press could be published. Those writers who had perished in Kolyma were disqualified as authors. Kozlov's determined efforts to prevail against the censoring authorities resulted in his being admitted to a psychiatric hospital with the diagnosis "obsession with the struggle for justice." The message that the authorities were sending was that either it was insane to try to challenge the system or the futility of the undertaking would drive one insane.

To make matters worse, even the attenuated and sanitized camp themes that had been initially approved were gradually weeded out from the collection. The final product was described by Kozlov as a "castrated book." When it was published under the title *Radi zhizni na zemle* (For the Sake of Life on Earth), Kozlov was listed as one of its editors, even though he had demonstratively removed himself from this position. Kozlov was deeply upset by this inclusion. The date of publication was September 1963; the city of publication was Magadan. The perceptive reader could infer the book's political tale by its omission of certain authors and subjects.

Despite the testimony of the coercive influence of the state in Kozlov's determined but failed struggle, Vilensky continued what he had already started—the collection of manuscripts of former zeks. In doing so, he was willing to risk his own life and freedom to preserve the stories of those who had lost both. Had he been found to possess even one manuscript, he would have lost his residence permit in Moscow and perhaps much more. Nevertheless, by the beginning of the seventies he had already gathered dozens of manuscripts, which he often placed with friends in villages outside of Moscow. This undertaking was particularly courageous because all the while Vilensky still suffered from recurrent nightmares about the camps. The stories that he believes must never be forgotten are also too traumatic to remember. In the interests of their mental health, he and other ex-zeks have become accustomed to practicing a useful form of denial. He says that when he meets ex-zeks, "we don't talk about the terrible things. We all know them. We talk about the amusing things,"—a particularly poignant example of gallows humor. He also wistfully admits that whenever he sees people of the age that he was when he was arrested, he realizes that he can never replace his lost youth. But he has achieved a different form of potency. Semyon Samuilovich Vilensky has been able to validate the suffering and salvage some of the pride of his constituency of ex-zeks, most of whom feel that they remained second-class citizens.[70] Through his efforts, he has made a reluctant world bear witness to their sacrifice and in so doing give it some redeeming value.

Camp Culture

The experience of the camp put its subcultural stamp on all of its inmates, who acquired distinctive clothing, language, and traditions. Generally those who had shared the experience were marked for life, and their camaraderie reflected the cohesiveness borne of sharing a common ordeal. They had spent so much time learning how to stay alive in a diabolic world that the conventional world often seemed strange to them. An ironic convergence of these two worlds can be found in the tale of Snegov's return, or rather, the tale of his being brought back. After Beria's arrest, it was necessary to find witnesses who would implicate Beria for his early activities as first secretary of the Transcaucasian Committee of the CPSU. After searching prisons and camps, the authorities finally tracked down Aleksandr Snegov, who had worked under Beria in Tbilisi.[71] This prize witness was actually brought to the Kremlin as he was found—in prison garb with numbers on his back and sleeves! Apparently, the camp supervisors did not know the purpose of Khrushchev's summons.[72]

The ex-prisoners who came back from the camps were not the same people who entered them. They had a different past and a different future and often felt alienated from the larger society. That society also felt apprehensive in their presence because the returnees disturbed the world into which they came with reminders of the world from which they came. So there was sometimes pressure on both sides to avoid each other. In questionnaires done for this project, we found that returnees often preferred the company of former zeks because they felt that no one else could understand what they had seen, done, and endured. While some were greeted with compassion by old friends, others concealed their status from friends in the interests of reestablishing their relationships.

It was difficult for those who had not been imprisoned to engage the prison experience, even second hand through contact with a survivor. This was made even more difficult because those ex-prisoners who had survived, and what it was that survived in those ex-prisoners, could be very disagreeable. In his realistic novel *Forever Flowing*, Vasily Grossman describes the ambivalence and pangs of conscience of Nikolai Andreevich who is about to see his recently liberated cousin, Ivan, for the first time since his return. The meeting generated an unwanted antipathy toward someone whom he expected to welcome back into the fold:

... with Ivan there in front of him, he experienced a turnabout of feeling. This man in a padded jacket, in soldier's shoes, his face eaten away by the cold of Siberia and the foul air of overcrowded camp barracks, struck him as alien, spiteful, hostile.[73]

Because many of the ex-zeks no longer fit into their previous social and vocational networks and because they shared a common experience of suffering, many developed and maintained what might be called a post-liberation sub-culture. According to Isaak Moiseevich Filshtinsky, the ex-zeks celebrated their ritual holidays—their day of liberation, the anniversary of Stalin's death (March 5)—and shared unique linguistic expressions. This "language of symbols" referred to things that had meaning only to those who had been in the camps.[74] Evgeniya Ginzburg has described this phenomenon:

> Even now, many years later, as I am writing these memoirs, all of us who have tasted the blood of the lamb are members of one family. Even the stranger whom you meet on your travels, or at a health spa, or at someone else's house, immediately becomes near and dear to you when you learn that he was *there*. In other words, he knows things that are beyond the comprehension of people who have not been there, even the most noble and kind-hearted among them.[75]

The uniqueness that united zeks and distinguished them from others was also sustained by their jargon and special uses of language. In the greeting ritual among former zeks, the phrase, "Where did you come from and when did you get back?" was often used to establish orientation points, and to confirm the common experience.[76] Additionally, special words entered the daily lexicon of former zeks. Words like *tufta* (exaggerating results to fulfill norms), *dokhodyaga* (goner, prisoner on his last legs) and *lagernaya pyl* (camp dust, an expression describing what prisoners were to become, since they were not properly buried when they died)[77] resonated with meaning even to those who had not been through the camps.

Other words were invented for collusive communication to evade detection by the authorities. For example there were coded terms for "knife" (a forbidden object), or "message," or "letter," or "meeting," or to indicate a lower-ranking official, or a person who hides the truth, or the act of concealing something, and so on.[78] Much of the covert communication was not particularly political, but rather criminal slang. This touches upon the issue raised earlier of criminalization that results from incarceration. Perhaps the adaptation of criminal language not only reflects the linguistic aspects of criminalization, but also reflects a certain psychosocial adaptation to the criminal status.

Tamara Davidovna Ruzhnetsova

An example of how some aspects of camp culture remained a part of the returnee and how other people responded to this can be found in the story of two sisters, one of whom was incarcerated. Tamara Davidovna Ruzhnetsova (interviewed for this project) grew up with her older sister, Rita, after they were orphaned in 1931. Tamara was fourteen at that time. They had been born Jewish, but their father converted to Christianity and had them baptized, because he wanted a military career.[79] In 1938 Tamara was arrested as an English spy. The charges seemed to have originated from the fact that she had danced with a musician from a Western jazz band at the restaurant National in Moscow.[80] She was shifted back and forth between camps and exile until her release in 1946. Her sister Rita was not arrested, but she was harassed by the authorities. They demanded that she denounce Tamara, which she refused to do. For her refusal she was stripped of the medals that she had earned for working as an interpreter in the Spanish Civil War.[81]

Upon her return, Tamara was not permitted to live inside Moscow because of her passport restrictions. However, she secretly visited Rita in her Moscow apartment. Fortunately, the building elevator operator whose function it was to report on residents' activities, was sympathetic toward Tamara, and would run into the apartment and tell her to hide whenever passports were about to be checked. On Tamara's first visit to Moscow, Rita arranged a whole "festival of art" for her sister's entertainment. They went to the theater, to exhibitions, and to concerts. There was an activity planned somewhere for every evening.

According to Tamara, on her second visit, a year later, things were different. She recalls that they sat home on the first night and some friends stopped by. On the second night friends visited again. By the fourth day, Tamara could no longer contain her curiosity and exclaimed, "Rita, last time I was here you got me tickets for everything, and now I'm just sitting at home—with your friends. How come?" Rita's answer surprised Tamara and reflected the personal and social problems created by the camp culture that still resided in returnees:

> Tomochka, please don't be insulted. The thing is that when you came last year you were such a *lagernitsa* [camp inmate], that I was simply ashamed to show you to my friends.

You barely spoke a sentence without cursing, you were full of camp jargon. Now you have already returned a bit to your former self, and once again become an interesting person. And my friends want to socialize with you.[82]

To add to the misery of the returnee, the ordeal of the camp had not elevated Tamara to the status of heroine, let alone martyr, but rather profaned her in the eyes of "proper" society. She was an outcast. Rita was not anticipating that her friends would experience discomfort or anxiety when confronted with her ex-zek sister. Rather, she feared their revulsion. It was not the fact that Tamara had been in the camps that would impress this complacent group, but rather that the camps were still in her. Tamara evoked images of a world that they did not want to deal with. Though it appears that her sister Rita also felt repelled, their family bond was strong enough to overcome it. Many returning zeks had no such family bonds and suffered in isolation.

The rest of the details revealed by Ruzhnetsova's story do not specifically relate to the culture of the camps. However, since they address the larger issue of this chapter—the effects of repression—it adds to our understanding of returnees and will be chronicled here.

When Rita was handed Tamara's rehabilitation certificate in July 1956, she received along with it a request from the authorities that she convey their apologies for past mistakes to Tamara. Tamara's response was that she would like to excuse them, but she could not because their cruelty was too great. She went on to explain that during her incarceration she developed night blindness. The prisoners were forced to work from dawn until dusk, so they went to and from the work site in the dark. A misstep to the right or left was considered an escape attempt, so Tamara lived in constant fear. She had reason to be afraid. Tamara recalls the brutality of the guards:

We worked from darkness to darkness. There were cases in which the guards shot prisoners. We were not allowed to tell anyone, although many of us were questioned. We had to answer, "attempted escape." Otherwise the next day it was your turn. Our shooters also amused themselves by shouting the commands: "lay down, stand up, lay down, stand up...." And since it was damp, dirty and cold, we went to work already exhausted and wet. We had to work like that until it was dark again.[83]

More than once, Tamara's life was saved by her camp-mates when they kept her from falling during the journey to and from work. But they could not save her eyesight. Tamara had dreamed of becoming a heart surgeon ever since her father's death from a heart attack. But after camp, instead of becoming a surgeon, she became a typist. Eventually she lost the vision in one of her eyes. "So what should I forgive," she asks, "forgive a ruined life?" I have no family [her sister died in the 1990s]. I have no children. At that time they deprived me of everything of which a person could be deprived."[84]

Today Tamara lives in Moscow and works with Memorial, transcribing oral histories. When asked on the eve of the May 1996 Russian presidential elections her opinion regarding the Communist Party candidate Zyuganov's popularity, Ruzhnetsova replied: "I'm seventy-eight years old. I can't cut wood, I can't do anything. They shouldn't waste a bullet on me."[85] She had been asked her opinion of the politician. Her answer did not address the question that was posed, but rather reflected her own feelings of worthlessness and her persistent fear of the political system that he represented. Tamara Ruzhnetsova's story illustrates why the burden of the camp experience could never be lifted. It justifies the expansive title of the book in which her memoirs have been included, *Our Whole Life*.

Adaptation to the environment is one of the basic survival mechanisms for all life forms. But it can create a number of problems. The adaptation to one environment can result in a maladaptation to another environment. Survival in the camps necessarily required the incorporation of attitudes and behaviors which could not and, indeed, should not be tolerable in a humane society. In consequence, this "zekification" of individuals who have experienced incarceration in Soviet labor camps sometimes resulted in dysfunctional behavior after release. The following fictitious tale illustrates well how difficult it is for prisoners to escape their past and their identification with prisoner (or victim) status. It is as if returnees come to belong to a different world, a secret clan of former zeks. In "Karzubyi," as the story is told, there was a man who served a term in the camps as the son of an "enemy of the people." Upon release, he could not resume a normal life—he could not find work, he could not reunite with his family, etc. His feelings of hatred toward everything that was not like the camp further hindered his adjustment to society. He arranged his own room like a cell, he ate primitive food, and he apportioned it into camp rations. Meanwhile, all of his efforts were directed at helping relieve the suffering of those who still remained in the camps. The ex-zek wrote letters and leaflets, told people of the horrors of the camps, and publicly accused the authorities of inhuman behavior toward prisoners. He was not arrested, but his efforts yielded nothing.

One day the former prisoner made the acquaintance of a man who belonged to a group of people wanting to change the system. They did not expect to accomplish this through agitation and propaganda, but rather through a (successful) Decembrist type revolt. But first it was considered necessary to man important posts in the government in order to work from within the establishment. On the group's orders, the former prisoner joined these "Soviet Decembrists," changed his name, fabricated a new biography, and got a job in the camp administration. But he could not play the assigned role. His inability to free himself from his past allegiances impeded his ascent in the Gulag career hierarchy. He could not find common ground with his co-workers, his "fellow" supervisors felt estranged from him, and he got into conflicts with those who were supposed to be his peers. In the depths of his being, he remained a victim of the regime, and despite his avowed intentions, was unable to overcome his past and convincingly play the part of victimizer.[86] While this story is fiction, we do know that former victims did, indeed, join the Soviet establishment, even the Gulag administration. The story is overdramatized, but it demonstrates how victims experienced an inherent and lasting sense of belonging to the world of ex-zeks.

Family Reunion

A primary goal for most returnees was to reunite with their families.[87] House and home are the physical, psychological, and social place to which they would most naturally be drawn. Because the family is the most likely point of reentry into society, the first problems of assimilation often manifested themselves in the familial setting. The family-returnee interactions were often difficult and complex. Many families waited vainly for the return of loved ones who had perished in the camps. One returnee who went to visit the families of his friends who had not survived felt guilty about his own survival. He could hardly bring himself to tell them what he knew.[88] Sometimes the equation was reversed and prisoners returned to find that their families had not survived the terror. All that they could do then was to try to find work, repair their legal status, and attempt to create new families. Many women who had been in Kolyma and were in their fifties when they were released, took up with strangers for shelter and protection, and married them within a month.[89]

As a rule the prisoners returned in a completely deteriorated state. One unfortunate returnee who had been in prisons and camps from 1936-41 and again from 1948-54 was finally allowed to go back to Moscow in June of 1954 at the age of fifty-six. He was reunited with his wife and daughter, but was too debilitated by the ravages of camp life to enjoy his freedom. Two days after his arrival in Moscow, he dropped dead of a heart attack in the middle of the street.[90] This was clearly an extreme case, but the same hardships that had killed so many prisoners left those who survived with enduring health problems for the rest of their lives.

The official organs of communication had not acknowledged the cause of the returnees' problems, nor had the government provided a socially approved procedure for attempting to heal these problems. On a practical and emotional level, families did not quite know how to deal with the readjustment of their returning loved ones. Once again let us turn to literature for a glimpse into some realities of the returnee experience. Okudzhava might just as well have entitled his *Devushka moei mechty* (Girl of My Dreams) "Mothers and Sons," (like Turgenev's [1862] work on generational conflict, *Fathers and Sons* [Children]), since it poignantly portrays the plight of the generation of surviving widows of "enemies of the people" who returned from the camps and sought their children. Bulat Okudzhava's narrative is filled with the kind of authentic detail that only an autobiography can supply. It describes the return of a mother to her son in 1947, after ten years of separation. It portrays the incapacity of outsiders (even family members) to fully comprehend what it meant to be inside, which complicated family unification and contributed to functional problems among returnees. The narrator prepared himself psychologically for the arrival of his mother from Karaganda, expecting a physically frail, but emotionally intact old woman to step off the train and greet him warmly. He anticipated that he would pick her up at the train station, they would have dinner at home, she would tell him about her life, he would tell her about his, and then they would go to the movies where she could relax.[91]

What might have been an appropriate homecoming for a return from a trip, was inappropriate for a return from the ordeal of the Gulag. The narrator did not find his mother at the station, so he returned home. When he arrived he was surprised to see his mother, tall of stature and graceful of movement, walking toward the house.[92] Her looks were at once familiar and yet deceiving. He had anticipated that their meeting would be a tearful reunion, and rehearsed how he would comfort his mother by saying that he was healthy, that everything was going well, that she was healthy and just as pretty, and everything would be okay. But when he looked into her eyes, they were dry, and her expression was one of detached aloofness. With bewilderment, he recalls, "she looked at me, but didn't see me, her face was hardened, frozen..."[93] When he asked her if she wanted to eat, she replied, "what"; when he repeated the question, she asked, "me?" She was alive, but something warm and vibrant and open to emotional experience had died. They went to the movies, but his mother needed to leave in the middle of the feature. And so it went.

The narrator realized that her experience "there" was hard for him to understand and even harder for her to talk about. The survivor who was standing before him could not let him inside her emotional life because even she dared not go there. We are reminded of the character in Shalamov's *Kolyma Tales* who did not want to go back to his family because of what he had seen and what he knew. The comfort of the homestead stood in such stark contrast to the destitution of the camps that returnees had difficulty fitting in again. The adjustments necessary for survival in one atmosphere are often ill-suited for survival in a different one.

It could be assumed that the family would exert a salutary and normalizing influence on the returnee. But it was also possible for the reverse to happen—for returnees to have an unsettling influence on their families, and particularly on their spouses. This was especially the case when the spouses of prisoners had formed other attachments.

Viktor Nekrasov's novella *Kira Georgievna*, one of the better known returnee tales, portrays this predicament. Interestingly, the book was published in 1961 and was initially favorably received by the critics, but a year later, Nekrasov was attacked for it.[94] Apparently the issues raised were still too politically unsettling to be presented to the public, even as a work of fiction. The protagonist, Kira, is married to a successful well-known artist and enjoys the good life. But the past intrudes on her idyllic life with a summons from the NKVD. In 1936 Kira had been married to Vadim, who was arrested in 1937 and charged with being an "enemy of the people." Shortly thereafter, she received a letter from her husband releasing her from the marriage.

Kira accepted her husband's altruistic offer and divorced him. She put her life with Vadim behind her, and eventually married someone else. But Vadim did not perish in the camps. One day, he returned to Moscow in connection with his rehabilitation process. He had been living in Kolyma for twenty years and had a wife and two-year-old son there. (He was probably released between 1953 and 1955 and had been restricted to that region.) When Vadim and Kira met again, their youthful love was rekindled. They wanted to forget the last twenty years and start all over again. But Vadim's outlook on life was too thoroughly shaped by twenty years of camp experience for him to start anew. Even for his beloved Kira, he could not take on the social trappings of a "rehabilitated person." One emigré literary critic, D. Burg, insightfully describes what was expected of such a role. "In accordance with the unwritten law of the last few years [late fifties, early sixties], the 'rehabilitated person' should express joy and thank the Party for its kindness. He should strive to restore his membership in the Party, and 'look forward into the future.'"[95] The problem was that Vadim could not give up his past. He never ceased talking about the past, not out of anger, but because he was not able to put aside such an authentic part of his being. His impassioned entreaty to himself and to his listeners was, "this cannot happen again, you understand, this cannot be repeated."[96]

In an effort to restore their lost compatibility, Vadim and Kira travelled to Kiev, the city of their youthful ardor. But the friction between them increased. It was difficult to share the present and future because they each had such a different past. She could not understand his preoccupation with the past; he could not understand her obliviousness to the past. Vadim agreed to try to look ahead and start thinking in terms of the future, but Kira reluctantly came to believe that he just did not understand contemporary life, and that his attitudes and judgments were outdated. For the past twenty years they each had lived in different worlds and each had married spouses who were from those different worlds. Kira's new husband was from Moscow; Vadim's new wife was from Kolyma. Each spouse brought with them the experience that came with these territories. In the end,

Kira and Vadim were unable to revive their old bond, and reluctantly parted. Still, Kira longed for what she and Vadim had once had. She became restless and, like the problems of reentry faced by ex-prisoners, could not resume living as she had prior to their reunion. It would take a long time for her to find a new balance in life, and even then, maintaining stability would be a balancing act.

Once again the emigré literary critic Burg provides us with a contrast between the official returnee literature and realistic literature. According to the Party line, normal "Soviet people help the 'victim of the personality cult' to take his position in society."[97] Burg observes that in this novel, the writer reverses this situation by revealing how the zek Vadim's experiences in the camps affected the normal life of Kira. This realistic story portrays the impact that victims had on the society to which they returned. It was not simply the case that those who stayed behind affected changes in the lives of returning victims. It was also the case that the victims, by virtue of their camp socialization, affected changes in the lives and perspectives of those to whom they returned. It appears that generally no one in the social network escaped being a victim. All were affected. It was just a matter of degree.

In Kira's case, her husband Vadim had released her from marriage and she had accepted. This practice was fairly widespread. Husbands were uncertain that they would survive their incarceration and wanted to protect their wives and families from being harrassed and ostracized as relatives of "enemies of the people." For their part, wives of an arrested spouse might be able to protect themselves by denouncing their husbands and divorcing them. But even this might not guarantee their safety. A number of wives did maintain their marriages to their incarcerated husbands, but the stresses of separation and the deforming acculturation to the camp life took its own toll on the marriages. According to Medvedev, few men returned to their previous wives after camp. Snegov, for example, married a nineteen-year-old. Although Shalamov did return to his wife, they divorced within a few years.[98]

When it happened that returnees were reunited with spouses who were also returnees, their chances for compatibility were better because they each had been "there." One former victim recalls the vicissitudes of her parents' marriage. Her father was released in 1951, with five years "deprivation of rights" (numerous restrictions includ-

ing loss of civil liberties), while her mother was still serving a fifteen-year sentence. They had been divorced, and her father had acquired a new wife and son. When her mother was released under a
1955 amnesty, her father returned to his first family even though his
second wife never officially granted him a divorce.[99]

The circumstance of wives of "enemies of the people" remaining
incarcerated, even after their husbands' liberation, was rare, but it
happened. One memoirist tells of a camp-mate whose husband was
released and rehabilitated while she lingered on in the camps for
another two years. Despite the fact that her imprisonment had been
related purely to her husband's "crime," they were unable to budge
the process of her release.[100] Another prisoner serving an eight-year
term in Akmolinsk as the wife of an "enemy of the people" received
a letter in her third year from her husband in Moscow. To her amaze-
ment, his rights had been fully restored, and their apartment was
given back. Even with his apparently privileged status, it took this
former prisoner at least a year to obtain the release of his wife.[101]

In spite of the official inducements to sever the marital bonds, the
years of separation, the uncertainty of return, the forming of other
alliances, and the problems of incompatibility associated with return, some marriages not only endured, but prevailed. Evgeny
Aleksandrovich Eminov, an accomplished engineer, was drafted into
the army as a specialist in 1941. According to his biography, he survived many brushes with disaster. Eminov's division was crushed by
the Germans in the fall of 1941. He sustained a serious stomach wound
and was taken into captivity. He was then sent to a POW camp and
operated on by a captive surgeon. He survived, but contracted ty-
phoid. He was thrown into the morgue, but again survived because he
was saved by a nurse. The following year he refused to work for the
Germans and was sent to Auschwitz and then Buchenwald. In 1944
he was sent to an invalid camp to be destroyed, but he escaped. In
1945 he was liberated by the Americans and sent for convalescence
first to an American hospital in Hamburg and then to a Soviet hospital
in Breslau. He then returned to Moscow and was reinstated in his
former high position of chief engineer. In 1952 Eminov was arrested
and sentenced to twenty-five years of hard labor and five years of
deprivation of rights. He believes that the reason for this was that he
had let the Germans capture him alive. He was sent to Vorkuta. He
survived all of that and was released in May of 1956.[102]

When Eminov came home he was greeted by a wife who had waited for him and who had also endured her own set of problems. At the time that he was sent to Vorkuta, their son was a student at the Mendeleev Institute, but the arrest had so damaged his son's standing at the institute that he was dismissed. Now he was in the army in the Far East. Eminov's wife was not permitted to defend a dissertation that had already been completed. In addition, she was forced to leave her position as a specialist in the All-Union Central Council of Professional Unions, where she had worked for twenty years. In order to keep the apartment, she took a lowly engineering job. The authorities had provided her with divorce papers that she was encouraged to fill out and file, but she never completed them.[103] This spouse did not take the opportunity to distance herself from her "criminal" husband in order to avoid hardships. There were a number of others who had that kind of determination, but such does not seem to have been the rule.

One ex-prisoner, Evgeny Edvardovich Gagen, returned to his wife after a fourteen-year separation. He spent from 1937-47 in Kolyma, and from 1947-54 in exile in the Magadan province. He said that his wife could have joined him when his exile began, but she did not want to leave the children alone in Moscow and she was afraid to bring them. Only when their daughter entered the university did she join her husband in exile. Despite the fact that they had a son nine and a half months after their reunion, the fourteen-year interval, and the experiences associated with it were difficult to overcome. Gagen's wife could not relate to his friends, and avoided meeting with them. He felt that he had grown in those years while she had remained the same.[104] Although his life in the labor camp was harsher than her life at home, as the spouse of a prisoner she had endured considerable social stigmatization. While it might have been accurate for Gagen to say that they grew apart, he was incorrect in his assessment that his wife remained the same. No one associated with the repression remained the same.

The pathological consequences of repression extended to the lifetime of the victim and beyond that in ever widening circles. The large and small difficulties created by repression found their way into every corner of the psychological, social, and political life of the victim. Some returnees attempted to blend back into the social fabric; other returnees would not go gently back into a society that had taken their freedom and now wanted to deprive them of dignity. These returnees rightfully demanded whatever small entitlements the state would allow.

In the immediate post-Stalin era, there was only a slight drift toward liberalization but not a clear direction nor a clear policy. Old repressive attitudes still prevailed, but there was recognition (exemplified by Khrushchev's secret speech to the XX Party Congress) that in order to continue functioning, the system's characteristic adaptation to repression had to change. Eventually it did, but lasting change was a long time in coming for the returnees. Gorbachev's two favorite concepts *glasnost* (publicity, openness) and *perestroika* (restructuring) were still three decades away.

Though the lot of returnees improved significantly as a result of the era of rehabilitation, the effects of their experience of Soviet repression continued to haunt their lives and the lives of everyone in their network. In the following chapter we will explore Khrushchev's "de-Stalinization" of 1956 and subsequent years, and the implicit social contract it made with returnees.

Notes

*Some passages from this chapter appeared in, "Life in the 'Big Zone': The Fate of Returnees in the Aftermath of Stalinist Repression," *Europe-Asia Studies*, 51, no. 1 (1995):5-19.

1.   Varlam Shalamov, "Inzhener Kiselev," *Grani* 76 (1970): 25.
2.   Edwin M. Yoder, Jr., "Looking Back in Anger: 5 Marines After Vietnam," *International Herald Tribune*, 28 February 1996, p. 9.
3.   Mikhail Baitalsky, (trans. Marilyn Vogt-Downey), "Notebooks for the Grandchildren: Notebook II," *Bulletin in Defense of Marxism* (New York, 1987), p. 43. See also Mikhail Baitalsky, *Notebooks for the Grandchildren: Recollections of a Trotskyist Who Survived the Stalin Terror* (New Jersey: Humanities Press, 1995). The Russian manuscript was donated to Memorial, and can be found in its collection of memoirs (f. 2, op. 1, d. 8 and 9).
4.   Isaak Moiseevich Fil'shtinskii, *My shagaem pod konvoem* (Moscow: Vozvrashchenie, 1994), p. 189.
5.   Khava Vladimirovna Volovich, "Povest' bez nazvaniia," Memorial, f. 2, op. 1, d. 36, l. 0001 2909 1325.
6.   Herbert M. Adler, "The History of the Present Illness as Treatment: Who's Listening, and Why Does it Matter?" *Journal of the American Board of Family Practice* 10, no. 1 (January-February 1997).
7.   Stevan M. Weine, Alma Dzubur Kulenovic, Ivan Paukovic, Robert Gibbons, "Testimony Psychotherapy in Bosnian Refugees: A Pilot Study," *American Journal of Psychiatry* 155, no. 12 (December 1998): 1720-26.
8.   Guillermo O'Donnell, "On the Fruitful Convergences of Hirschman's *Exit, Voice, and Loyalty* and *Shifting Involvements*: Reflections from the Recent Argentine Ex-

perience," in *Development, Democracy, and the Art of Trespassing* (Notre Dame, IN: University of Notre Dame Press, 1986), p. 251.

9. Some victims of China's Cultural Revolution are only beginning to tell their stories of terror, after thirty years of silence. See "Recalling 10 Years of Madness: Cultural Revolutionaries Do Lunch," *International Herald Tribune*, 17 May 1996, p. 2.

10. Dierk Juelich, Hrsg., *Geschichte als Trauma* (Frankfurt am Main: Nexus Verlag, 1991), p. 24.

11. Louis Fischer, *Russia Revisited: A New Look at Russia and her Satellites* (Garden City, NJ: Doubleday and Company, Inc., 1957), pp. 48-49.

12. Roy Medvedev, transcript of interview with S.F. Cohen, early 1980s, p. 45.

13. N.N. Krasov, Jr., *The Hidden Russia: My Ten Years as a Slave Laborer* (New York, 1960), pp. 93-94.

14. V.V. Lapshin, "Vsë techët, vsë izmeniaetsia...," Memorial, f. 2, op. 1, d. 80, l. 1993 0810 0697.

15. Iosif Il'ich Peiros, "Chast' 3: 'Poluvolia'," Memorial, f. 2, op. 1, d. 93, l. 1993 1510 0894.

16. *Dodnes' tiagoteet*, Vypusk 1, (Moscow: Sovetskii pisatel', 1989), p. 134.

17. Eugenia Ginzburg, *Within the Whirlwind*, pp. 97-98.

18. Larisa Nikolaevna Suprun, deputy chief doctor of endocrinologic therapy, interview held at Hospital No. 60, Moscow, October 6, 1997.

19. Suprun, interview, and Irina Aleksandrovna Berdisheva, department chief, interview.

20. For more on the woman's recollection of the camp experience vs. the man's, see Irina Sherbakova, "The Gulag in Memory," in Luisa Passerini, ed., *Memory and Totatitarianism* (Oxford: Oxford University Press, 1992), especially pp. 113-14.

21. Julia Wishnevsky, "The Last Days of Varlam Shalamov," *RFE-RL research report* 38/84, 24 January 1984, p. 2.

22. Since 1992 "Compassion" has had a status independent of Memorial, although they still work together.

23. Eduard Kariukhin, report delivered during the XII Training Seminar on Rehabilitation of Torture Survivors and Their Families, Copenhagen, Denmark, 1993.

24. A.S. Korotaev, M.I. Berkovskaia, E.V. Kariukhin, "Opyt organizatsii mediko-sotsial'noi pomoshchi pozhilym i starym liudiam-byvshim uznikam GULAGa," *Klinicheskaia Gerontologiia* 3 (1996): 67-68.

25. Kariukhin, Copenhagen report.

26. Alexander N. Michailov, Nikolai V. Vostroknutov, Marina I. Berkovskaya, "The Correlation Between the Kinds of Repression and the Current Psychosomatic Status of Torture Victims," paper, Humanitarian and Charitable Center "Compassion," Moscow, Russia, 1993, pp. 4-5.

27. Ibid., pp. 4, 6, 10.

28. Marina Iosifovna Berkovskaia, interview held at the "Compassion" office in Moscow, October 7, 1997.

29. Lisa Grinshpun, interview held at her Moscow home and at Hospital No. 60 October, 1997.

30. Kariukhin, interview held at his Moscow office, April 21, 1998.

31. Ibid.

32. Anatolii Karelin, "GULAG—ne tol'ko proshloe," *Trud*, 16 May 1995.

33. Evgenii Tsvetkov, "Khranitel' Drevnostei, pamiati Iuriia Iosifovicha Dombrovskogo," *Vremia i My* no. 30 (1978): 119.

34. Memorial's headquarters at Malyi Karetnyi Pereulok 12 in Moscow house a museum containing a number of works of repressed artists that were donated to the organization by their families. The collection also includes tattered dresses, shoes,

glasses, handcrafts, photos and other remnants and reminders of camp life. After years in production, a catalog was published in 1998 under the title, *Tvorchestvo i byt GULAGa. Katalog muzeinogo sobraniia obshchestva 'Memorial'* (Moscow: Zven'ia, 1998). See Anna Iakovleva, "Iskusstvo pod okhranoi gosudarstva," *Russkaia Mysl'*, 29 October - 4 November 1998.

35.   *New Times* 27, 1990.

36.   It seems that Nazi concentration camps scenes have been more vividly portrayed in art. See for example, "The Holocaust, 'Spat Out' by Artist Who Survived," *International Herald Tribune*, 2 November 1995, p. 22. Of course, the political climate in the post-Stalin Soviet Union influenced the artist's choice of subjects. See also, *Teatr Gulaga: vospominaniia, ocherki* (Moscow: Memorial, 1995) for biographies of artist-prisoners in particular I. Sooster (pp. 91-102) and B.M. Erbshtein (pp. 111-122) who could not get work through the Artists' Union after release. Erbshtein committed suicide in 1963.

37.   Vilenskii, discussion held at Chapkovskii home in Moscow, April 22, 1998.

38.   Fil'shtinskii, "Raskovannaia Dusha," article prepared for publication by "Vozvrashchenie," Moscow, April 1998.

39.   Evfrosiniia Antonovna Kersnovskaia, *Naskal'naia Zhivopis'* (Moscow: Kvadrat, 1991), pp. 293-307.

40.   See *Ogonëk* nos. 3 and 4, 1990; also *Znamia*, nos. 3, 4, and 5, 1990.

41.   Igor' Moiseevich Chapkovskii, Daria Igor'evna Chapkovskaia, interview held at their Moscow home, April 22, 1998.

42.   Valentina Aleksandrovna Tikhanova, "Introduction," *Tvorchesto i Byt*, p. 14.

43.   Viktor E. Frankl, *Man's Search for Meaning: An Intoduction to Logotherapy* (London: Hodder and Stoughton, 1964).

44.   Vadim Shavrov, "Vesennie mysli i vospominaniia," *Grani* 63 (1967): 103.

45.   Many of Eduard Kariukhin's clients talked of this, interview.

46.   Zoia Dmitrievna Marchenko, response to questionnaire designed for this project, April 6, 1995.

47.   Anonymous response to project questionnaire, December 12, 1995.

48.   Pavel Albertovich Ivensen, response to project questionnaire.

49.   A poignant illustration can be found in the rumors circulating in the camps of cases in which "convoy" guards committed suicide after having recognized their father or mother among the prisoners (Maia Ulanovskaia, Cohen questionnaire, Jerusalem, 1980).

   On the fine line between loyalty to individuals and loyalty to the system, and on the struggle for survival in a totalitarian system, see Tina Rosenberg, *The Haunted Land: Facing Europe's Ghosts After Communism* (New York: Random House, 1995).

50.   See Iurii Druzhnikov, *Informer 001: The Myth of Pavlik Morozov* (New Brunswick: Transaction Publishers, 1997). See also Serge Schmemann, "Soviet 'Hero' Informer, 13, Leaves a Bitter Legacy," *New York Times*, 16 September 1982, p. 2. The panic-stricken response of informers to returning zeks is well described by Nadezhda Mandelstam in *Hope Against Hope* (New York: Atheneum, 1970), pp. 48-49.

   For a discussion on the function and practice of denunciation in the Stalin era, see Sheila Fitzpatrick and Robert Gellately, "Introduction to the Practices of Denunciation in Modern European History," in *The Journal of Modern History* 68, no. 4 (December 1996): 747-767; Vladimir Kozlov, "Denunciation and Its Functions in Soviet Governance: A Study of Denunciations and Their Bureaucratic Handling from Soviet Police Archives, 1944-1953," Ibid., pp. 867-898.

   See also Etkind's essay on Aleksandr Fadeev in "Sovetskii pisatel' i smert'," (*Vremia i My* 26 (1978): 132-46). The General Secretary of the Writers' Union, whose signature condemned many writers to death and imprisonment, committed suicide in 1956. Etkind argues that the return of these writers put Fadeev in an unbearable situation.

51. Polina Furman, response to Cohen questionnaire, May 1982.
52. Roy Medvedev, letter to Stephen F. Cohen, 25 September 1983.
53. Nikita Petrov, interview, March 7, 1997.
54. Solomon Shulman, "Tupikovaia Situatsiia," *Vremia i My* 27 (1978): 23-39.
55. Leonid Ivanov, "Chelovek iz GULAGa," *Trud*, 24 January 1996.
56. Elena Egereva, "Pavel Sudoplatov: 'Iz menia sdelali kozla otpushcheniia'," *Novoe Vremia* no. 39, 1996, pp. 40-42.
57. The information in this section has been gleaned from personal interviews carried out by the writer over the course of several years. Most of the interviews were held at the home of Semën Samuilovich Vilenskii, which also served as the headquarters of "Vozvrashchenie," Moscow, December 2 and 5, 1995, May and November, 1996, September-October, 1997, April, 1998.
58. See "Goriachii kartser diktatury," *Vecherniaia Moskva*, 28 October 1995. p. 2.
59. Vilenskii, interview held at his Moscow home, April 4, 1995.
60. Ibid, December 2, 1995.
61. The "liters" like KRD (counter-revolutionary activities), KRTD (counter-revolutionary Trotskyite activities), SOE (socially dangerous element) and others were eventually replaced by articles.
62. "Goriachii kartser diktatury."
63. See Lidiia Golovkova, "Tikhaia Obitel' (Sukhanovka)," Biblioteka Zhurnala *Volia* 1 (Moscow: Vozvrashchenie, 1996).
64. See Conquest, *The Great Terror: A Reassessment*, pp. 123-24.
65. Vilenskii, interview, December 2, 1995.
66. Varvara Mikhailovna Azarova, "Chernoe krylo," Memorial, f. 2, op. 1, d. 3, l. 0001 2909 0121.
67. Boris L'vovich Brainin, "Vospominaniia Vridola," Memorial, f. 2, op. 1, d. 27, l. 0001 2909 0258.
68. "Reabilitatsiia Vracha R.," materials from Anton Antonov-Ovseenko sent to Stephen F. Cohen, May 14, 1980.
69. Vilenskii, interview, December 2, 1995.
70. Details of Vilenskii's story were also added in interviews held at his Moscow apartment in May and November of 1996 and on later occasions.
71. "Listki iz bloknota: Trudnye voprosy vremeni," *Novoe Russkoe Slovo*, 17 March 1977.
72. Medvedev, interview, pp. 6-7.
73. Vasily Grossman, *Forever Flowing* (New York: Harper & Row, Publishers, 1972), p. 45.
74. Isaak Moiseevich Fil'shtinskii, interview held at his Moscow home, April 20, 1995.
75. Ginzburg, *Within the Whirlwind*, p. 157.
76. Nina Ivanovna Gagen-Torn, Memorial, f. 1, op. 1, d. 967, l. 0013 0612 0907.
77. Lev Razgon, "Pamiati Ne Vernuvshikhsia...," transcript of interview with Memorial oral historians, 1990, p. 45.
78. Evsei Moiseevich L'vov, "Vospominaniia," Memorial, f. 2, op. 1, d. 84, l. 1993 0810 1574 and Gleb Iosifovich Anfilov, "Materialy k biografii: vyderzhki iz pisem, dnevnikov i drugie dokumenty," Memorial, f. 2, op. 1, d. 4, l. 0001 2909 0269.
79. Tamara Davidovna Ruzhnetsova, interview held at her Moscow home, April 21, 1996.
80. Ruzhnetsova, transcript of interview with Memorial members, 1990, pp. 7-8.

81. Galina Ivanovna Levinson, *Vsia nasha zhizn'* (Moscow: NIPTs Memorial, 1996), pp. 78-79.
82. Ruzhnetsova, transcript, pp. 23-24, and Levinson, p. 78.
83. Levinson, p. 76.
84. Ibid., p. 79.
85. Ruzhnetsova, interview, April 21, 1996.
86. Mikhail Iakobson, "Karzubyi," (Paris-New York: Tret'ia Volna, 1983). Iakobson was incarcerated for nine years in the camps of the Northern Urals in the post-Stalin era (Maia Muravnik, "Lagernyi Don-Kikhot," *Strelets* 1 (January, 1984): 20-21.)
87. This is listed as the first goal for many upon return in Cohen's questionnaires, though there were some respondents whose primary desire was to rematriculate at institutes or be rehired at their jobs. They may have returned together with their families (from exile, for example), or their families may not have survived.
88. Grigorij V. Kravtschik, *Dornenwege: Ein Leben unter Stalin* (Bremen: Edition Temmen, 1989), pp. 129-30.
89. Elinor Lipper, "Nuns, Thieves, Speculators and Lovers," in *Eleven Years in Soviet Prison Camps* (Chicago: Henry Regnery Co., 1951), pp. 159-161.
90. Ekaterina Safonova, "Nesmotria ni na chto, sud'ba otnositsia ko mne po-materinski," *Ogonëk* 10, March 1996, pp. 48-51.
91. Bulat Okudzhava, *Devushka moei mechty: avtobiograficheskoe povestvovanie* (Moscow: Moskovskii Rabochii, 1988), p. 111.
92. Ibid., p. 113.
93. Ibid., p. 114.
94. Viktor Nekrasov, *Kira Georgievna* (Cambridge: Cambridge University Press, 1967), p. 6. See also interview with the author, "Viktor Nekrasov: to chto massovyi chitatel' za Berlinskoi stenoi—eto nashe gore," *Novoe Russkoe Slovo*, 16 June 1985.
95. D. Burg, "Moral'noe bankrotstvo sovetskikh konformistov," *Grani* 53 (1963): 122.
96. Nekrasov, p. 79.
97. Burg, p. 125. See also Manya Harari, "From the Other Shore," *Encounter* vol. XIX, 1 (July, 1962): 89.
98. Roy Medvedev, letter to Cohen, February 10, 1984, pp. 2-3.
99. Anonymous oral history, recorded and transcribed by Memorial, 1990, pp. 16, 18.
100. Vera Dmitrievna Uspenskaia, "Povest' moei zhizni," Memorial, f. 2, op. 1, d. 119, ll. 0007 3111 1178-79.
101. RTsKhIDNI, f. 560, op. 1, d. 37, l. 308.
102. Evgenii Aleksandrovich Eminov, "Smert' - ne samoe strashnoe," chast' 2, Memorial, f. 2, op. 1, d. 142, l. 0008 3111 1041.
103. Ibid., ll. 0008 3111 1213-1215.
104. Evgenii Edvardovich Gagen, "Vospominaniia," tom 4 (1955-1956), Memorial, f. 2, op. 1, d. 45, l. 1993 0510 1253.

5

The Politics of Readaptation and Resocialization Procedures: Policy and Practice before and after the XX Party Congress

Introduction

The political climate in the Soviet Union in the 1950s was sardonically portrayed by a popular joke circulating at the time. It divided the Soviet Union into three classes: prisoners, former prisoners, and future prisoners.[1] While it is true that after Stalin's death, ex-zeks were less likely to be arrested and were less harassed, it is also true that in the post-Stalin era many felt an ongoing sense of injustice related to their status as ex-prisoners, or even rehabilitated persons. Their history of incarceration made it difficult to find proper work and housing. Moreover, while the XX Party Congress led to changes in the physical and legal status of zeks and returnees, it was still an era characterized by contradictory ethos. The disparity between official policy and unofficial practice resulted from and reflected the pervasive ambivalence at all levels of the government (and society). But there was a gradation in the government's commitment. The upper levels were more reform minded, but were often not so committed to it that they were willing to fight very hard. Because first-line bureaucrats still hewed to the old Party line, discrimination against returnees continued at lower levels long after it had been rescinded from above.

John Keep accurately described the ambivalent quality of rehabilitation in the post-Stalin years as having a "superficial, grudging character." He adds that "it was less a legal than a political matter, subject to the vagaries of the struggle in the Kremlin and the interests of the Party as interpreted by the victors."[2] Rehabilitation was not carried out in the spirit of justice, but rather as a rear-guard action to preserve entrenched power, especially at lower levels. Even after legal reform was enacted, many old repressive attitudes still remained. In *The Gulag Archipelago* Solzhenitsyn railed against the continuing injustice endured by many ex-zeks. He cites the tale of one former prisoner who suffered fifteen years in camp, and another eight years in silence about the experience. In 1960, when this returnee dared to share his memory of camp conditions with his fellow employees, it triggered a KGB investigation during which a KGB major had this to say: "Rehabilitation does not mean that you were innocent, only that your crimes were not all that serious. But there's always a bit left over!"[3] The bit that was presumably "left over" could always be employed to justify further harassment. For many returnees justice was a train which was always late.[4] In this chapter we will continue on the road to and from the XX Party Congress, tracing the victims' journey back into society through their search for housing, work, social rehabilitation and personal recovery. We will describe both official "top-down" pronouncements regarding returnee issues and the victims' "bottom-up" experience created by these policies. We will find that people who left for the camps were changed so that they were not the same ones who returned, and the place to which they returned was not the same place they had left.

Housing

Adequate housing was a persistent and serious problem for the Soviet citizenry in general. It was an even greater problem for returnees. Among the consequences of Soviet repression was not just a loss of one's residence permit, but a loss of one's residence. This problem plagued most returnees. One former prisoner recounts that his apartment was occupied by staff members of the MGB: "even as my interrogation was being conducted in the Lefortovo prison, an MGB agent took the lock off of my apartment and moved in with his family."[5] The prisoner's family was left with one fourteen-square-meter room, where his wife and son lived together. After release in May 1955 he was allowed to return to Moscow, but he had no legal grounds on which to demand the return of the apartment. There was a decree in Moscow that apartments of the repressed which were occupied by MGB people would not be returned to the rehabilitated former residents.[6]

One returnee recalls that even after the housing policy was liberalized, the practice of denying them housing continued. In 1955, the executive committees were obligated to give returnees priority in housing. However, none of this ex-prisoner's efforts to retrieve his room (probably in a communal apartment) succeeded. He continued to live with three other family members in a seventeen-square-meter room.[7]

The requests that were finally honored generally required a considerable amount of petitioning. One woman who was arrested for anti-Soviet agitation by the counter-intelligence division SMERSH in 1944 and released in 1947, spent the next eight years trying to register to live with her mother in Moscow. In a 1955 letter to the president of the USSR, Voroshilov, she pleads for reevaluation of her case, because her son suffers from tuberculosis and she needs to be near a Moscow clinic. She points out that she spends all of her free time working on her rehabilitation, and that the date of reevaluation is constantly postponed. (We are reminded of the "accused" in *Der Prozess* who spends all his time desperately trying to extricate himself from the bureaucratic maze.) This ex-zek adds a patriotic note: "How I want to live, work, and feel like an equal citizen of this great motherland!"[8] A number of files in this fund (the USSR Supreme Soviet), especially those containing correspondence with the USSR Procuracy on citizens' petitions for reexamination of their cases (or those of their relatives), could not be investigated because they are still classified. A handwritten instruction on the letter requests that Procurator Rudenko look into the matter. This returnee's sentence was revoked on July 7, 1955.[9] It is not clear if the exoneration resolved her problems, but at least one of the countless obstacles was removed.

Even among unequals, some were more unequal than others. Distinctions based on former political associations influenced, for better and worse, the treatment of some returnees. Some of the more prominent returnees did receive a "hero's welcome," compared to the reception accorded to ordinary citizens who came back from the camps. This preferential treatment extended to a wide range of needs. There were cases in which higher officials were willing to intervene, most often on behalf of formerly privileged Party members. Aino

Kuusinen, the wife of Otto Kuusinen, a Finnish communist and member of the Presidium of the Supreme Soviet, arrived in Moscow in October of 1955 after being liberated from the women's camp at Potma. She went to the KGB reception office on Kuznetsky Most and told an official that she had just gotten out of camp and did not know how to begin a new life. When he saw her name, the official asked if she was related to the Presidium member. Upon hearing that this returnee was indeed Kuusinen's wife, he advised her to go to her husband and live with him. She explained that her pride would not allow her to return. The KGB official had no other advice to offer.

Through old friends, Aino found a "guardian" official to guide her through the labyrinthine process of legal return. Even so, she spent eight months going from one institution to another. The lines of petitioners extended to the ends of long corridors. At one agency, she saw an old woman faint upon hearing that many of the people who came there every day had been coming for as long as five years. Eventually, because her estranged husband still occupied his official position, and because she had help, Aino Kuusinen was offered the apartment of her choice in Moscow. In her memoirs, she addresses both her own difficulties in reassimilating and those of others less fortunate: "it was quite difficult for me, a [well-known] political prisoner to return to a normal life. How much more complicated, and indeed even impossible, it must have been for simple people who did not have the support I did."[10] Indeed the hardships for ordinary citizens upon return, like the hardships of ordinary citizens in Soviet society, were immeasurably greater than were those of the formerly privileged. Still, even the latter group had to endure the trials and tribulations of reentry. Let us turn to one more such example.

Roza Yakovlevna Smushkevich

The wife of an executed Soviet Army general, Yakov Smushkevich, appealed personally to Voroshilov for help for herself and her daughter (Roza). Up until Smushkevich's arrest in June 1941, the family had lived in the building of the Council of Ministers, the Dom na Naberezhnoy (House on the Embankment). When his widow, Basya Solomonovna Smushkevich, and their daughter, Roza, returned from their eleven-year sojourn in Karlag and exile in Kazakhstan, Roza recalled (in our 1996 interview) that they were immediately offered their old apartment.[11] However, according to materials that have recently emerged from the archives, the process was not quite so immediate nor automatic. In a May 1954 urgent plea to Voroshilov, Basya Solomonova writes, "In my old age I don't have any place to rest my head, no corner, no roof under which I can spend my last years ... you remember my husband well ... please don't leave us in this miserable situation without help or attention."[12] In the interests of accuracy, it should be noted that when confronted with this document Roza insisted that it was a fabrication because she contended that her mother would never have written—nor would she have any need to make—such a plea to Voroshilov.[13] It may be that this disparity can be accounted for by the known problems associated with reconstructed memories and selective recall, because it does not seem logical that a letter of this nature would be falsified and preserved in the archive of the Supreme Soviet. Furthermore, Voroshilov's subsequent action supports the authenticity of the written request. He ordered that the matter be investigated immediately.

It was ascertained that Yakov Smushkevich had been executed without trial on the "criminal orders" of Beria. The case of Smushkevich was suspended by the General Procurator, Rudenko. This suspension of criminal status was extended to his widow and daughter as well, and they were to be offered their confiscated property, the pension appropriate to the family of a deceased general, and a place to live.[14] Roza recalled that Malenkov met with her mother personally, gave them some money, and offered them their former residence. Her mother refused to live there. Roza maintains that this decision was based on emotional considerations—her mother wanted to avoid painful memories. Her refusal was not due to an aversion to living in an official Soviet building. While her mother's refusal was based on sentimental considerations, Roza's refusal was more of a political protest. She thought they were better off not living in that "accursed building where every apartment counted three, four or five arrests in its turnover of tenants."[15] Though they chose to live elsewhere, Roza often visited, and still visits, those friends of her youth who managed to survive in the House on the Embankment.

Work

Returnees as well as the family members of (former) "enemies of the people" continued to be oppressed at work even when this was no longer officially allowed. Complaints by returnees were either ignored or handled by pro-forma investigations which produced little meaningful improvement in the lot of the complainants. The archives have yielded some interesting paper trails that illustrate this deceptive practice.

Genri Grigoryevich Levin, who was a senior lecturer at the Kazakh Pedagogical Institute, was fired on March 18, 1953. He wrote a letter to Voroshilov challenging the grounds for his dismissal. He argued that his dismissal was not based on his work, as had been officially claimed. Rather, it was politically motivated. No evidence had been provided by the officials to substantiate the alleged "political mistakes" in his teaching and scientific work. However, he was in fact a relative of the "enemy of the people" Zinoviev (the nephew of Zinoviev's wife Zlata Ionovna Lilina, who had died in 1929).[16] Voroshilov ordered that the the USSR Ministry of Culture investigate the matter.

The Ministry, for its part, twice asked the Kazakh Minister of Education for the reasons for Levin's dismissal. The minister did not provide a substantive answer, but merely confirmed the institute director's decision. The Culture Ministry could go no further, and passed the case on to the Kazakh Council of Ministers. The Division of Schools of the Central Committee of the Kazakh Communist Party studied the question and presented what it called an "exhaustive" reply to its USSR counterpart in January of 1954.[17]

In the meantime Levin was not able to find other employment because of the *kharakteristika* that he was given when he was fired. He also lost his permanent residence when he lost his job. Because he had no job, he could not register to live anywhere, not even with his mother in Leningrad. In consequence, he had no place to live.[18] This was typical of the bureaucratic obfuscation with which many returnees and their family members were confronted.

The conclusions that were presented to the head of the division of schools of the Central Committee of the CPSU (in a certificate dated January 6, 1954) list Levin's family relationship to Lilina as the first reason for his dismissal. Second on the list is the fact that the majority of Levin's relatives were repressed at one time or another. It enumerates five relatives. At the end of the first page, the certificate reads, "besides that, Levin permitted political mistakes in his work ... and did not properly guide students in field work in the summer of 1952."[19] The schools division concluded that Levin's dismissal was justified. A copy of this certificate was later sent to Voroshilov's deputy.

Interestingly, in a January 26 letter from the Secretary of the Central Committee of the Communist Party of Kazakhstan to Voroshilov, the chronology of reasons was changed in order to disguise the blatant political rationale for his dismissal. The first reason he presents for Levin's dismissal was his professional performance. He writes that Levin's lectures were theoretically poor and his field work with students was careless. Besides all of that, he points out, Levin was a relative of Zinoviev. The Kazakh Central Committee of the Communist Party deemed the institute's decision to have been proper.[20] The documentation of Levin's case stopped there. We can assume that the decision for his dismissal was upheld. True, that was 1953, and the matter was related to a member of an oppositionist's family. Since Zinoviev was rehabilitated only under Gorbachev in 1988, it was to be expected that those connected with him would be subjected to many official and unofficial obstacles. But how was it for more ordinary people, those who were neither politically active nor well known?

We can look at the lot of ordinary repressed citizens who were no longer considered enemies to see if there is any discernable difference in treatment between them and those still *officially* considered enemies. In a 2,000-page handwritten memoir Evgeny Edvardovich Gagen (see also chapter 4) takes us through his ten-year journey in Kolyma (1937-47), his seven years of exile in the Magadan province (1947-1954), and his year-long struggle for rehabilitation and reinstatement in the Party (1955-56). His confrontations with the ever suspicious Soviet officials and his struggle to find work reveal the problems faced by ordinary citizens who are dealing with a system adapted to repression.

In the summer of 1955 Gagen lived in the Borovsk district of the Kaluga province, and wanted to find work as a journalist. In pursuit of this, he went to the Moscow reception room of the RSFSR Ministry of Internal Affairs to try to acquire temporary registration (pending rehabilitation) so that he could work in Moscow. Witness this revealing exchange between an official (C) and this former prisoner (G):

C: "Why are you here?"

G: "My case is being reexamined and I would like to request temporary registration in Moscow."

C: "Do you have article 58?" the colonel lazily [more likely passive aggressively] asked while yawning.

G: "I have a decree of the Special Conference."

C: "KRD?" [counter-revolutionary activity, a "liter"]

G: "Yes, KRD."

C: "That's one and the same thing." [art. 58 and KRD]

G: "You may think that, but I think it is quite another thing."

C: "And why is it a completely different thing?" asked the colonel.

G: "Because I was not tried. According to our constitution nobody can be condemned without a trial, in absentia, and without the right to defense."

C: "Oh, is that what you think? Well I think that the Special Conference is also a court," the colonel looked at me suspiciously. "And why do you want to register in Moscow anyway?"

G: "Because my family lives here."

C: "So have your family come to you."

G: "Is that how you see it?"

C: "Yes, that is how I see it."

G: "But my case is being reviewed! And I am a Moscovite."

C: "But the case has not yet been reevaluated."

G: "If it had been, I wouldn't be coming to you...."[21]

The conversation continued in the same obstructive vein, and ultimately led nowhere for Gagen. It is interesting to note that this particular representative of the authorities claimed that he considered the Special Conference to be a court. This, in spite of the fact that the Special Conference had already been officially condemned in early 1954 (see chapter 3). Apparently a change in the law did not necessarily mean that there would be a change in practice, because officials at this level were often able to flout the law with impunity.

At most of the official places Gagen felt that he was treated like a "second-class citizen," even by people twenty years his junior.[22] There were, however, some exceptions. In early September of 1955, Gagen was summoned to the regional social services office of the Borovsk district. His pension papers had arrived from Magadan and he had to come in to fill out forms. The head of this governmental agency was actually interested in learning about Gagen's history of repression, and showed compassion when he heard the tale. When Gagen mentioned that he expected to be rehabilitated, the official confided that he had received an instruction briefing him on the privileges of the rehabilitated. First of all, they were entitled to receive a compensation of two-months salary (at current rates), based on their wages at the time of arrest. Secondly, they were to be given priority for apartments, and thirdly, those who were incapable of working could receive pensions which would be calculated so that the length of service would include the time spent in incarceration (*trudovoy stazh*).[23] What was especially kind about the agency head's sharing this information was that he expected that this document would never be publicized, and he wanted Gagen to know his rights.[24]

However, in spite of the inertia of the system, the swing toward liberalization was gaining momentum, and the document was made public. On September 8, 1955, the Council of Ministers of the USSR issued decree No. 1655.[25] It set down directives "On the length of service, job placement, and pensions for citizens who were incriminated without due cause and subsequently rehabilitated." Even so, questions and problems regarding the implementation of this decree continued for the next forty some years. One former victim who had been released in 1946 and rehabilitated in 1963 still had not obtained this financial compensation when he wrote to Memorial in the late eighties. In his letter, he ridiculed the state's paltry and arbitrary compensation: "Why two months and not two years or two days?"[26]

Gagen eventually obtained temporary registration in Moscow in the fall of 1955, but, in a Kafkaesque bureaucratic twist, his "temporary" status was considered legitimate grounds for denying him employment. To make matters worse, returnees often could not resume their old jobs because their places had been taken.[27] But any number of reasons could be cited to refuse to give ex-zeks work, and any number of jobs could be considered inappropriate for them. Former prisoners had no opportunity to return to jobs they formerly held as school teachers[28] (conveyers of information). Returning to a poorly paid library or museum job that afforded little contact with people was a more likely, but by no means guaranteed, option.[29]

In addition to the general prejudice against returnees, there was a specific prejudice against Jews. This reservoir of anti-Semitism could be tapped at any time to justify a refusal of privileges. One Jewish doctor returnee in the Kiev region of Moscow was frankly told by a potential employer, "listen, I have a Jewish husband, I wish you no ill, but your efforts are in vain, we were given a directive 'from above' not to employ Jews and nobody has withdrawn that yet."[30]

The employment problem for the ex-zeks was compounded by the fact that the executive committee demanded that ex-zeks get work, or they could be expelled from Moscow for "parasitism." They were often doubly confounded, because while they were required to have work, they could not get it. As one returnee letter to Voroshilov attests, "I can only get work after I have been registered in Moscow, and the police will not register me because I don't have proof of a job."[31] Trotsky's granddaughter, who had a similar experience after returning to Moscow from Kazakhstan in 1954, described this phenomenon as a "vicious circle." At the reception room of the Supreme Soviet, she lamented to an official: "you took my parents away, I don't have an official marriage, I can't get work, how am I supposed to live? Do I have to become a prostitute?" Apparently unmoved by her story, the official replied, "do you want to go back there again?"[32]

Returnees could be frustrated in pursuing their rights at every turn, since policy often differed from practice, and since officials did not feel particularly obligated to enforce the decrees on granting them their rights. One memoirist writes of her ex-zek father's dogged efforts to find work in Kharkov: "the powers that be made it quite clear to him that full rehabilitation was only theoretical."[33] Gagen's struggles exemplify this predicament. He had been rehabilitated in November of 1955. According to the decree of September 8, he was entitled to a new (clean) passport. Armed with a new passport, Gagen would have been permitted to seek work, receive a pension, and obtain a permanent residence. When he went to the police with completed forms to exchange his passport, the head of the division told the ex-prisoner that he saw no reason to issue a new passport. When Gagen referred to the September decree, the official told him to write a declaration about why he was incarcerated. Gagen refused to return to that stage of the rehabilitation process because his status was now changed. At his next visit, Gagen asked why there was such a delay and again reminded the official of the decree. Whereupon the official retorted, "So what? This is Moscow, not the countryside."[34] In fact, the same rules applied to both. The official was not right, nor did he have the legal right to block Gagen, but he apparently had the power to do so and he exercised it.

Gagen's subsequent efforts to find work, now with the status of "rehabilitated" were still met with frustration. As soon as it was mentioned that he was rehabilitated, the conversation changed. The potential employer would suddenly realize that he did not have time to talk to Gagen at that moment, but asked that he come back later. When he did, he was turned away. One potential employer did not even mask his prejudice. Gagen recounts, "without being roundabout, he told me that the only reason he was not hiring me was that, even though I was rehabilitated, in his eyes I was still a person with a dark past."[35] After being refused job after job, Gagen concluded that, "everyone seemed to fear one word: 'rehabilitated.'"[36] Like the returning prisoners in the late forties and early fifties, what they had been labeled and where they had been sent were reasons enough to make them undesirable to potential employers. It appears that the status of being rehabilitated had come to be a "negative" label.

This was true even for some of the formerly privileged. Yadviga Iosifovna Verzhenskaya, the wife of a Red Army General who, she subsequently learned, had been shot, spent three exasperating years after release trying to acquire housing, work, rehabilitation, and an identity different from that of an outcast. In 1951 she appealed to an NKVD officer, asking to be sent back to camp. She explained that at least if she worked there, she could get bread, an option not available to many other returnees. He found work for her, and was later arrested himself.[37]

Rehabilitation in 1956 did not significantly improve Verzhenskaya's life. She could choose to live in one of a selected number of military areas but was provided only one room for herself, her son, and her mother. Because her husband had been demoted before arrest, the pension she received was lower than that of a general's family. Cultural and other official agencies were still wary of employing her. Their collective response seemed to be: "Rehabilitation, rehabilitation—but she was in prison!"[38]

Indeed, the fact that someone carried the status of "rehabilitated" meant that they had been arrested and that they had once had prisoner status. Rehabilitation could not erase that stigmatized history, not for the former victims, and not in the eye of the public at large. People knew that in order to have the status of "rehabilitated" the person first had to become a prisoner. What they did not examine was how it was that this person became a prisoner. Not until the criminal behavior of the officials who decreed the imprisonment was revealed would the stigma of the prisoner be lifted.

Intellectuals fell into a category of their own. Some were praised and honored, some were reluctantly accepted, and others were merely tolerated. Under Khrushchev there was a trend toward supporting the intellectual work of returnees, which culminated in the publication of Solzhenitsyn's *One Day in the Life of Ivan Denisovich* (see below). However, it is hard to infer a uniform policy from these experiences. One scientist who spent from 1938-1948 incarcerated in Norilsk, and the subsequent seven years in exile, organized and worked in a laboratory even during his term. In 1955 he received complete rehabilitation and restoration of Party membership, with no loss of continuity in his pedagogical record. He went on to teach at prominent Moscow institutes.[39] Another scientist, Pavel Oshchepkov, who had worked in a research laboratory developing radar in the thirties, a project supported by Tukhachevsky, was subsequently arrested. He continued his scientific work after return from the camps. It is not surprising that a biography of this returnee that appeared in a Soviet journal skips his years of incarceration. What is surprising is that the piece was entitled, "The heroic deed of a scientist."[40] Such high regard for returnees was hardly the norm, but it sometimes happened.

Isaak Moiseevich Filshtinsky

Isaak Moiseevich Filshtinsky (see also chapters 1 and 4), a professor of Arabic philology, was incarcerated from 1949-1956. While imprisoned, he was plagued with personal and professional losses:

his mother died ("of an incomprehensible illness, probably simply from grief"[41]), his wife left him, his father lost his job, and his doctoral dissertation was declared invalid. After his release he was well received in a social setting by both his friends and the people with whom he shared a communal apartment. However, if it happened that he were to meet these same neighbors in the work place, in their official capacity, he was treated much differently—more like the former "enemy" that he was. Official establishments, he asserted, treated those who had been repressed like "second class citizens."[42] Filshtinsky was treated even worse.

In a chapter of his memoirs entitled, "That Bitter Word Called Freedom," Filshtinsky recounts an exchange between him and an official regarding the invalidation of his doctoral dissertation. The official justified the invalidation by arguing, "You're a scientist, you should understand that in the course of six years science has moved ahead and your findings have become outdated. Write a new dissertation!"[43] Though he had negative feelings about Party membership, the former prisoner undertook the task of getting rehabilitated and reinstated in the Party. Eventually he succeeded, but was later excluded from the Party because of his human rights work. Unable to secure an academic position as a professor, he was only able to gain employment as an editor in the Library of Foreign Languages. The director of this institution, Margarita Ivanovna Rudomino has been praised by a number of former prisoners for having had the courage to employ them. Later, Filshtinsky worked in the Academy of Sciences, but in 1978, his apartment was searched and he was expelled from this organization. He was not invited to teach again at Moscow State University until 1992.

Lev Emmanuilovich Razgon

Some returnees were able to resume working at their previous place of employment, albeit at a lower salary and with a lower status. The writer Lev Emmanuilovich Razgon was one such case. Before his 1938 arrest (at age thirty) Razgon had worked as an ideological editor at a publishing company. His history is typical of the plight of many returnees who were initially well received upon return. After his release and rehabilitation in 1955, he was taken back to work at the same organization, taken back into his communal apartment, and taken back into the Party. Lev Razgon is among the small group of returnees who were, indeed, treated as "heroes." But he, too, sustained irremediable loss. No matter how much society may have eased Razgon's transition back toward his previous status, it could not compensate him for his personal tragedy—Razgon's wife never returned from the camps, having died during transit in 1938.[44] Not until 1990 was Razgon permitted to see his KGB file. What it revealed was a case study of the death of a family, and the destruction of its supporting social network. These victims were his friends and others connected with him who had belonged to the upper echelons of the Party. These were "people who created this Party, made the revolution, built and governed this society...."[45] Razgon made constructive use of both his talents and his experience by becoming one of the founding members of Memorial. In so doing, he helped himself as well as others toward rehabilitation.

Another ex-prisoner, Yuri Dombrovsky, released in 1955, employed the literary style of Aesop's fables. In one work, "Obezyana prikhodit za svoim cherepom" (The Monkey Comes for His Skull), for example, he portrayed racist Nazi Germany in a thinly veiled criticism of Russia under Stalin. Although he did manage to get published, few copies were printed. Dombrovsky was given a room in a communal apartment, a pension, and membership in the Union of Writers. But he was isolated from other writers, not allowed to go abroad, and discouraged from making public appearances. The reluctant acceptance by his colleagues provided just enough reward to prevent him from rebelling—using his public medium to recount his experiences in the camps.[46] In some cases employers used the coercive power of employment and the fear of unemployment to "guide" returnees in the proper direction.

Official Regulations Regarding the Employment of Ex-Zeks

The bureaucratic practice of establishing and maintaining systematic obstacles to the reassimilation of returnees had been insititutionalized in 1953-1955 (see chapter 3). The Soviet authorities were aware of it, but did little to correct it. A 1955 report on the activities of the reception room of the RSFSR Supreme Soviet quotes the following statistics: 7,601 individuals came with registration (*propiska*) restriction problems, 6,263 people sought assistance in work-related problems. There is no indication as to what percentage of these visitors were ex-zeks, though the problems with registration restrictions would suggest that ex-zeks comprised most of this group (as discussed above, their status often hindered their job prospects, and without work they could not get residence permits. On top of that, many still had passport restrictions). Moreover, this report to Voroshilov concedes that there were many problems with the job placement of citizens, "in particular invalids released from places of incarceration ... there were cases where they could not get work for many months."[47]

One of the systemic causes of the unofficial opposition to the official position on rehabilitation was the authorities' reluctance to accept moral responsibility. To do so would have shifted the stigma of criminal behavior from the returnees to the authorities, especially the "infallible" CPSU, and that they were not yet prepared to do. Therefore, despite the promising September 1955 decree on work-placement and other official gestures, the problems of ex-zeks persisted. One memoirist recounts that he wanted to return to the factory where he had worked prior to his second arrest, but he was received with extraordinary hostility by the director: "despite the September 8 stipulation requiring the employment of those who were rehabilitated, he refused to hire me, indignantly explaining that he does not want and is not required to hire former prisoners at 'his' factory. He didn't take me."[48]

The returnees' complaints were, however, reaching the top. This issue is acknowledged in an April 1956 document found in the "Special Files of Khrushchev" on "questions of work placement of those who were released from places of incarceration." It begins,

> The instructions of the directive organs that obligate local Soviet organizations as well as directors of economic institutions and enterprises to render all possible assistance in job placement to those who have been freed from incarceration are being carried out unsatisfactorily, a fact which is attested by numerous complaints and declarations from ex-prisoners.[49]

It goes on to enumerate a number of cases. Moreover, it discloses that many offices assigned to distribute manpower were even given explicit instructions by the organizations which they served that they should not hire "those who had been convicted." Similar problems with registration were highlighted in this report.

Official policy on the employment of returnees was relatively unambiguous. This issue is treated by the USSR Procuracy in an October 1956 draft of Regulations regarding correctional labor camps. The report generally deals with continuing official violations with regard to transport of prisoners, camp discipline, and camp conditions. In the section on "release and employment" the document states, "The committees [presumably executive committees, factory collectives, etc.] are obligated to help the liberated [prisoner] to register at his residence, and to quickly find work ... so that the discharged prisoner would be employed in socially useful work activity."[50]

A May 1957 letter from the Supreme Court of the USSR to the Council of Ministers outlines even more specific legal and organizational rules with regard to this question:

> Those who have been liberated from correctional labor institutions should be employed with consideration of their specialization no later than two weeks from the day of their petition for assistance.... The responsibility for timely employment of those who are liberated ... lies with the Council of Ministers of the Union and Autonomous republics, and the krai, provincial, city, and regional executive committees of the councils of labor deputies.[51]

Still, as numerous cases in that same year attest, it remained hard for ex-zeks to find work. Documents of the reception room of the Chairman of the Presidium of the RSFSR Supreme Soviet report that in 1957 the most difficult group to assist in acquiring employment was "citizens who had been imprisoned ... who did not have a place of residence."[52] They go on to state that the reception room, however, did manage to find a position for them. It is not clear to which category of prisoners this account is referring, though it is almost a moot point since many people did not distinguish between those imprisoned for political offenses and those imprisoned for other crimes.

A report for 1958 claims that "as a rule those who are petitioning for work do not have a place to live or a permanent address.... Moreover, many of them do not want to work honestly, change their jobs often, and violate labor discipline."[53] While these petitioners were not all ex-zeks, the combination of employment problems as well as residence problems suggests that ex-zeks constituted some part of the group.

The claim that ex-zeks did not desire to work can also be found in the correspondence of the USSR Ministry of Internal Affairs to the Central Committee dated December 24, 1959: "many individuals who have been released early from their places of imprisonment do not wish to enter the working world; many of them who have acquired jobs quit them and commit crimes again."[54] Even if this were true, it could be argued that the very difficulty in finding appropriate jobs may have been a causal factor in the "repeat offenses." A January 1961 document of the Supreme Court supports this latter view. It states that the lack of work for ex-zeks leads to criminal acts, and that "certain supervisors of organizations and institutions refuse to give them work. When they [ex-prisoners] turn to the police for help in these matters, they are not rendered [officially] obligatory assistance."[55] The unwillingness of officials to respond to the legitimate needs of the returnees was evident early in the process of rehabilitation and persisted throughout. Despite their official mandate to facilitate the timely release of prisoners and aid the (ex-) zeks in their efforts to gain employment, the commissions of executive committees of councils of labor representatives did very little.[56]

Thus, the process of discriminating against former prisoners started early, and continued for a long time. These attitudes were still (and again) extant in the seventies. For many, the official doctrines only succeeded in creating false hopes. One returnee recalls that by the time she finished the pedagogical institute in 1960 it was very hard to find work because "the fashion for us was over."[57]

Pavel Negretov recalls his job frustrations even twenty years after his release, in 1975. When the head of the archive of the Vorkuta coal combine (plant) retired, he had hopes of replacing her. The person in charge of hiring was enthusiastic about his prospects because Negretov had a degree in history. However, when he heard that the applicant was not officially rehabilitated, "he saddened and pensively looked out the window at the statue of Kirov."[58] Wittingly or unwittingly, the author presents the ironic image of the potential employer rejecting the clearly qualified ex-zek while looking at a statue of Sergey Kirov, whose murder helped set the Soviet terror apparatus in motion. It may be that Negretov was not hired because he was an "unrehabilitated" person, but there are many instances in which the status of "rehabilitated" made no more than a marginal difference in the returnee's struggle for reentry.

An old saw has it that "A man convinced against his will is of the same opinion still." Many of the Soviet citizenry had an ingrained attitude toward their government such that if a person was arrested and imprisoned by the socialist state, one had to assume that they must have deserved it. From this perspective, rehabilitation was an undeserved reward for wrongdoing. Until the government could admit its malfeasance in the imprisonment itself there would be little reason for the populace to reevaluate their attitude toward ex-prisoners. As the stories in these sections demonstrate, every potential employer in an enterprise, factory, university, or office could serve as judge and jury with regard to work opportunities. Regardless of official guidelines, returnees remained vulnerable on a number of different scores.

Status and Rights

Returnees did not always understand their rights, and even when they did and argued for them, officials often refused to grant them. In fairness, not all of the official opposition was purposely subversive, but rather was the result of the circumstance that officials did not always understand returnees' rights. Still, despite all the mid-level official-unofficial opposition, the issuance of the September 1955 decree was a major concession on the part of the state. However, the lack of clarity of the regulations became a source of frustration for officials as well as for former victims. This problem is addressed in the correspondence of the USSR Procuracy for 1955 and 1956. The issues in question centered on returnees' rights to the two-month compensation as well as their social and legal status. The most frequently raised question was whether a person who had been incarcerated and released a number of times, and then subsequently received rehabilitation on each of the different charges, was entitled to a two-month compensation from each of the previous pre-arrest employers.[59] The final decision was that the two-month compensation is only granted once.[60] Those who were freed from special settlement (exile), and the relatives of posthumously rehabilitated prisoners were also entitled to this benefit.[61] Applicants were required to show a rehabilitation certificate and proof of their employment and position on the day of arrest.[62] The compensation did not extend to ex-prisoners who were unemployed at the time of arrest.[63]

The XX Party Congress and Its Aftermath: How Actions of the Congress Affected the Status of Returnees

At the end of 1955 the Presidium of the CPSU Central Committee formed a special commission, under secretary of the Central Committee Pospelov, to study materials on the mass repressions of 1935-1940. After examining cases and documents and conducting interviews with interrogators, the commission presented its damning report to the Presidium of the Central Committee on February 9, 1956.[64] Khrushchev argued in favor of making "a clean breast of the abuses committed by Stalin"[65] by presenting the findings in a closed session of the Congress. To this information would also be added the revelations of rehabilitated Old Bolsheviks like Shatunovskaya and Snegov. It was decided that the Party would take responsibility for the repression, but culpability would be attributed to Stalin. The "Secret Speech" inveighed against the "cult of personality," and focused on the crimes of and under Stalin against Communists. Notable by their absence were crimes against the oppositionists and, significantly, against the ordinary citizens who were repressed by the punitive policies of the Stalinist regime. In criticizing the cult of personality, Khrushchev limited his attack to the "personality" and glossed over the offenses of the complicit "cult," the Party members who supported the repressions. By making the speech anti-Stalin rather than anti-Stalinist, the system itself was spared criticism. Khrushchev expected that the potentially damaging testimony of the returning zeks might be counterbalanced by the fact that the Party had liberated them.[66] However, Voroshilov was fearful of the impact of the revelations on the present officeholders, and argued in favor of presenting the speech only after elections to the Central Committee Presidium had been conducted.[67] Elections were held on February 24 and on the following day the speech was presented to delegates of the congress and newly elected members of the Central Committee. The shock, dismay, and anger of the delegates to the "Secret Speech" is beyond the scope of our present discussion. Instead, we will examine its consequences for the lives of prisoners and returnees.

One of the first consequences of the revelations was an improvement in the procedure by which those who had been declared innocent were released from the camps. At the end of 1953, the camps and prisons contained 475,000 people who were held for "counterrevolutionary activities." By January 1, 1956, 114,000 political prisoners still remained incarcerated.[68] These figures, of course, do not reflect the population of exiles and special settlers. According to documents of the USSR Procuracy, liberation commissions of the Supreme Soviet were being formed as early as February 7, 1956. On this date Procurator Rudenko presented a draft of a directive "on the regulations regarding work of the commissions for verification of the grounds for detainment of prisoners at places of deprivation of liberty." In contrast to the work of the earlier teams described in chapter 3, it outlines specific procedures and emphasizes that cases should be examined for "their essence and the data that characterizes the personality of the prisoner."[69] Furthermore, the commissions were obligated to speak with every prisoner. The camp administration was charged with the responsibility of so informing those prisoners who were denied liberation.[70] It was also to provide released prisoners with a certificate of release and a certificate of withdrawal of sentence.

The (accessible) archives have provided slightly different figures than have the historical accounts on how many people liberated how many prisoners. We will offer only a very brief sketch of these figures here, since different documents contain different information, and a number of Russian historians do not indicate the sources for their assertions, nor do they explain on what basis certain figures were derived. Moreover, since our focus is on the victim's experience, the scope of the commissions' work is secondary.

The USSR Procuracy attempted to be as bureaucratically inclusive as possible. Accordingly, sixty-seven commissions were to be made up of three to seven persons each, for a total of 291 participants. This group would include: members of the staff of the Central Committee, secretaries and heads of divisions of central committees of republics, krais, provinces, and cities, high functionaries of the Presidium of the Supreme Soviet, the Procuracy, the Supreme Court, the Ministry of Justice, and the Ministry of State Security of the USSR and RSFSR, rehabilitated Party members, and deputies of the Supreme Soviet of the USSR and republics.[71]

One historian contends that ninety-seven commissions of the Supreme Soviet were charged with the liberation of prisoners.[72] Another puts the number at 100 commissions comprised of three persons each (one rehabilitated Party member, one person from the Procuracy, and one Central Committee representative), travelling the country.[73] Writing about the political aftermath of the Secret Speech, Russian historian Naumov (see also chapter 1) estimates that approximately one million prisoners and exiles were released, but he does not specify whether these releases were immediate.[74] Elsewhere, he points out that hundreds of thousands returned from prison and exile shortly after the speech.[75] Gorbachev, in a 1996 speech, claimed that Khrushchev initiated the release of *millions* of prisoners as well as the "rehabilitation of those who were turned into 'camp dust.'"[76] (What a difference these nine years had made in Gorbachev's public estimate of the number of victims! See chapter 1.)

More specific figures have also come to light. A November 1956 document (from the Special Files of Khrushchev) states that 107,979 prisoners (50,562 of whom were politicals) were released by the commissions in that year.[77] It does not mention rehabilitation. One Russian source contends that as a result of the "broadening rehabilitative practices," 232,000 persons were rehabilitated by mid-1957, and between 1954-1961 a total of 737,182 rehabilitations were carried out.[78] (See chapter 1 for more statistics on rehabilitation.) He does not specify, however, whether these numbers included posthumous rehabilitations (since relatives were also petitioning for exoneration of perished prisoners). Nor does he make it clear how many of these cases were politicals, and if they were released by decision of the commissions.

Turning from numbers to qualitative assessments, let us examine the effect of the commissions' decisions on the prisoners' experience. Prisoners' accounts have generally been critical of the rehabilitation procedure. One memoirist recalls that a common impression among zeks was that the commission disliked those who claimed that they had been arrested without good cause. Nor, according to this ex-prisoner, were they willing to hear about the lawlessness and torture in the camps. They just wanted the prisoner to listen passively, and answer the questions asked.[79] Solzhenitsyn is indignant as he contrasts what should have happened with what did happen:

> Should not the commission have stood before a general line-up of prisoners, bared their heads, and said: "Brothers! We have been sent by the Supreme Soviet to beg your forgiveness. For years and decades you have languished here, though you are guilty of nothing.... Accept our belated repentance, if you can."[80]

He goes on to remonstrate that the "unloading commissions" were "no way to lay new moral foundations for our society," since "the prisoner is put in a position of one forgiven, not one who forgives!"[81] What could they have realistically expected? Given the time and place of the commissions, the message of the Secret Speech, and the system's adaptation to repression, the grudging character of this work is not all that surprising.

In the summer of 1956, a tidal wave of released prisoners was washing over the land: "[I]n railway trains and stations there appeared survivors of the camps, with leaden grey hair, sunken eyes and a faded look; they choked and dragged their feet like old men."[82] They were sometimes strangers even to themselves.[83] They were no longer prisoners, but neither were many of them really free. Still they were better off than their comrades who continued to languish in prison. It was an unsettling time for officials as well as prisoners. Officials had to reexamine the legal and moral assumptions that had previously justified the repression. Prisoners and ex-prisoners had to reassess their allegiances to a system that had imprisoned them and had to find ways of putting their shattered lives back together.

In the confusion of shifting directions and changing directives, some instructions defied what had come to be common sense. An October 1956 letter from the Krasnoyarsk krai Procuracy to the USSR Procuracy complains that since the publication of the March 1953 amnesty, they have repeatedly asked what they should do with article 7-35'ers (mostly children of "enemies of the people") who had been exiled for ten-year terms in 1948, and with the "especially dangerous criminals" who received exile from the Special Conference after release in that same year. In a reversal of what might have been expected, the answer was: "If there are any [of the latter category of] exiles in the krai at this time ... you must take measures to liberate them," because the directive that detained them was abolished in 1954. The 7-35'ers would have to be reviewed on an individual basis.[84]

Some returnees could not yet hope for rehabilitation, but they could strive for more privileges. One letter from the Estonian Procuracy to the USSR Procuracy addresses the issue of the legal status of the article 58'ers who were accused of having collaborated with the occupying forces during the "Great Patriotic War." A March 10, 1956 decree of the Supreme Soviet released this group from exile. To the extent that they were entitled to rights under the September 17, 1955 amnesty (which provided release for 55,480 prisoners in 1955 and 4,130 in 1956[85]) the ex-prisoners were protesting the fact that they were only granted limited passports. The Estonian police were refusing to exchange these citizens' passports, "because the order of the General Procuracy of the USSR, the Ministry of Internal Affairs of the USSR and the Chairman of the KGB of the Council of Ministers of the USSR states that the charges are not cleared from individuals freed from exile on the decree of March 10, 1956."[86]

The reform-minded Estonian Procuracy did not concur with the Estonian police because, according to their interpretation, the September amnesty provided for the rescinding of sentences and the restoration of rights. They even wrote a follow-up letter to the USSR Procuracy urging that they quickly expedite the matter because the Estonian Procuracy was becoming inundated with complaints.[87] The USSR Procuracy responded that the Estonian police had acted incorrectly in not issuing clean passports to those who were freed under the September 1955 amnesty. Cases relating specifically to the March 10 decree would have to be considered on an individual basis.[88] With questions abounding, the Supreme Soviet had to issue a clarification on the September 17 directive.[89] There was not only conflict between governmental and judicial bodies but confusion within both establishments. However, through all this turmoil, ex-prisoners were becoming more aware of returnees' rights, and it was becoming more difficult for officials to blatantly violate them.

Achieving the status of rehabilitation became especially important to the returnees because their compensation was contingent upon this status. A bureacratic barrier to this was the confusion regarding whether those prisoners freed by the 1956 commissions of the Presidium of the Supreme Soviet of the USSR were to be considered as amnestied or rehabilitated, because the only documents they were given were a release certificate, and a paper stating their entitlement to the privileges outlined in the September decree.[90] The confusion of the release process with the rehabilitation status made accurate calculation of compensation for the latter exceedingly difficult. A September 1956 letter from the Kazakh SSR Procuracy to a regional sub-division is unambiguous regarding this issue:

> individuals who were freed from their places of incarceration by decision of the commissions of the Presidium of the Supreme Soviet of the USSR for being convicted without due cause are considered rehabilitated and are entitled to all privileges, including the two-month allowance in accordance with the decree of the Council of Ministers of the USSR of September 8, 1955.[91]

These official rules were clear, but whether they were considered to be equitable by subordinates and whether they would be carried out were entirely different issues.

While some in the upper levels of government were recoiling from the horrors of Stalinist repression and moving toward reform, many of those at lower levels remained uninformed of the justification for reform. In consequence, they resisted dispensing what they considered unwarranted privileges to undeserving criminals. This resulted in a systemic passive resistance in the bureaucracy charged with overseeing release and rehabilitation. Moreover, resistance, passive and otherwise, was already built into the program for dealing with ex-prisoners.

While prisoners freed by the commissions were entitled to privileges, they were indeed not automatically rehabilitated. Since the camps did not issue *rehabilitation certificates*, ex-prisoners still had to apply for that status. One prisoner who was released by a commission in May of 1956 was not accepted again at the university, because she did not have a rehabilitation certificate. She petitioned the Presidium of the Supreme Soviet, which in turn sent her letter on to the Procuracy. They responded that, "there is no basis for reexamining your case."[92] It subsequently took this returnee nine years to achieve rehabilitation. The fact that this group of returnees had already been reviewed by committees apparently had little bearing on the pace of their process of official exoneration. Still, it is likely that they fared better in threading their way through the rehabilitation maze than did those who were released under one of the amnesties. One returnee who had been freed under the 1953 amnesty and had unsuccessfully petitioned for rehabilitation from July 1955 - July 1956, complained, "I don't understand why I should be punished twice. The first punishment was camp and exile; the second was the refusal to rehabilitate me."[93] She added that now that she was seventy-three years old, rehabilitation would soon no longer be necessary.

As noted earlier, one of the systemic problems that impeded the progress of reform was that the government did not adequately address its ambivalence. The same people who had overseen the persecution of yesterday's "enemies of the people" were now being asked to treat them as victims or martyrs—without the government's acknowledging its own culpability. In consequence, while there were some genuine efforts toward reform at one level, new repressive measures were still being implemented at another level. In order to conceal this political ambivalence, a good bit of internal and external propagandizing was necessary. A September 1956 article in *Izvestiya* entitled "'Today Inmates Are Criminals': Butyrka as Model Jail," boasts of an improved prison environment. After claiming that all the present inmates had indeed committed crimes, it describes the sumptuousness of their daily menu: "mashed potatoes with vegetable oil and herring for breakfast, sour cabbage soup with meat and barley porridge with butter for dinner, and millet porridge with vegetable oil for supper."[94] The credibility of the menu has the same standing as the claim that all of the inmates have committed crimes. During this time, arrests were still being carried out for such transgressions as the reading of Marx, out of fear that his texts would be given a different interpretation than that dictated by the Party line. Consequently, such intellectual activity was treated as "a struggle for violent overthrow of the existing social structure."[95] However, in the liberalized post-XX Party Congress atmosphere, the sentence for such a criminal offence was now merely incarceration rather than execution!

While the preposterous *Izvestiya* account was not true to the facts of the prison environment, it did reflect the efforts of some—failed efforts one might say—at policy reorientation. Still, for the most part, Stalinist practices continued. Official repression even extended to those who had only recently been released from the camps. A December 19, 1956 Central Committee letter to party organizations, for example, cautions that there may be "anti-Soviet elements" among this group:

> there are people among the returnees who are unfavorably disposed to Soviet authority, especially among the former Trotskyites, right opportunists, and bourgeois nationalists. They surround themselves with anti-Soviet elements and politically unreliable persons, try to renew their hostile anti-Soviet activity.[96]

In terms of true "oppositional" elements, it should be noted that quite often many of those who were convicted as Trotskyites, for example, were rather arbitrarily categorized as such. The label did not reflect their own political orientations as much as that of their relatives, friends, or the quota of the day. However, taken at face value, the December 1956 Central Committee letter reflected the (not altogether unwarranted) paranoia of a repressive system whose inability to tolerate dissent keeps creating the enemies it attempts to destroy. It led to the drafting of a Supreme Court regulation "On the elimination of mistakes in the work of the courts on reevaluation of cases of counter-revolutionary crimes."[97] After a pro-forma preamble on the necessity to rehabilitate those who were convicted without due cause in the Stalin years the document goes on to note that

> certain courts, especially recently, sometimes allow serious mistakes ... that attest to dulled vigilance and underestimate the danger of counter-revolutionary activities. ... These mistakes [are reflected in] groundlessly closing a number of cases ... and acquitting those who are guilty [— actions that are the] result of incorrect political and juridical evaluation of their activities.[98]

The concluding instructions reflect the persisting ambivalence of the system. Like the contradictory double messages conveyed in 1954-55 (see chapter 3), they urge increased vigilance in the "merciless struggle" against these types of crimes, but also caution against permitting the "conviction without due cause of honest Soviet people."[99] In a democratic political system, this admonition might simply have been an attempt to strike an equitable balance, although democratic governments have also encountered the problem of determining "right" from "wrong" citizens or acts. (The post-World War II efforts of the Dutch government to ascertain which of its citizens had been Nazi collaborators is one such example.) In the Soviet system, the "merciless struggle" to weed out "counter-revolutionary" tendencies was used as a license to continue repression. In February 1957, the KGB responded to the draft regulations by emphasizing the need for the courts to "carefuly examine all the circumstances of a case [to insure that] enemies of the Soviet government will not receive acquittal or lighter punishments [when they should in fact be receiving] more severe punishments."[100]

Not surprisingly, this was followed by an increase in the prosecution of cases of counter-revolutionary activities in 1957. Memorial researcher Nikita Petrov, one of the first scholars given access to the KGB archives, found an exceedingly high number of political convictions in the year 1957.[101] Another Russian researcher found that in comparison to 1954 there was a 25 percent increase in convictions, that there were twice as many convictions compared to 1955, and as many as four times the convictions compared to 1956. He quotes the figure of 2,948 convictions for 1957,[102] though he does not record the number of arrests. This researcher also asserts that a 1958 Supreme Court summary on the results of judicial practices with regard to cases of counter-revolutionary crime was one of the "central documents that paved the way to new punitive policies."[103] It provided the basis for new approaches to consolidating the "law on state crimes" that had been passed on December 25, 1958 as part of the new Soviet Penal Code. It is unclear whether this provision was inititated by the Supreme Court or the Central Committee, since the materials that might answer this question are located in archives that are still inaccessible.

Others have also described the inconsistencies and turmoil of this period. Naumov cites the ruthless shootings of peaceful demonstrators in Tbilisi (1956) and Novocherkassk (1962) [not to mention Hungary in 1956] as just a few of the many examples of the employment of brutal repression under Khrushchev, a leader who presented himself as a reformer. Considering the changes that were being attempted within a short time period with the same entrenched leaders, with the same political system, and without the cleansing consequences pursuant to a military defeat, it is little wonder that the pace of reform lurched and veered. Antonov-Ovseenko, a historian whose father was a prominent victim of the terror, asserts that the rehabilitation campaign was greeted with some degree of satisfaction only at the center, and even then many officials only feigned their approval of the abrupt reversal of the Party line. In the provinces, he goes on to point out, an attitude of fear and mistrust prevailed.[104] It often seemed that the right hand did not know what the left hand was doing. For example, while the victims of repression of the thirties and forties were being rehabilitated, new political prisoners were being created. Such contradictions could not continue indefinitely, and it was the rehabilitation process that was curtailed. Naumov points out that after reexamining many thousands of cases in 1956-1957 there was such a sharp drop that in 1962 there were only 117 (not necessarily individual) reviewed. Of these, 25 percent of the petitioners were refused rehabilitation or reinstatement in the Party. In 1963, 13 percent (seven of the fifty-five) of the cases reviewed were rejected, while 1964 saw only twenty-eight case reviews. By 1965 the process had virtually halted.[105]

A further sign of the inconsistency of the rehabilitation process, according to Semyon Vilensky, was the burning of hundreds of thousands of prisoners' dossiers in the sixties, under Khrushchev. The motivation for this action was that "people wanted to eliminate the traces of their crimes." Vilensky added that certain books that might have aided in establishing the number of arrests were being destroyed in Moscow during this period.[106]

The Social Contract of Rehabilitation

In the absence of a program to change the perceptions of the bureaucracy and to inform the populace of the injustices committed by the government, official directives instituted from above and implemented from below were bound to founder. Ambivalence about rehabilitation and the rehabilitated was reflected at all levels. Arseny Roginsky (see chapter 7), was born in the camp zone because his father, a political prisoner, had been released with restrictions. He went on to become a historian, dissident, prisoner, ex-prisoner, and one of Memorial's founders. He offers an insider's perspective of this period. "Rehabilitation," Roginsky observed, "became a sacred word; the rehabilitation certificate became a sacred document,"[107] and the rehabilitation status occupied a central place in mass consciousness. In consequence, for personal, social, and political reasons, many ex-zeks waged a principled struggle to achieve a status equal to those who were not viewed with suspicion. Roginsky maintains that "that status influenced the concrete factors by which you measure how someone returned: finding an apartment, job, and so on."[108] The rehabilitation process progressed through three stages: release (physical separation from the camp), attainment of the certificate (recovering one's personal status), and finally reinstatement in the Party for those who had been members (recovering political/social status). A revoked sentence, for example, was similar to rehabilitation because it offered certain privileges, but in Soviet consciousness it was not equivalent to rehabilitation. Those who were not rehabilitated experienced "eternal instability," a status which required repeated explanations, for example, every time they had to fill out a questionnaire.[109] Some, however, did not even dare to apply for rehabilitation, so ingrained was their fear of any kind of contact with official authorities.[110] Others did not want to "humiliate" themselves by requesting reconsideration from the Soviet authorities.[111]

All this notwithstanding, there was often an ironic futility to the struggle to attain the rehabilitation status, because, as we have seen, it was still politically stigmatized and it often had little positive influence on landlords or employers. One returnee characterizes "so-called rehabilitation" as "phony" because, he maintains, all former zeks, even Party members, remained on a special register and were under surveillance.[112] One former zek was told by the KGB that "the mark was removed, but the stain remained."[113] They told him that he could forget about returning to his field of specialization, that he should just be happy that he got a pension and an apartment and leave it at that. Another describes what happened when he received his "so-called rehabilitation" certificate in 1957:

> after eighteen years of suffering, I was given a two- month teacher's salary by the Moscow Historical Archive Institute where I worked until my arrest. I was put in line for an apartment, and led a miserable homeless existence for two years inside and outside Moscow.[114]

There were many social and political factors that complicated the rehabilitation process. Roginsky contrasts the differences between the "*glasnost aresta*" (the public openness with which arrests were carried out) and the "*tainaya reabilitatsia*" (the poorly publicized, almost secretive process of rehabilitation).[115] When the victims were repressed by the State, the action was public knowledge; when the State recanted, it was a private matter. What was consistent in both procedures was that victims were still stigmatized. They were a political embarrassment because the very status of rehabilitation confronted the State with a past it was still trying to deny. The rehabilitated served as a reproach regarding both a past which the Party could not defend and a present to which the Party was not adapted. As the rehabilitated attempted to take their places in the community, these same issues were confronted at lower levels of society. As one ex-prisoner observed, "even if we were heartily greeted, we knew that society as a whole still lived by previous laws. Nothing essentially changed.... We were given back our freedom, but it was done very quietly."[116]

The public's attitude toward returnees was especially relevant when the returnees applied for rehabilitation because testimonials regarding their character were sometimes required. In a general atmosphere of social disapproval, favorable testimonials could be hard to come by. It was also hard to get the plight of the returnee before the public, even in literary works. Ivan Lazutin's "Chernie Lebedi" (Black Swans), a fictional tale that dealt with this and other returnee themes, had its own history of repression. Lazutin's detailed account of the problems encountered by returnees was apparently too controversial for the authorities to abide. It was published in installments in the journal *Baikal* in 1964, but discontinued in 1965 after receiving a rather critical review in *Voprosy Literatury*.[117] The final thirty pages, perhaps in a face-saving gesture, were included in a 1966 installment.[118]

According to the story, in order to initiate the rehabilitation process the Military Procuracy required character references from people who knew the returnee well. The testimony of a rehabilitated former camp-mate was acceptable, but only as a supplement to the references of others who knew the person in question before 1937.[119] Lazutin portrays the predicament of Rodimov, a Deputy People's Commissar arrested in 1937. Years later, he runs into an old camp-mate who is surprised to see him, because Rodimov was supposed to have been executed. In fact he was taken out for execution but was only wounded by the bullet. He managed to crawl away, bury himself in a pile of coal on a freight train, find a soldier's uniform (it was 1941), and even fight in the war.

After that, Rodimov lived with his sister under an assumed identity until 1955, when she received a certificate of Rodimov's posthumous rehabilitation. When he went to the MGB to declare that he was still alive (and rehabilitated), they said they needed proof from others that he was indeed the person he professed to be. Rodimov's four remaining former colleagues at the Ministry refused to identify him.[120] Through this episode, Lazutin conveys the pathos of people unwilling and/or unable to help a person in political trouble, either because of their allegiance to the Party or their fear for their own safety.

Lazutin dramatically portrays the duplicity of a Party more interested in rehabilitating its public image than in rehabilitating people. It was the dead Rodimov, not the living Rodimov who was rehabilitated. Rodimov had, after all, been executed by official decree. Now that he stood before his peers, they would only rehabilitate the living Rodimov if they got an official directive. Lord Acton's dictum that "Power tends to corrupt and absolute power corrupts absolutely,"[121] is widely accepted. The obverse is also true: weakness corrupts and absolute weakness corrupts absolutely. The support of former colleagues was withered by their fear of the government. Posthumous rehabilitation was generally less challenging to the system than accounting to the living, remembering, talking survivor in their midst.

Eventually Rodimov received assistance from below. The cloak-room attendant recognized him and had the courage to step forward on his behalf. Thereafter, he was restored to the Party, and was offered his old job as Deputy Minister. A major theme of this tale is that the people in entrenched positions of authority were more interested in protecting their Party position than in helping returnees. Such portrayals may well have contributed to the impediments Lazutin's writing encountered.

Rodimov's story described the ethos that prevailed in 1955, prior to the XX Party Congress. In the aftermath of the XX Party Congress people were much more willing to be character witnesses. In a letter to Memorial, one woman provides a success story. In 1955 she approached the Military Collegium of the Supreme Court to request (posthumous) rehabilitation for her husband. They had no documents whatsoever on him. She managed to gather the testimonies of high officials at the Zhukov Military Aviation Academy where he had worked. Two letters of reference written in June of 1956 secured her husband's 1956 posthumous rehabilitation.[122] This was a heartening but not typical experience.

Sometimes the authorities tried to render the living rehabilitated returnees as politically inactive as their posthumously rehabilitated comrades. A number of rehabilitated returnees were cautioned that they should leave the past behind. One returnee, released in 1960, was given a passport without limitations, but with one restriction: he was not to talk about what he had seen in "the zone" (camp).[123] Another ex-zek was pressured by the authorties into signing a pledge when she was released in 1956. In it, she acknowledged that she could be imprisoned for three years if she were to carry out requests from campmates, or if she were to disseminate information about the way the regime ran the camp.[124] Though these silencing practices could not have had any legal basis, they were clearly still being enforced.

In spite of the threat of reincarceration, it was often difficult to refrain from expressing the anguish created by the experience of arbitrary repression. It was even more challenging to keep silent in the era of rehabilitation, with its facade of liberalization. A former exile, the daughter of an "enemy of the people," was indignant when she finally received her father's posthumous rehabilitation certificate in 1957. She protested to an official at the Military Tribunal, "It took you twenty years to clarify that he was innocent, and I always knew it ... so tell me how this monstrous injustice that destroyed so many honest, devoted people could have occured!"[125] The major tried to mollify her, at the same time telling her very pointedly that the certificate entitled her to a number of privileges, but asking such questions was not one of them. For this woman and others like her, rehabilitation required a tacit agreement to keep quiet about the past in exchange for privileges in the present.

Yuri Aikhenvald, the son of repressed parents, was arrested in 1949 and exiled. He was rearrested in 1951 and committed to the Leningrad Psychiatric Hospital, where he was kept until 1955, at which point he was discharged and later rehabilitated. In his collection of memoirs and poetry, he describes the experience of a woman who returned to Moscow after rehabilitation. Some people could not look her in the eye, because ten years earlier they had condemned her as an "enemy of the people." Aikhenvald poignantly conveys the double jeopardy of the returnee who is first stigmatized by repression and then stigmatized because she stirs up unwelcome memories in the society that repressed her. The prevalent feeling that he inferred from the public's response was "enough, already, about 1937."[126]

The public's reaction may be less callous than it seems because it may be at some level a misguided response to an unbearable guilt. Freud illustrated the paradox of sensitivity presenting as callousness by quoting a humorous story. A beggar walking in a wealthy neighborhood found a door ajar, walked in, and found himself face to face with the rich owner of the mansion. Before the rich man could say anything, the beggar poured out his tale of misery. The rich man immediately rang for his butler and said, "I have never before heard such a tale of compelling misery. I can't stand it. Please, throw him out."[127] Bearing witness to the plight of the victims of repression not only carried political risks, but was also emotionally taxing. Isolating and blaming the victim was an easy, albeit cruel solution.

The literary works whose themes deal with the problems of rehabilitation tend to contain at least two messages: first, rehabilitation is essentially a conditional pardon,[128] second, full rehabilitation tends to silence people. How accurate was this depiction? In the words of Shatunovskaya, many of those who were reinstated in the Party and secured important positions were "very careful" not to talk about the past.[129] Stephen Cohen describes this "unwritten but often-spoken social contract" offered by the Soviet government to Gulag survivors thus: "Having freed you, we now will meet your welfare and work needs within limits, and we will let you live in peace. In return, you must not make political demands or clamor about the past."[130]

The recognition that rehabilitation was bought and sold for silence—a kind of Khrushchevian deal—was sometimes dealt with quite explicitly as a fictional plot, for lack of a safer venue. A tale written by a returnee, Iosif Aronovich Bogoraz, will be illustrative. His personal history attests to his right to speak about repression as an insider. He witnessed the repression spreading around him in widening circles to engulf his network. A Memorial questionnaire filled out by his daughter, the well-known former dissident Larisa Bogoraz, lists nine family members who were incarcerated. They included Bogoraz' first husband, Yuli Daniel, whose 1965 trial ushered in the dissident movement, and her second husband, Anatoly Marchenko, a political prisoner who died in incarceration in 1986.[131]

Josif Bogèraz opens *Otshchepenets* (The Renegade) with the funeral of an ex-prisoner, Pavel. It was attended by many returnees whose stories of Soviet society after Stalin are explored through flashbacks. By the use of vignettes he examines the personal choices of returnees, recounts their arguments, and attempts to explain why so many ex-prisoners remained silent. The story raises the question of why the moral principles that had been for many such a sustaining source of courage throughout the prison years failed to lead to a firm stand and active search for truth when the tyranny was officially over.[132] The answer it offers is essentially that the Party under Khrushchev offered political prisoners a deal to which years of grinding deprivation made them amenable—rehabilitation in exchange for silence. Silence in exchange for never having to go back. Many ex-prisoners wanted to put their hardships behind them and return to the positions of authority they had once enjoyed, or perhaps to gain new privileges. Moreover, many had always considered themselves loyal to the Party, even to Stalin and even while in camp, and were ready to serve the Party. Indeed, we have seen a number of prisoners who, upon release, took jobs with the MVD authorities if they were offered.

Through two characters, Bogoraz offers two contrasting ways by which returnees could resolve the issues of rehabilitation. Pavel, the main character, remained an ideologue. He could not adjust to his returnee status, did not want restoration of Party membership, and was unforgiving. In contrast, another character was pragmatic. His approach was essentially "you're back from that cold and bitter Vorkuta earth, forgive, and get yourself a decent place in the Party."[133] Accordingly, he helped returnees to reassimilate. In one particularly revealing scene, Pavel inveighs against the pragmatic ex-prisoners, "pathetic comedy ... you've been paid off [with]... two months compensation, rehabilitation, good jobs, ... apartments, dachas, personal pensions ... Vorkuta never existed ... don't raise it from the ashes ... you've sold out."[134] Later he remonstrates "they shut your mouths, be silent [since you are] in an enviable position."[135] This work was fictional, but the issues it depicted were true to the reality of returnee life.

Zorya Leonidovna Serebryakova

In spite of the difficulties encountered by many returnees, there were a number of them who fared well under Khrushchev. They insist that there was no commitment of silence, implicit or explicit. Zorya Serebryakova, daughter of "enemy of the people" Leonid Serebryakov, lost her father and step-father, Grigory Sokolnikov, (both high Soviet officials) to the Great Terror. Her mother, Galina, a Party writer, spent twenty years in camps and prisons.[136] (Cohen cites Galina Serabryakova as an example of a returnee who "rose high in the Soviet establishment by outwardly forgiving or forgetting the Gulag."[137]) Zorya's father was arrested in 1931, and by the time she was sent to an orphanage in 1937 at age thirteen, her father had already perished.[138] Like other children of "enemies of the people," in this children's home, where the windows had bars, she was fingerprinted and photographed with a number.[139] Zorya went on to join her mother in exile in Semipalatinsk. She studied there from 1945 to 1947 and was married in 1948. Her husband, a Polish Jew, was arrested in 1949 because of connections with a family member of the "enemy of the people" Serebryakov. During this time, her mother had been in camp, then in exile, then in a "political isolator" in Vladimir, then exiled to Dzhambul, Kazakhstan and then arrested again.

When Zorya returned to Moscow in 1950, she too was arrested. Apparently the authorities considered her suspect because she was married to an "enemy of the people," her mother was a political prisoner, she had corresponded with an "enemy of the people" Sokolnikov, and she had preserved a photo of the "enemy of the people" Serebryakov. In the nineties, when Serebryakova was allowed to see her *delo* (dossier), she noted that there was no mention of the fact that these charges against her were for corresponding with men who were respectively her step-father and father. She spent two months in isolation, and in the meantime, the KGB ordered that her baby son be put in a children's home. In November of that year, Zorya was reclassified from Article 58-10 to Article 7-35 and sentenced to ten years of exile into which she was allowed to take her son as well. Serebryakova recalls that she was so happy upon hearing her new status of detainment that she jumped up and kissed the man who read the sentence. In exile in Dzhambul she worked as a teacher of Russian at a Kazakh school on a kolkhoz. In 1952, she managed to get a job teaching English, but could not get a job in her own field of history.

In 1955, Zorya Serebryakova's sentence was halved, permitting her immediate liberation under the 1953 amnesty. Zorya's mother, who had been in the Potma camps, was also released into exile. In the summer of 1955 Zorya returned with her son to the home of friends in Moscow. Serebryakova asserts that "When Stalin died the terror ended ... there may have been repression, but there was no terror. You could say everything under Khrushchev. [She adds] We did not have this horrible corruption that we have today [1996]."[140] She also recalls that shortly after her arrival in Moscow in 1955, the police came to the home where she was staying with friends and demanded that this "politically compromised" person leave the capital within 72 hours.[141]

Despite her early personal history, or maybe because of her later personal history, Serebryakova disagreed with the view that the Soviet system was adapted to repression. Zorya was rehabilitated in February of 1956. Then, on February 14, 1956 the first day of the XX Party Congress, Zorya's mother, Galina, was also rehabilitated. At that time the Military Procuracy would not consider her father's posthumous rehabilitation, but they did treat Zorya politely. Serebryakov's rehabilitation came under Gorbachev. Zorya defended her candidate dissertation under Khrushchev, and her doctoral dissertation under Gorbachev. After rehabilitation she was even called by the Academy of Sciences and invited to join. Interestingly, the place of our interview—Serebryakova's spacious dacha on the out-skirts of Moscow—had its own history of repression and adaptation. This dacha had been taken over and occupied by Procurator Vyshinsky until Zorya and her mother regained their privileges. It is ironic, but not unusual, that this victim's house was occupied by a henchman, and then once again by the victim.

Zorya contends that from the end of 1955 until 1964, the rehabili-tated were treated as heroes.[142] Indeed, some formerly high func-tionaries were released, immediately rehabilitated, reinstated in the Party, and officially honored as Party veterans and builders of com-munism.[143] One military engineer who was incarcerated from 1938-1948 was lauded with official certificates congratulating him on his 70th and 75th birthdays (1971 and 1976), and commemorating the 30-year anniversary of the victory of the Soviet armed forces. Ab-sent from these certificates of praise for his service to the country was any mention of his incarceration.[144]

This stance on the celebrated returnee is also shared by Serebryakova's fellow historian and colleague at the Gorbachev Foundation, Vladlen Terentevich Loginov. Loginov challenges the credibility of the presentation and representation of the victims' ex-perience that has been disseminated by organizations such as Me-morial. Since returnees were really afforded a "hero's reception" under Khrushchev, he argues, their stories to the contrary cannot be true.[145] In opposition to his position is the evidence presented by many former victims. That evidence regarding their stigmatized sta-tus is so abundant and so consistent with corroborating data, that it has both face validity and convergent validity. Nevertheless, to the extent that Loginov's data are accurate, this illustrates the variability and unevenness of the process of rehabilitation.

The Return Of Confiscated Property

As it was with the restitution of social and legal status, so it was with the return of property confiscated at the time of arrest. Resto-ration of property to the previous owners was impeded by the grudg-ing attitude on the part of Soviet officials as well as honest confusion. Since inventories made at the time of arrest were often as arbitrary and illegitimate as the arrest itself, even if officials were willing to be help-ful, it was difficult for them to know what to give back. Thus, the recovery of valuables now in the hands of the state often became a matter of the victim's word against the official document.[146] We have already seen how little credibility the state extended to the victims.

According to the Procuracy, early in 1956 there was no direct law governing the question of whether rehabilitated persons should be reimbursed for the 1956 value of their confiscated property or for the NKVD 1937-38 assessment of its worth.[147] One memoirist describes what was seized at the time of her grandfather's arrest: an antique carpet, a porcelain tea set, a Swiss hunting rifle, a gold watch and an engagement ring, among many other items. The value assigned to the truncated inventory—not all of the items were listed—was so "ridiculous," the author tells us, that when her grandmother presented this document during the rehabilitation procedures, "even the lawyers were indignant."[148] Gold watches, for example, were often described as "yellow metal" watches, and valued accordingly.[149] When confiscated items could not be returned, officials often based financial compensation on these descriptions, despite their apparent knowledge of this deceptive practice. Moreover, even though the family members who stayed behind sometimes received a copy of the inventory, this, too, was seized if they themselves were arrested.[150] Some clearly incomplete inventories were signed by family members who, in the confusion and shock of the arrest of a loved one, did not bother to read the document. Upon seeing the inventory of her property that was confiscated in 1957, the widow of a posthumously rehabilitated Old Bolshevik protested, "Judging by this description, we were sitting on stools and eating from earthen bowls with tin spoons. At the time I did not pay any attention and just signed what they gave me to sign."[151]

By the end of 1956, no doubt as a result of the chaotic practice of restitution, the USSR Ministry of Finance instituted a process of reassessment of the value of confiscated property. The November correspondence of this agency attests to numerous "expert assessments" to determine how much more money the state owed to the returnee. Each object was evaluated in terms of its quality, its 1937 value, and its 1956 cost. The difference was to be paid to the returnee.[152]

There were some instances in which petitioners insisted on the return of property that was not listed on the inventory. This presented a problem that had to be investigated. Yekaterina Ivanovna Muravieva maintained that a number of items, including a painting, were not returned. Her daughter identified other missing materials, such as documents and letters, that were seized by the MGB during its 1948 search. The investigation into this matter resulted in a decision for the henchmen and against the victim. An August 1956 KGB letter to the Presidium of the Supreme Soviet asserts that the former MGB agents who carried out the search and listed the inventory, as well as others who were present, confirm that Muravieva never owned such things. With regard to the documents and letters to which her daughter referred, they had been "indiscriminately destroyed."[153] The outcome of this case and many like it must have discouraged other returnees from pressing their legitimate claims. Also discouraging was the impunity with which officials engaged in deceptive practices and subverted their own laws. The conclusions in this case were perhaps a reflection of the same type of passive aggressive bureacratic behavior observed in 1953-1955 (see chapter 3).

These practices did not, however, escape official notice. An October 1956 provincial Procuracy document to the General Procuracy complains about a particular directive which gave the KGB a wide latitude in deciding these disputed matters. The provincial division requested that the courts should make the final decision on confiscated property, and that the KGB should only be responsible for verifying the petitions. The General Procuracy's dismissive response was that a different KGB directive governed compensatory practices, and that the provincial procuracy official should familiarize itself with it.[154] The General Procuracy's response was a flimsy attempt to rebut the obvious fact that the KGB had a conflict of interest in judging its own cases. The KGB along with the Ministry of Finance continued to determine the outcome of these cases.

All this notwithstanding, it would be a mistake to conclude that petitioners were always honest about their confiscated property. Clearly there must have been cases in which items were claimed to have been seized, when in fact they never even existed. Quite often, the facts of the matter were hard to ascertain, but sometimes the authorities were right. In one case, in 1957 and 1958 Vasily Kotlov tried to claim compensation on behalf of his wife, whose father was posthumously rehabilitated. He insisted on a reassessment of his father-in-law's confiscated property. In 1956 Kotlov's wife began the petitioning process with a claim for reimbursment for a car, a piano, and three bicycles that supposedly belonged to her father. These items were not listed on the inventory. The KGB checked into this claim and found that he had owned a motorcycle and two bicycles. Furthermore, they contended that while he did own a piano, he had sent it to his daughter in Moscow in 1936—a year before his arrest in Ufa. According to a Supreme Soviet document, witnesses at his former place of work and residence also attested to these facts, and confirmed that he did not have a car.

Kotlov went to the reception room of the Supreme Soviet fifteen times between the end of 1957 and April of 1958. To the extent that the documentation is credible, there were good grounds to challenge the legitimacy of his request. Kotlov was arrested in 1952 for swindling. His chief offence was "underground advocacy"—he pretended to be a lawyer and took money to write citizens' complaints to official institutions. He was then sent to the Serbsky Institute to establish whether he could be held accountable for his actions. He was declared accountable and sentenced to ten years of correctional labor camp. Subsequently, his sentence was lowered and he was released under the amnesty in 1953.[155] In this instance, it seems indeed possible that the official assessment of the falsity of Kotlov's claims may have been correct. However, because it was often the case that officials lied, ordinary citizens may also have felt justified in lying. In a system so flagrantly exploitative of the repressed, the victims felt warranted in finding ways to manipulate the system in order to gain some small recompense. It might be added that those who survived the camps well enough to return would likely have had to acquire manipulative and deceptive practices. As in any other social organization, some were more likely than others to bend the rules to their advantage.

Not all problems with obtaining compensation were official in origin. Sometimes domestic problems complicated the process of compensation. In one such case, Dmitry Danilovich Golovin, an opera soloist of the Bolshoi Theater, was arrested in 1944, sentenced to ten years of correctional labor camp, and released in 1953. Golovin's son and brother had also been convicted with him, but they were released earlier and were rehabilitated in 1956. Upon his release, Golovin was told that he could not return to his family in Moscow because they wanted nothing to do with him. Golovin claimed that his former wife's "slander" hindered his rehabilitation. Many highly placed artists petitioned on his behalf, and rehabilitation was finally granted in November 1965. In the meantime, Golovin remarried in 1956. The family from his previous marriage maintained their distance, and only started to show some interest in him after his 1965 official exoneration. When Golovin died in 1966, his ex-wife did not attend the funeral. She did, however, make an immediate claim to inherit the money he had received in compensation after rehabilitation.[156] It is not clear what the outcome of this case was, since these documents were part of a Memorial dossier, rather than an official archive which generally would have included both complaints and responses. It is, however, entirely possible that this matter lingered on for years. This is one of the many examples of how personal and domestic issues interacted with the camp experience to influence the compensation process.

In a country where service to the motherland was intensely promoted by propaganda, the symbols of that service in the form of awards were an important indicator of social status. For many ex-prisoners the strongest confirmation of their acceptance back into Soviet society was the restitution of their state honors. The return of previously awarded decorations was a special kind of acknowledgement of their rehabilitated status. It was the official and public emblem of legal exoneration and regained social status. Armed with their medals, ex-prisoners could display their regained status and once again feel proud of their past service to the motherland. That is why this issue ranked high in the concerns of many returnees. That is why Stalinist henchmen had moved so quickly to strip victims of their official decorations. After robbing them of the symbols of state service, it became easier to stigmatize them as enemies. In the years between 1938-1958, 72,791 citizens were stripped of their decorations.[157] The process of restoration of these honors began in 1953 but progressed very slowly. Between 1953 and 1958 the Presidium of the Supreme Soviet granted only 2,125 ex-prisoners the right to retrieve their medals. This figure included the return of decorations to the families of posthumously rehabiliated victims of the terror like Tukhachevsky and Iona Yakir.[158]

The Co-Existence of De-Stalinizing and Re-Stalinizing Policies

The years between the XX Party Congress in 1956 and Khrushchev's ouster in 1964 were characterized by ambivalent attitudes, inconsistent directives, and sometimes contradictory policies toward returnees and the rehabilitated. Still, during this period there was evidence that the old repressive bureaucracy was lumbering toward reform. A number of new regulations were instituted to accommodate the needs of the growing segment of society comprised of ex-prisoners. One such accommodation was the establishment of legal provisions for supporting the financial and other needs of returning prisoners. In July of 1956, a new law on state pensions was proposed. Though it did not refer specifically to returnees, the recommended budgetary reforms were tailored toward incorporating large masses of pension-seekers into the system.[159] Moreover, in a gesture toward clearing returnees' names, the Academy of Science's Institute of State and Law published an article arguing that interrogators do not have the right to coerce confessions, and that verdicts based on confessions of guilt (Vyshinsky's theories) were a "gross violation of socialist justice."[160] The article defended the presumption of innocence—a major departure from the Stalinist presumption of guilt without the right to prove one's innocence.

However, many reforms did not go very far. In 1956 the restrictions that had been placed on a number of deported peoples were lifted, but that did not necessarily give them the right to return to their homelands. Zemskov has characterized these half-measures thus: "The directives on the abolishment of the special regime with regard to deported peoples and other groups were distinguished by indecisiveness, and attempts to avoid being subjected to the slightest criticism of the previous policies of mass deportation."[161] Tens of thousands of Chechens and Ingush returned to their homelands without official permission. Some of the turmoil created by these mass returns to places Russians had occupied has been recounted earlier (see chapter 3). Finally, in November of 1956 the Chechens, Ingush, Kalmyks, Balkars, and other national groups did receive official autonomy which entitled them to return.[162] Even after their official return, problems abounded. For example, despite numerous Central Committee directives on the work placement of these returnees, by April of 1957, only 1/6 of the Chechens and Ingush were able to find employment.[163]

The returning deported peoples generally aspired toward the reestablishment of their national identity and the restoration of their rights rather than reassimilation. Ongoing conflicts to resolve the problems related to the return eventually led to massive bloodshed.

It is in this context no coincidence that the Chechen separatist leader, Dzhokhar Dudaev, like most of his cohorts, was a returnee.

As with much of the reform process, it was variable in its application. In 1967, the Volga Germans received legal rehabilitation, though they were not permitted to return to the Volga region.[164] The Crimean Tatars were partially exonerated in 1967, though they were not granted autonomy at that time, nor were they permitted to return en masse to their homeland.[165] In the sixties and early seventies, dissidents like Pyotr Yakir, son of the executed Red Army commander Iona Yakir, were to jeopardize their own legal standing by campaigning for restoration of the rights of the Crimean Tatars. For his support of this unpopular cause, General Pyotr Grigorenko was committed to a Special Psychiatric Hospital.[166] The Volga Germans, like the Crimean Tatars, were not fully rehabilitated until late in the Soviet era. The problems associated with the return of the deported peoples lingered for decades (see chapter 7).

Various amnesties through the years resulted in the staggered release of prisoners. A 1957 amnesty in celebration of the fortieth anniversary of the October revolution, for instance, liberated 196,713 prisoners. The November 1958 document from the Khrushchev Special Files that reveals this statistic, does not specify, however, what percentage of these releasees were political prisoners.[167] Moreover, the amnesty was primarily aimed at prisoners with terms of under three years, so it did not appear to be dealing with Stalin's zeks. However, it did improve returnees' status since it revoked the sentences of those who were freed, reduced by half the terms of those still in camp, and provided release for exiles who had finished their prison terms.[168] There was thus a considerable movement of ex-prisoners back into society during these years. Again, according to the Khrushchev Files, in the period between 1953 and 1958, a total of 4,118,414 prisoners were released from correctional labor camps and colonies by decree of the Presidium of the Supreme Soviet.[169] This number includes many ordinary criminals, and states only that they were released; it discloses nothing about their rehabilitation status. Elsewhere it is recorded that the number of incarcerated "counter-revolutionaries" declined from 480,000 in the fall of 1953 to approximately 11,000 on January 1, 1959.[170]

In the spring of 1958 the restrictions were lifted from 25,000 special settlers, including former kulaks and family members of "leaders and participants in the nationalist underground." This regulation did not necessarily carry the implication that these ex-exiles were entitled to return to their homeland or to the return of their confiscated property.[171] This is typical of the half-way measures taken toward reform. Typical also were the back and forth oscillations of the reform movement. While the process of de-Stalinization under Khrushchev often moved two steps forward and one step backward, it sometimes moved one step forward and two steps backward. While the government was releasing old political prisoners it was arresting new ones. And although the numbers of new political arrests were low by historical standards they attest to an ongoing policy of official repression during this 'period of liberalization.' According to Memorial researchers, materials culled from the KGB archives have revealed that in the year 1958 alone, 1,416 people were arrested and convicted on the basis of Article 70 ("anti-Soviet agitation and propaganda," a new version of 58-10).[172] And these were only the documented cases. In that same year, Boris Pasternak was forced to decline the Nobel Prize for *Doctor Zhivago* for fear of deportation. The novel's criticisms of the political system had not been sufficiently disguised by the fiction.

In this climate of censorship, camp city reports, starting in the late fifties and published from regions like Kolyma/Magadan, revealed precious little on their history of forced labor. These *gosizdat* (i.e., official) publications generally portray what went on there as the heroic, self-sacrificing conquest of the wildnerness, but do not refer to the conquest of the laborers who conquered the wilderness. When the camp labor is addressed, the references are usually oblique, misleading, and euphemistic. One work, *Notes on the History of the North-East RSFSR (1917-1953)* tells us that in Dalstroi "there was ... large and intense work aimed at the reeducation through socially useful work of a contingent of former criminals and other socially dangerous elements."[173] It does not detail the principle of pedagogy employed in the effort at reeducation. Another book, *A Historical Chronicle of the Magadan Province*, employs local archives in its historical description. It mentions the fact that Magadan provincial and city organizations met in March 1956 to discuss the results of the XX Party Congress.[174] This was probably the time when the Secret Speech was read in Magadan. A later work on the industrial development of Siberia published in 1982 strives to refute Western claims that Siberia was developed exclusively through the use of forced labor.[175]

While the repressive policies emanated from Moscow, it was mostly in the geographically peripheral regions that they came to reside. It was also in these regions, the places where the Gulag was being dismantled, that the political climate was slower in thawing. An example of this is the troubled history of the publication of a collection of memoirs from Kolyma victims and survivors described by Semyon Vilensky (see chapter 4). Also revealing were some works whose subject matter and place of publication allude to the personal history of their author. A book published in Perm in 1963, regarding recent developments in lumbering,[176] was very likely written by someone who had found out more than he ever wanted to know about chopping down trees! Likewise, we need not stretch our imaginations to recognize that the editor of the 1967 *Handbook of Selection and Seed Growing of Oil Plants* is a returnee.[177]

At the same time, through veiled (or not so veiled) criticism, important steps were being taken in the direction of examining the Stalinist terror. In 1961, for example, the journal *Novy Mir* published a review of a book, edited by the Soviet General Procurator Rudenko, on the Nuremberg trials. It stressed the importance and "timeliness" of the publication of such documents, because they "reveal the crimes of German imperialism." It summons us to "be vigilant about any attempts at new *German* [my italics] imperialist aggression."[178] Considering the year, the place, and the subject matter of the publication, one wonders if there was not an implicit question raised about the trial of Soviet henchmen.

In contrast to his more careful speech at the XX Party Congress in 1956, Khrushchev's indictment of Stalin at the XXII Party Congress in the fall of 1961 was relatively open and broad. He also revealed the complicity of Molotov, Kaganovich, Malenkov, and Voroshilov in Stalin's crimes by showing their signatures on death sentences of even the wives of "enemies of the people."[179] Such was the anti-Stalin mood at the Congress that Dora Lazurkina, a delegate who had spent seventeen years in the Gulag, disclosed that in her daily contact with Lenin he had expressed to her, "I do not like being next to Stalin, who inflicted so much harm on the Party."[180] The motion to remove Stalin's body from the Lenin Mausoleum, where it had been since 1953, was proposed and accepted, and Stalin was relegated to a place alongside the Kremlin wall. A proposal to build a monument to victims of the terror was also submitted. The fulfillment of this sentiment would not be realized until three decades later, and it was not the state that inspired or created this commemoration of the victims of Soviet terror—it was the organization Memorial.

The silence from above had been broken by the XX Party Congress, and the muted struggle from below to deal with the history of repression and the histories of the repressed could now be expressed. Medvedev characterizes the period that immediately followed the XXII Party Congress as a "time of memoirs."[181] Two of the more stirring publications of 1962 were Solzhenitsyn's story, *One Day in the Life of Ivan Denisovich*, and Yevgeny Yevtushenko's poem, "The Heirs of Stalin." Solzhenitsyn's tale, published in *Novy Mir*, was about a typical day in a Siberian labor camp during the war as described by a prisoner.[182] Yevtushenko's poem, written after Stalin's removal from the mausoleum, warned of the dangers of Stalin's spirit escaping the grave. It was published in *Pravda* in October of 1962. The taboos against speaking and writing about the Gulag had been removed. The terror, the camp theme, and anti-Stalin sentiments found their way into literature, memoirs, film, and theater. Fiction followed a more cautious, but no less effective approach to treating these issues. For this reason the present research has incorporated many of these stories.

Stephen Cohen describes the effect of the pivotal discussions that ensued in this period thus:

> The magnitude of the unfolding picture shattered the corollary fiction that only Stalin and a few accomplices had been guilty. Publicizing the camps meant publicizing the conduct of millions. Face-to-face confrontations between victims and their former tormentors were being portrayed in literature and on the stage. And this raised the question of present-day Stalinists...[183]

The contemporary Stalinists, many of whom were still in positions of influence, tried to stem the tide of anti-Stalinism. The publication of *Ivan Denisovich* led to a debate between its "friends and foes,"[184] who had opposing opinions on this approach to the examination of the Soviet past. When Solzhenitsyn's book was nominated for the Lenin Prize for Literature in 1963, conservative forces realized that the popularity of a book with such a potentially incriminating theme was a sign that things were getting out of hand—at least out of the Party's hands.

A letter to the editor published in *Kazakhstanskaya Pravda* pro-vides an example of the "foe" view. The writer, presents himself as a returnee who disputes Solzhenitsyn's portrayal and expresses the hope that a journalist (whom he names) will write a true story about zeks in the Gulag. This true story should not dwell on the inmates' struggles for survival, as Solzhenitsyn had, but rather should em-phasize their sense of comraderie, humaneness, and communist con-victions.[185] The "returnee," if indeed he was a genuine returnee, must be counted among the true believers, one of those who felt that they were the builders of socialism, no matter that they were impris-oned in its edifice.

Another sign from the literary front that the times were changing was a change in the editorship of the *Concise Literary Encyclopedia* (*CLE*). This general reference work on literature, the first volume of which appeared in 1962, provided biographical and terminological in-formation. A number of editors and consultants were returnees who brought with them the perspectives of their own personal histories of repression as well as a wealth of information on other repressed writers. The editorship had its own history of repression. In the fall of 1964 one of the editors who had spent ten years in prisons and labor camps, was expelled on orders of the KGB from the Institute of World Literature and the Writers' Union, and stripped of his editorial posts.

Despite this Stalinist measure, and despite the fact that the staff still had to accommodate more to the demands of Party critics than to those of scholars, some of the early traditions of the encyclopedia were maintained. One significant illustration of continuity of the scholarly tradition was that later volumes of the *CLE* did include entries on some returnees, though their personal history was some-times referred to in the Soviet tradition—euphemistically. The entry on Galina Serebryakova, for example, reads "She was one of the first in Soviet literature to create a picture of the founding father of scientific communism, K. Marx, in the novel 'Marx's Youth' (books 1-2, 1933-34). After a twenty-year interval she returned to literary activity."[186] Volume 9, however, published in 1978, abandoned the policy of referring to anyone's history of repression.[187]

By 1964, officials began to harness the forces that they had un-leashed, and the de-Stalinization process from above ended abruptly with the end of the regime of Khrushchev. "The screws were so tightened," observed one ex-zek, "that the rehabilitated no longer felt rehabilitated."[188] Brezhnev made the Khrushchev regime's political ambivalence, even with all of its impediments, retrospectively look good to reformers. The discrepancy between reform policy and reform practice which characterized the ambivalent efforts of Khrushchev was replaced by unfettered consistency in the Brezhnev years. It was a consistency of retrenchment. There was no equivocation with regard to returnees' rights, because the new leadership did not purport to resolve the lingering problems associated with returnee status. Among the more visible signs of re-Stalinization (and practice reflecting policy) in this period were the trial and conviction of the writers Andrei Sinyavsky and Yuli Daniel in 1966, and the placement of a marble bust of Stalin on his gravesite in 1970. Cohen contends that this official gesture was not "unequivocal rehabilitation ... but it was rehabilitation nonetheless.... Governments do not erect monuments, even small ones, to people they consider to be criminals."[189]

Significantly, one of the few real rehabilitations of the period was Molotov, who had been expelled from the Party after the XXII Party Congress and restored to membership in 1984. At a 1984 Politburo meeting attended by Gorbachev, a discussion about "illegal rehabilitations" was raised. This referred to prisoners who were "rightly punished," and therefore whose official transgressions did not deserve exoneration. Solzhenitsyn was named as one such example. Furthermore, taking a stance that further reflected the resurgence of political conservatism, Gorbachev supported restoring Party membership to Malenkov and Kaganovich.[190]

In the Khrushchev years, reform policy often differed from practice because the problems presented by returnees could not be fully and consistently dealt with until the political issues represented by their repression were addressed. To acknowledge that these former "enemies of the people" were really innocent victims of repression by the state is to undermine the moral foundations and legitimacy of the state. If criminals caused the problem, and the inmates were not the criminals, then where should one look for the malefactors? They would not be hard to find because many of them were still in office. The politically expedient partial truth was that the blame rested with Stalin. A more honest appraisal of the repression was not to happen for nearly four decades.

Repression had been used as a significant instrument of governance. Moreover, even after this was officially recognized, repression continued to be used as an instrument of governance. The political system was not ready to correct its fundamental flaws. This ambiguity from the "top-down" was also present from the "bottom-up." So it was that many people (employers, landlords, officials) who had not been directly victimized believed in the system, supported the Party, and had trouble confronting the historical reality, or at least adjusting to it. This attitude was consequently reflected in their antipathy toward the returnees.

That people who had not been incarcerated continued to believe in and support the Party is not surprising. What is surprising is that so many prisoners, despite their lost youths, lost families, and long years of hard labor under deplorable conditions, were not politicized by their experience to the extent that they challenged the legitimacy of the governing system. On the contrary, many individuals retained their belief and strove for restoration of Party membership not just on practical but on ideological grounds. Their political convictions and the way that repression affected the political system will be explored in the next chapter.

References

*Some passages from this chapter appeared in, "Life in the 'Big Zone': The Fate of Returnees in the Aftermath of Stalinist Repression," *Europe-Asia Studies*, 51, no. 1 (1995):5-19.

1. Lipper, *Eleven Years in Soviet Prison Camps*, p. 162. A former camp inspector's slightly different version is also quoted in Helmut M. Fehling, *One Great Prison: The Story behind Russia's Unreleased POW's* (Boston: The Beacon Press, 1951), p. ix.
    This joke is also employed in a 1997 *Izvestiia* article. In a commentary on Stalinist repression and Stalinism, it cites increasingly limited access (reclassification) to Party archive documents as one of the enduring consequences ("Vechnyi Rab: Pravda o 37-m gode vnov' zasekrechivaetsia," Eternal Slave: the Truth about 1937 is Once Again Classified," *Izvestiia*, 6 September 1997).
2. Keep, *Last of the Empires*, pp. 79-80.
3. Solzhenitsyn, *The Gulag Archipelago*, volume three, p. 451.
4. Max Hayward and Edward L. Crowley, eds., *Soviet Literature in the Sixties: An International Symposium* (New York and London: Methuen, 1965), p. 51.
5. Leonid Furman, response to Cohen questionnaire, May 30, 1982.
6. Ibid.
7. Iosif Il'ich Peiros, "Poluvolia, Vospominaniia, chast' 3," Memorial, f. 2, op. 1, d. 93, l. 1993 1510 0887.
8. GARF, f. 7523, op. 107, d. 123, ll. 59, 56-58.
9. Ibid., ll. 60-61.
10. Aino Kuusinen, *Gospod nizvergaet svoikh angelov: vospominaniia 1919-1965* (Petrozavodsk: Izdatel'stvo Kareliia, 1991), pp. 203, 198-216.
11. Roza Iakovlevna Smushkevich, interview held at her Moscow home, November 30, 1996.

12. GARF, f. 7523, op. 107, d. 255, l. 54.
13. Smushkevich, interview, May 16, 1997.
14. GARF, f. 7523, op. 107, d. 255, l. 56.
15. Smushkevich, interview.
16. GARF, f. 7523, op. 107, d. 255, ll. 1-4.
17. Ibid., l. 5.
18. Ibid., l. 11.
19. Ibid., ll. 7-8.
20. Ibid., l. 9.
21. Evgenii Edvardovich Gagen, "Vospominaniia," Memorial, f. 2, op. 1, d. 45, ll. 1993 0510 1018-19.
22. Ibid., ll. 1050-1051.
23. see also GARF, f. 8131, op. 32, d. 4754, l. 2.
24. Gagen., ll. 1034-1035.
25. "O trudovom stazhe, trudoustroistve i pensionnom obespechenii grazhdan, neobosnovanno privlechennykh k ugolovnoi otvetstvennosti i vposledstvii reabilitirovannykh," *Sbornik zakonodatel'nykh i normativnykh aktov o repressiiakh i reabilitatsii zhertv politicheskikh repressii* (Moscow: Izdatel'stvo 'Respublika', 1993), pp. 168-70.
26. Aleksandr Dmitrievich Levshin, undated open letter to Memorial.
27. See, for example, Aleksandr Kron's fictional "Bessonitsa," in *Novyi Mir* 4 (April, 1997): 41.
28. M. Narymov, "Nespetaia Pesnia," *Grani* 48 (1960): 107.
29. Kirill Kostsinskii, "Nabroski k budushchei knige," *Kontinent* 21 (1979): 160-61.
30. Polina Furman, Cohen questionnaire, pp. 2-3.
31. GARF, f. 7523, op. 107, d. 123, ll. 84-85.
32. Aleksandra Zakharovna Moglina, (transcribed) interview with Laura Starink and Marc Jansen, November 27, 1988, p. 10.
33. David Moiseevich Rakhlin, "Griaznaia istoriia: vospominaniia," Memorial, f. 2, op. 1, d. 101, l. 1993 1510 1242.
34. Gagen, ll. 1071-1073.
35. Ibid., l. 1105.
36. Ibid., l. 1106.
37. Iadviga Iosifovna Verzhenskaia, "Vospominaniia," Memorial, f. 2, op. 1, d. 33, ll. 2909 1068-1073.
38. Ibid., l. 1095.
39. Aleksandr Petrovich Grinberg, Memorial, f. 1, op. 1, d. 1279, ll. 0014 0712 1993-2016.
40. A. Erokhin, "Podvig uchënogo," *Baikal* 3, May-June, 1964, pp. 19-36.
41. Fil'shtinskii, *My shagaem pod konvoem*, p. 186.
42. Ibid., interview held at his Moscow home, April 20, 1995.
43. Ibid., p. 187.
44. Lev Emmanuilovich Razgon, interview held at his Moscow home, April 16, 1995.
45. Razgon, "Pered Raskrytymi Delami," (Moscow: Biblioteka 'Ogonëk' No. 39), p. 10.
46. I. Shenfeld, "Krugi zhizni i tvorchestva Iuriia Dombrovskogo," *Grani* nos. 111-112 (1979): 351-378.
47. GARF, f. 385, op. 25, d. 151, l. 2 and ll. 1, 4, 5, 36.
48. Sergei Bondarevskii, *Tak bylo..., Memuary* (Moscow: Invar, 1995), p. 119.
49. GARF, f. 9401, op. 2, d. 479, ll. 379-380.
50. GARF, f. 8131, op. 32, d. 4957, l. 123, also ll. 78-80, 82-87, 97, 121-129.

51. GARF, f. 9474, op. 16, d. 604, l. 81, also ll. 104, 105, 217, 218.
52. GARF, f. 385, op. 25, d. 154, l. 7, see also d. 150, ll. 39, 40; d. 152, ll. 1, 2, 16; d. 153, ll. 18-26; d. 154, ll. 1, 2, 6, 15, 16, 18.
53. Ibid., d. 155, l. 8, and also ll. 1-3.
54. GARF, f. 9401, op. 2, d. 507, l. 87, and ll. 85, 86, 88.
55. GARF, f. 9474, op. 16, d. 723, l. 16.
56. Ibid., l. 2.
57. Materials sent by Roy Medvedev to Stephen Cohen, early 1980s.
58. Negretov, *Vse Dorogi Vedut na Vorkutu*, p. 18.
59. GARF, f. 8131, op. 32, d. 4847, ll. 90, 91, 116, 181.
60. Ibid., l. 182.
61. GARF, f. 8131, op. 32, d. 4754, ll. 4, 2.
62. GARF, f. 411, op. 4, d. 80, l. 6.
63. Memorial, f. 1, op. 1, d. 1693, ll. 0016 1612 1878-880, 1893-1912.
64. See N.A. Barsukov, "XX S"ezd v retrospektive Khrushcheva," *Otechestvennaia Istoriia* 6 (1996).
65. Nikita Khrushchev, *Khrushchev Remembers* (London: Little, Brown and Company Inc., 1971), p. 349.
66. Ibid., p. 348.
67. V.P. Naumov, "K istorii Sekretnogo Doklada N.S. Khrushcheva na XX S"ezde KPSS," *Novaia i Noveishaia Istoriia* 4 (1996): 162.
68. Barsukov, p. 171.
69. GARF, f. 8131, op. 32, d. 4581, l. 3.
70. Ibid., l. 31.
71. Ibid., l. 7.
72. Z.L. Serebriakova, "Ottepel', zamorzki, ottepel'...," in *XX S"ezd: Materialy konferentsii k 40-letiiu XX S"ezda KPSS* Gorbachev Fund, February 22, 1996 (Moscow: izdatel'stvo April 1985, 1996), p. 93.
73. Medevedev, transcript of Cohen interview, pp. 13-14.
74. Naumov, "K istorii...," p. 153.
75. V.P. Naumov, "N.S. Khrushchev i reabilitatsiia zhertv massovykh politicheskikh repressii," *Voprosy Istorii* 4 (1997): 31.
76. M.S. Gorbachev, "Vstupitel'noe slovo," *XX S"ezd: Materialy Konferentsii...,"* p. 6.
77. GARF, f. 9401, op. 2, d. 482, l. 69.
78. Barsukov, p. 175.
79. A.I. Kaufman, *Lagernyi Vrach: 16 let v Sovetskom Soiuze, vospominaniia zionista* (Tel Aviv: Izdatel'stvo AM OVED, 1973), p. 328.
80. Solzhenitsyn, pp. 489-90.
81. Ibid., p. 490.
82. Keep, *Last of the Empires*, p. 79, citing E. Nosov, "Kostriuma ne Aiova," in *Nikita Sergeevich Khrushchev: Materialy k biografii* (Moscow: Izdatel'stvo politicheskoi literatury, 1989), p. 98. Nosov goes on to assert that many returnees died soon after release because they were unable to adapt, alienated as they were from their families, from whom they were separated by barbed wire for the best years of their lives.
83. Some very poignant scenes from this first journey have been described in memoirs. Former prisoners were not only confronted with society, and vice-versa, but they were also confronted with themselves. In *Kino: Politika i Liudi (30-e gody)* (Moscow: Materik, 1995), for example, one ex-zek describes a touching scene from the train ride home: "In liberty we had the good fortune of riding in passenger trains. I went into the bathroom to clean up a bit. I am washing my face, and peering at me from the mirror is an unfamiliar old woman with short hair ... and a slight face. I was

frightened and ran out into the corridor, where an officer asked me: 'what's with you?' I pointed to the bathroom. There's some old woman in there. He opened the door—no one was there. And then I understood: that woman was I...."(p. 179).

84. GARF, f. 8131, op. 32, d. 4847, ll. 185-187.
85. Ibid., f. 9401, op. 2, d. 500, l. 319.
86. Ibid., f. 8131, op. 32, d. 4847, ll. 142-43.
87. Ibid., l. 144.
88. Ibid., l. 145.
89. "Vedomosti Verkhovnogo Soveta Soiuza Sovetskikh sotsialisticheskikh respublik," 20 September 1956, pp. 410-411.
90. GARF, f. 8131, op. 32, d. 4847, ll. 90, 198, 199.
91. Ibid., l. 201.
92. Memorial, f. 1, op. 1, d. 47, ll. 0008 3111 2027-28.
93. Ekaterina Ivanovna Murav'eva, GARF, f. 7523, op. 107, d. 184, l. 28.
94. *Izvestiia*, 13 September 1956, p. 3.
95. "My otstali navsegda," *Prizyv* (Vladimir), 7 June 1996, pp. 1-2.
96. Naumov, "N.S. Khrushchev i...," p. 33.
97. Aleksandr Georgievich Papovian, "Tematicheskii Obzor Dokumentov po istorii politicheskikh repressii v SSSR v 1956-1958 gg.," unpublished manuscript (diplomnaia rabota RGGU), Moscow, 1995, pp. 63-64.
98. Ibid., p. 64.
99. Ibid., p. 65.
100. Ibid., p. 66.
101. Nikita Petrov, lecture, Institute for Russian and East European Studies, University of Amsterdam, June 23, 1997. See N.P. Petrov, "Pervyi predsedatel' KGB General Ivan Serov," *Otechestvennaia Istoriia* 5 (1997): 37.
102. Papovian, p. 67. According to Memorial researchers this figure is 2,498 (A. Daniel', A. Roginskii, "Spravka o rezul'tatakh obobshcheniia sudebnoi praktiki po delam o kontrrevoliutsionnykh prestupleniiakh," *Memorial-Aspekt*, nos. 10-11, September, 1994).
103. Ibid., p. 111.
104. Letter to Stephen Cohen from Anton Antonov-Ovseenko, Iurii Larin, Anna Larina, October 5, 1984.
105. Naumov, "N.S. Khrushchev i...," p. 34.
106. Semën Vilenskii, interview held at his Moscow home, October 16, 1997.
107. Arsenii Roginskii, interview at Memorial headquarters, Moscow, April 26, 1996.
108. Ibid.
109. See Vladimir Voinovich, "The Questionnaire," *Radio Liberty Research*, October 5, 1984.
110. Memorial, f. 1, op. 1, d. 4088, l. 0028 2201 1896.
111. Maia Ulanovskaia, "Konets sroka - 1976 god," *Vremia i My* 10 (August, 1976): 170.
112. "Reabilitatsiia Vracha R.," materials from Antonov-Ovseenko sent to S. Cohen, April 3, 1980.
113. Nadezhda Mikhailovna Dabudek, "Donoschik: materialy semeinogo arkhiva," Memorial, f. 2, op. 1, d. 51, l. 1993 0511 0634.
114. M. Frenkin, response to Cohen questionnaire, (Jerusalem), October 29, 1983.
116. Nina Baital'skii, response to Cohen questionnaire, July, 1980.
117. *Voprosy Literatury* 12 (1964): 223-27.
118. The information on Lazutin's work was made available by Stephen Cohen, Princeton archive.

119. Ivan Lazutin, "Chernie Lebedi," *Baikal* 1 (1966): 88.
120. Ibid., pp. 95-105.
121. John Emerich Edward Dalberg-Acton, Letter to Bishop Mandell Creighton, April 5, 1887.
122. Memorial, f. 1, op. 1, d. 610, ll. 0011 0113 1396-1407.
123. Iurii Alekseevich Anokhin, response to questionnaire for this project, December 12, 1995.
124. Ulanovskaia, p. 176.
125. Nina Dmitrievna Zlenko, "Vospominaniia o bylom: avtobiograficheskaia povest'," chast' 3, 1960, 1989, Memorial, f. 2, op. 1, d. 66, l. 1993 0710 1058.
126. Iurii Aikhenval'd, *Po Grani Ostroi* (Munich: Echo Press, 1972), p. 54.
127. Sigmund Freud, "Wit and its Relation to the Unconscious," *The Basic Writings of Sigmund Freud* (New York: Random House, 1938).
128. See, for example, Vladimir Rybakov, "Vrag," *Vremia i My* 35 (1978): 66.
129. Lidiia Shatunovskaia, "Zagadka odnogo aresta," *Vremia i My* 5 (1976): 210.
130. Cohen, "The Victims Return," p. 12.
131. Memorial, f. 1, op. 1, d. 498, ll. 0011 0113 0422-24. See "Ekhali po nebu oblaka...," *Ogonëk*, no. 12 (March, 1991) for a portrait of Larisa's mother (Ol'ga Grigor'evna) and her artistic endeavors while in camp.
132. Bogoraz' family had clearly always taken an active stand against Soviet repression. On the 20th anniversary of the Moscow Helsinki group, Larisa Bogoraz related the following exchange that she had had with Gorbachev. In a forum in which she was talking about Soviet abuses of human rights, Gorbachev proudly quipped: "Who freed the political prisoners?." Bogoraz retorted: "I did." Moscow, May 13, 1996.
133. Iosif Bogoraz, *Otshchepenets* (Jerusalem: Stav, 1976), p. 5.
134. Ibid., p. 8.
135. Ibid., p. 14. The writer Mikhail Aleksandrovich Naritsa-Narymov was outwardly an "integrated" rehabilitated returnee, complete with job and security, but inwardly he never accepted such a deal. See "Delo Mikhaila Aleksandrovicha Naritsa-Narymova," *Grani* 51 (1962): 3-13.
136. See Harrison E. Salisbury, "Stalinist Purges Over 20 Years Left Wide Mark in All Sections of Soviet Society," *New York Times*, 3 October 1967, pp. 1, 18.
137. Cohen, "The Victims Return," p. 11.
138. See "Ostalsia Bolshevikom: Leonidu Petrovichu Serebriakovu 11 iiunia 1988 goda ispolnilos' by sto let. On ne prozhil i poloviny etogo sroka," *Sotsialisticheskaia Industriia*, 10 June 1988, p. 3.
139. Zoria Leonidovna Serebriakova, interview held at her dacha outside of Moscow, November 29, 1996.
140. Id., interview.
141. Id., "Ottepel', zamorzki, ottepel'...," p. 91.
142. Id., interview.
143. Khrushchev personally intervened on behalf of individuals like Ol'ga Shatunovskaia. She, in turn, assisted others (materials on rehabilitation from Antonov-Ovseenko to Stephen Cohen, complete with the instruction not to publish during the lifetime of 'O.G.Sh.').
144. Edvard Frantsevich Kondrat'ev, Memorial, f. 1, op. 1, d. 2333, ll. 0020 2712 0430-443.
145. Vladlen Terent'evich Loginov, interview held at Serebriakova's dacha outside of Moscow, November 29, 1996.
146. See M. Dereeva, "Za polbykhanki rzhanogo: prodali razvaliukhu moego rasstreliannogo ottsa, poka ia sobirala spravki na vozvrat konfiskovannogo nasledstva," *Rossiiskaia Gazeta*, 11 November 1995.

147. GARF, f. 8131, op. 32, d. 4847, l. 139.
148. Elena Petrovna Smaglenko, "Vospominaniia," Memorial, f. 2, op. 1, d. 111, l. 0007 3111 0137.
149. Comments of a rehabilitated person, materials given to Stephen Cohen by Roy Medvedev, early eighties. See also Bondarevskii, p. 118.
150. GARF, f. 7523, op. 107, d. 123, l. 49 (ob).
151. Zinaida Davidovna Usova, "ChSIR: Vospominaniia," Memorial, f. 2, op. 1, d. 118, l. 0007 3111 1087.
152. GARF, f. 7733, op. 45, d. 520, ll. 1-123. The fact that the 1956 correspondence of the USSR Ministry of Finance regarding such issues fills over thirty-two volumes attests to the enormity of the problem.
153. Ibid., d. 184, ll. 26-31.
154. GARF, f. 8131, op. 32, d. 4847, ll. 195-97.
155. GARF, f. 7523, op. 107, d. 74, ll. 4, 99-14, 19-22, 24, 25.
156. Memorial, f. 1, op. 1, d. 1136, ll. 0014 0712 0607, 608, 619-22, 624, 625, 634-37, 646, 647, 653, 654, 677-79.
157. GARF, f. 7523, op. 107, d. 136, l. 100.
158. Ibid., ll. 95, 99.
159. *Pravda*, 12 and 15 July 1956.
160. R.D. Rakhunov, "Dokazatel'stvennoe znachenie priznaniia obviniaemogo po sovetskomu ugolovnomu protsessu," *Sovetskoe Gosudarstvo i Pravo* 8 (1956): 34.
161. V.N. Zemskov, "Massovoe osvobozhdenie spetsposelentsev i ssyl'nykh (1954-1960)," *Sotsiologicheskie Issledovaniia* 1 (1991): 16. See also pp. 14, 15, and 18.
162. Michel Heller and Aleksandr Nekrich, *Utopia in Power* (London: Hutchinson, 1986), pp. 534-535. See also "'Punished Peoples' of the Soviet Union: The Continuing Legacy of Stalin's Deportations," *A Helsinki Watch Report*, New York, September 1991.
163. *Istochnik* 4 (1997): 49.
164. "Decree Removes Stigma from Volga Germans," *Current Digest of the Soviet Press*, 27 January 1965, p. 13.
165. See Alan Fisher, "The Crimean Tatars: A Struggle for Survival," *Inquiry*, January 7 - 21, 1980, pp. 20-23.
166. In a sign of full official recognition, the anniversary of Pëtr Grigorenko's ninetieth birthday was commemorated in the 'House of the Russian Army' on October 16, 1997. Speakers included the human rights activist Liudmila Alekseeva, and Grigorenko's son, Andrei Petrovich who came to Moscow from New York for the presentation of Grigorenko's memoirs on this occasion. In addition to speaking about his father's life and struggle for human rights (which ended in New York), Andrei Petrovich voiced a plea in support of more humane conditions for the impoverished Russian armed forces.
167. GARF, f. 9401, op. 2, d. 500, l. 316.
168. *Vedomosti Verkhovnogo Soveta SSSR* 24 (891), November 6, 1957, pp. 694-695.
169. GARF, f. 9401, op. 2, d. 500, l. 318.
170. Davies, *Soviet History in the Yeltsin Era*, p. 184.
171. GARF, f. 9401, op. 2, d. 497, ll. 335, 337.
172. Arsenii Roginskii, Nikita Okhotin, "About Various Sources on the History of the Dissident Movement," speech, Moscow, August 26, 1992.
173. Nikolai Aleksandrovich Zhikharev, *Ocherki istorii severo-vostoka RSFSR (1917-1953)* (Magadan: Magadanskoe knizhnoe izdatel'stvo, 1961), p. 212.
174. *Istoricheskaia Khronika Magadanskoi oblasti: sobytiia i fakty, 1917-1972* (Magadan: Magadanskoe knizhnoe izdatel'stvo, 1975), p. 198. See also *Vremia, sobytiia, liudi*

5 volumes (Magadan: Magadanskoe knizhnoe izdatel'stvo, 1967, 1968, 1970, 1973, 1983) for occasional references to camp labor.

175. *Industrial'noe Razvitie Sibiri v gody poslevoennykh piatiletok (1946-1960)* (Novosibirsk: Izdatel'stvo Nauka, Sibirskoe otdelenie, 1982), pp. 213-222.

176. V.V. Shmidt, *Novoe prikhodit v lesoseky* (Perm: Perm'skoe knizhnoe izdatel'stvo, 1963).

177. V.S. Pustovoit (ed.), *Handbook of Selection and Seed Growing of Oil Plants* (Moscow: Izdatel'stvo "Kolos," 1967).

178. "Sud Narodov," *Novyi Mir* 6 (June, 1961): 274.

179. Heller and Nekrich, p. 597.

180. *Current Digest of the Soviet Press, Current Soviet Policies IV. The Documentary Record of the 22nd Congress of the Communist Party of the Soviet Union* (New York: Columbia University Press, 1962), p. 215.

181. Medvedev, Cohen interview, p. 30. See also Van Goudoever.

182. In 1963 prisoners in the camps were allowed to read *Ivan Denisovich*. For their reactions, see Leonid Sitko, "Dubrovlag pri Khrushcheve," *Novyi Mir* 10 (1997): 160.

183. Cohen, *Rethinking the Soviet Experience*, p. 115.

184. These terms were used in the title of an article by V. Lakshin in *Novyi Mir* 1 (January 1964): 223-245.

185. "My ostalis' liud'mi," *Kazakhstanskaia Pravda*, 6 October 1963, p. 4.

186. Barry Lewis and Michael Ulman, "The Soviet Concise Literary Encyclopedia: Its Evolution and Achievement," *Slavic Review* 39, no. 1 (March 1980): 109, 104-110.

187. Ibid., p. 108.

188. Aleksandr Chachulin, response to Cohen questionnaire.

189. Cohen, *Rethinking*, p. 121.

190. Davies, p. 213.

6

The Effect of Repression and Readaptation on Both the Returnees and the Political System

Thus far we have explored the nature of the terror, the experiences of early and late return, the passive aggressive behavior of the Procuracy and other officials, the psychological and moral impact of repression, the practical problems, that is, living and working conditions, attendant to reassimilation, and the discrepancy between official policy and unofficial practice with regard to returnees. Throughout this discussion we have presented evidence of the system's dependence on and adaptation to repression. Moreover, the fact that the persecution of returnees continued even after the putative reforms of the XX Party Congress indicates that repression and the threat of repression were still used by the Soviet regime as maintenance tools and as a prophylaxis.

Considering all of the personal, social, and ideological frustrations endured by those who had survived the Gulag, the subsequent allegiance to the Party by some of them is counter- intuitive. That allegiance was displayed by their motivation and efforts to gain reinstatement in the Communist Party. The behaviors of this group spanned the spectrum from those who died singing Stalin's praises and ex-zeks who waxed poetic about the restoration of their Party membership, to those who merely sought career advancement. As would be expected, different people sought Party rehabilitation for different reasons. Their motivations included fear of persecution, a conviction in the rightness of the system, the practical necessity for social adaptation, and the belief that only when the *Partbilet* (Party membership card) was returned would their rights be fully restored. For balance, it should be noted that some returning zeks made no request for rehabilitation, because they wanted nothing more to do with the Soviet system. Many of their later rehabilitation appeals resulted from the circumstance that they changed their minds as the political situation began to change in 1989.[1]

In considering the impact of the policy of repression on the political system it is relevant to examine the impact that the returning Stalinist-era zeks had on dissidents or the dissident movement. It might have been expected that many ex-prisoners would have been so politicized by the camp experience that they consequently challenged the legitimacy of the Soviet system in the form of protest (i.e., active dissidence). This expectation was only partially realized. Returnees of the fifties as well as dissidents of the sixties have described themselves as constituting two completely separate groups, with separate histories and separate agendas.[2] This is not entirely correct because there was considerable overlap between the groups. While not all returnees became dissidents, a number of them did, and it also happened that the children and grandchildren of some returnees became dissidents and human rights activists. Still, there were other survivors who became Party activists, and their children followed in their footsteps. The vicissitudes of the returnees can be most clearly illustrated by examining some of their individual stories.

Fear, Belief, and Disillusionment

Iosif Bogoraz

It might seem that one could infer the sentiment of individuals toward the Soviet system by noting their attitude toward Party membership, but in a repressive system that deduction could be misleading. Iosif Aronovich Bogoraz was arrested on charges of Trotskyism and spent from 1936-1957 in camps or exile.[3] Upon release he was rehabilitated, and he applied for and was granted reinstatement in the Party. Considering his history of incarceration and his later activities, which included writing such works as *Otshchepenets* (see chapter 5), published in samizdat, one wonders what impelled him to rejoin the Party.

On a cold Moscow night in the late 1990s, at a gathering reminiscent of the atmosphere of the dissident era, this question was raised with his grandson, Aleksandr Daniel, who runs a Memorial project covering the dissident movement from the fifties to the eighties. After agreeing that his grandfather's behavior was puzzling, Daniel accounted for it by explaining that Iosif Bogoraz was not motivated by a desire to support the Party, but rather by a fear of the consequences of not requesting reinstatement. The official ideology at the time dictated that everyone was supposed to want to be part of the Communist Party. Added to this pressure was the fact that Bogoraz was also weary of fighting against the persistent impediments that resulted from his not having the legal status of Party rehabilitation. According to Daniel, his grandfather's new-found Party membership did not last long. Bogoraz left the Party in the early seventies.

(The political course of the next generation tells its own compelling story of what resulted from the convergence of returnees with dissidents. Bogoraz' daughter [and Daniel's mother], Larisa, true to her heritage, went on to become a major dissident and human rights activist. She was also first married to Yuli Daniel and then to Anatoly Marchenko, two well-known dissidents [see chapter 5].)

Present at this gathering was also another former dissident, Andrey Grigorenko, son of General Pyotr Grigorenko whose own dissident activities resulted first in his internal exile, then in his incarceration in a Soviet psychiatric hospital, and finally in his expatriation to New York. Andrey Petrovich concurred with Daniel's assessment that fear was a primary motivating factor for many returnees. Still, as Arseny Roginsky correctly pointed out, the memoirs do not tend to reflect this sentiment.[4] In fact, the writings of many returnees profess a genuine desire for reinstatement on ideological grounds.

Lev Kopelev

Lev Kopelev received a ten-year term of incarceration in the wave of postwar repressions of the military, and then was released and rehabilitated in 1956. He was restored to Party membership in 1957.[5] Kopelev and his wife Raisa Orlova, also a dissident, continued to believe in the "healthy socialist nature of society," and thought that the illness of the cult of personality could be cured.[6] In his memoirs Kopelev rationalizes his (earlier) steadfast stance, "my Party, right or wrong," by recalling that he had always been an honest communist.[7] Elsewhere he claims that "none of us returnees felt the need for revenge,"[8] an attitude that is consistent with his early attempts to work within the Party. He and his wife were initially convinced that the reform movement of the Soviet system was irreversible.[9] In 1964

Kopelev wrote, "the movement begun by the XX and XXII Party Congresses could not be stopped ... liberated thoughts and awakened consciousness would not permit a return to Stalinism."[10] He was wrong.

Early on, it might have been apparent to Kopelev that in spite of official pronouncements to the contrary, governmental behavior had not changed in any significant way. For example, at a spring 1956 meeting of translators and critics, his recommendation that Kafka be published was considered strange and inappropriate.[11] (Kafka's depictions of the robotic tyranny of bureaucracy were always a little too close to the Soviet Communist reality for political comfort.) Things did improve, though. What Kopelev could not do for Kafka he did for Solzhenitsyn by promoting the publication of *Ivan Denisovich*.[12] These two former campmates shared a similar political history. Indeed, Solzhenitsyn's character, Lev Rubin, in *The First Circle* was based on Kopelev. Because of their opposition to the governing policies, they were also to share a similar political future.

Up until the mid-sixties, Kopelev tried to maintain his faith in the reform movement, but the Brodsky affair and the trial of Sinyavsky and Daniel changed his thinking. Then, in May of 1968 his "hopes of thaw" were decisively crushed when he was expelled from the Party, ironically, for expressing his fears about a return to Stalinism.[13] Indeed, this and subsequent actions confirmed his fears. In short order, he was fired from his job and no longer permitted to publish, even though his works at the time were primarily translations of German literature. Kopelev's petitions for the freedom of Aleksandr Solzhenitsyn and Andrey Sakharov further jeopardized his standing with the government, and he was expelled from the official Writer's Union in 1977. By then he reluctantly came to realize that the absolute power wielded by the Communist Party was inherently corrupt, that it stifled self-correction, and that it led inevitably to repression, mass arrests, and the camps. The system was at fault and so, too, were those who helped construct it. In a 1979 interview Kopelev expressed this rueful sentiment: "The more I thought things over, the more I became convinced that we had embarked on the wrong road from the very beginning, that the way things turned out was not only Stalin's fault but mine, ours."[14]

No longer willing to support the regime, Kopelev was pushed to the periphery of Soviet society. After the returnee-dissident emigrated to West Germany in 1980, he was stripped of his Soviet citizenship in 1981.[15] In the West, Kopelev remained true to his former countrymen while actively opposing the system under which they still lived. He supported fellow human rights campaigners by helping translate and publish dissident East European writers. In 1990 he participated in the Henrich Böll Stiftung's cooperation programs with Memorial.[16]

Still, there were among ex-prisoners those who continued to believe in the system. Some of them fared better than Kopelev. Some of the returnees who were restored to Party membership were elevated to prominence, and were subsequently used by the regime for propaganda purposes to counter such figures as Solzhenitsyn and the forces that were released by *Ivan Denisovich*. Galina Serebryakova, who spent twenty-one years in Siberia, is cited by one author as "one of the regime's pawns in the tragicomedy of the aftermath of the Stalinist camp system."[17] Rather than addressing her incarceration by the Stalinist (Soviet) system, Serebryakova instead focused on her release and praised the "Leninist Central Committee" for her liberation. In an article in *Molodaya Gvardiya* in 1964 she gushed, "of course I am in love with my time, with my generation. Practically every day new cities and waterways emerge, important scientific discoveries are taking place.... New relationships between people are developing, the new man of the communistic tomorrow."[18]

Those returnees who praised the Party were the most useful for propaganda purposes—for Khrushchev and for the regime that long outlasted his reign. Such ex-prisoners as Dora Lazurkina, who attested to her belief in the Leninist cause at the XXII Party Congress, provided especially effective propaganda support for the Party. If ex-prisoners could still profess faith in the system after everything that they had endured, so reasoned the ideologues, then the system must really be good. In 1962 *Izvestiya* published a poem written two years earlier and dedicated to the "beloved Party." Its author, Sofiya Dalnyaya, had been arrested in 1937 and spent nearly twenty years in prisons and camps.[19] The poem's theme was that the Bolsheviks had been successful in their struggle to become a world force. Poetry expressing the joys of the restoration of Party membership can even be found in the Memorial memoirs, an unlikely place in which to praise the regime. These expressions were quite probably heartfelt, since this is a non-public-oriented venue.

Pyotr Yakir

The story of Pyotr Yakir, in contrast to many of the biographies presented in this work, is rather well known. It is, however, a unique and tragic tale of the effect that repression can have on the returnees' political views, their physical health, and their emotional stability, and will therefore be included in our examination. Pyotr's father, Iona, was a celebrated Red Army commander who was shot in 1937 as an "enemy of the people." Iona Yakir's last words before his execution were reportedly "Long live Stalin!"[20] We will never know whether he was expressing his true belief in the leader, simply hailing the system with a customary expression, or protecting his surviving, incarcerated family. It may be that he died still believing in the Soviet system that he had helped to construct. It is unlikely, however, that, as a high military man, Iona Yakir would have been unaware of Stalin's role (or for that matter his own) in the terror.

Also in 1937, the same year that his father was executed, Pyotr Yakir, then age fourteen, was arrested as a "socially dangerous element." He was forced to grow up in the Gulag—spending the next seventeen years in orphanages, prisons, camps, and exile.[21] After Stalin's death, he and his parents were eventually rehabilitated. Iona's rehabilitation was posthumous. Pyotr's history caught Khrushchev's attention, and he even referred to the fate of the executed general's son at the XXII Party Congress. Pyotr was subsequently to become one of "Khrushchev's zeks," that is, a returnee who received privileges, and was used for propaganda purposes to promote Khrushchev's de-Stalinization campaign. He was given a post at the Institute of History[22] and offered a good apartment in Moscow.[23]

By 1969, however, concern over the emergence of neo-Stalinism compelled Pyotr to actively support the dissident movement. Yakir wrote a letter to the Party journal *Kommunist* in which he outlined all of the crimes of which Stalin would have been guilty under Soviet law, concluding that Stalin was one of the greatest criminals of the century. Thereafter, as he continued his human rights campaigning, he was subjected to increasing harassment by the KGB. Still vivid in his mind was the nightmare of an adolescence and young adulthood spent in the camps. The fear of arrest constantly plagued him.[24] Finally, the inevitable did happen; Pyotr Yakir was arrested in 1972.

His testimony, together with that of Viktor Krasin, provided the KGB with more than 200 names of fellow dissidents. In addition to the consequences that these disclosures had on the individual lives of the targeted dissidents, the dissident movement itself suffered a setback because the KGB was able to force the suspension of an important underground journal of human rights activities—*Khronika Tekushchikh Sobytii)* (The Chronicle of Current Events).

At his 1973 trial Pyotr Yakir pleaded guilty to charges of "anti-Soviet agitation and propaganda." This returnee's last words to the court were "I do not want to die in prison."[25] In exchange for his cooperation, he received a reduced sentence of three years of incarceration, and three years of internal exile. He was pardoned after one year. After liberation, Yakir was unable to pursue his profession, because he had become physically debilitated as a result of alcohol abuse. Nor could he return to his former friends or to human rights activities. Pyotr Yakir, a consummate victim of the Soviet system of terror, lost his father, his youth, his friends, his integrity, his self-esteem, and his health. Broken in body and spirit, he died in 1982. Pyotr's personal and political trajectory provide a microcosm of the repressive times in which he lived.

In the post-Soviet era, Pyotr's life and fate could be reevaluated in light of what was learned about the treacherous workings of the system. A 1995 article in the journal *Kengir*, written by L.P. Petrovsky, former dissident and grandson of an "Old Bolshevik," argues in favor of posthumously conferring the degree of Candidate of Historical Sciences on Yakir, who was never given the opportunity to defend his completed dissertation. The author further supports granting an honorary diploma to Pyotr's daughter Irina, also a former dissident, who was not readmitted to the Historical Archive Institute.[26] The story of the Yakirs demonstrates the intergenerational reach of the Soviet political system—from Iona, a general who helped fight for it, to Pyotr, a historian who believed, however briefly, that it might work, to Irina who experienced her own share of KGB harassment for her work on the *Khronika*. The saga of this family also illustrates the Soviet system's reliance on ruthless repression as a maintenance tool. The system betrayed the trust of its early architects and disillusioned its most passionate believers. Little wonder that it was weakened by lack of support.

Ruf Bonner

The Bonners are another family whose early commitment to socialism ended in disillusionment. Ruf Bonner, Yelena Bonner's mother and Andrey Sakharov's mother-in-law, grew up in a family so devoted to the revolutionary cause that they chose to live in an exile town in eastern Siberia in order to be close to relatives incarcerated in Tsarist prison camps. She went to Moscow as a teenager in 1917 to support the Bolshevik revolution, joined the Red Army in the Civil War, and later worked at the Institute of Marxism. Ruf was arrested in 1937 and spent seventeen years in camps and internal exile. Her husband, Gevork Alikhanov, was a highly placed Comintern official who was arrested and executed.[27] Ruf's daughter (and Alikhanov's step-daughter), Yelena, despite her status as the daughter of a "traitor to the motherland" was accepted as a volunteer to defend the country in the "Great Patriotic War." Both mother and daughter were rehabilitated after Stalin's death. Subsequently, Mikoyan arranged for medical treatment for Yelena's war wounds (an eye injury), and provided a good apartment for Ruf. In anticipation of a new political thaw following Khrushchev's overthrow, Yelena joined the Communist Party in 1964. That thaw did not materialize.

The Soviet tanks that rolled into Prague in 1968 dispelled the Bonner family's belief in humane socialism. As Ruf recalled "for people with social sentiment, it caused a complete crushing of all hope for any change from within. They had to seek something outside of the system [i.e., the dissident movement]."[28] Ruf Bonner asserted in a 1984 interview that when the Kremlin retreated from de-Stalinization, many returnees fell silent, but those who continued their criticism became the earliest dissidents. Her own family's political history reflected the erosion of faith in Communism caused by the Soviet system's continued dependence on repression. Even as she spoke, her son-in-law Andrey Sakharov was on a hunger strike in internal exile while her daughter, Yelena, struggled to obtain travel permission for medical treatment in the West. (In recognition of the contributions of Sakharov to the dissident movement, he was later to become the honorary chairman of Memorial.)

Builders of Socialism

A number of returnees maintained a "parental" faith in the Soviet system because they had participated in constructing it. Ideologically committed Party members[29] could use their enduring belief in the Communist Party that they helped build as a source of solace to help them bear the deprivations of the camps. More altruistically, some even considered their camp labor to be a direct contribution to the Party's welfare. One ex-prisoner, who served thirteen and a half years of a fifteen-year sentence, described his sentiments thus:

> Right up until 1951 I manually extracted so many precious metals that I could have become a multi-millionaire. That is my contribution to the communist system. But the most important factor that secured my survival in those harsh conditions was my unflinching, ineradicable belief in our Leninist party, in its humanist [!] principles. It was the Party that imparted the physical strength to withstand these trials. [The Party] nourished the brain, [and our] consciousness, helped us fight. Reinstatement in the ranks of my native Communist Party was the greatest happiness of my entire life!"[30]

Numerous camp memoirs contain similar declarations couched in similarly laudatory phrases, extolling patriotism to the motherland and loyalty to the Party. Witness the final sentence of a short autobiography written in 1967 by a female returnee who had spent from 1937-1954 in camps and exile: "during all the years of prison I never lost faith in our Great Communist Party and hopes for restoration of the truth and my good name as a communist and as a fighter for the Soviet regime."[31] She was reinstated in the Party in 1956.[32]

One returnee memoirist describes how another ex-zek even waxed nostalgic about his camp experience: "in recent years Leonid Artyemevich lives in Kislovodsk and, like all the Norilskians from that time, always remembers with a sense of sorrow and patriotic pride the years he spent in this city, where his labor went into every meter of the street and every building."[33] (A contrasting view is presented by the grim statement of some returnees that these frozen, inhospitable Arctic cities were literally "built on top of prisoners' bones."[34])

It is easy to understand why people who have been repressed by a system turn away from it. One such returnee referred to ex-prisoners who maintained their belief in the Party as "maniacs."[35] But the continued and sometimes reinvigorated commitment of those who have been imprisoned seems paradoxical. From a common-sense point of view, it would seem that a political system should deliver on its political promises and if it does not, faith in that system should be abandoned. However, as the endorsements above attest, allegiance to a belief system can have deep non-rational (not irrational) roots which have little to do with political promises kept. The emotional

satisfactions attendant to membership in a belief system may be un-
related to material outcomes.

Indeed, people may persist in supporting a system that oversees
their physical suffering so long as it provides them with a sense of
meaning, an apparently essential ingredient for the quality of life.[36]
For many idealists, the Communist Party was the only institution
that provided their lives with a sense of meaning. In other countries
this sense of meaning could be provided by the institution of religion—another act of faith that does not depend on good material or
political outcomes for continued devotion. Once one accepts the
assumptions of a belief system—such as the conviction that God or
Communism is good, then everything that subsequently happens
can be interpreted to support it. Organized religion, which is the
most widespread institution for providing meaning to people's lives,
had been systematically debilitated by the Soviet state, leaving the
field of "meaning" to the Party.[37]

At root, comprehensive belief systems such as religion and communism provide two psychosocial essentials: a conceptual framework for making events meaningful and a supportive social group—
actual or imaginary.[38] After the Holocaust, many people questioned
the existence or the nature of God, but in spite of this cataclysmic
event, many, although not all, persisted in believing in the existence
of a force larger than themselves that they entrusted to govern them.
As Viktor Frankl argued, people cannot live in a world that they
consider meaningless.[39]

Once a belief system comes to satisfy the need for meaning, that
system cannot easily be given up, even if its adherents suffer hardship under it, and maybe especially if they suffer hardship, because
the hardship may make people even more needy. For ex-zeks as
well as for the Soviet citizenry in general, there were not many alternative systems of meaning to which they could legitimately sub-
scribe. Therefore, even when the Communist Party could be seen as
the overseer of so much individual and mass misfortune, it could
still be perceived as a transcendent force that provided a set of guidelines for living and a package of material and social benefits that
could accompany the status of being a good Communist.[40] Moreover, when a Party controls its members' social lives, livelihood,
physical existence, and the panhuman need for "meaning," it is difficult to challenge.

Other sources of reinforcement for hewing to the Party line were the thick journals of the sixties.[41] They propagated "heroic epoch" tales which extolled the virtue of victims of the terror who, despite it all, "returned home having preserved the flame of their devotion to the revolution."[42] What is largely absent from these devotional accounts is a critical examination of what it was that these victims were preserving, and how disparate the modus operandi of the Soviet system was from the ideals of its founders as well as the ideology putatively espoused by its leaders.

For believers, if there was any reason to assign blame, the blame was directed at individuals such as Yezhov or Beria or Stalin, viewing their behavior as an abrogation of the "humanist principles" of socialism on which the Soviet Union was supposedly based. It is true that such individuals did contribute to, and were responsible for their role in the terror. However, it is also true that the system of government was indeed responsive not to the governed but only to the governors. Under these circumstances, there was no accountability to the citizenry and governmental repression became an integral part of the system.

While the continued devotion of some returnees to the Communist Party was something akin to religious faith, it still required reinforcement. Convictions of Party loyalty were exploited wherever possible. The Soviet propaganda machine persistently extolled the virtues of the "builders of communism." In 1959 *Pravda* published a number of letters on "awakening benevolence and consciousness in the builders of communism." According to the Khrushchev Files, active discussions of these letters were promoted in the correctional labor institutions. We do not know how assertive the prison authorities were in encouraging prisoners to write politically correct responses, but we can assume from other prison practices that they were under some pressure to do so. The Ministry of Internal Affairs used selected responses of prisoners for propaganda purposes. These responses were reported to the Council of Ministers and to the editor in chief of *Pravda*. One [criminal] prisoner's statement includes the following text about how they were still full Soviet citizens despite their physical status:

...If you are a Soviet citizen, then you remain a Soviet citizen under any conditions and you can always make your contribution to the construction of Communism. The letters published in *Pravda* ... inspire me to work even better, give me the assurance that after liberation I will be able to find work, and if I have any trouble, I will go to Party and Soviet organizations, they will help me.[43]

Assuming this was not coerced—in itself an act of faith—it would be another example of the cruel disappointments that lay ahead for ex-zeks (political or criminal). We have seen how little help and how many impediments they experienced from the Party and other Soviet organizations. Still, if we are to accept this statement as an authentic attestation of loyalty, then we must understand it as part hope, part faith, and part practical accommodation.

Party Membership as Social Status

Despite their anti-Stalinist sentiments and hostility toward the Soviet system, some ex-prisoners and children of ex-prisoners sought Communist Party membership or reinstatement as a means of reassimilating into Soviet society. For those with a stigmatized personal or family history, membership in the CPSU was instrumental to career advancement.

Andrey N. Sakharov

Professor Andrey Nikolaevich Sakharov, who rose to the position of director of the Institute of Russian History of the Russian Academy of Sciences, was the son of an "enemy of the people." Other members of Sakharov's family also had a history of repression. His grandfather, a poor village clergyman who resided in the church, had been arrested and executed in 1937. Sakharov's father had studied at a seminary before the revolution, and was later trained as a social scientist. At the end of the twenties, however, it became apparent that people who were in any way connected to pre-revolutionary Russian ways of life, or, like his family, had suspect backgrounds, were particularly vulnerable to persecution. So Sakharov's father retrained himself for a profession that seemed more neutral. He became an engineer. Even so, as the son of an executed priest, he began to have problems with the authorities at the end of the thirties. According to Andrey Nikolaevich, the person responsible for informing on his father was someone who was motivated by a romantic interest in his mother.[44] It was not uncommon for people to turn their friends and neighbors over to the authorities for personal as well as political motives. The co-opting of spouses ranked high on the motivation list, along with the opportunistic acquisition of jobs and apartments. Sakharov's father was arrested in 1940.

The family who stayed behind—Andrey, his brother, and his mother—suffered all the usual restrictions imposed on relatives of an "enemy of the people." They were not permitted to live in any big cities, the three of them had to share one room, his mother was excluded from the Party, and she had trouble finding or keeping a job as a history teacher. Sakharov's father survived the camps and was liberated in the wave of postwar releases. After release, he worked as an engineer in a small town in the province of Gorky where many other ex-zeks resided. Sakharov noted that his father did not seek Party membership, since he no longer needed to advance in his career and apparently felt no particular allegiance to the CPSU.[45] It is also doubtful that he would have had the option of Party membership at that time.

In spite of his superior qualifications, Andrey Nikolaevich had difficulty gaining admission to Moscow State University in 1948. Even after he got in, he had trouble staying in and advancing in his studies. Despite a perfect grade point average, he had to wage a battle for acceptance as a graduate student in the history department, because his father was an ex-zek. This same stigmatized family history foreclosed Andrey Nikolaevich's ability to join the Party. This was important to his career because Party membership was a necessary prerequisite to getting into the Academy of Sciences and getting a good job as a historian. In spite of these obstacles, he managed to complete his studies. When Stalin died the situation improved for Sakharov and his family. His father was rehabilitated in 1956-57 and Andrey was permitted to join the Party under Khrushchev.

Despite the impediments associated with his family background, Andrey Nikolaevich Sakharov was successful in climbing the career ladder, and eventually rose to a very prestigious position in his field. In fact, he was one of the few who was able to succeed in spite of the pervasive social and political handicaps imposed on the repressed and their families.[46] We should note that while Sakharov suffered from the social and political consequences of a stigmatized family history, he did not have the additional social burden of being himself an ex-prisoner.

Sakharov claims that he lost his belief in the system during the regime of Brezhnev. In a 1997 interview, Sakharov said that he concluded that the system should have been set up by the elite leaders of society, that is, the intelligentsia. (Though Lenin was a member of the intelligentsia, Sakharov apparently did not consider him a good example.) They might have cultivated better instincts in people. Instead it was created by Lenin, who was essentially no different than Stalin. They were equally ruthless. Furthermore, while the repressive system had been created by Lenin, it was implemented by hordes of self-serving bureaucrats, and it found an excellent breeding ground in the mentality of the people. Instead of stimulating the development of the best qualities of people, the historian maintained, the Soviet system brought out the worst in them.

In essence, Sakharov asserted, the Soviet system was adapted to the people, but it maintained itself not just by repression but by misshaping its citizens to adapt to repression. The state encouraged people who were struggling for apartments and jobs to cultivate their most selfish and vile tendencies. Thus the culpability for massive repression lay not just with the Party or with Stalin, but with the millions of impoverished, ill-informed individuals who rose to positions of authority, and with the workers and peasants from the countryside who aspired to live like the people in the cities. He did not quarrel with their aspirations but with their methods. They had been indoctrinated to mistakenly believe that they could improve their lives by destroying others. Sakharov went on to observe,

> In Russia a man's life was cheap ... today you can kill a priest, a nobleman, an entrepreneur, tomorrow [that same system will lead you to] inform on your friend, and on your comrade ... the mentality of the people played an integral part in this repressive apparatus, they never learned the system of respect for the individual that is necessary to setting up a civil society and rule of law state.[47]

Sakharov's perspectives on the nature of the system gain credence from his position as a student of history and from his own family's history. His post-Soviet reflections and condemnation of the system should, however, be considered in light of how much and how well he would have had to accommodate to that system in order to ultimately reach one of the highest academic ranks in the country in his field. These views are now politically correct. Sakharov could not have ascended to his present position unless his previous views were also politically correct for the previous times.

Memorial and Vozvrashchenie

In the mid-nineties, questionnaires for this project were administered to people who had some connection to the organizations Memorial and/or Vozvrashchenie. In response to the question of whether they had ever been members of the Communist Party of the Soviet Union, approximately 75 percent of the respondents answered with an emphatic "No, never."[48] While these post-Soviet responses may not necessarily have been truthful with regard to the past, at the very least, they represented present sentiments that were clearly anti-Party. Those in the survey who admitted to having been members of the Party said that they had been primarily motivated by "self-preservation," that is, fear of the consequences for not accommodating to the system. As one ex-zek explained, he rejoined the Party, "because adaptation would have been even harder without it."[49]

"Full-Fledged Citizens"

Arseny Roginsky, historian, ex-dissident, and chairman of Memorial's Scientific Research Center cautioned that the requests for reinstatement in the CPSU by the returning zeks of the fifties should not be misinterpreted as evidence of mass loyalty to Communist ideology. Nor did questions of ideology particularly interest the applicants. Such requests were often attempts to achieve an otherwise unobtainable social status. Only after the restoration of Party membership could one participate in Party meetings and would one's rights (along with *lgoty*—the privileges that constituted the material expression of rehabilitation) be truly restored.[50] This sentiment is reflected in a number of the memoirs with phrases like, "only after I got Party membership did I feel like a full-fledged citizen of my motherland!"[51] The power to grant or withhold privileges proved to be an effective way of forcing support of the Party.

For some ex-zeks, CPSU membership was connected not just with their external social status, but with their pride and their sense of self. Consider the case of Anna Larina, Bukharin's widow, whose determined struggle for her husband's party rehabilitation continued into the Gorbachev era.[52] Ordinary citizens were similarly motivated. One ex-prisoner in Norilsk, for example, recounted that after rehabilitation, his dismissal from work was overturned. Armed with his rehabilitated status and a job, he explained, "Now my biography became completely clean, and I could leave Norilsk to request Party reinstatement with a clear conscience."[53] As so often happened, this former prisoner's equation of a clear conscience with a clean political biography illustrates the hold that the political system had on the interior lives of its citizens. In the absence of viable competing institutions such as religion or rival political parties to validate the individual's self-esteem, the Party had a monopoly control over it.

A letter of gratitude to Khrushchev in 1959, published in *Pravda*, used this very public forum to convey a similar confirmation of the Party's ownership of social validation and, through it, individual self-esteem:

> I am not a [Party] member because 20 years ago, when I had already obtained recommendations for membership, my father was jailed. Now he has been posthumously rehabilitated. For this let me voice tremendous thanks to the Party and to you personally, the initiator of the review of many old cases. Even though it be posthumously, a man's memory has been cleared.... I am writing you the truth that I have told to no one (except my husband, before we linked our lives). I concealed this from people... From the time of my childhood Father did not live with us. None of my friends knew anything about him. But I did not join the Party. I could not mark my entrance into the Party with a lie. And who would have recommended me for membership if I had told the truth?[54]

The satisfaction connected with the restoration of Party membership sometimes required a degree of politically correct amnesia. The wife of an "enemy of the people" who spent twelve years in Akmolinsk described her sense of pride after receiving her husband's pension and (posthumous) Party reinstatement thus:

> I finally felt that I was a politically and civilly full-fledged person. Moreover, I was in a certain sense a "hero of the day." We rehabilitated persons were "elevated," we were given first place in line for living quarters, trips, financial assistance, etc.[55]

As her subsequent problems attest, the Party also developed a degree of amnesia for the benefits that it had promised to rehabilitated people. She goes on to admit that these benefits were short-lived. However, as often happens with a totalitarian mindset, she, like the state, blames the victims. Not only did the state betray its promise of benefits, but it faulted the victims for bringing this to their attention. This author opines that the change in attitude toward returnees can be attributed to "the immodesty and criticism of certain comrades" which ultimately had a negative effect. "Gradually we went 'out of fashion'. The Party and government still helped us, but not as readily as in the beginning. Having exposed the cult of personality of Stalin, the Party nevertheless acknowledged his achievements in the construction of socialism and especially his role in the Great Patriotic War."[56] This rehabilitated, reinstated returnee's memoirs were not to be found in the Memorial or Vozvrashchenie collections. She donated them to the Institute of Marxism-Leninism.

The Soviet invasion of Hungary in 1956 resulted in a major setback to the Party's prestige, at least among the critically minded. As one of the detractors put it, "the Party wasn't worth five kopecks after Hungary."[57] However, others were reappraising their country from a more differentiated perspective. In the late fifties and sixties, writers like Yevgeny Yevtushenko were trying to rekindle the revolutionary ideas of 1917 and promoting the point of view that while Stalin was bad, the Party was still good. Arseny Roginsky pointed out that "placing blame for mass repression on the system itself was only a later construct."[58]

In the fifties and sixties the ex-zeks and Party propagandists who preferred to focus on the "heroism of Communists" rather than on the repression of the communists greeted Khrushchev's efforts toward liberation with great enthusiasm. In turn, prominent Party and Komsomol returnees were accorded the status of heroes. These Party people focused on efforts to reform the political system and put aside the issue of how Stalin should be judged. Their criticism was directed at particular, correctable deficiencies in the system. Following Khrushchev's lead, individuals like Shatunovskaya and others maintained their loyalty to the Party, while still advocating reform. Their ideas were rejected by the conformists after Khrushchev's ouster.[59]

Party Membership Application in the Second Half of the Fifties

Not everyone who applied for Party membership or reinstatement received it. Among the requirements were: good recommendations from known Party members, a clean record (i.e., rehabilitation), timeliness of the application,[60] proof of work in local Party organizations, demonstrated loyalty, *partinost* (party-mindedness), and so on. At their discretion, Party officials could delay or block reinstatement on the grounds of long-term (in some cases eighteen years) absence from its ranks.[61] The officials were technically correct in holding that the applicant had not participated in Party life during

the years of incarceration, but considering the involuntary circumstances of their absence, the withholding of membership on these
grounds was an example of blatant discrimination against former
zeks.

A 1957 report of the Central Committee Party Control Commission covering the year 1956 states that 55.5 percent of the appeals
of individuals who were "excluded from the Party on unfounded
political accusations" were honored with reinstatement. From another statement that appeared in that same report, there is evidence
indicating that Party membership was withheld from applicants who
were deemed to be too critical of the Party's history. Witness the
reason for the following rejection:

> The Party Control Commission confirmed the exclusion from the CPSU of P.I.
> Gudzinsky (member of the CPSU since 1918), senior engineer ... who during a Party
> meeting where the conclusions of the XX Party Congress were being discussed, ex-
> pressed anti-Party revisionist sentiments. He slanderously asserted that in the course of
> thirty years the Party and the country experienced a [dark chapter] in the history of its
> development and that this history was not condemned at the XX Party Congress, that
> the report on the cult of personality at the XX Party Congress "doesn't teach the Party
> anything."[62]

Consistent with its history, the Party was continuing to respond to
the message by banishing the messenger. Moreover, even the status
of juridical rehabilitation did not help applicants who "during the
period of heated struggle with Trotskyites, Zinovievites ... actively
acted against the Party in defense of the opposition." Their exclusions were upheld.[63]

In some instances, when officials could not legitimately reject an
appeal, they found administrative means of postponing the process
of reinstatement. A 1957 inquiry into practices of the Party Control
Commission based on letters and declarations of workers revealed
that many appeals were "artificially delayed" in the *apparat* of the
Central Committee, because they were sent for implementation to
officials who were on business trips, were sick, or were on vacation.
In consequence, processing of these requests was delayed for long
periods of time. The same bureaucratic obstacles were used to impede appeals for assistance. This was a particularly egregious be-
trayal of the government's promises because sometimes these appeals came from rehabilitated victims who had been reinstated in
the Party, but needed help in arranging pensions or better living con-

ditions.[64] While such practices occur in every bureaucracy, their application to returnees is consistent with the passive-aggressive policy of the Soviet Procuracy in the early years of the rehabilitation process.

In spite of these obstacles, during the period following the XX Party congress, thousands of Party rehabilitations were applied for and granted. Between February 1956 and June 1961, according to a report of the Party Control Commission, 30,954 Communists, many posthumously, were reinstated. This group included Party and Komsomol leaders.[65] The same report undertakes to assess accountability for the apparently illegitimate exclusions. Not surprisingly, the focus was on *who* was to blame rather than *what* was to blame, that is, the system itself:

> Great responsibility for the massive exclusion from the Party of Communists based on flimsily falsified materials lies with the former staff of the ... Central Committee Party Control Commission. Materials of the Party Control Commission indicate that in the past, especially from 1936-1940, the Party Control Commission did not verify the grounds for the political accusations made against Party members, and basically, indiscriminately excluded them from the Party with the formulations: "enemy of the people," "counter-revolutionary," etc. In many cases the decision on exclusion from the Party was made on the basis of lists of arrestees sent by the NKVD.[66]

If there had to be a culprit in the system, the Party wanted it to be the NKVD.

Thus far we have explored a number of psychological and emotional reasons why former zeks would seek CPSU membership or reinstatement but put very simply and pragmatically, Party membership made Soviet life a lot easier. Roginsky pointed out how something as routine as filling out a questionnaire—a common Soviet requirement—rendered rehabilitated status (preferably with Party rehabilitation, that is, restored membership) particularly relevant. When applying for apartments or jobs, or for admission to the university, for example, applicants had to fill out forms detailing their personal history. Roginsky observes that this was a defining psychological event: "Just imagine the eternal instability that returnees felt every time they had to fill out a questionnaire ... their status was a little similar to that of being a Jew [a group against whom discrimination was the rule]."[67] A rehabilitation certificate or Party card could permit a returnee to avoid revealing the details of a stigmatized history. Arseny Roginsky spoke not only as a historian, but as a participant-observer. He could speak from experience.

The Effect of Repression on the Formation of a Dissident:
Arseny Roginsky

Arseny Borisovich Roginsky is the chairman of Memorial's Scientific Research Center, an authority on victims of Soviet terror, a former victim, and the son of a father who was a victim. The organization he heads is the most wide-reaching in representating victims. During our interview, conducted in 1996, he joked, "I should be a *lagernik* (camp inmate) in my blood, but I'm not."[68] In this and other statements, he denied that the camp was still a part of him. To the question of whether the returnees he met had significantly influenced his development, he answered "those old people [fifties returnees] who sat on the bench quietly singing Civil War songs in the apartment building courtyard when I was growing up had no effect on me at all." Furthermore, the subject of Stalinist repressions did not interest him at that time of his life. Let us examine his personal history in light of his assertion that this group's experiences did not influence his thoughts and actions with regard to the system.

Roginsky's father was a Jewish engineer and a Talmudic scholar. He was arrested in January 1938 and sentenced to six years in camp. While incarcerated he was able to do some work in his specialty as an electrical engineer. He served eight years—two years longer than his sentence—because prisoners who were due for release in 1944 were sometimes retained because of the war. Arseny was born outside the camp, in the "zone"—a territory under the jurisdiction of the NKVD, in 1946. At first the family was forced to live in this remote area, three hundred kilometers from Leningrad, because of the "minuses" in his father's passport. But by 1948 the family decided to leave and began to move to different places. In January 1951, Roginsky's father was arrested again, probably for violating his passport restrictions and living too close to Leningrad. This time he did not survive the incarceration. Boris Roginsky died in prison, three months after his second arrest.

In spite of her status, which she never tried to conceal, Roginsky's mother got a job as a German teacher in 1952. Her German was not fluent, but there was a shortage of people who could speak foreign languages. She started working in the village, and then four years later moved to the city. By then the family finally acquired a room in a communal apartment where Arseny, his mother, his sister, and his grandmother shared a living space of seventeen and a half meters. Roginsky recalled that a neighbor, who was a building representative, complained to his mother about how badly he behaved, "I was a real street hooligan, I was always anti-society."[69] He was accepted as a Pioneer in the fourth class, but by the time he reached the seventh class, was dropped from its ranks for hooligan acts. Unlike most young people of his generation, Roginsky did not become a Komsomolets.

In 1962 when Arseny wanted to continue his studies, he could not gain admittance to Leningrad University and so went to Tartu University instead. Roginsky attributed this rejection from his native city to his own biography but not to his father's status.[70] "After all, this was the time of *Ivan Denisovich*," he explained. Roginsky was relegated to studying in the Estonian SSR because he was a Jew, because he was not a Komsomolets, and because he did not have a sufficiently long record of work achievement. By 1966 when he was twenty years old, the young student started to become skeptical of the regime, but his skepticism was not accompanied by an interest in politics. He began associating with other students who, for various reasons, had not been accepted at Moscow State University. Among these students was Aleksandr Daniel, whose father was Yuli Daniel, the man whose Moscow trial sparked the growth of the dissident movement. At that time, also, Roginsky met Nikita Okhotin, with whom he would later develop Memorial.

Roginsky graduated in 1968. In the sixties and seventies Arseny befriended Natalya Gorbanevskaya, and a number of other Leningrad poets and philosophers who were subsequently arrested. The human rights movement started to grow, and though he says he was not particularly involved at the time, Roginsky submitted materials to *Khronika Tekushchikh Sobytii* (see also above), a journal of current human rights offenses. It had been started by Gorbanevskaya in 1968 and dealt with the persecution of dissidents and related issues. Larisa Bogoraz and Sergey Kovalyov were also active in the development of *Khronika*. Up until then Roginsky's activities were primarily academic with a special interest in nineteenth-century history and the preservation of history through archives. However, his growing awareness of what was happening to his circle of friends and, by extension, to the country, made him realize how limited was the ideological vacuum in which he lived. So, using his interest in history, he began exploring the early alternatives to Bolshevism and the roots of the repression. Subsequently, Roginsky started to develop his own political point of view: "I found my heroes. They were somewhere in between Social Democrats, Mensheviks and Popular Socialists. There was a third way that wasn't White or Red." By integrating their perspectives, Roginsky formulated an instrument for measuring the Soviet system.

In pursuit of his new interest, Roginsky met many former zeks in the following years. He collected materials from people who were connected with any kind of opposition such as Troskyites, anarchists, Mensheviks, and those who had taken part in the resistance at Solovki or the camp strikes. He was only interested in the stories of these particular groups. The history of ordinary citizens who landed in the camps for no particular civil infraction or for no particular political orientation, and who did not participate in acts of resistance, seemed to him to be too undifferentiated to find a pattern that interested him.

By 1976 Roginsky and his circle of friends—Aleksandr Daniel, Larisa Bogoraz, Mikhail Gefter, and others connected with the *Chronicle*—were moving in the direction of a historical inquiry which would eventuate, a decade later, in Memorial. Their focus was on the history of the repression rather than the immediacy of the repression, but the relevance of their work to the political agenda of the dissident movement did not escape the government. The power to write history is the power to control whose story is told. The Soviet system maintained itself not only by repressing people but by repressing ideas; the state's power was used to control the flow of knowledge. Roginsky, his friends, and the regime understood that there is no politically neutral pursuit of history, so Roginsky anticipated that he might be arrested. He was already being harassed regularly by KGB searches of his apartment. Finally in 1981, Roginsky was summoned to OVIR, the visa office, and told he had permission to emigrate within ten days. Roginsky did not accept the offer, nor did he mistake it for a gesture of good will. On August 12, 1981 Arseny Roginsky was arrested on Article 196—"the forgery and the production and sale of forged documents," and also accused of sending materials abroad to anti-Soviet publications such as *Pamyat*, a historical journal.[71] The documents in question were letters needed to obtain permission for the use of the Leningrad archives for research. (Roginsky had been barred from working in Soviet research institutions because he was a Jew and the son of a former political prisoner.)[72]

Roginsky was sentenced to four years in a labor camp. Considering his family history of repression and the experiences of his current social group, it might have been expected that Roginsky would have been prepared for the experience of incarceration. He confessed that he was not:

> I probably knew more about the Gulag than all the dissidents combined, but the first time I entered a cell—that horrible world—despite all of my erudition and all of my knowledge I felt like I was an absolutely helpless child who knew nothing. I had never really asked about the camps, I asked about internal life and philosophy and heard about the external horrors. But I never realized the main thing—that camp is degradation from the first moment to the last, and all of camp life comes down to a struggle to resist humiliation.... People talk about the rats, but what is not in a standard memoir is that the individual is completely trampled upon. The camp is a place for collective loneliness.[73]

After surviving five camps in four years[74] and down to fifty kilograms, Roginsky went back to Moscow at the end of his term in 1985. Even with camp jargon and all, he was received as a hero. It was the fashion for returnees of the eighties to be received as heroes. Roginsky lamented about his father's generation, "No one applauded them when they came back." Only after enduring his own incarceration four decades later did Roginsky fully understand why his father told his mother that he could not survive a second arrest. This hypersensitivity to a repeated experience of trauma, a characteristic of the Post-Traumatic Stress Syndrome, may provide some insight into the reluctance of returnees to resume their ideological pursuits with its attendant exposure to rearrest.

In the early nineties Roginsky joined with Sergey Kovalyov on a human rights inspection of the Butyrka, but he did not accompany him when he visited the camps. He could barely tolerate the prison visit, so nightmarishly reminiscent were its smells and sounds.

Roginsky's early tendency toward rebelliousness manifested itself in later life as 'anti-Soviet' activity. He now works as a historian and as the supervisor of Memorial's research. In this capacity, he has irregular access to the KGB archives, and oversees an organization that defends the interests of returnees and ensures that stories of Soviet repression are recorded and preserved. In view of Roginsky's current mission in life, it would seem that he has underestimated the impact on his life of his family history and of his youthful exposure to those old people in the courtyard. However, given his sincerity in discounting such early influences on his formation as a dissident and on his present life, it is relevant to note that people often deal with the effects of early experience through behavior rather than words.

The Gulag/Returnee Legacy

Throughout this chapter we have explored how the Gulag, as an experience and as a threat, continued to influence and politicize survivors, their families, and the larger society. More specifically we have cited a number of examples that attest to both a direct and an indirect connection between returnees and the dissident movement. Organizationally, they were two separate groups, but their membership overlapped: many dissidents were incarcerated; after release from prison, especially if they were not granted full rehabilitation, a number of returnees were politicized into the dissident movement; the presence of returnees and the stories they told generated a societal revulsion to the lawlessness with which the Soviet government governed.

Yuri Aikhenvald (see also chapter 5), a Stalinist-era returnee and the son of repressed parents, was fired from his job in the late sixties because of his involvement in the human rights movement. Aikhenvald's offence consisted of the fact that he had signed some petitions to the courts on behalf of accused writers and activists. In his writings, Aikhenvald makes it clear that the demands made by the returnees and dissidents that the law be observed and applied equitably were a direct response to the Stalinist lawlessness under which they had suffered.[75] It was the painful knowledge of what had happened to them and their social networks as a result of Stalinist repression that led them to support the human rights movement in the post-Thaw era. Calls for reform also came from people who had been part of the apparatus that administered the repression. These included former interrogators of the Procuracy, who had previously dealt with rehabilitations and subsequently became dissidents.[76] Some returnees never flagged in their opposition to the system despite a continuing series of rearrests and reincarcerations.[77] Other returnees never looked back and had nothing to do with the previous generation of prisons and prisoners.

Leonard Borisovich Ternovsky

Leonard Ternovsky's story is that of a true idealist whose dissident behavior stemmed more from liberal convictions than from personal experience with repression. As a dissident who had no personal connection to fifties returnees, Ternovsky's tale offers insight into the motivation of this group. Based on his own experience, he does not believe that the majority of later human rights defenders developed their convictions as a result of Stalinist repression. No one in Ternovsky's family had suffered under the Stalinist repression, and until Stalin's death, almost until Khrushchev's "unmasking" of his "cult," Ternovsky grew up believing in the basic righteousness of the Soviet system. In 1956, however, at age twenty-three he experienced an intellectual awakening through which he came to realize that "it was the system itself, that is, the totalitarianism and the absence of freedom that begat the monstrous repression."[78] It was then that he felt impelled to make a commitment to civic responsibility.

Ternovsky completed his medical studies and worked as a radiologist in the sixties. He became increasingly disturbed by what was happening in the world around him—the persecution of Pasternak, the trial of Brodsky on charges of "parasitism," the trial of Sinyavsky and Daniel. For him, the last straw was the Soviet occupation of Czechoslovakia in September 1968. The handful of courageous citizens who demonstrated in Red Square made a great impression on him. Ternovsky could no longer remain on the sidelines. He wrote an article under a pseudonym in samizdat sharply criticizing the Soviet invasion. Soon Ternovsky was openly signing petitions in defense of the convicted demonstrators.

This "taste of freedom" inspired Ternovsky with an even greater feeling of dedication and motivated him to become engaged in further acts of defiance. He was a signatory to a number of letters in defense of human rights, joined the Moscow Helsinki Group, and in 1978, he became a member of the working commission to investigate the abuse of psychiatry for political purposes. By that time the doctor had become convinced that this branch of medicine was being appropriated by the government. By that time, also, Ternovsky's motivations were more personal. Some of his friends were imprisoned, others were incarcerated in psychiatric hospitals, still others had saved themselves only by leaving the country, and one, unable to withstand the persecution, committed suicide.

Ternovsky's own arrest was inevitable. In 1980 he was sentenced to three years of camp on Article 190-1 (deliberately circulating fabrications defaming the Soviet political and social system). Ternovsky was placed with common criminals in order to isolate him from his peers.[79] Witness his final words in court:

> I anticipated my arrest and this trial. Of course that does not mean that I tried to get into prison. I am not fifteen, but almost fifty and I don't need that kind of "romance." I would have preferred to avoid years of imprisonment. But to have done so would have meant acting in a way that would have been unworthy of what I consider my duty.... I am going to prison with a good conscience.[80]

Reflecting on his prison years Ternovsky later said, "I was free in an unfree country."[81] The sentiment that had developed in this dissident's consciousness is reminiscent of Henry David Thoreau's words in his 1849 tract on *Civil Disobedience*: "Under a government which imprisons any unjustly, the true place for a just man is also a prison ... the only house in a slave State in which a free man can abide with honor."[82]

Though his initial entrance into the dissident movement may not have been influenced by Stalin's zeks, his own imprisonment created a setting in which he was forced to think about their experience. In contrast to many of Stalin's zeks, Ternovsky knew why he had been incarcerated, and in knowing why, he had a sense of purpose that was often absent from their experience. He also knew that when he came out his friends and family would be waiting for him, even the West would be waiting for him. Ternovsky realized that the contrast between his experience and that of Stalin's zeks was considerable, because they could not depend on anyone or anything when they came out. Still, readapting to the "big zone" in 1983 required an extensive effort for Ternovsky as well. He was not permitted to live in Moscow, he was a professional outcast, and he was unable to get formal employment. The only work the radiologist could find was temporary, so he experienced long periods of unemployment. This, of course, made him vulnerable to charges of "parasitism." Ternovsky decided to apply for retirement, since the eligibility age in his field of specialization was fifty. After pursuing this for almost a year, he attained this status.[83] The fact that this was granted at all in the Brezhnev era was more likely determined by the government's desire to remove him from circulation than out of any adherence to the principles of justice. Ternovsky was rehabilitated in 1991.

In the sixties and seventies those who could not openly petition for their rights could still express their protest in the form of Aesopean language in fiction and samizdat—an increasingly political venue after 1964.[84] Throughout this study we have looked at a number of these literary works with thinly veiled political messages. Literary criticism was yet another effective means of addressing tabooed topics. A 1964 essay on Kafka describes the surroundings in which Kafka's protagonists find themselves as "deformed and conditional."[85] It inveighs against a robotic, labyrinthine bureaucracy with its own rules and its own momentum, which Soviet citizens must have recognized as all too familiar.[86] Moreover, the article discusses *The Trial*, a theme that must have been on the minds of many a victim. Given the timing and the subject matter it is reasonable to assume that this publication reflected some implicit criticism of the Stalinist repression and the regretted end of de-Stalinization.

The Camp Regions

The camp regions, of course, experienced their own "haunting of the present by the past."[87] In his *Arctic Tragedy*, written in the first half of the seventies, Grigory Svirsky, whose critical writing was banned in the Soviet Union after 1964, provided some insight into the atmosphere of this "land whose terrain and population are permanently scarred by the marks and memories of the Stalinist labor camps."[88] One of the main points of these short stories was that little had changed in Siberia since Stalin died. Many of the zeks stayed on as employees for lack of any other place to go or means to get there. According to Svirsky, the command structure and the arbitrary use of power were still the same.[89] In its review of Svirsky's work, Radio Liberty provided the following commentary on the persistent problems which continued to influence life in the Yenisei region: "Former prisoners still continue to settle scores with former camp guards, state law still contrives to make criminals of the innocent, protest is suppressed, and there is a general sense of misrule by authority and grievance and demoralization among the ordinary citizens."[90]

This raises the question of why some former prisoners remained in spite of the often harsh climatic conditions[91] and generally hostile sociopolitical environment of the remote camp regions. (These cases would be subject of a study in itself.) Let us briefly explore their reasons for staying. Svirsky's answer to this question is that the prisoners were conditioned to hopelessness. In his documentary short story "Lyova Soifert, Friend of the People..." someone asks the ex-prisoner Soifert what kind of masochism it is that makes one stay in this Northern city, 'where even the clay on the hillocks seems to be soaked with blood.' He grinned and said, "and where is there not a prison?... The only good places are where we aren't!"[92] This explanation seems to suggest that no matter where ex-zeks end up, they carry their prison with them and the good life is elsewhere. It may also allude to the fact that the Soviet society itself was a prison.

Mordovia and Dolinka (Karaganda, Kazakhstan) are fairly representative examples of what life is like after the camp experience when people still live near the camp sites.[93] Mordovia was a part of the Gulag that was also widely used to incarcerate dissidents. The camps later functioned as penal colonies rather than political prisons. According to a 1997 article in *Nezavisimaya Gazeta*, every family in that region was in one way or another still connected with the camp zone. Some even counted three or four generations of camp laborers. While earlier generations had served time in the camps for anti-Soviet activities, their children and grandchildren were now employed by the Dubravlag (Dubravny lager, Mordovia) system.[94] In Dolinka, the capital of the Karlag (Karaganda camp complex), the post-Soviet residents were people who had once been either prisoners or guards, or were the children of prisoners or guards, or were the children of both. However, neither side of the prisoner-guard divide talks much about the past. The pragmatic motto is, "the less you say, the more peaceful your life will be."[95]

Regardless of whether or not old attitudes are expressed in words, they persist. A former guard claimed in an interview that only criminals were incarcerated in the Karlag. Moreover, he maintained that they were well taken care of, that they were fed "three times a day, 5,250 calories per person. In the morning bread, tea, soup or oatmeal. At lunch an appetizer and main course," and so on. Interestingly, the 1993 pension of the NKVD veterans was rather high—comparable to that of soldiers who served at the front. It was higher than the meagre compensation and pension allotted to former prisoners.[96]

One incentive for families to remain in the area of the camps was the relatively good wages and benefits available for those who were still able to work. Other factors included the socialization to the camp, travel restrictions, and the lack of alternatives. Some prisoners went into the camps and did not come out until five, ten, or even seventeen years later. They had spent their youth and young adulthood in these areas and felt too old to leave.[97] As we have seen, the prisoners who left the camps were not the same people they had been when they entered, and many lacked skills or initiative to start over in another place. Moreover, when they initially came out of the camps they were usually held back by passport restrictions which limited or prohibited travel outside of the region. In addition to the special restrictions attendant to their ex-prisoner status, the residency registration (*propiska*)—a tsarist regulation that applied to everyone in the Soviet period—superimposed further impediments on their mobility. It was also the case that many former prisoners had acquired camp-spouses with whom they established new families, and for reasons referred to in earlier chapters, they either did not have the option of returning or did not want to return to their old families in the places from whence they had come. Hence, even if the camps had politicized the prisoners and motivated them to challenge the legitimacy of the government that had incarcerated them, the physical, psychological, and social means to do this were not always attainable. As one former prisoner noted when asked why he remained, "You'd have to ask Stalin why we are still here."[98]

Conclusion

In this chapter we have explored the effect that repression had on the attitudes of former prisoners toward the Soviet system. We have also examined whether former prisoners influenced the way others viewed the system as well as whether they had a more direct effect on the system itself. Some former prisoners who had once embraced the Party were not embittered by their camp experience to the extent that they subsequently rejected the Party. Evidence for this conclusion is based on their written memoirs and their acts of petitioning for restoration of Party membership. While some of those who requested membership did so out of fear of the social and professional consequences of not doing so, others requested reinstatement out of a lingering belief in the system. Some of this group became very disillusioned.

To all outward appearances, in the immediate aftermath of release, the political system was not significantly weakened by the presence of these survivors of the repression or by their activities. And though returnees may have had some influence in stimulating the dissident movement and adding to its ranks, there was little progress toward real political reform. On the contrary, the retrenchment of the Brezhnev years made it seem as if the presence of returnees had no corrective effect, and certainly no destabilizing effect, on the Soviet political system. Apparently, and "apparently" is an important qualifier, the system of repression was not changing in response to its casualties and failures. As the propaganda machine continued in its efforts to erase history, the people were not permitted to openly examine the past or be critical of the present. But some did, and they formed a nidus for future change. Under Gorbachev, when the populace were finally permitted to look back at the past lawlessness of their government, the explosion of revelations combined with the burgeoning discontent to make it no longer possible for the Soviet propaganda machine to continue steamrolling the facts into a fraudulent version of history. In our next and final chapter we will explore how the returnees reemerged in the eighties and nineties, eventually to become a powerful force in challenging the legitimacy of the Soviet system.

Notes

1. For example Izrail' Mazus, who was imprisoned from 1948-1954 for being a member of an anti-Soviet organization. Interview held at Vozvrashchenie headquarters in Moscow, November 26, 1996. See also Mazus, *Gde Ty Byl?* (Moscow: Vozvrashchenie, 1992).
2. Semën Vilenskii (Stalinist-era zek), Arsenii Roginskii (dissident), and many others from both groups maintain this stance.
3. S.P. de Boer, E.J. Driessen, H.L. Verhaar, eds., *Biographical Dictionary of Dissidents in the Soviet Union 1956-1975* (The Hague: Martinus Nijhoff, 1982), pp. 56-57.
4. Discussion held at the home of Arsenii Borisovich Roginskii in Moscow, October 14, 1997.
5. For more on Kopelev's political and professional development see Bruno Naarden, "Literatuur en geschiedenis bij Lev Kopelev: een Russische germanist aan het woord," *Theoretische Geschiedenis* 22, no. 4 (1995): 498-509.
6. Raisa Orlova, Lev Kopelev, *My zhili v Moskve* (Ann Arbor, MI: Ardis, 1988), p. 33.
7. Lev Kopelev, *Khranit' Vechno* (Ann Arbor, MI: Ardis, 1975), p. 578.
8. Orlova and Kopelev, p. 58.
9. Ibid., p. 77.
10. Ibid., p. 104.
11. Ibid., p. 133.
12. Viktor Nekrasov, "Twenty years since the publication of *Ivan Denisovich*," RFE-RL (radio liberty research) v. 27, no. 1, 5 January 1983, p. 2.
13. Orlova and Kopelev, p. 159.
14. "Lev Kopelev, a Soviet Dissident Who Does Not Want to Emigrate, Speaks Out," *New York Times*, 29 July 1979.

15. See also *International Herald Tribune*, 19 June 1997.
16. He spoke, for example, at an April 1990 Memorial-Böll Stiftung workshop in Köln attended by, among others, Arsenii Roginskii, and East German historians. Memorial was struggling at the time for legal status. Such support made it more difficult to officially ignore the organization.
17. Peter Benno, "The Political Aspect," in Hayward and Crowley, eds., *Soviet Literature in the Sixties: An International Symposium*, pp. 196-197.
18. Galina Serebriakova, "Voidi Khoziainom," *Molodaia Gvardiia* 1 (1964): 6.
19. *Izvestiia*, 16 December 1962, p. 5.
20. Lyudmila Alekseeva, Radio Liberty Background Research Report, December 8, 1982.
21. See Petr Ionovich Yakir, *A Childhood in Prison* (London: Macmillan, 1972).
22. Details of his life story come from various reports, including "Petr Yakir: the Making and Breaking of a Soviet Dissident," Radio Liberty Research, November 18, 1982.
23. According to his daughter, Irina (also a former dissident), Pëtr Iakir was even offered a larger apartment. He modestly declined, because a three-room apartment was suitable for himself and his family (conversation with Irina Petrovna Iakir, October 8, 1997). At the time of our meeting, Irina still lived in that same apartment with her husband, Iuli Kim, and her daughter and grand-daughter.
24. Alekseyeva, p. 3.
25. Ibid., p. 4.
26. L.P. Petrovskii, "Desiat' iz 1001 'Prestupleniia' Petra Iakira," *Kengir* 1 (1995): 74-75.
27. See Elena Bonner, *Mothers and Daughters* (London: Hutchinson, 1992).
28. James Ring Adams, "Sakharov's Mother-in-Law Remembers," *Wall Street Journal*, 26 July 1984.
29. Mikhail Baital'skii, for example, was still supportive of the October Revolution and Bolshevism under Lenin and Trotsky—even after two incarcerations. He still believed that socialism would ultimately triumph when he died in 1976. See Mikhail Baitalsky, (edited and translated by Marilyn Vogt-Downey), *Notebooks for the Grandchildren. Recollections of a Trotskyist Who Survived the Stalin Terror* (New Jersey: Humanities Press, 1995). See also *Europe-Asia Studies* Vol. 49, No. 7 (1997): 1362-65.
    Baital'skii's notebooks were donated to Memorial (f. 2, op. 1, d. 8).
    Aleksei Kosterin had similar views. This veteran of the Civil War who spent seventeen years in camps from 1938 on was a committed Marxist-Leninist Bolshevik. See Tamara Deutscher, "Intellectual Opposition in the USSR," *New Left Review* 96 (March-April 1976): 105.
30. Anatolii Brat, "Zhutkie Gody," (1989) Memorial, f. 2, op. 1, d. 29, l. 0001 2909 0477.
31. Evgeniia Martinovna Borian, Memorial, f. 1, op. 1, d. 556, l. 0011 0113 0913.
32. Vasilii Aksënov, a writer and the son of Evgeniia Ginzburg, also included in at least one of his stories the true to life image of a former political prisoner who did not return depressed, broken or embittered. On the contrary, after camp the returnee maintained his former patriotism and belief in the system. Vasilii Aksënov, "Pravo na ostrov," (St. Petersburg: Ermitazh, 1983), p. 157.
33. Pëtr Osipovich Sagoian, "God 1937 v moei zhizni—vospominaniia," Memorial, f. 2, op. 1, d. 104, l. 1993 1510 1639.
34. This expression can be found in numerous memoirs, but is here excerpted from a letter from D. Glikshtein to Stephen Cohen, May 23, 1983.

35.   Nadezhda Markovna Ulanovskaia, response to Cohen questionnaire, Jerusalem, July 1980.
36.   Viktor E. Frankl, *Man's Search for Meaning: An Introduction to Logotherapy* (London: Hodder and Stoughton, 1964).
37.   American communism has also been placed in the religion niche. Witness one writer's observations: 'American communism seems best understood not as a political movement but as a quasi-religious one, whose members lived in a world where strategies and tactics were accepted as matters of faith, where only very narrow debate was ever permitted, and where even a hint of public skepticism was regarded as punishable heresy.' Sam Tanenhaus, "Keeping the Faith," *New York Review of Books*, June 25, 1998.
38.   Herbert M. Adler, "Crisis, Conversion, and Cult Formation," *American Journal of Psychiatry* (1973).
39.   Frankl, *Man's Search*....
40.   Looking back on his belief in communism, a Spanish communist later admitted to having rationalized much of Russia's misbehavior, thereby falsifying his perception (See Angela van Son and Mireille Sennef, "Vrouwenoorlog om Ravensbruck," *Historisch Nieuwsblad* (May 1998): 25.)
41.   These journals were guided by the spirit of the times. They also served as a medium for political communication in the absence of competing political parties, civic organizations, and a free press. Thus, camp stories (*Ivan Denisovich*) or 'fictional' returnee tales were also "thick" journal readers' fare in the sixties.
42.   Iurii Zubkov, "Nravstvennost' geroicheskoi epokhy," *Znamia* 3 (March 1963): 206.
43.   GARF, f. 9401, op. 2, d. 506, l. 236.
44.   Andrei Nikolaevich Sakharov, interview held at the Institute of Russian History, Russian Academy of Sciences, Moscow, September 30, 1997.
45.   Ibid.
46.   We should add that almost everyone, high and low, has a relative who was in the camps. Gorbachev, for example, had a grandfather who was a victim of the dekulakization campaign.
47.   Sakharov, interview.
48.   The survey was not large-scale, and is mostly an indication of sentiment in the ranks of the respective organizations, rather than a representation of popular sentiment.
49.   Anonymous responses to questionnaires especially designed for this project.
50.   Arsenii Roginskii, interview held at Memorial headquarters in Moscow, April 26, 1996.
51.   Galina Mikhailovna Paushkina, "Tragediia Nevinovnykh," Memorial, f. 2, op. 1, d. 92, l. 1993 1510 0630.
52.   See Anna Larina, *This I Cannot Forget: The Memoirs of Nikolai Bukharin's Widow* (London: Hutchinson, 1993).
53.   Sagoian, Memorial, f. 2, op. 1, d. 104, l. 1993 1510 1633.
54.   *Current Digest of the Soviet Press*, vol. XI, no. 27 (August 5, 1959): 22.
55.   RTsKhIDNI, f. 560, op. 1, d. 37, (tom II), l. 487.
56.   Ibid.
57.   Roginskii, April 26, 1996.
58.   Ibid., May 7, 1996.
59.   Ian Rachinskii, co-chairman of the Moscow Memorial and chairman of the council of the Memorial Human Rights Center, interview held at Memorial, May 4, 1996.
60.   A number of ex-zeks reported trouble with reinstatement in the Party because they applied for it a few years after return. The irony was that they could not apply earlier because of the cumbersome rehabilitation process which had to be successfully

negotiated first. See, for example, Memorial, f. 1, op. 1, d. 5224, l. 0034 1002 1593.

61.   This was the response that one former prisoner received in March, 1956. He was eventually reinstated. Gagen, "Vospominaniia," tom 3 and 4, Memorial, f. 2, op. 1, d. 44 and 45, ll. 1993 0510 1123-1124, 0001 2909 1866.

62.   TsKhSD, f. 6, op. 6, d. 1077, ll. 4-5.

63.   Ibid., d. 1165, l. 10.

64.   Ibid., d. 1099, ll. 3-4.

65.   Ibid., d. 1165, l. 2.

66.   Ibid., l. 9. The collusion of the NKVD and the Party was not further examined in this document. Nor did the Party necessarily need the NKVD data since it kept its own archives. One former prisoner asserts that the Party archives contained much more information on his "opposition past" than the NKVD ever knew. This ex-zek believed that if the NKVD had known what was in the Party archives on him when he was arrested, then he might have been shot. E. Osipov, "Partiinaia Reabilitatsiia," *Pamiat'* 1 (New York, 1978), pp. 348-350.

67.   Roginskii, interview held at Memorial headquarters, April 26, 1996.

68.   Ibid., May 7, 1997.

69.   Ibid.

70.   He did not, however, indicate his father's status on his university application.

71.   In the 1990s when he was given access to his KGB dossier, Roginskii found the decision to arrest him—it was dated December 1980.

72.   See Boris Gasparov, "Poteriannoe pokolenie uchënnykh," *Russkaia Mysl'*, 15 October 1981, p. 7. See also "The 'Crime' of Arseny Borisovich Roginsky," *New York Times*, 28 August 1981.

73.   Roginskii, interview, May 7, 1996.

74.   Roginskii claims that he was the only Jew in the camps where he was placed.

75.   Aikhenval'd, *Po Grani Ostroi*.

76.   See *Khronika Tekushchikh Sobytii* no. 9, p. 232.

77.   Many of these arrestees were "nationalist oppositionists" who continued their battle for recognition throughout the Soviet period. See, for example, Antanas Terliatskas, "Eshchë raz o Evreiakh i Litovtsakh," *Kontinent* 21 (1979): 213-227.

78.   Leonard Borisovich Ternovskii, letter to this author, June 1997.

79.   Id., interview held at Vozvrashchenie headquarters in Moscow, May 15, 1996.

80.   Id., "Poslednee slovo Leonarda Ternovskogo, proiznesënnoe v sude 30.XII.1980g.," in "Mne bez vas odinoko...," *Volia* 3 (Moscow: Izdatel'stvo Vozvrashchenie, 1997): 5.

81.   Id., letter.

82.   *Bartlett's Familiar Quotations* (Boston: Little, Brown and Company, 1980), p. 558.

83.   Ternovskii, interview.

84.   See Tamara Deutscher, "Intellectual Opposition in the USSR," *New Left Review* No. 96 (March-April 1976): 101-113.

85.   Boris Suchkov, "Kafka, ego sud'ba i ego tvorchestvo," *Znamia* 11 (1964): 240.

86.   Ibid., p. 238.

87.   "Grigorii Svirsky and His 'Arctic Tragedy,'" A Radio Liberty Special Report, January 24, 1975, p. iii.

88.   Ibid., p. ii.

89.   Grigorii Svirskii, *Poliarnaia Tragediia* (Germany: Posev, 1976).

      Interestingly, the city of Norilsk requested reinstatement of its status as a "closed city" in 1998. Norilsk's intention to reintroduce the travel restrictions that were eliminated in 1991 was unprecedented. See Frank Westerman, "Russische stad wil communistisch blijven," *NRC Handelsblad* (Rotterdam), 28 January 1998.

90. "Grigorii Svirsky and His 'Arctic Tragedy,'" p. iii.
91. For a glimpse of life in Norilsk in the post-Soviet period, see Michael R. Gordon, "Siberia Tests Russia's Ability to Profit from Privatization," *New York Times*, 9 December 1997.
92. Svirskii, *Poliarnaia Tragediia*, p. 145.
93. For more on these camp systems, see N.G. Okhotin, A.B. Roginskii, eds., *Sistema ispravitel'no-trudovykh lagerei v SSSR, 1923-1960. Spravochnik* (Moscow: Zven'ia, 1998), pp. 217-19, 285-86.
94. "Ot sumy i ot tiur'my ne zarekaisia: Pochemu Mordovii ne prozhit' bez lagerei i zon," *NG-Regiony* No. 2, 1997, p. 7.
95. Hella Rottenberg, "Onverwerkt verleden in Karlag," *de Volkskrant*, 25 September 1993.
96. Ibid. For more on how both former Stalin-era prisoners and ex-guards share a common lot as hostages of the North, see Sjifra Herschberg, "De gijzelaars van het Russische hoge noorden," *Vrij Nederland*, 5 June 1999, pp. 34-38. After the collapse of the Soviet Union, the special financial incentives that motivated many people to stay in the region were eliminated. Moreover such resources as heating oil became scarce. In the brutal Magadan winter, many residents were forced to endure indoor temperatures of no more than 4 degrees Celsius.
97. See Chrystia Freeland, "The Gulag Grand Tour," *Financial Times*, 23-24 August 1997.
98. Adam Tanner, "Some Stalin Prisoners Still Stuck in Gulag Region," *Johnson's Russia List*, August 11, 1997.

7

The Victims Strike Again:
The Reemergence of Returnees in the
Eighties and Nineties

The story of the ex-prisoners who started trickling back into society in the fifties, as recounted in the preceding chapters, has a logical sequence: this is the story of the public return of these repressed people as well as the public revelation of their repressed history in the eighties and nineties. This final chapter documents what happened. After the death of Stalin, state policy traversed the spectrum from de-Stalinization to re-Stalinization to de-Stalinization to de-Sovietization. While all these phases touched upon the issue of the Stalinist past, if even by glaring omission, the post-Soviet period was particularly challenged by the need to come to terms with the past. Indeed, the creation of a democratic Russia would involve the task of eradicating deep-rooted Soviet attitudes.

Yet, as the Soviet Union struggled to maintain stability and, later, to survive, the government could not acknowledge the culpability of massive crimes on the part of the Soviet system itself. Thus, the questions raised by the presence of returnees could not be adequately addressed. On a societal level, people could no longer excuse their own complicity or silence by claiming ignorance once the truth about the terror was in the open. (The problem of the Soviet people at that time was similar to that which the Germans faced after the Holocaust had become public.)

The victims of the Soviet system, by virtue of their very presence and status, compelled society to face an ignominious national past that extended well beyond the camp internments of the Stalin era. But the times (the fifties to the eighties)—and the political and social system—were not ripe for coming to terms with that past. This is evidenced by the fact that, for the most part, from the top down and from the bottom up, ex-prisoners were either persecuted, ignored, or, at best, merely tolerated. A proper acknowledgement of the returnees' problems would have required a moral indictment of the system.

At a 1997 Academy of Sciences presentation of the book *The Gulag in the System of Totalitarian Government,* Semyon Vilensky, chairman of Vozvrashchenie, made the following comment on the achievements of national historians: "Our Soviet historians were truly great. They managed to record the history of the country without ever mentioning the Gulag."[1] Indeed, despite the victims' lingering problems, the returnee and Gulag questions were essentially relegated to the recesses of *official* memory in the sixties, seventies, and early eighties. Not only had returnees gone "out of fashion," but recognition of their existence and needs became politically incorrect. In this atmosphere of official amnesia, victims were compelled to suppress their memories and to become silent witnesses once again.

The Soviet repressive mechanism, meanwhile, regained momentum. A new generation of prisoners and returnees was created. Many of them, such as Arseny Roginsky, Aleksandr Daniel, Andrey Sakharov, and Sergey Kovalyov were later to join—and lead—the organization Memorial. That organization retrieved the history of Soviet repression, opened the discussion of its consequences, and defended the rights of its surviving victims. Kovalyov and Sakharov were not only Memorial chairmen, they were also elected to the Congress of People's Deputies, where they continued to exercise their moral influence as watchdogs of human rights.

The Need to Remain Vigilant: Sergey Adamovich Kovalyov

Sergey Kovalyov exemplifies a vital social force that propelled change. As an individual who consistently provided the self-corrective feedback in alerting the governors to remove sources of discontent among the governed, he came to be known as "the conscience of Russia" and "the second Sakharov."[2] For reasons that should be evident, Kovalyov's history will serve as a basis for concluding our discussion of the fifties to the nineties. Let us begin by examining the environment which helped shape the thinking of this dissident turned politician.

Unlike some other dissidents' development, Sergey Kovalyov's was not directly influenced by the returnees of the fifties. In fact, he had his first real contact with Stalinist-era zeks only after he had already joined the dissident movement and, more importantly, in the late eighties through Memorial.[3] However, the silence and fear created by the Stalinist repression had an early impact on him, and he ended up being one of the most outspoken opponents of the social injustice and lawlessness that characterized the Soviet system. By extension, he also championed the returnee cause. Sergey Kovalyov went from Soviet dissident to Memorial co-chairman to parliamentarian to Russian government official (Commissioner for Human Rights)—a position from which he was eventually compelled to resign. Ironically, in post-Soviet Russia, Kovalyov was dubbed by some officials as an "enemy of the state" for his criticism of Russian military actions in Chechnya.[4] Kovalyov was just being himself, but so, too, were they. He took a critical stance, and Russian officials responded by labelling him a "state criminal." Witness Kovalyov's deliberations on the question of Russian democracy, as addressed in a 1998 *Izvestiya* article:

> Will we finally become free people? Are human rights being observed in Russia today? Can the concepts of freedom, democracy, rule of law, and human rights even be applied to our country? Many people are asking these questions now. I have always asked these questions. At one time this interest led me to imprisonment; later to a high government post...[5]

Sergey Adamovich Kovalyov was born in 1930 and had the good fortune of having escaped the Stalinist repression, and his family remained untouched as well. Looking back on his childhood, Kovalyov recalled (in our 1998 interview) that his parents were very careful not to talk to Sergey and his brother about anything that would not be safe to repeat to others. Even, and maybe especially, the subjects that the children were being taught in school—history, literature, physics, etc.—had to be avoided, because Kovalyov's parents did not want to lie, nor did they want to say that the teachers were lying. Nevertheless, the message that something was wrong with the system did come across to him. Kovalyov recollected how, in 1936, when the first Soviet elections were held, the radio reported, "all the Soviet people are rejoicing because they are headed for the polls. Everyone is united in their vote for the Communist bloc." When his mother came home, visibly not "rejoicing," Kovalyov asked why she looked so somber. She answered, "I just voted." Kovalyov remembers saying, "Yes, but on the radio they said everyone was thrilled, and you're not." Kovalyov does not remember his mother's exact response, but he does recall sensing that already at the age of six, he had touched upon an awkward, even taboo theme.[6]

While Stalin's death did not effect Kovalyov greatly, he later realized that his indifference was potentially risky. Sergey was invited, for example, by his fellow university students to accompany them in paying their respects to the dead leader. As it happens, on that same day he had heard from a friend about a dog in a pound that was about to be put to sleep, because it had no owner. When Kovalyov explained to the students that he could not go with them, because he was going to pick up the dog, there was a painful silence. That silence was broken by Kovalyov's comment: "Better a live dog than a dead lion."[7] There were no detrimental consequences for living by his own principles at that time, though there easily could have been and, indeed, later were.

The larger questions connected with the "rule of law" government did not occur to Kovalyov in that year. Though he did not believe the charges that Beria was a British spy, he did think that Beria's arrest and execution signified the elimination of one of the worst exponents of the former regime. He never asked himself at that time if lawlessness was the proper way to combat lawlessness. In retrospect, Kovalyov concluded that his attitude was evidence of how far people were removed from any sense of legal consciousness. That consciousness became well developed in Kovalyov in the ensuing years. He noted, "In 1993 if Rutskoy or Khasbulatov had been accused of espionage for China, I would have used all my energy to support them, despite the political antipathy I had toward both of these figures."[8]

What had happened in the years in between? According to Kovalyov, the courts provided him with a ten-year opportunity to ponder the relationship between human rights and politics.[9] Let us briefly backtrack to the events that led to his incarceration. In the beginning of 1966, Kovalyov signed an open letter protesting the trial of Sinyavsky and Daniel on the grounds that it threatened the constitutionally guaranteed rights and freedom of the citizen. More letters in defense of other writers were to follow. Kovalyov also signed a letter in defense of the demonstrators convicted for protesting the

Soviet invasion of Czechoslovakia in August of 1968.

How did these petitioners define themselves? According to Kovalyov, the words "dissident" and "human rights activist" did not really exist at the time. Instead, the word "democratic movement" was sometimes used, though Kovalyov considers "movement" to be too strong a description, since this group had no program, no particular social basis, no ideology, and no structure:

> We were more like a loose union of various circles of friends who were really only united by the rejection of the official lie as well as the preparedness to publicly protest the officially ordained lawlessness ... the Soviet human rights movement was initially united by one thing: its moral irreconcilability with the governing regime.[10]

In fact, these were the very principles that united Memorial twenty years later. As Roginsky pointed out, the direction of what would later be Memorial began to be determined in these years.

Kovalyov's name was a common denominator on most petitions for human rights. He signed a letter in protest of the psychiatric internment of Zhores Medvedev in 1970, worked on the *Chronicle of Current Events*, joined the "Initiative Group in Defense of Human Rights," supported Solzhenitsyn, Bukovsky, Plyushch, the return of the Crimean Tatars to their homeland, and just about every other person or issue that called into question Soviet compliance with law and basic human rights.[11] Finally, in December of 1974 Kovalyov's home was searched by KGB agents, who confiscated samizdat literature.

After the search, Kovalyov and his wife were invited to come to KGB headquarters. By this time, Kovalyov's attitude toward this organization and the Soviet system of governance that it represented had taken shape. Witness the following story of his interrogation: In the course of his interview with KGB Captain Trofimov, Kovalyov declared that he refused to cooperate with the investigation. His refusal was noted, and Kovalyov and his wife were sent home. Kovalyov had another appointment to be interrogated the next day. He appeared at the appointed time, but after waiting for an hour, he grew impatient. When he asked an official about the delay, he was told that the interrogators were busy. Kovalyov replied, "tell them that I, too, am a busy man and I will no longer wait." With that, he left. Trofimov called Kovalyov later that day, offering his apologies for the delay. They made a new appointment, but on the morning of that day, something else came up that Kovalyov considered much more attractive than appearing before the KGB—Andrey Sakharov had summoned Kovalyov to meet with him. Defying convention, Kovalyov once again adhered to his own sense of values and rescheduled his appointment with the rather annoyed KGB captain.[12]

Five years later, when Kovalyov was being tried by the Lithuanian Supreme Court for "anti-Soviet agitation and propaganda," Sakharov, who had travelled to Vilnius to testify in Kovalyov's defense, was not permitted to gain entrance into the courtroom. Subsequently, Kovalyov refused to remain in the courtroom for the rest of his trial, because the witnesses who had come on his behalf were not admitted. When he was summoned for sentencing, Kovalyov declined to go to the courtroom with the comment: "What should I do there? Don't you think I know that you are giving me seven years?" Kovalyov was wrong about his sentence. They gave him seven years strict-regime camp plus three years of exile.[13]

Having served his term, it was not until the fall of 1987 that Kovalyov could legally move back in with his wife in their Moscow apartment. A month earlier, the Memorial initiative group had begun collecting signatures in support of a monument to victims of totalitarianism. Kovalyov took part in Memorial meetings and conferences and was elected as one of its co-chairmen in 1990. Three days before Sakharov's death in December 1989, the revered dissident told Kovalyov, "it is your duty to run for parliament."[14] The next year, Kovalyov was elected as a People's Deputy to the Parliament of the RSFSR. When the RSFSR Supreme Soviet was dissolved in 1993, Yeltsin appointed Kovalyov as Chairman of the Presidential Commission on Human Rights. He was also head of the parliamentary committee on human rights. However, in March 1995, after Kovalyov's sharp criticism of Russian military intervention in Chechnya, the Duma removed him from this post, and the following January he resigned from his presidential appointment.

A number of Kovalyov's experiences in Russian government provide insight into the nation's attempts to come to terms with its past. The reform of the security services is a particularly telling illustration. In 1994, Kovalyov participated in the work of a commission that ascertained whether officials were qualified for higher posts in the state security service (FSB, formerly KGB). Other members of the commission included the president's National Security Adviser Baturin, Secretary of the Security Council Lobov, and Director of the Federal Security Service Stepashin. The commission's mandate serves as an example of the Russian government's "democratic" efforts to reform itself. What Kovalyov ultimately discovered, though, was that the Russian government was not willing or prepared to recognize that real progress could only be made by first exposing the crimes, and then distancing itself from the criminal system that had perpetrated them. We might recall that the same sequence occurred in the first and second periods of de-Stalinization. Former victims continued to be plagued by their status because the Soviet government was reluctant to officially recognize who the criminals were and what the crime was.

Kovalyov's criterion for the advancement of officials to supervisory functions was quite simple. He would not recommend those candidates who had served in the "fifth directorate" of the KGB (responsible for interrogating dissidents and waging the battle against "ideological diversion"), because of their tainted pasts. Kovalyov distinguishes this practice from that of lustration. "Lustration," or "ritual purification,"[15] also defined as "clarifying things by bringing them to light,"[16] as it was practiced in East Germany and Czechoslovakia, amounted to the exposure and the subsequent banning from all public service jobs of officials, and a wide range of others, who had collaborated with the state security service. Kovalyov made this distinction, because the commission's aim was not to forbid individuals from working in the state service, but rather to prevent them from fulfilling important functions or working in sensitive divisions.

(Kovalyov was principally against lustration in Russia, because he did not believe that a democratic state should begin its existence with a witch-hunt, and that it was even a morally dubious and dangerous undertaking for a young democracy. He voiced this opinion in the public discussions on this theme in 1991-92. Later, as he drove past the ruins of houses in Grozny on his way back to Moscow in 1995, Kovalyov began to wonder if his rejection of lustration was justified.[17])

Kovalyov was initially convinced that Yeltsin really was determined to clean up his security service. As it turned out, all kinds of reasons were found—for example, that someone was close to retirement age, etc.—to allow candidates with a dubious record to stay on, and even move up in the ranks. According to their testimonies and the subsequent official approval, Kovalyov remarked, "it seems that none of them played any part in the Soviet repressive appara- tus—except for the fact that I knew some of them personally." Kovalyov's principle stance was not surprising: "A person who com- mitted repressive acts has no place in an organization that claims that it no longer intends to commit repression."[18]

All of his attempts to foster change were met with stubborn resis- tance. "I was a fool," Kovalyov regretfully admitted, "I thought Boris Nikolaevich wanted to make decisive changes in these special ser- vices ... when in fact he just wanted to remain surrounded by the trusted KGB people with whom he had maintained a close relation- ship since he was first secretary of the Moscow Provincial Commit- tee." Kovalyov ended up disappointed by the commission's cosmetic purges and disillusioned with Yeltsin. On an ironic note, in 1994, Kovalyov's interrogator, Trofimov, became Chief of the Federal Se- curity Service for the city and district of Moscow.[19]

Sergey Kovalyov's story has been chronicled in this concluding chapter because it brings a number of issues to the fore. Kovalyov's personal history is one of the better illustrations of Thomas Jefferson's principle that "eternal vigilance is the price of liberty." He tested the limits first of de-Stalinization and then of de-Sovietization, and more generally, he monitored the moral state of the nation. Kovalyov served as a corrective mechanism to both the Soviet and the Russian gov- ernment. His goal was to pressure government officials to respect the Constitution and the law, and to acknowledge and deal with the fact that the principles laid down in both had been violated. Sergey Kovalyov was an early and consistent "bottom-up" proponent of this philosophy. In the late eighties and early nineties, many more joined in his crusade. The consequences of decades of arbitary rule had become too great to conceal.

"Top-Down" Influences and "Bottom-Up" Pressures

The political atmosphere in the Soviet Union of the first half of the eighties proved to be anything but a predictor for what was to come. Let us briefly sketch the state of the government's adaptation to repression just before it opted to allow the return of repressed history and the reemergence of repressed people: Stalin was once again revered in Georgia[20] and many other places; Soviet psychia- try had been transmogrified into a political tool for reshaping "those

who thought differently"; loyal Stalin followers like (the rehabilitated) Molotov were buried in honor; the Procuracy was stating that
"the USSR has never had, nor does it have now, any 'concentration
camps' or 'special camps' whose 'horrors' are described by ... 'experts'";[21] Anatoly Marchenko, Sergey Kovalyov, Arseny Roginsky,
Pavel Negretov, and numerous others were still or were once again
political prisoners; eight months prior to his appointment as General
Secretary, in a 1984 Politburo meeting, Gorbachev supported the
restoration of Party membersip to Malenkov and Kaganovich.[22] The
list goes on and on, but the practices could not.

According to Kovalyov, reform was imminent because:

> totalitarian methods were no longer sufficient in suppressing society. An economically
> dissatisfying and morally dubious regime, which was also internationally isolated and
> had lost a great deal of public support, simply could not go on in the old form. It either
> had to change or collapse. It ended up doing both.[23]

But let us not get ahead of ourselves. First, the returnee question
will be briefly examined through the prism of the Gorbachev years
in order to provide insight into both the continuity and the change in
the Soviet system.

There was a great contrast in the political atmosphere before and
after Gorbachev launched perestroika. Nevertheless, after perestroika
began, it was not the immediate past—indeed the long-term legacy
of Stalinism—that became the focus of discussion. It was Stalin's Gulag
(the revelations about which ultimately exposed the nature of the Soviet system itself). Once it was initiated, discussion of Stalinist repression could neither be ignored nor avoided, because the many stories
that had been suppressed for decades began to surface. Oral accounts and memoirs were being corroborated and publicly verified.

The returnee experience, however, was not being highlighted.
Arseny Roginsky points out that once the official silence was broken in 1987, the main focus of discussion among former prisoners
centered on the camp experience. He went on to say that "the [pre-
sumably officially and publicly accepted] mythology" dictated this
focus.[24] This phenomenon is noteworthy, because many individuals endured a five-year prison term, but suffered the consequences
for thirty-five years thereafter. For most of their lives they were
plagued by fear, a sense of "eternal instability," memories of the
camp experience, and their status as ex-prisoners. Yet the focus was
on the five years of imprisonment.[25] While the camp experience

was more traumatic than their post-camp experience, we know that returnees endured a number of prolonged ordeals as a result of their status. It may well be that officials hewed the public focus on repression to that which took place some time ago in the camps, because it was the existing system itself that was responsible for the difficult plight of returnees in the post-Stalin era.

The reemergence of returnees in the eighties and nineties, like the emergence of earlier returnees, posed demands on the government—demands for rehabilitation, restitution, privileges, information about the fate of lost loved ones, and revenge. There were scenes so aptly described by Anna Akhmatova when she wrote, "Two Russias are eyeball to eyeball—those who were imprisoned and those who put them there."[26] Some angry victims wanted only apologies,[27] but others were calling for trials of Stalinist henchmen. Witness the railings of one former victim at the meager attempts at justice, as expressed in her 1988 memoirs: "Sure, some people have been fired from their jobs, or sent into retirement—but with [good] personal pensions. They still have their nice apartments, dachas .... [T]hose guilty of repression should be named, and Stalin should be condemned."[28] (Former victims often lamented that the pensions of KGB agents were higher than the compensation allotted to the rehabilitated victims of "unlawful repression.") Others used much stronger language and had much greater demands—for trials and sentencing, even capital punishment, for those who were guilty of repression. The trials never took place. This outcome was encouraged and influenced by authoritative figures like Sakharov and Afanasyev. The former contended that the moral recovery of the nation could not be achieved by revenge, and organizations like Memorial should not play prosecutor; the latter essentially argued that Stalinism was so deep-rooted that there were too many Stalinists to try.[29]

The Reverberation of Revelations and Rehabilitations

There are still long lines to obtain rehabilitation certificates and permission to request the paltry compensation of two-months' salary.[30] Outside of Moscow, the process is even more drawn out. In 1999, in Magadan alone 3,000 files awaited review.[31] A 1996 article in a Buryatiya newspaper entitled, "Thousands are still waiting in line," addresses the problems related to assisting those who were refused rehabilitation because of the "unproven facts of repression." It comments that over 2,000 people (in this region) have to turn to the courts to establish juridical facts based on evidence. Considering that more than sixty years have passed since the moment the repression was carried out, this presents no simple task.[32] Numerous ex-prisoners also experienced problems in obtaining documents on the *trudovoy stazh* (work record), which were necessary to establish compensation. Many of them requested and received help from Memorial in these matters.[33]

For the most part, the government met the need to know about the fate of a family member. In the late Soviet and post-Soviet period, relatives were granted access to the relevant KGB files. Victims' families could also send inquiries to the KGB. The following was written in the 1990s:

> I sincerely request that you devote attention to my letter and inform me of the subsequent fate of my father: for what was he arrested and when? Which year did he die, is the date of death certified at the place where he is buried? If he is innocent, I request that you send me his certificate of rehabilitation ... if the documents cannot be sent, then at least send a photograph of him, I don't even know what he looks like...[34]

Her request was honored and she became acquainted with the materials related to her father's life that had been concealed for sixty years. She was also given a photograph of her father, dressed in a prison uniform in the Butyrka. This was the only picture she had ever seen of him. Her father received posthumous rehabilitation in 1994.

Requests like these were about more than obtaining the necessary documentation for rehabilitation. On an individual level, finding out the truth that had been concealed for decades was the first step in coming to terms with the past. People needed to know what had happened to their relatives in order to put them, and themselves, to rest. Sometimes they needed a place to bring flowers, to mourn, or to say a prayer. Moreover, most children of "enemies of the people" endured their own share of avoidance by society, and fear of the "all-hearing ear" and the "all-seeing eye,"[35] so it was important that they be officially recognized as having certain rights, such as the right to know. We will recall that the children of "enemies of the people" who had been in exile or orphanages were themselves declared "victims of repression" in the nineties.

Mass Graves

Any official attempt to supress history could not hide those aspects of the terror that were too big to either ignore or even to minimize. Mass graves began to be discovered and from 1988 on they were written about in newspaper articles on a regular basis. Memorial even appointed a special coordinator for mass grave discovery projects. The grisly burial sites were widely scattered—in places like the Kuropaty forest near Minsk, Bykovnya outside of Kiev, Kolpashevo, alongside the Ob River in the Tomsk region, on "Golden Mountain" near Chelyabinsk, Butovo, near Moscow, and in the Katyn forest near Smolensk.[36] The search continues even today. As late as 1997 a mass grave was discovered in a pine forest north of St. Petersburg.[37]

Deported Peoples

The unresolved problems associated with the deported peoples are yet another major challenge. The enormity of this problem can be seen from the numbers. A 1989 census records the following numbers of some of the former ethnic deportees: 957,000 Chechens, 2,039,000 Germans, 237,000 Ingush, and 85,000 Balkars.[38] In 1989, after decades of equivocation about their legal status, the Supreme Soviet passed a law "on recognizing as illegal and criminal the repressive laws against peoples who were subjected to forced resettlement, and on the securing of their rights." In 1991, the legislation was reformed to include further abolition of the decrees that had served as the basis for the "anti-legal" deportations. The 1991 resolution also permitted fuller inquiry into past abuses by providing for the declassification of the related state and KGB documents.[39] Though this law envisaged full rehabilitation for the repressed nations in the Russian Federation, it also stressed that, "In the process ... the rights and lawful interests of the citizens currently residing on the territory of the repressed people mustn't be infringed."[40] In effect, it acknowledged a problem, but did not resolve it.

In 1995, a decree issued by President Yeltsin "on measures for the realization of territorial rehabilitation of the repressed peoples," went further. It not only recognized the problem, but it also recommended the broad use of regional and local self-governance, the development of which the federal government would support.[41] Indeed, the issue had become too large to remain unresolved without having a destabilizing effect. For example, between 1989-1997 approximately 250,000 Tatars returned to the Crimea (now part of Ukraine), a migration that created considerable tensions with their Russian and Ukrainian neighbors.[42] In the late Soviet and post-Soviet period many of the Volga Germans, never having been restored their autonomous republic on the Volga River, opted to leave for Germany.[43] The problems associated with the deported peoples are among the most visible legacies of Stalinism because they remain too complicated to permit a simple resolution.

Victim Compensation

Financial assistance and privileges, however inadequate, are among the state's only means of compensating former victims for their suffering in the camps and for their years of living with a "tainted past." In February of 1998, the amount of compensation for victims of Stalinism was up for discussion in the Russian State Duma. At issue was the Russian Duma's decision to reduce by half the compensation that was planned by the government "for the defense of the rights of those who suffered illegal repression." In the debate that ensued, witness the raving of Vladimir Zhirinovsky in support of reducing or eliminating restitution to deported peoples:

> Comrade Stalin, head of our government, did not just deport people. When the KGB informed him that thousands of Kalmyks organized brigades, joined the ranks of the Red Army, and destroyed thousands of Soviet fighters, yes, then he naturally deported those who were still alive...[44]

In addition to justifying the deportations, Zhirinovsky also went on to declare that there were no "victims of repression," and that all of Russia was repressed in the twentieth century. Although this performance barely merited a response, Memorial objected to the fact that Zhirinovsky's "scandalous" behavior did not summon indignation or condemnation among the majority of deputies. In fact, even after the deputy's outbursts, the Duma still voted in favor of the reduction in compensation for which he had argued. More significant and worrisome, however, was what Memorial called the "gradual rehabilitation of Stalinism," a trend which was actively supported by some, and passively observed by others. Memorial registered its protest by sending petitions to the Duma, and organizing hundreds of demonstrators who picketed in front of the parliament building with signs like: "Stalin imprisoned [them], the deputies robbed [them]." Official reaction was reminiscent of Memorial's early days—the organizers were rounded up and taken to the police station for carrying out an unsanctioned activity. Memorial then appealed to its constituency to approach their elected officials for clarification on the question of reduced compensation.[45] Letters of protest from regional Memorial organizations against Zhirinovsky's statements and the Duma's decision were published in *Nezavisimaya Gazeta*, *Moskovskie Novosti*, and other influential newspapers.[46] One of these letters, signed by 155 Memorial members, made the following point: "It's funny to think that economizing on the compensation allotted to victims of repression could improve the economy of the country, and resolve the problems in industry, science, and education."[47] Indeed, while not significantly improving the country's economic health, the decreased compensation could certainly have a harmful effect on a great number of individuals. According to a list compiled by Memorial, there were approximately 2,000 survivors of political repression in Moscow alone in 1996. This estimate did not include exiles, deportees, or the children of "traitors of the motherland."[48]

The Ambivalent Struggle to Come to Terms with the Past

Remembrance

Acknowledging past injustices, restoring rights, and providing compensation to victims all consititute concrete efforts at coming to terms with the past. Organizations like Memorial and Vozvrashchenie have aided in further promoting the moral-ethical, non-material expression of rehabilitation.[49] In this context, the ever-vigilant Semyon Vilensky, chairman of Vozvrashchenie, brings our attention to the fact that Magadan has the dubious honor of being the only city in the world to have erected a monument to the former supervisor of a labor camp.

Magadan began to be constructed in 1932 under the supervision of Edvard Berzin, who was the first person to head the NKVD division called "Dalstroy." Vilensky recounts that Berzin was considered a "liberal," despite the fact that he commanded the "thousands of new prisoners" who were brought to Magadan. A number of these prisoners subsequently died of illness or exhaustion from forced labor, or they were simply executed. Like many others before and after him, Berzin himself eventually came to be counted as one of the victims of the terror, since he too was arrested and executed.[50]

On June 12, 1996, "The Mask of Sorrow," a monument to the victims of Stalinism designed by the sculptor Ernst Neizvestny, was also erected in Magadan. With regard to the continued presence of Berzin's statue, Vilensky notes how the two monuments "look at each other, like the [Memorial] Solovetsky stone and the Lubyanka in Moscow"[51]—indeed, Anna Akhmatova's "two Russias" all over again.

Rehabilitation for Henchmen

A highly controversial issue presented itself in 1998 when the Russian Supreme Court declared that a reevaluation of the cases of Stalin's henchmen would take place. This, in turn, had the potential to lead to their rehabilitation, or at least partial rehabilitation.[52] Yagoda, Yezhov, Beria, and Abakumov (Minister of State Security from 1946-1951) had been arrested, tried, and executed under the same types of trumped-up charges that they themselves had used against many innocent victims. These charges included espionage, sabotage, Trotskyism, treason, and other "anti-Soviet" activities. The four under discussion were guilty of a host of other crimes, but not these. According to the Court, some of these key figures in the implementation of the Soviet terror should have received twenty-five-year prison camp terms rather than the death penalty.[53]

Each of the men in question had sowed such "immeasurable evil" that new words, like "*Yezhovshchina*," (the bloody reign of Yezhov) had to be created in the Russian language to describe the phenomenon.[54] Posthumous rehabilitation of these men who had personally committed and/or ordered atrocious criminal acts, but who were indeed not guilty of the crimes of which they were charged, raises a tricky legal question in Russia's quest to be a "rule of law" state. As Kovalyov stated with regard to Beria's trial and execution: injustice cannot be rectified with injustice. That may be so, but the rehabilitation laws of the 1990s did not envisage benefits to (former) henchmen. They were established in order to restore the honor of innocent people who had suffered the consequences of Stalinist repression for crimes that they did not commit. With all the crimes that can be attributed to these Stalinist henchmen, their exoneration would be an afront to their victims. Russian human rights activists also argued that this action would set a bad example for a country that is struggling to establish a democratic state. (Yezhov was ultimately denied posthumous rehabilitation,[55] but the very contemplation of even partial exoneration raised considerable ire among those striving to build a civil society. The Supreme Court ruled that Yezhov could not be considered a victim of the terror which he himself organized.[56] Abakumov received partial rehabilitation.[57] To date, Yagoda's case is still open. Another former henchman, high state security officer Pavel Sudoplatov, spent years after his 1968 release struggling for rehabilitation. He defended his terrorist acts as "military operations carried out against evil opponents of the Soviet government."[58] He eventually received rehabilitation, in 1991.[59])

An *Izvestiya* article analyzes the problem. It points out that it is incumbent upon society to be aware of the political and moral consequences of the fact that, according to the Soviet Criminal Code of the thirties to the fifties—the legislation which must guide the reevaluation of their cases—these four men were not guilty of state crimes. However, the article goes on to argue that "common sense, conscience, memory, and historical responsibility to the past and the future" dictate against such reasoning, because the consequences would be too great. If the culpability of the Lubyanka henchmen were to be minimized, by extension, the blood would also be removed from the "generalissimo's" hands. This issue makes clear, according to the article's author, how necessary a Russian "Nuremberg Trial" would have been. The court would have been able to render judgement on the nature of Stalinism, and to

> determine the personal culpability of the main inspirer and organizer of genocide against his own people, the personal culpability of his comrades in arms ... as well as those who carried out orders (let us remember that the International Military Tribunal at Nuremberg decreed that the execution of a criminal order does not free one from the burden of responsibility.)[60]

The author goes on to explain that the oft-quoted expression "'Stalin died yesterday,'" essentially means that the system

> invented by him was not yanked out by its roots, the people did not condemn it, a [cancer grew] in our society. ... Signs at demonstrations like "Glory to the Soviet state," portraits of the "leader of all peoples," and the nostalgic longing for a "firm hand" prove that society did not recover from its ailment.[61]

He cautions that the threat of a return to a repressive regime is not unrealistic.

Apparently such arguments proved influential, and some of the abovementioned issues found partial resolve when Beria's case was finally decided in the summer of 2000. While the sentences of three of the "Beria band" of seven were posthumously revised from capital punishment to twenty-five years of deprivation of liberty, Beria's death sentence remained unchanged, and he was denied rehabilitation. It was determined that the law on the rehabilitation of victims of political repression could not be applied to Beria and the three others because "they occupied high posts in the government and organized repression—actually genocide—against their own people."[62]

The judgement criterion for rehabilitation raises complicated questions. The rehabilitation procedures have been criticized by Memorial for legitimizing Stalinist laws, because they generally focus on whether the sentences were appropriate to the laws that existed at the time. That means that those who committed acts against the Soviet system are not eligible for rehabilitation.[63] It also means that those who did not commit acts against the Soviet system are eligible for rehabilitation.[64]

Commemoration

What we choose to publicly remember and commemorate is largely determined by the direction in which the political wind is blowing. In a gesture marking continuity with the Soviet past, at the end of 1995, Yeltsin decreed that December 20 would be officially recognized as the "Day of Secret Service Workers."[65] It was on this day in 1917 that Lenin's dreaded secret police organization, the "Cheka," was established. It is remarkable that an organization with so much blood on its hands would be celebrated by a president who claims to be striving for democratization.

November 7, the Day of the Revolution, is still a free day in Russia. On this holiday, Soviet leaders traditionally took the opportunity to use the October Revolution for legitimizing whatever their current political situation was.[66] On the eightieth anniversary of the Bolshevik Revolution, Yeltsin proposed that this day henceforth become the "Day of agreement and reconciliation."[67] That raises a number of interesting questions, considering that Stalin is still buried in the Kremlin wall, and Lenin's mummy still rests in the mausoleum on Red Square. Aleksandr Yakovlev, one of the architects of perestroika, and later head of the rehabilitation commission, re-marked,

> With whom should we reconcile, with whom should we agree? [Should we] reconcile with people who still adore Lenin and honor Stalin? The state should make it clear that the country suffered under a criminal regime from 1917 on. [It should state] that Lenin was a murderer and Stalin was a mass-murderer. I can imagine November 7 as a day of mourning and repentance.[68]

Yeltsin's proposal never got off the ground.

The Trial Issue: Who or What was Responsible and What Should be Done about It

Throughout this book, we have been dealing with the compli-cated issues surrounding exoneration and restitution—concepts that Stephen Cohen aptly defined as the "official admissions of colossal official crimes" (see chapter 1). We have shown that the grudging nature and contradictory quality of rehabilitation were directly related to this reality. To date the problem of culpability has not been adequately resolved. It stands to reason that the omission of this admission of guilt in the rehabilitation process has not escaped the victims. Witness the sentiments of the son of an executed "enemy of the people," who spent years in various state orphanages. After expressing regret that the culprits could no longer be punished, he argued that they could and should be exposed, as should the malfeasance of the system itself: "They did that in Germany and they are doing it in South Africa ... how can someone be [considered] a victim of a regime that has not been officially declared criminal?"[69]

Herein lies a complex question. Soviet Russia could not condemn its own system of governance, because in many instances, people would be judging themselves. But what about post-Soviet Russia? Though the 1992 trial to establish the constitutionality of banning the Communist Party might also have used this legal forum to exam-ine the Communist system itself, it did not venture beyond the issue at hand. Sergey Kovalyov maintains that if at that time national or international legal proceedings, made up of unbiased participants, had been held to assess juridically the Communist Party, they would have constituted nothing short of a Nuremberg Trial: "The CPSU would have been declared a criminal organization, and any activity, under any possible past or present name, would have been forbidden." He maintained that it would have been very healthy for a young democracy to do so.[70] Kovalyov lamented the fact that incriminating documents from the Party archives that "unambiguously showed the Party to be the main organizer of large-scale terrorist activity against its own people," were ruled inadmissable at the 1992 trial, because it was not a "historical trial."[71]

Kovalyov was called as a witness at these proceedings. In his testimony, he accused the Party of gross transgressions of the law. He also added that a part of the responsibility lay in every individual. Much to his dismay, Kovalyov was thanked afterwards by a Communist official for his honest testimony about everyone's complicity. Apparently it had made the Party itself seem less culpable. In the ensuing years, the Communist Party was reinvigorated, and even thrived, as worsening economic conditions turned the public attitude away from its Gorbachev-era anti-Stalinist orientation. After the outcome of the trial of 1992, Zyuganov's candidacy (Russian Communist Party) in the later presidential elections was no surprise to Kovalyov. (Zyuganov's opinion on the repressions of the past was that they did not concern him or his party: "We are a new generation. We can't answer for the mistakes of the past." Those who would challenge that attitude held up a poster in the December 1995 parliamentary elections that read: 50,000,000 victims of civil war, collectivization, and repression would not vote for Zyuganov."[72] The Communists ended up doing well in the elections, the liberals did not.)

Pro-communism also gave way to pro-Stalinism. In a 1998 poll taken by *Argumenty i Fakty*, 34 percent of the 6,000 respondents gave Stalin a positive assessment.[73] "Stalin didn't die yesterday ... he's still alive," remarked the ninety-year-old ex-prisoner Lev Razgon.[74]

The Public Record in Russia and Elsewhere

In post-Soviet Russia there seems to be an official and public tendency toward forgetting, or at least not being reminded of the tragic aspects of the Soviet past. There are a number of explanations for this trend. On a political level, opening or keeping open old wounds could undermine, rather than strengthen, a new democracy and the building of a civil society. The question, then, arises as to what ends would be served by continued or new discussions of past repression. A trial at this stage would be complicated for at least three reasons: many of the victims and perpetrators are already dead, the totalitarian mechanism was so pervasive that a number of victims were also at some level implicated, and the scope and duration of the Soviet Communist dictatorship would make the reach of the trial enormous.[75] On a societal level as well, remembrance is complicated. In Lev Razgon's words, "people wish to avoid spiritual discomfort," and develop anew a sense of national pride.[76] In an already divided society, the truth about the criminal nature of a regime that represented the only belief system known to many people for much of their lives could prove even more divisive.

Despite all the problems associated with dredging up an onerous past, understanding past mistakes may well help to prevent their repitition. Memorial is well recognized for its efforts at chronicling the history of Soviet terror. This organization has succeeded in documenting tens of thousands of individual cases of repression through its questionnaires, and it has also examined the bases for mass repression by ascertaining official policy and practice through research in the KGB and Party archives.

The French publication of the work *Le Livre Noir du Communisme*[77] (*The Black Book of Communism*) was timed to coincide with the eightieth anniversary of the Bolshevik Revolution. Lest there be any doubt as to the criminal nature of Communism as it has been practiced, this 800-page volume documents the crimes of the regimes of the Soviet Union, Eastern Europe, Communist China, Cambodia, North Korea, Vietnam, and others. Though these countries varied in their brand of communism, the facts indicate that mass murder to force conformity, to serve as a prophylaxis for potential opposition, or simply to sow fear and obedience, was a common denominator to all of these governments.[78]

The unwanted legacy of association with crimes against humanity also is a challenge for non-Communist formerly autocratic nations, such as Chile, Argentina, and South Africa, where a different kind of state tyranny had to be overcome. South Africa ambitiously followed the lead taken by Argentina in 1983 and Chile in 1990. The new government set up "truth and reconciliation" commissions, which have the power of granting amnesty (from *amnestia* – [to be] forgotten) to perpetrators, in exchange for a full confession. The philosophy behind these "public morality plays" is to achieve a kind of "collective catharsis," and then put the experience behind.[79] Not surprisingly, the operation of these commissions evoked mixed emotions.[80] Some South Africans, like Russians in the eighties and nineties, were shocked at the truth on the extent of the crimes, and incensed that the torturers could remain free.[81] But while some experienced shock and outrage, others relived their pain. Rather than helping the victims to recover, the process of truth-telling merely opened old wounds.[82]

Newspapers are filled with stories of twentieth-century totalitarianism and the accounts of terror's children: the survivors of those who disappeared in Argentina, or those who were murdered in Cambodia, or those who fell victim to the death machine of the Nazi Holocaust, or the repression of the Soviet state, or the Chinese Cultural Revolution. Issues of remembrance and compensation still rage. For example, more than half a century later, the children of Holocaust victims are still trying to reclaim confiscated property, bank accounts, and moral restitution. Moreover, only in 1998 did the German parliament pass a law that in effect provided moral rehabilitation in the form of a mass pardon to people who were punished unjustly by Nazi courts. This category included resistance fighters, homosexuals, and deserters.[83] For the victims and survivors, recognition of their rights is a matter of dignity.[84] Governments, too, have the need to regain dignity, even in the face of acknowledgement of tremendous national wrongs. Japan, for example, is still battling with the ghosts of Imperial Japan's wartime atrocities. As late as 1998, Emperor Akihito was snubbed by British war veterans on an official visit to England. They demanded financial compensation and an imperial apology for their wartime victimization.[85]

Rethinking Soviet History Again

History is once again being rethought in Russia. This liberalizing process has also, as in the past, been followed by the reemergence of old, questionable practices. One of them is that a number of archives that were once declassified have become reclassified. The quest for freedom of information is an ongoing part of the battle against forgetting. After August of 1991, many of the archives documenting the terror became accessible to researchers and family members of the repressed, and the Soviet tradition of providing as little documentation as possible was replaced by new procedures.[86] These procedures made stacks of inventories and their corresponding documents available upon request. Part of the research for this book was indeed facilitated by the de-classification of the "Special Files" of Khrushchev and materials of the Party archive. However, documents of the Party Control Commission containing information on Party reinstatement (in the former Party archive) that were provided to me in 1996 were no longer available in 1997, because they had become reclassified. When I pointed out that I had already had access to these materials and simply wanted to reexamine them, my request was denied, with the qualification, "well, you've already seen them." These new restrictions were not specifically directed at foreign researchers.

Memorial researchers spotted this trend and even wrote about it in *Izvestiya* and *Nezavisimaya Gazeta*. The chairman of the Krasnoyarsk Memorial, Vladimir Sirotinin, writes, for example, that he and his colleagues have encountered problems in working in the archives since 1996. He laments that certain documents are being withheld on "legal" grounds:

> The joke is that the "Law on archives" is formulated very cleverly. The preamble is marvelous, [it basically reads that] any Russian citizen or foreigner for that matter may become acquainted with the materials that are preserved in the archive. But then the "buts" begin. Access to personal files is prohibited. This is motivated by the fact that materials on individuals can be used for ignoble ends .... [T]here is no mechanism for contesting the rules.[87]

He goes on to say that access to the former Party archive (the archive of the CPSU Central Committee, now in the Center for Preservation of Contemporary Documentation) is especially blocked. The director examines all the documents and if they mention the repression, "they are immediately treated as personal files, to which access is prohibited." Furthermore, only with great difficulty did these researchers manage to obtain (declassified) documents on the camps from the former KGB archive. Another author with similar experiences concludes in *Izvestiya* that this trend may be attributable to the increasing mid-level and perhaps high-level influence of the Communist Party.[88]

On the other hand, there are also some encouraging developments on the archival front toward rediscovering the past. In April of 1998, Yeltsin ordered the transfer of documents on Soviet repression from the largely closed Presidential Archive to the Rehabilitation Commission for further examination.[89] These documents, some containing Stalin's personal markings, consist of lists of victims, letters of individuals who were arrested and convicted, and transcripts of hearings, among other evidence of terror. When the transfer would take place was still in question. As Memorial researchers warned, "at present it is only a promise."[90] It is also not clear as to how broad the access to these materials will be.

A Museum at Perm

In the postscript to her book, *The Gulag in the System of Totalitarian Government*, historian G.M. Ivanova notes that postwar Europe made the concentration camps an important theme in its efforts to expose the ideology and practices of fascism.[91] Post-Soviet Russia has the potential to do the same. The beginnings are evident: the camp in the Urals, approximately 950 miles east of Moscow and 130 miles northeast of the city of Perm, is now a historical site.[92] The physical structure of the Gulag itself, a "visible trace of [Russia's] recent, harrowing past,"[93] serves as a significant condemnation of the nature of the Soviet system. For that reason, closely observing its mandate as a historical enlightenment society and watchdog organization, Memorial is in the process of transforming the partially bulldozed ruins of the notorious Perm 36 (opened in 1946, closed in December 1987) from a Soviet labor camp into a living museum of Russia's past—"The Memorial Museum of the History of Poltical Repressions and Totalitarianism in the USSR: Perm-36," or simply the "Museum of totalitarianism." The complex will constitute a memorial to those who perished as a result of Soviet repressive practices. As one journalist wrote in 1997, "In a nation bent on forgetting, the museum is the most tangible attempt to illustrate the darkest corners of the Communist system."[94]

The Perm project is partially being completed by historians. This has caused consternation among some survivors, because they feel that people who did not experience the Gulag personally cannot really understand. Historians may have some comparative perspective to add, though. Speaking about the significance of the project for the historical record, Viktor Shmyrov, historian and organizer of the restoration effort, points out that no films or photographs of the Soviet prison system exist, "unlike the Nazis, who were proud of their actions, our government knew it was doing something wrong. They hid what they were doing."[95] He further revealed some interesting information on arrest policy in the Stalin era, which he had unearthed in the KGB archives in Perm. There he found a telegram from Moscow ordering the arrest of an additional 100 people in order to fulfill a work quota at a particular camp. Shmyrov pointed out that, "they'd literally just take the phone book and go through it until they found a foreign-sounding name, then go and arrest them for spying ... the saying was 'Give us the man, we'll find the statute to convict him.'"[96]

The Perm camps housed such dissident-era political prisoners as Josef Begun, Vladimir Bukovsky, Sergey Kovalyov, Natan Sharansky, Gleb Yakunin, and Anatoly Marchenko and Vasily Stus, both of whom died during incarceration.[97] Visitors to the museum will be able to visit their dismal barracks and cells, see the prisoners' uniforms, feel the flimsiness of the blankets that were allotted to them in sub-zero temperatures, and view the so-called "exercise blocks" (essentially steel cages), punishment cells, and holes in the floor that functioned as latrines.[98] Semyon Vilensky cautions, however, that it will be very difficult to portray the real conditions in the camp, because rebuilt structures and fresh paint could make the place appear to be less brutal than it actually was.[99]

Perm seems as good a site as any, maybe even better than most, for the museum.[100] By 1995 Perm had not yet changed its Soviet street names. Perm's primarily dissident-era ex-prisoners experienced many of the same kinds of obstacles to reassimilation as their Stalin- and Khrushchev-era predecessors. Witness the ironic circumstance conveyed by one former prisoner who received his rehabilitation document in 1994: "I was rehabilitated in the Dzerzhinsky district of the city of Perm, on Communist Street. That says it all."[101]

The museum was initiated and dedicated in 1995, after which construction efforts began. Organized tours of specialists and foreign groups as well as excursions for the local public began in 1998. In that year, 1,500 visitors in all came to the Perm museum. The aims of the museum, much like those of Memorial itself, are research, exhibition, and public education activities. Exhibition plans include the following themes: "Strict Regime Political Incarceration," "Living Voices of the GULag," and "The People and Power in Russia." The "Living Voices" exhibition will feature photographs, documents, and other materials on the arrest, exile, and deportation of the Stalinist-era prisoners. These visual documents will eventually be accompanied by oral memoirs in the form of recorded interviews of life stories.[102]

Thus far, the funding for conservation and rebuilding efforts at Perm-36 has been provided by the local government and local businesses, by start-up grants from the Ford Foundation, by special project support from, among others, TACIS, the Open Society Institute, Soros, and the Jewish Community Development Fund, and by revenues from the sawmill that Memorial revived (in fact, the very place in which Kovalyov had labored).[103] The list of people outside of Perm who are involved in the project looks a bit like a *Who's Who* of former Soviet political prisoners. The Perm memorial museum is being overseen in Moscow by Arseny Roginsky, Aleksandr Daniel, Sergey Kovalyov, and Semyon Vilensky, among others, while the Board includes such well-known dissident figures as Vladimir Bukovsky and Aleksandr Solzhenitsyn.

Conclusion

The returnee question is one of the keys to understanding the nature of de-Stalinization. It may even provide a clue to understanding the Soviet system itself. Throughout this book, we have travelled with returnees on their journey from the camps back into society, from the late Stalin era, through the Khrushchev and Brezhnev eras, and into the Gorbachev era. We have also explored the reemergence of returnee questions in the post-Soviet era. A rather consistent trend has presented itself with regard to former victims of Soviet terror. With some exceptions, returnees' efforts at reassimilation and readaptation were by and large impeded by individuals, officials, and even family members, to say nothing of their own psychological scars. Family reunion was exceedingly difficult, because both sides of the equation had changed in the course of the prisoners' incarceration. Jobs were hard to find and hard to keep, because employment depended on the political climate. So, too, did housing and rehabilitation.

Rehabilitated status was all but unattainable for some early and even some late returnees. A number of former prisoners had to wait four decades for exoneration and official recognition of their plight. In the course of these decades, most of the ex-zeks had numerous confrontations with the often clashing rehabilitative and repressive forces of Soviet officialdom. Their thwarted efforts to attain a social and legal status equal to that of individuals who had not experienced incarceration led to an ongoing sense of injustice among many returnees. When asked his opinion on the status of former Soviet political prisoners, Russian poet and activist Yevgeny Yevtushenko concurred with their own description of "second-class" citizenship. He pointed out that, with the exception of Sergey Kovalyov, very few of them made it to high positions—and look what happened to Kovalyov when he did reach the top.[104]

In the continued debate on whether the Soviet system can be defined as totalitarian, the experiences of returnees contribute an excellent illustration of how total the system indeed was—from the "top-down," from the "bottom-up," and horizontally. As a political system adapted to repression and generally intent on denying the extent of its history of repression for purposes of self-preservation, de-Stalinization often proved cosmetic. This was well reflected in the individual and official attitude toward returnees over the course of time.

The existence of returnees discredited the Soviet system for reasons that have been amply elucidated. But it was not the Stalin-era ex-zeks or the dissidents that ultimately brought about the major changes, and later the downfall of the Soviet system. It was the nomenklatura. As noted by Kovalyov, forced with economic crisis and international isolation, the Soviet leadership implemented change in the system in their own interest, so that it would serve to strengthen their position nationally and internationally. Yet, this was not to be the long-term result, a fact that was apparently anticipated by some. Aleksandr Yakovlev, for example, concluded as early as 1987 that "the building was rotten internally in all its most important parts," and what was necessary were new foundations.[105]

Once public discussion of the camp and returnee themes had been inititated, overt and covert efforts at damage control (like Gorbachev's low-range public estimates of victims and subsequent limitation of Memorial) did little to stem the tide, or rather tidal wave of revelations. The mass of evidence of the systemic and systematic repression that came to characterize Soviet governance presented a serious challenge to its legitimacy. The newly reformed leadership was not well equipped to deal with the challenge presented by this question, because it still wanted to maintain the Soviet regime. To this end, the CPSU did not assume moral responsibility for repression under Soviet rule. Thus, many issues involving responsibility lingered even after the collapse of the Soviet Union.

Let us briefly return to the concept of rehabilitation. With Russia's attempts to turn to democracy as well as to the rule of law—gradually and by stages—three options (or a combination thereof) for dealing with the sordid history of the Gulag seem to have been available to the government: the first, to do nothing; the second, to provide judicial redress by means of trials (higher levels, lower levels of accused); and the third, to establish truth and reconciliation commissions, as in South Africa, with or without subsequent trials. From Khrushchev through Yeltsin the Russians have followed, and likely will continue to follow, a fourth—unproven—path.[106] This particularly Russian variant is worth examining, for who would ever have entertained the thought of "rehabilitating" victims of Nazi terror? No one, because the system was pronounced criminal. In the West, even a ninety-year-old former Nazi will be pursued and tried, because there is no statute of limitations for crimes against humanity.

Such is not the case in Russia. For example, despite the fact that one of the executioners from a mass grave site outside of Moscow is still alive—his whereabouts known to the security services—the crime took place too long ago (1930s) to be prosecuted.[107] At most, recognized henchmen were excluded from the Communist Party. Furthermore, true rehabilitation would inevitably lead to arrests, because it would ascertain the guilty as well as the innocent. The act of rehabilitation would constitute examining individual dossiers, determining who the real conspirators were in cases of false accusation, and taking subsequent legal action against them. As it is practiced, Russian rehabilitation is issued in the spirit of a pardon to former victims of Soviet repression. Those who rebelled against the regime, for example the strikers at Norilsk, ultimately received rehabilitation, but they were not pronounced heroes.

Nearly half a century has passed since the rehabilitations were begun in 1954, and the process of granting paltry compensation has yet to be completed. It does not appear that this institution for dealing with past injustices will undergo any change. In keeping with the tradition of muddling through, the Soviet concept of rehabilitation is the most expedient option for the government because it does not implicate anyone.

At the beginning of the third millenium, Russia is still a long way from achieving democracy. In a February 2000 appeal in advance of the March elections, former dissidents cautioned that elections under the prevailing conditions of modernized Stalinism were a farce.[108] They cited the censor-like control of oligarchs in league with state authorities to determine the content of mass communication, for example, the frequent slur campaigns against serious opponents of the Kremlin. According to Yelena Bonner and others, under this growing authoritarianism, vote counts were being falsified, the military budget was being increased, and nationalist and anti-Western propaganda abounded. Moreover, there is evidence that the security agencies are gaining influence, despite the fact that they unabashedly demonstrate their kinship with the former agencies. In a gesture that leaves little room for ambivalence, Vladimir Putin personally laid a wreath on the grave of Andropov. Under this former KGB chief, the 1956 Hungarian uprising was brutally crushed and the practice of incarcerating dissidents in psychiatric hospitals was initiated and finely tuned. Former dissidents expressed fear of "shattering upheaval" under the Putin government with its persistent suppression of human rights, pointing out that major national and international policy shifts would be required for Russia to some day become a "safe and stable country, safe for other people and safe for its own population."[109]

The violent twentieth century was followed by new turmoil as the Russian government and people struggled to cope with the past, move forward, and prosper in the aftermath of over seven decades of Soviet rule. Lev Razgon, who survived seventeen years in the Gulag and most of the Russian century, pointed out that the mentality and political traditions of Russia were formed over a long period of time. As a result of that, the changes that have been made are too few and were too slow in coming. He went on to assert that a deeply ingrained element of that mentality and political tradition is that it suppresses the dignity of the individual. This is the element that Razgon believed must first be eradicated. In order for real changes to occur, it will take a new generation. This thinking has historical precedent. Moses led the Israelites within a short time across the Sinai desert to the "Promised land," but they were too timid to take it by force. So he took them back into the desert to wander for forty years until a new generation, not socialized to slavery, grew up, and it was they who took the "Promised Land."[110] At age ninety, Razgon concluded, "my hope rests on those who are entering the first class today."[11] Indeed, these six and seven years olds were born in Russia, not the Soviet Union.

Returnees of the Stalinist era are a dying breed. The task of this work was to record and investigate a number of their stories in search of commonalities. The evidence that former political prisoners in the Soviet Union largely remained in a stigmatized status is abundant and consistent with corroborating data. The Great Terror should have been followed by the Great Return of those it persecuted. As their hardships attest, this was only partially realized. In the year 2000 there were signs that the Great Return might not remain that of the victims, but of the kind of system that victimized them. It is therefore imperative that the Stalinist-era prisoners' experiences continue to be documented in Russia, along with the stories of their children, and those of the dissidents. The archives containing these damning testimonies on the Soviet brand of Communism should be stamped with the order: *"khranit vechno"* ("to be preserved forever"). These chronicles of the fate of victims of Soviet terror can help to serve as a safeguard against any kind of return to that system under any other name.

Notes

1.   Semën Vilenskii, Institute of Russian History, Russian Academy of Sciences, October 7, 1997.
2.   Sasza Malko, "Sergei Kovaljov: Een Geuzenpenning voor 'de tweede Sacharov,'" *Vrij Nederland* 14 March 1998.
3.   Sergei Adamovich Kovalëv, interview held at Memorial headquarters, April 14, 1998.
4.   Sergey Kowaljow, *Der Flug des weissen Raben: Von Sibirien nach Tschetschenien: Eine Lebensreise* (Berlin: Rowohlt, 1997), p. 222.
     This autobiography is written straightforwardly and with a sense of humor. The Russian version, which is considerably longer, was yet to be published in 1998. It includes an additional 100 pages on Kovalëv's dissident years.
5.   Sergei Kovalëv, "Kakie my demokraty—takaia u nas i demokratiia," *Izvestiia*, 14 April 1998.
6.   Kovalëv, interview.
7.   Kowaljow, p. 34.
8.   Ibid., pp. 36-37.
9.   Ibid., p. 108.
10. Ibid., pp. 55-56.
11. For enumerated details, see De Boer, Driessen, Verhaar, eds., *A Biographical Dictionary of Dissidents*, pp. 282-283, as well as Kovalëv's autobiography. See also *Chronicle of Current Events*, no. 39, pp. 212-13.
12. Kowaljow, pp. 89-91.
13. Ibid., pp. 96-99.
     While Kovalëv served his time in Perm, his son Ivan became active in the human rights movement and ended up in the same camp.
14. Ibid., p. 114.

15.   See Timothy Garton Ash, "The Truth About Dictatorship," *New York Review of Books*, 19 February 1998, pp. 37-38.
16.   Daan Bronkhorst, *Truth and Reconciliation: Obstacles and Opportunities for Human Rights* (Amsterdam: Amnesty International Dutch Section, 1995), p. 78.
17.   Kowaljow, pp. 160-161.
18.   Kovalëv, interview.
19.   Kowaljow, p. 90.
20.   See Serge Schmemann, "A Hometown Shrine to Stalin Pulls in the Tourists," *New York Times*, 8 July 1982.
21.   "Legal Official Praises Soviet Penal System," *Political and Social Affairs*, 17 December 1985.
22.   Davies, *Soviet History in the Yeltsin Era*, pp. 212-13.
23.   Kowaljow, p. 107.
24.   I encountered this same trend in numerous interviews. While I tried to steer the discussion to the post-camp experience, former prisoners tended to dwell on the incarceration itself in their oral histories. Once we finally did get into the post-camp sphere, their stories of the return and its aftermath were abundant.
25.   Arsenii Roginskii, interview held at Memorial headquarters, Moscow, April 26, 1996.
26.   Cohen, *Rethinking the Soviet Experience*, pp. 99-100.
27.   See, for example, Sergei Kiselev, "Kto zhe predal 'Moloduiu Gvardiiu': o dramaticheskoi sud'be odnogo iz deistvuiushchikh lits fadeevskogo romana," *Literaturnaia Gazeta*, 27 June 1990.
28.   Elena Petrovna Smaglenko, "Vospominaniia," Memorial, f. 2, op. 1, d. 111, ll. 0007 3111 0144, 0148.
29.   Adler, *Victims*, pp. 76, 79, 127.
30.   "V ocheredi za opravdaniem," *Moskovskie Novosti*, no. 12, March 24 - 31, 1996.
31.   Herschberg, "De gijzelaars van het Russische hoge noorden," p. 34.
32.   "Eshchë tysiachi del zhdut svoei ocheredi," *Buriatiia*, 12 December 1996.
33.   Numerous newspaper articles and letters to Memorial addressed this theme. See, for example, Memorial, f. 1, op. 1, d. 475, ll. 0011 0112 0159-176.
34.   Vladimir L'vovich Timoshin, "Obrashcheniia i zaiavleniia grazhdan po voprosam reabilitatsii zhertv politicheskikh repressii kak istoricheskii istochnik po izucheniiu mentaliteta rossiiskogo obshchestva," (Po materialam Upravleniia FSB RF po g. Moskve i Moskovskoi oblasti), diplomnaia rabota RGGU (Moscow, 1997), pp. 63-64.
35.   This is well described in some of the interviews conducted by the Memorial oral history group in 1990. See, for example, Aleksandr Danilovich Viaskov, "1937," transcribed by Memorial.
36.   Adler, pp. 26, 62, 65, 71, 87-88, 92-95.
37.   David Hoffman, "9-Year Search Uncovers Traces of 'Great Terror,'" *International Herald Tribune*, 14 July 1997, p. 5; see also John Varoli, "Russia Prefers to Forget," *Transitions* (July, 1997): 35-41.
38.   "'Punished Peoples' of the Soviet Union: The Continuing Legacy of Stalin's Deportations," *A Helsinki Watch Report* (New York, 1991), p. 6.
39.   *Izvestiia*, 14 March 1991, p. 2.
40.   *Moscow News* no. 28, 1991, p. 6.
41.   *Rossiiskaia Gazeta*, 19 September 1995, p. 4.
42.   See, for example, Frank Westerman, "Krim-Tataren: een moeizame terugkeer," *NRC Handelsblad* (Rotterdam), 17 June 1997; James Rupert, "Reversing the Trek of Stalinist Exile: Tatars Return to an Inhospitable Home in Crimea," *International Herald Tribune*, 11 January 1996.

43. See, among others, Serge Schmemann, "German? Yes, and a Touch Russian," *New York Times*, 3 July 1987; Isabelle Kreindler, "The Soviet Deported Nationalites: A Summary and an Update," *Soviet Studies* XXXVIII, 3 (July 1986): 387-405.

44. *Informatsionnyi Biulleten'*, vypusk 1, (Moscow: Rabochaia Kollegiia Mezhdunarodnogo istoriko-prosvetitel'skogo pravozashchitnogo i blagotvoritel'nogo obshchestva "Memorial," February 1998).

45. Ibid.

46. See, among others, "Zhertvy politicheskikh repressii protestuiut," *Nezavisimaia Gazeta*, 3 March 1998; "Pis'ma," *Moskovskie Novosti*, no. 8, 1 - 8 March 1998.

47. *Moskovskie Novosti*, 1 - 8 March 1998.

48. *Moskvichi v GULAGe* (Moscow: Memorial, 1996), pp. 51 - 128.

49. See Lidiia Golovkova's introduction to *Butovskii Poligon: Kniga pamiati zhertv politicheskikh repressii* (Moscow: Moskovskii Antifashistskii Tsentr, 1997), pp. 5-30; see also "Poliana nad kotlovanom smerti," *Russkaia Mysl'*, 25 - 31 December 1997; Wera de Lange and Wendelmoet Boersema, "Terreurmachine na decennialang zwijgen in kaart gebracht," *Trouw*, 9 February 1998.

50. For an insightful examination of Berzin's role in the construction of the Gulag, see David J. Nordlander, "Origins of a Gulag Capital: Magadan and Stalinist Control in the Early 1930s," *Slavic Review* 57, 4 (Winter 1998): 797-808.

51. Semën Vilenskii, "Maska Skorbi," in *Volia: Zhurnal uznikov totalitarnykh sistem* nos. 6-7 (Moscow: Vozvrashchenie, 1997): 9-14.

52. For revealing portraits and profiles of some of Stalin's executioners (not in line for rehabilitation) see Boris Sopel'niak, "Palachi: ikh litsa—poslednee, chto videli prigovorennie," *Novye Izvestiia*, 18 April 1998; Peter d'Hamecourt, "Een portret van Stalins beulen," *Algemeen Dagblad*, 9 May 1998.

53. Bert Lanting, "Stalins beulen worden wellicht gerehabiliteerd," *de Volkskrant*, 6 May 1998.

54. Boris Piliatskin, "Reabilitatsiia GULAGa: Peresmotreno delo stalinskogo ministra Abakumova. Na ocheredi—delo narkoma Ezhova," *Izvestiia*, 28 April 1998.

55. Lanting, "Geen postuum eerherstel voor beul van Stalin," *de Volkskrant*, 5 June 1998.

56. *Izvestiya*, 8 September 1998.

57. See Peter D'Hamecourt, "Geen rehabilitatie voor Stalin-beul," *Algemeen Dagblad*, 5 June 1998; Boris Piliatskin, "'Vrag naroda' Ezhov ostaëtsia vragom naroda," *Izvestiia*, 4 and 5 June 1998; "Ministra gosbezopasnosti SSSR Abakumova rasstreliali nezakonno: Ego nuzhno bylo posadit' na 25 let," *Kommersant-DAILY*, 28 February 1998.

    According to a staff member of the Russian General Procuracy, an official list of former NKVD officials exists, and those on it are by definition not subject to rehabilitation. If this is indeed the law, the public has not been sufficiently informed of its existence, as witnessed by the heated and emotional debates surrounding the question of exonerating Stalinist henchmen, see Anatolii Karpychev, "Kogda istina torzhestvuet," *Trud*, 26 January 1999.

58. Pavel Sudoplatov, *Razvedka i kreml': Zapiski nezhelatel'nogo svidetelia* (Moscow: TOO 'Geia', 1996), pp. 457, 469.

59. See Jansen and De Jong; Nikita Petrov and Tatyana Kasatkina, "Attempts are Being Made to Get It from KGB Archives: The Truth About Beria's Secret Laboratories," *Moscow News*, no. 39, 1990.

60. Piliatskin, "Reabilitatsiia GULAGa."

61. Ibid.

62. Evgenii Zhirnov, "Pican li zakon tovarishch Berii?" *Trud*, 6 June 2000; see also Sergei Leskov, "On ne byl shpion, On byl palachom," *Izvestiia*, 30 May 2000.

63. Consider, for example, the cases of disaffected East Europeans or Russians, who had spied on the Soviet government for the Americans. Rehabilitation and compensation is still denied to many of them, even though in hindsight, their anti-Soviet stance proved to be largely legitimate. See, for example, Jane Perlez, "Eastern Europeans Keep Ex-U.S. Spies in the Cold," *New York Times*, 22 January 1998.

64. Bert Lanting, "Vrijspraak voor Stalin," *de Volkskrant*, 26 July 1997.

65. *Sobranie Zakonodatel'stva Rossiiskoi Federatsii* 52, 25 December 1995.

66. See Bruno Naarden, "Het geloof en geweld van Oktober," *Internationale Spectator* (November, 1997): 587-592.

67. "O Dne soglasiia i primireniia," *Rossiiskaia Gazeta*, 10 November 1996.

68. Peter d'Hamecourt, "Stille getuigen van onbekende slachtoffers," *Algemeen Dagblad*, 1 November 1997. See also, Aleksandr Iakovlev, "Bez pamiati i kul'tury nam otvetov ne naiti," *Rossiiskaia Gazeta*, 29 May 1997.

69. d'Hamecourt, "Stille ...."

70. Kovalëv, interview.

71. Kowaljow, pp. 141-142.

72. Andrew Nagorski, "Repressed Nightmare," *Newsweek*, 19 February 1996, p. 18.

73. "Stalin—kandidat s togo sveta," *Argumenty i Fakty* no. 10, 1998.

74. Otto Latsis, "Lev Razgon: 'Ia napivaius' kazhdyi god piatogo marta'," *Novye Izvestiia*, 1 April 1998.

75. See Garton Ash, pp. 35-40; Assen Ignatow, "Vergangenheitsaufarbeitung in der Russischen Föderation," Berichte des Bundesinstituts für ostwissentschaftliche und internationale Studien, 42 (1997); Varoli, pp. 35-41.

76. Latsis.

77. Stéphane Courtois, et al., *Le Livre Noir du Communisme* (Paris: Robert Laffont, 1997).

78. Tony Judt, "Communism Was Mass Murder From the Outset," *International Herald Tribune*, 23 December 1997; see also Jonathan Mahler, "The Black Book," *Forward*, 5 December 1997.

79. Garton Ash, p. 38.

80. See Suzanne Daley, "South Africa Gambles on Truth, Not Justice," *International Herald Tribune*, 28 October 1996; see also Bronkhorst.

81. Anthony Lewis, "In South Africa, the Truth Sets Free the Torturers," *International Herald Tribune*, 8-9 February 1998.

82. Suzanne Daley, "In Apartheid Inquiry, Many Only Relived the Pain," *International Herald Tribune*, 18 July 1997.

83. Alan Cowell, "German Law Corrects Some Wrongs of Nazis: Moral Rehabilitation for Victims of Injustice," *International Herald Tribune*, 30-31 May 1998.

84. See, for example, among many others, A.M. Rosenthal, "Remember, and the Slain Return," *International Herald Tribune*, 8-9 February 1997; Menachem Z. Rosensaft, "Dignity for Holocaust Victims," *International Herald Tribune*, 7 May 1997; Lidia Schapira and Michael Schlossmacher, "Recalling a Viennese Tragedy," *International Herald Tribune*, 13 March 1998; Alan Riding, "Heirs Claim Art Lost to Nazis in Amsterdam," *International Herald Tribune*, 13 January 1998; Alan Cowell, "Germany Wants to Be 'Normal', but History Keeps Getting in the Way," *International Herald Tribune*, 25 November 1997; Alan Cowell, "Wall of Silence Falls as Guilt of Hitler's Army Is Displayed in Munich," *International Herald Tribune*, 4 March 1997; Henry Chu, "Jews Break Silence on Shanghai Era: Survivors Who Fled Nazis Recount Misery of Their Improbable Haven," *International Herald Tribune*, 17 July 1997; Thomas Crampton, "A Japanese Atonement Helps to Heal Wounds," *International Herald Tribune*, 10 October

1998; Daniel Goleman, "Terror's Children: Mending Mental Wounds," *New York Times*, 24 February 1987; Edward Schumacher, "Children of the Disappeared: Argentine Doctors Find a Syndrome of Pain," *New York Times*, 21 February 1984; Tina Rosenberg, "High Time to Dig Up and Examine the Cambodian Genocide," *International Herald Tribune*, 22 April 1997; Anne F. Thurston, "Victims of China's Cultural Revolution: The Invisible Wounds," Part I *Pacific Affairs* 57, no. 4 (Winter 1984-85): 599-620; Ibid., part II, 58, no. 1 (Spring 1985): 5-27; Paul Theroux, "Transportable Memory in Hong Kong, on the Way Elsewhere," *International Herald Tribune*, 13 June 1997; Molly Moore, "Dead Men Tell Grisly Tales: Atrocities in Guatemala's Civil War Are Bared," *International Herald Tribune*, 21 July 1998; Alan Cowell, "Opposition Turns Germany's Holocaust Memorial Into a Campaign Issue," *International Herald Tribune*, 27 July 1998; Mary Robinson, "A Permanent International Criminal Court at Last," *International Herald Tribune*, 15 June 1998; Anthony Faiola, "Pinochet Arrest Revives Latin Debate: Young Democracies Ponder Whether to Confront Authoritarian Ghosts," *International Herald Tribune*, 24-25 October 1998.

85. T.R. Reid, "Emperor Gets Mixed Reception: British War Veterans Protest as Queen Welcomes Akihito," *International Herald Tribune*, 27 May 1998.

86. For early discussions on the de-classification of archives, see V.P. Kozlov, "Publichnost' rossiiskikh arkhivov i problema rassekrechivaniia arkhivnykh dokumentov," *Vestnik arkhivista* 1 (1994): 43-50.

87. Vladimir Sirotinin, "Gasnet svecha pamiati: Pochemu snova stanovitsia nelegkim dostup k gebeshnym arkhivam?" *Nezavisimaia Gazeta*, 24 March 1998.

88. Aleksei Tarasov, "Vechnyi Rab: pravda of 37-m gode vnov' zasekrechivaetsia," *Izvestiia*, 6 September 1997.

89. "Yeltsin Releasing Papers From Stalin Era," *New York Times*, 1 April 1998.

90. Nikita Petrov, discussion at Memorial headquarters, Moscow, April 14, 1998.

91. G.M. Ivanova, *GULAG v sisteme totalitarnogo gosudarstva* (Moscow: MONF, 1997), p. 213.

92. As early as the 1920s, the Western Urals came to function as a "second Kolyma." It was there, in the northern province, that the NKVD created the USSR's first model labor camp of 10,000 prisoners. See Evgenii Kliuev, "Tam, gde zona byla, segodnia - muzei," *NG-Regiony* no. 10, 1998.

93. Alessandra Stanley, "The Ghosts of Russia's Past," *International Herald Tribune*, 30 October 1997.

94. Ibid.
     For an insightful probe into reforms in the penal system today, see Frank Westerman's (Dutch language) report on his visit to the Krasnoiarsk Prison Number 1. He describes, among others, a Center for Social Adaptation—a resettlement organization for former prisoners. The men he met there returned from their abnormally long prison terms as "zombies." This center in Siberia provides food, shelter, counselling, job assistance, and help in the search for family members. "Gekooid in Gevangenis Nummer 1: De moeizame hervorming van de Goelag gevangenissen in Siberië," *NRC Handelsblad*, 20 September 1997.

95. Ibid.

96. Carey Scott, "In memoriam: 14 million ghosts of the gulag," *Sunday Times*, 20 August 1995.

97. For the history of the Perm camps and a breakdown of which prisoners were housed in which of the camps, see "Informatsionnyi biulleten' Perm'skogo oblastnogo otdeleniia Vserossiiskogo dobrovol'nogo pravozashchitnogo, istoriko-prosvetitel'skogo i blagotvoritel'nogo obshchestva 'Memorial'," no. 4, 28 February

1998.
98.   Alan Philps, "Gulag is now a memorial to liberty," *Daily Telegraph*, 15 November 1997.
99.   Vilenskii, interview held at his Moscow home, April 15, 1998.
100.   Since the early 1990s, a small museum has been set up on Solovki (Marc Jansen, "Het eerst eiland van de Goelag Archipel," *NRC Handelsblad*, 18 August 1990.) A room in the Magadan museum is also devoted to the Gulag. Its exhibition includes photos of camp commanders, copies of execution orders, and the primitive tools used by the slave laborers (Bart Rijs, "In Magadan zijn beulen en slachtoffers buren, *de Volkskrant*, 3 December 1998).
101.   Andrew Nagorski, "Back to the Gulag," *Newsweek*, 25 September 1995, pp. 46-48.
102.   *Informatsionnyi Biulleten'*, p. 14.
103.   Scott.
104.   Yevgeny Yevtushenko, conversation in "Pravda," New York, October 1999.
105.   See Michael Ellman and Vladimir Kontorovich, "Memoirs and the Soviet Collapse," *Europe-Asia Studies* 46, 8 (1994): 270-71.
106.   My thanks to Professor G.O.W. Mueller for provoking this discussion.
107.   Mikhail Mindlin, *Anfas i Profil'* (Moscow: Vozvrashchenie, 1999), pp. 10-11.
108.   "The West Must Reexamine Its Policy Toward the Kremlin," *Johnson's Russia List*, 22 February 2000.
109.   Ibid.
110.   A similar sequence is decribed by Thomas Kuhn in his *The Structure of a Scientific Revolution* (Chicago: University of Chicago Press, 1962). He argued that new theories gain sway not primarily because of their scientific power, but because the old men who held the previous theory have died out.
111.   Mikhail Gokhman, "Iubilei L'vu Razgonu—pisateliu, obshchestvennoi deiateliu, avtoru i drugu 'MN'—ispolniaetsia 90 let," *Moskovskie Novosti*, no. 12, 29 March - 5 April 1998; Elena Kolovska, "Lev Razgon: Obshchestvo zabyvaet, chto byl 37 god," *Izvestiia*, 1 April 1998; Latsis, "Lev Razgon...." See also Lev Razgon, *True Stories* (London: Souvenir Press Ltd., 1997); Alexei Bukalov, "Stories from the Other World: At the Trial of History Lev Razgon will be one of the best witnesses for the prosecution," *New Times* (May 1998): 62.

The younger generation of Russians, with its focus on the future, does seem to be moving further and further away from (even awareness of) the Soviet past. In 1995 I gave a guest lecture on the returnee experience to first-year political science students at the Russian State Humanitarian University. To my surprise, this group knew close to nothing on the topic and had no family members who had been victims of the terror, although one claimed a grandfather who was an NKVD'er.

Selected Bibliography

Archives

GARF (State Archive of the Russian Federation)

Memorial (microfilmed collection at the International Institute of Social History in Amsterdam and at Memorial headquarters in Moscow)

RTsKhIDNI (Russian Center for Preservation and Study of Documents of Recent History, former Central Party Archive of the Institute of Marxism-Leninism)

TsKhSD (Center for Preservation of Contemporary Documentation, former Archive of the Central Committee of the CPSU)

Periodicals and Newspapers

Algemeen Dagblad
American Historical Review
Argumenty i Fakty
Baikal
Cahiers du Monde russe
Cahiers du Monde russe et sovietique
Europe-Asia Studies
Grani
History and Memory
International Herald Tribune
Istochnik
Istoricheskii Arkhiv
Izvestiia
Memorial newspapers: *Memorial-Aspekt, Gazeta Press Tsentra Moskovskogo Memoriala, Informatsionnyi Biulleten', Kotlovan, Svoboda, Vedomosti Memoriala, Vestnik Leningradskogo Obshchestva "Memorial"*

Moskovskie Novosti
New York Review of Books
New York Times
Nezavisimaia Gazeta
Novaia i Noveishaia Istoriia
Novyi Mir
NRC Handelsblad
Ogonëk
Otechestvennaia Istoriia
Pravda
Rossiiskaia Gazeta
Russian Review
Slavic Review
Sobranie Zakonodatel'stva Rossiiskoi Federatsii
Sotsiologicheskie Issledovaniia
Svobodnaia Mysl'
Times Literary Supplement
Trud
Vecherniaia Moskva
Volia
de Volkskrant
Voprosy Istorii
Voprosy Literatury
Vremia i My
Znamia

Books

Adler, Nanci. *Victims of Soviet Terror: The Story of the Memorial Movement.* Westport, CT: Praeger Publishers, 1993.

Aguilar, Paloma; Barahona de Brito, Alexandra; and Gonzalez Enriquez, Carmen, eds. *The Politics of Memory: Transitional Justice in Democratizing Societies.* Oxford: Oxford University Press. 2001.

Aikhenval'd, Iuri. *Po Grani Ostroi.* Munich: Echo Press, 1972.

Bacon, Edwin. *The Gulag at War: Stalin's Forced Labour System in the Light of the Archives.* Houndsmills: Macmillan Press Ltd., 1994.

Becker, Howard S. *Outsiders: Studies in the Sociology of Deviance.* New York: Macmillan, 1963.

Bitov, Andrei. *Pushkinskii Dom.* Moscow: Sovremennik, 1989.

Boer, S.P. de; Driessen, E.J.; Verhaar, H.L. eds. *Biographical Dictionary of Dissidents in the Soviet Union, 1956-1975.* The Hague: Martinus Nijhoff, 1982.

Bogoraz, Iosif. *Otshchepenets*. Jerusalem: Stav, 1976.

Bondarevskii, Sergei. *Tak bylo... Memuary*. Moscow: Invar, 1995.

Bronkhorst, Daan. *Truth and reconciliation: Obstacles and opportunities for human rights*. Amsterdam: Amnesty International Dutch Section, 1995.

Buruma, Ian. *The Wages of Guilt: Memories of War in Germany and Japan*. New York: Farrar, Straus & Giroux, 1994.

Butovskii Poligon: Kniga Pamiati zhertv politicheskikh repressii. Moscow: Moskovskii Antifashistskii Tsentr, 1992.

Cohen, Stephen F. *Rethinking the Soviet Experience: Politics and History Since 1917*. New York: Oxford University Press, 1985.

Conquest, Robert. *The Great Terror: A Reassessment*. London: Pimlico, 1992.

Cordon, Diana R.; Edelman, Lucila I.; Lagos, D.M.; Nicoletti, E.; and Bozzolo, R.C. *Psychological Effects of Political Repression*. Buenos Aires: Sud-Americana Planeta, 1988.

Davies, R.W. *Soviet History in the Yeltsin Era*. London: Macmillan Press Ltd., 1997.

Des Pres, Terrence. *The Survivor: An Anatomy of Life in the Death Camps*. New York: Oxford University Press, 1976.

Dodnes' Tiagoteet, Vypusk 1. Moscow: Sovetskii Pisatel', 1989.

XX S"ezd: Materialy konferentsii k 40-letiiu XX S"ezda KPSS. Moscow: izdatel'stvo April 1985, 1996.

Eitinger, Leo, and Strom, Axel. *Mortality and Morbidity after Excessive Stress*. Oslo-New York: Universitet Fologet, 1973.

Fentress, James, and Wickham, Chris. *Social Memory: New Perspectives on the Past*. Oxford: Blackwell, 1992.

Fil'shtinskii, Isaak Moiseevich. *My shagaem pod konvoem*. Moscow: Vozvrashchenie, 1994.

Frankl, Viktor E. *Man's Search for Meaning: An Introduction to Logotherapy*. London: Hodder and Stoughton, 1964.

Freud, Sigmund. *The Basic Writings of Sigmund Freud*. New York: Random House, 1938.

Ginzburg, Evgeniia. *Krutoi Marshrut*. Moscow: Sovetskii Pisatel', 1990.

Ginzburg, Eugenia. *Within the Whirlwind*. CA: Harcourt Brace Jovanovich, Publishers, 1981.

Goffman, Erving. *Stigma: Notes on the Management of a Spoiled Identity*. Engelwood Cliffs, NJ: Prentice-Hall, 1963.

Grossman, Vasily. *Forever Flowing*. New York: Harper & Row, Publishers, 1972.

Haimson, Leopold H. *The Making of Three Russian Revolutionaries: Voices of the Menshevik Past*. Cambridge: Cambridge University Press, 1987.

Hayward, Max, and Crowley, Edward L., eds. *Soviet Literature in the Sixties: An International Symposium*. New York and London: Methuen, 1965.

Heller, Michel, and Nekrich, Aleksandr. *Utopia in Power*. London: Hutchinson, 1986.

Hilberg, Raul. *Perpetrators, Victims, Bystanders. The Jewish Catastrophe: 1933-1945*. New York: Harper Collins Publishers, 1992.

Hochschild, Adam. *The Unquiet Ghost: Russians Remember Stalin.* New York: Penguin Books, 1994.

Ito, Takayuki, ed. *Facing up to the Past: Soviet Historiography under Perestroika.* Sapporo, Japan: Hokkaido University Slavic Research Center, 1989.

Ivanova, G.M. *GULAG v sisteme totalitarnogo gosudarstva.* Moscow: MONF, 1997.

Jansen, Marc. *A Show Trial Under Lenin: The Trial of the Socialist Revolutionaries, Moscow 1922.* The Hague: Martinus Nijhoff Publishers, 1982.

Jaspers, Karl. *Die Schuldfrage.* Zürich: Artemis-Verlag, 1947.

Juelich, Dierk, Hrsg. *Geschichte als Trauma.* Frankfurt am Main: Nexus Verlag GmBH, 1991.

Kafka, Franz. *Der Prozess.* Frankfurt am Main: Fischer Taschenbuch Verlag, 1980.

Keep, John. *Last of the Empires: A History of the Soviet Union 1945-1991.* Oxford: Oxford University Press, 1995.

Kersnovskaia, Evfrosiniia. *Naskal'naia zhivopis'.* Moscow: Kvadrat, 1991.

Khrushchev, Nikita. *Khrushchev Remembers.* London: Little, Brown and Company, Inc., 1971.

Kopelev, Lev. *Khranit' vechno.* Ann Arbor: Ardis, 1975.

Korotkov, A.V.; Melchin, S.A.; and Stepanov, A.S. *Kremlëvskii Samosud: Sekretnie Dokumenty Politbiuro o Pisatele A. Solzhenitsyne.* Moscow: Rodina, 1994.

Kowaljow, Sergej. *Der Flug des weissen Raben: eine Lebensreise.* Berlin: Rowohlt, 1997.

Kurlansky, Mark. *A Chosen Few: The Resurrection of European Jewry.* Reading, MA: Addison-Wesley Publishing Company, 1995.

Kuusinen, Aino. *Gospod nizvergaet svoikh angelov: vospominaniia 1919-1965.* Petrozavodsk: Izdatel'stvo Kareliia, 1991.

Laqueur, Walter. *Stalin: The Glasnost Revelations.* New York: Charles Scribner's Sons, 1990.

Larina, Anna Mikhailovna. *This I Cannot Forget: the Memoirs of Nikolai Bukharin's Widow.* London: Hutchinson, 1993.

Levinson, Galina Ivanovna. *Vsia nasha zhizn'.* Moscow: NIPTs Memorial, 1996.

Lewin, Moshe. *The Making of the Soviet System.* New York: Pantheon Books, 1985.

Lipkin, Semën. *Dekada.* New York: Chalidze Publications, 1983.

Lipper, Elinor. *Eleven Years in Soviet Prison Camps.* Chicago: Henry Regnery Co., 1951.

Loftus, Elizabeth F. *Eyewitness Testimony.* Cambridge, MA: Harvard University Press, 1996.

Löwenhardt, John. *The Reincarnation of Russia: Struggling with the Legacy of Communism, 1990-1994.* Essex: Longman Group Ltd., 1995.

Mazus, Izrail'. *Gde ty byl?* Moscow: Vozvrashchenie, 1992.

Mandelstam, Nadezhda. *Hope Against Hope.* New York: Atheneum, 1970.

Medvedev, Roy. *Let History Judge: The Origins and Consequences of Stalinism*, revised edition. New York: Columbia University Press, 1989.

Medvedev, Roy. *Khrushchev*. Oxford: Basil Blackwell, 1982.

Medvedev, Roy A., and Medvedev, Zhores A. *Khrushchev: The Years in Power*. London: Oxford University Press, 1977.

Menninger, Karl. *The Crime of Punishment*. New York: Viking Press, 1968.

Millar, James R., ed. *Politics, Work , and Daily Life in the USSR: a Survey of Former Soviet Citizens*. Cambridge: Cambridge University Press, 1987.

Moskvichi v GULAGe. Moscow: Memorial, 1996.

Negretov, Pavel. *Vse dorogi vedut na Vorkutu*. Vermont: Chalidze Publication, 1985.

Nekrasov, Viktor. *Kira Georgievna*. Cambridge: Cambridge University Press, 1967.

Nove, Alec, ed. *The Stalin Phenomenon*. London: Weidenfeld and Nicolson, 1993.

Nyeformaly: Civil Society in the USSR. A Helsinki Watch Report. New York: February 1990.

Okhotin, N., and Roginskii, A., eds. *Sistema ispravitel'no trudovykh lagerei v SSSR*. Moscow: Zven'ia, 1998.

Okudzhava, Bulat. *Devushka moei mechty: avtobiograficheskoe povestvovanie*. Moscow: Moskovskii Rabochii, 1988.

Orlova, Raisa, and Kopelev, Lev. *My zhili v Moskve*. Ann Arbor: Ardis, 1988.

Orlowa, Raissa, and Kopelew, Lew. *Wir lebten in Moskau*. München: Albrecht Knaus Verlag GmbH, 1987.

Passerini, Luisa, ed. *Memory and Totalitarianism*. Oxford: Oxford University Press, 1992.

Rappoport, I.L.. *Na rubezhe dvuch epoch: Delo vrachei 1953 goda*. Moscow: Kniga, 1988.

Razgon, Lev. *Nepridumannoe*. Moscow: Kniga, 1989.

Razgon, Lev. *True Stories*. London: Souvenir Press, Ltd., 1997.

Reabilitatsiia: Politicheskie Protsessy 30-50kh godov. Moscow: Izdatel'stvo Politicheskoi Literatury, 1991.

Reabilitirovan Posmertnyi: Vozvrashchenie k pravde, Vypusk 1-4. Moscow: Iuridicheskaia Literatura, 1988.

Remnick, David. *Lenin's Tomb: The Last Days of the Soviet Empire*. New York: Random House, 1993.

Rosenberg, Tina. *The Haunted Land: Facing Europe's Ghosts after Communism*. New York: Random House, 1995.

Sbornik zakonodatel'nykh i normativnykh aktov o repressiiakh i reabilitatsii zhertv politicheskikh repressii. Moscow: Izdatel'stvo 'Respublika', 1993.

Shalamov, Varlam. *Graphite*. New York and London: W.W. Norton, 1981.

Smith, Kathleen E. *Popular Memory and the End of the USSR*. Ithaca, NY: Cornell University Press, 1996.

Solomon, Peter H., Jr., ed. *Reforming Justice in Russia, 1864-1996: Power, Culture, and the Limits of Legal Order*. New York: M.E. Sharpe, Inc., 1997.

Solomon, Peter H., Jr. *Soviet Criminal Justice Under Stalin*. Cambridge: Cambridge University Press, 1996.

Solzhenitsyn, Alexander. *The Gulag Archipelago*, volume three. New York: HarperCollins Publishers, Inc., 1992.

Soprotivlenie v GULAGe. Moscow: Vozvrashchenie, 1992.

Stettner, Ralf. *'Archipel GULag': Stalins Zwangslager —Terrorinstrument und Wirtschaftsgigant, Entstehung, Organisation und Funktion des sowjetischen Lagersystems 1928-1956*. Paderborn: Ferdinand Schöningh, 1996.

Sudoplatov, Pavel. *Razvedka i kreml': zapiski nezhelatel'nogo svidetelia*. Moscow: TOO 'Geia', 1996.

Svirskii, Grigorii. *Poliarnaia Tragediia*. Germany: Posev, 1976.

Thompson, Paul. *The Voice of the Past: Oral History*. Oxford: Oxford University Press, 1978.

Thurston, Robert. *Life and Terror in Stalin's Russia: 1934-1941*. New Haven, CT: Yale University Press, 1996.

Tvorchestvo i byt. Moscow: Izdatel'stvo 'Zven'ia', 1998.

Ugolovnii Kodeks RSFSR. Moscow, 1950.

Van Goudoever, Albert P. *The Limits of Destalinization in the* Soviet Union: Political Rehabilitations in the Soviet *Union since Stalin*. New York: St. Martin's Press, 1986.

Vesëlaia, Zaiara Artëmovna. *7-35*. Moscow: Moskovskii Rabochii, 1990.

Volkov, Oleg. *Pogruzhenie vo t'me*. Moscow: Molodaia gvardiia, 1989.

Whitehead, Tony Larry and Conaway, Mary Ellen, ed. *Self, Sex, and Gender in Cross-Cultural Fieldwork*. Chicago: University of Illinois Press, 1986.

Yow, Valerie Raleigh. *Recording Oral History: A Practical Guide for Social Scientists*. Thousand Oaks, CA: SAGE Publications, Inc., 1994.

Zelizer, Barbie. *Remembering to Forget: Holocaust Memory through the Camera's Eye*. Chicago: University of Chicago Press, 1998.

Zhigulin, Anatolii. *Chernie Kamni*. Moscow: Moskovskii Rabochii, 1989.

Zven'ia: Istoricheskii Al'manakh, volumes 1 and 2. Moscow: Progress, Feniks, Atheneum, 1991, 1993.

Index